Designing
SVG Web
Graphics

Andrew H. Watt

D1697899

New Riders

201 West 103rd Street, Indianapolis, Indiana 46290

Designing SVG Web Graphics

Copyright © 2002 by New Riders Publishing

All rights reserved. No part of this book shall be reproduced, stored in a retrieval system, or transmitted by any means—electronic, mechanical, photocopying, recording, or otherwise—without written permission from the publisher. No patent liability is assumed with respect to the use of the information contained herein. Although every precaution has been taken in the preparation of this book, the publisher and author assume no responsibility for errors or omissions. Neither is any liability assumed for damages resulting from the use of the information contained herein.

International Standard Book Number: 0-7357-1166-6

Library of Congress Catalog Card Number: 20-01090517

Printed in the United States of America

First Printing: September 2001

05   04   03   02   01   7   6   5   4   3   2   1

Interpretation of the printing code: The rightmost double-digit number is the year of the book's printing; the rightmost single-digit number is the number of the book's printing. For example, the printing code 01-1 shows that the first printing of the book occurred in 2001.

Trademarks

All terms mentioned in this book that are known to be trademarks or service marks have been appropriately capitalized. New Riders Publishing cannot attest to the accuracy of this information. Use of a term in this book should not be regarded as affecting the validity of any trademark or service mark.

Warning and Disclaimer

Every effort has been made to make this book as complete and as accurate as possible, but no warranty of fitness is implied. The information provided is on an "as is" basis. The authors and the publisher shall have neither liability nor responsibility to any person or entity with respect to any loss or damages arising from the information contained in this book.

Publisher
David Dwyer

Associate Publisher
Al Valvano

Executive Editor
Steve Weiss

Acquisitions Editor
Theresa Gheen

Development Editor
Victoria Elzey

Technical Editors
ElShaddai Edwards
Richard F. Cecil

Product Marketing Manager
Kathy Malmloff

Book Packaging
Justak Literary Services

Copy Editor
Rebecca Whitney

Cover Designer
Aren Howell

Interior Designers
Wil Cruz
Rebecca Harmon

Compositor
Bill Hartman

Proofreader
Lara SerVaas

Indexer
Sherry Massey

Contents at a Glance

Table of Contents

About the Author

Andrew Watt is an independent Web consultant with an interest and expertise in XML and SVG who created the world's "first" SVG-only Web site, accessible at http://www.SVGSpider.com/default.svg. He is a contributing author to *Platinum Edition Using XHTML, XML and Java 2, XHTML By Example* (published by Que), *Professional XSL, Professional XML* (2nd Edition), and *Professional XML Meta Data* (published by Wrox).

Andrew first viewed the Web using a text-only Lynx browser and has dark memories of the dullness of the Web before bitmap graphics. Having tasted the power of SVG, he is an enthusiastic evangelist for the advantages of SVG over bitmap graphics and saw in a flash a serious competitor to proprietary vector formats, particularly for the XML-based Web.

When he wrote his first programs in 6502 assembly language, he failed to see that his interest in graphics would one day merge creatively with his interest in programming. With the arrival of SVG, the day of the visually creative programmer is here—as well as the day of the programmatically literate Web designer.

Dedication

To the memory of my late father, George Alec Watt, a very special human being.

About the Tech Editors

ElShaddai Edwards is a Product Manager at Jasc Software, the developers of Paint Shop Pro and WebDraw. Since joining Jasc in 1996, he has managed a wide range of digital imaging software as well as sales and marketing programs—responsibilities that have given him significant understanding of the people who want and need the company's products. ElShaddai is responsible for the strategic market and product planning of the company's Web Publishing product line.

Before his work at Jasc, ElShaddai held positions in the product development and marketing departments at Coda Music Technology. He holds a degree in music from Carleton College and has been active in several local orchestras.

Richard F. Cecil is a visual designer and producer at `hesketh.com/inc.` in Raleigh, North Carolina. In his role as Visual Designer, he draws on his understanding of website composition, typography, usability, optimization techniques, and current graphic design trends. He works closely with programmers, other visual designers, and information architects to design sites that are eye catching, elegant, and extensible.

Working at hesketh.com, Rick is confronted with many of the same challenges most web designers face: making sites that are user-friendly and visually appealing while working within the technological constraints of Web browsers and markup. He believes that SVG is a powerful and simple solution to many of those challenges, a technology that builds on the future of markup to meet the needs of the present day.

Rick has written for *Digital Web* magazine and can be reached at rick@hesketh.com.

Acknowledgments

I want first to thank Tom Arah, whose prophetic 1999 article on the then embryonic SVG so excited my interest that I couldn't resist dabbling with the emerging child that is SVG. Thanks, Tom.

I also want to thank the members of the SVG-Developers mailing list. The many discussions there are a great source of interest and education for me. I guess that it is invidious to single out individuals, but I particularly appreciate the patience and assistance of the editor of the SVG Recommendation, Jon Ferraiolo. The input on the list from Jon and from Chris Lilley, the chair of the W3C SVG Working Group, showed how open interaction with W3C can work well. Thanks, too, to Wade, Kevin, Stefan, Tobi, Michael, and all the others. You are a great bunch.

And I wouldn't want to forget to thank the young lady who posed the question to me, "You wouldn't remotely be interested in writing this, would you?" in a slightly different context. And the rest, as they say, is history. Thanks, Victoria!

Oh, and I need to thank Victoria Elzey again for being Development Editor on this project. The best development editors know how to handle their authors. Victoria has that art off to perfection.

I also want to thank the technical editors ElShaddai Edwards and Rick Cecil for their constructive comments and for spotting those little "slips" that it is all too easy for an author to make.

Thanks too to Steve Weiss, Executive Editor, and Theresa Gheen, Acquisitions Editor, for doing all the things that are best kept away from authors but are essential to turn a book from idea to reality. Thanks, too, to the many people at New Riders whom I have had no direct contact with but whose contributions helped make this book happen.

Introduction

In this chapter:

SVG in Perspective

Welcome to the exciting new graphics world of Scalable Vector Graphics!

Designing SVG Web Graphics explains to you the principles of SVG and shows you how to create SVG graphics for the Web. You might find it hard to believe, but, with the arrival of SVG, the world of Web graphics will never be the same. SVG will replace many uses of bitmap graphics on the Web—as Web page "furniture," such as navigation bars and graphics, animations, and banner ads— and provide serious competition to graphics produced in a proprietary vector graphics format, such as Flash.

In *Designing SVG Web Graphics*, my primary aim is not to sell you on the benefits of SVG (many articles in print and on the Web have hyped SVG); I aim primarily to show you *how* to design for the Web using the power and flexibility that SVG provides. However, although I am focusing on the practicalities of using SVG, I am also excited by the creative possibilities that SVG brings to the Web. And I hope that you soon will be excited by those creative possibilities too.

SVG source code is open for inspection, and just as the arrival of HTML released a surge of creativity on the Web, the arrival of SVG might also be part of a creative surge in the Web-based (and paper-based) graphics world! SVG, like HTML, is *open source*—the source code for SVG graphics can be read by those viewing SVG images, so skills in the basics of creating SVG will transfer rapidly to tens of thousands of potential SVG graphics designers. Tens of millions of Web users will be able to access SVG images within months. Adobe is planning to have distributed 100 million copies of its SVG viewer within about six months of the publication date of this book, in addition to the distribution of SVG toolkits from other groups, which will allow the embedding of SVG in cross-platform Java applications. The rapid transference of the technologies underpinning SVG as well as of SVG knowledge mean that SVG will take off rapidly. Don't be left behind.

SVG is radically open source. Here is the SVG source code for an SVG image:

Listing 0.1 (IntroTurbulence01.svg)

```
<?xml version="1.0" standalone="no"?>
<!DOCTYPE svg PUBLIC "-//W3C//DTD SVG 1.0//EN"
     "http://www.w3.org/TR/2001/PR-SVG-20010719/
     DTD/svg10.dtd">
<svg width="400" height="500">
<defs>
 <filter id="Turbulence1"
filterUnits="objectBoundingBox">
  <feTurbulence  type="turbulence" baseFrequency="0.01"
   numOctaves="1" seed="0" >
  </feTurbulence>
 </filter>
</defs>
<rect x="0" y="0" width="400" height="500"
style="filter:url(#Turbulence1)"/>
</svg>
```

That code, short as it is, produced Figure 00.01, using only a simple SVG filter.

Mastering SVG and the technologies that work with it is not a trivial task, but the new creative potential is enormous. I invite you to join me on that exciting exploratory journey into a new Web graphics world. Just as an aspiring concert pianist has to spend time practicing scales, you need to master basic techniques and skills in SVG in order to use SVG to its full creative potential. Empowering you with that foundational knowledge and basic skills is the reason that this book is written.

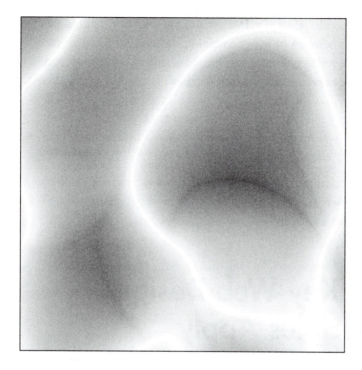

Figure 00.01

An SVG image (slightly zoomed) created by using the SVG `<feTurbulence>` filter primitive.

To fully release the creative potential latent in SVG, you are likely to find that you need to approach at least part of SVG with a different mindset than you might bring to some other graphics design tasks. You need to think partly like a traditional graphics designer, partly like an animator, and partly like a programmer. The power of SVG is likely to be best focused by those who invest time in understanding SVG at a level that goes beyond its surface appearance, important though that is, and who explore the XML-based roots of SVG and how they can be harnessed. You can use SVG alone, but its full power and flexibility are available when you use it with other XML-based languages.

The idea of having to combine a programmer's and a designer's skill set to move forward in the new Internet graphics world is likely not new to you. Many Web graphic designers, including Flash designers, appreciate that they will have to begin to think more like programmers and acquire new skills. Designers who have experimented with or become skilled in using Dynamic HTML, DHTML, or ActionScript in Flash are likely to have some appreciation of how combining design and programming thought processes yields new and important benefits. I encourage you to adopt that forward-looking mindset as you read this book and as you begin to explore and apply SVG in your creative graphics endeavors. Just as programmers increasingly think of their task as being to combine components, graphics designers will increasingly find that they will be spending time reusing and combining *visual components*.

Graphics designers and programmers will work more closely together, with programmers having to understand more about design and SVG in particular to make use of SVG in their applications.

The Key Web Design Principles Apply

Web graphics must download quickly. With SVG, you can create attractive animated or static graphics that download quickly and therefore don't resemble those Flash sites where the protracted `Loading...` message causes the user to act out a `Leaving` message. SVG provides a unique combination of qualities to empower you in creating exciting, static, animated, and interactive Web graphics, but I want to emphasize that the key principles of good design still apply. SVG provides you with lots of creative power, but does nothing to stop you from using that flexibility in a way that is inappropriate.

For example, the following code describes an animated SVG gradient that behaves a little like a disco light and could be horribly intrusive on many Web pages; yet, if you adapt that visual component and produce it in a smaller version and keep the repeat count down to 2 or 3, the component might be a useful visual attention grabber (see Figure 00.02). Alternatively, in a pop music site, this type of SVG animation might usefully mimic a disco environment.

Listing 0.2 (IntroGradient01.svg)

```xml
<?xml version='1.0'?>
<!DOCTYPE svg PUBLIC "-//W3C//DTD SVG 1.0//EN"
     "http://www.w3.org/TR/2001/PR-SVG-20010719/
      DTD/svg10.dtd">
<svg width="300" height="400">
<defs>
<linearGradient id="GradientH" x1="0" y1="0"
x2="120" y2="0"
 gradientUnits="userSpaceOnUse">
 <stop offset="0%" style="stop-color:black" />
 <stop offset="20%"
style="stop-color:rgb(255, 102, 153)" />
 <stop offset="50%" style="stop-color:yellow" >
  <animate attributeName="stop-color" begin="0s"
dur="0.5s" values="yellow; #FF6699; yellow;"
   repeatCount="indefinite"/>
 </stop>
 <stop offset="80%"
style="stop-color:rgb(255, 102, 153)" />
 <stop offset="100%" style="stop-color:black" />
</linearGradient>
</defs>
<svg x="10" y="0" width="120" height="240">
 <rect x= "0" y="0" width="120" height="240"
  style="fill:url(#GradientH)" />
</svg>
</svg>
```

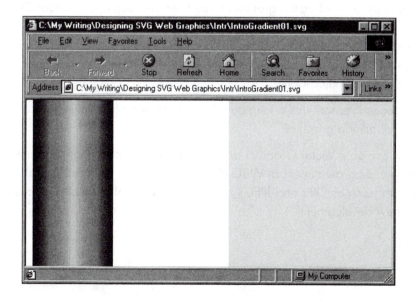

Figure 00.02

A view of an animated SVG gradient, which looks onscreen like a pulsating light.

Good design is customer centered. If the design that you and your colleagues create does not provide what the customer wants or needs, your Web site will soon be history. Only you know your customers and their needs, so this book presents a variety of techniques you can apply in various settings. Whether you look on some of the designs as dull or understated or alternatively lively or obnoxious depends on your taste and who your target audience is. Underestimating the variety of tastes present among Web users today would be a mistake.

Why Was SVG Needed and Created?

Many existing graphics technologies are focused mainly or exclusively on the Web. If you already have GIFs, JPEGs, PNGs, or Flash, for example, what possible reason can there be for the creation of a new graphics format?

SVG was developed for two basic reasons. The first was the perception that with the arrival in 1998 of parts of the XML (Extensible Markup Language) family of technologies, the need (and an exciting opportunity) existed for an XML-based graphics format. As you begin to consider SVG and its background in XML, I hope that you begin to appreciate that a text-based, vector graphics format raises a variety of new issues and creates an exciting range of new creative opportunities. I return later to the idea of a text-based graphics format.

The second reason was a long-standing recognition of the limitations of traditional bitmap graphics.

So, if Scalable Vector Graphics arose in part from a combination of the long-standing awareness at W3C of the shortcomings of bitmap graphic formats, such as GIFs and JPEGs, what were the problems that stimulated this new development?

Limitations of Bitmap Graphics

Bitmap graphics have several limitations. Inevitably, a trade-off occurs between quality (and therefore the size of an image file) and download time. If you want to create bitmap graphics of any size and of good technical quality, the files are large and, for any given connection, are downloaded more slowly. For a fortunate minority with high-speed Internet access, that is not a significant disadvantage. For the majority, however, because of modem speeds, the only viable access to graphics on the Web is low-resolution GIFs, for example. If you compare the visual quality that you would find unacceptable in print with what you routinely accept on the Web, you begin to appreciate the subconscious compromises you make in the Web medium.

Do bitmap graphics provide a quality visual experience?

Look critically at typical bitmap graphics on a Web page. Aren't they generally of pathetic quality? They have low resolution with a limited color range. If the Web had not colored your judgment so that you accepted such poor-quality images, where else would you tolerate such tiny, fuzzy images? A photographer would turn up his nose at graphics of the quality you accept as the norm on the Web. You don't need to continue to tolerate those.

I wasn't around in the 1890s when people listened to music played from wax cylinders. Nor was I there a decade or two later when shellac records were the state of the art. The sound quality was poor, but the fact that any sound could be heard was considered exciting and entertaining. Are your positive reactions to having GIFs and JPEGs on the Web any different? You tolerate poor visual quality because you are impressed that any graphics are possible on the Web, so you suspend your critical visual faculties. I wonder whether you will look back in a few years with a fond nostalgia for the then discarded GIFs and JPEGs? Or will you be honest enough to admit that they were, in many cases, a visually poor experience?

Now take a look now at how SVG originated in the context of the important Web developments that have taken place—and are still to take place—with the advent of the Extensible Markup Language, or XML.

The Birth of SVG

In February 1998, the World Wide Web Consortium (W3C) released the Extensible Markup Language (XML). XML is a meta-language—a language to create other languages—designed for use across the World Wide Web. One aim of XML was simplicity, an aim that is arguably a distant memory given the number and complexity of W3C Recommendations that have emerged since 1998. However, although simplicity might have been eroded, the creation of languages based on XML opened up possibilities to integrate a variety of technologies on the Web, all of which were XML based. More specifically for your purposes, the emergence of XML gave the W3C opportunities to create a new graphics format, which has emerged as Scalable Vector Graphics. It is founded on well-formed XML documents, which would develop further a number of W3C goals for the World Wide Web.

Scalable Vector Graphics are scalable in two senses. First, because the visual appearance of an SVG graphic is stored as a text-based description and its display is recalculated when it is rendered, you can zoom an SVG image while preserving image quality. Second, SVG is a technology suited for the Web, with the potential for a multiplicity of uses for a multiplicity of users.

To give you an impression of the scalability of SVG compared to bitmap graphics, compare Figure 00.03, a piece of 12-pt. bitmap text magnified 16 times, to Figure 00.04, a piece of similarly sized SVG text magnified by a similar amount. Notice how the quality of the bitmap text is degraded with magnification, whereas the quality of the SVG text is maintained (apart from the slight flaw in the font on the bottom of the V).

Figure 00.03

*Bitmap text,
12 points high,
magnified 16 times.
Note the loss of
image quality.*

Figure 00.04

*SVG text of compara-
ble size magnified to
a similar degree (as
seen in the Batik SVG
viewer). Note the
preservation of the
outline of each glyph.*

The first public Working Draft of the Requirements for Scalable Vector
Graphics was released in October 1998. You can see the original document at http://www.w3.org/TR/1998/WD-SVGReq-19981029. From the
beginning, the W3C envisioned a radical effect on the Web graphics scene
because it viewed SVG as a format "which can be widely implemented in

browsers and authoring tools and which is suitable for widespread adoption by the content authoring community as a *replacement* for *many* current uses of raster graphics." Note the emphasis I placed on *replacement* and *many* in the preceding quote. SVG, created by W3C to have an impact in the Web graphics community, was a conscious intention that *many* uses of bitmap graphics were *intended* to be replaced by SVG. In addition, SVG was designed, from the beginning, to be accessible to a wide range of devices "from small mobile devices through office computer monitors to high-resolution printers." The scalability of a vector graphics format made that cross-platform targeting possible. At the time it was first discussed, this focus on multiple browser types was far seeing. Now you take for granted the existence of various mobile platforms for viewing the Web, although the creation of bitmap graphics for multiple platforms, even when bitmaps can be displayed, is a potentially tedious, time-consuming process.

Internationalization

You might have been involved in creating multiple images that have many similarities but must be created as separate images to suit each language version of your company's or your client's Web site. SVG can free you from much of the repetitive work involved in internationalizing a corporate Web site. Imagine creating graphics that can be used in English and that, by simply changing the text to that of another language and providing information about which language it is, you can customize in multiple languages by using relatively simple variants of a single image.

Five years ago, the Web was arguably a North American, English-language medium. Major corporations now see the need to reach, in their native language, the one billion native speakers of Chinese and the speakers of many European languages, for example. To reach an international, multilingual audience, you need built-in facilities for internationalization. XML and SVG have those. Bitmap graphics don't. If your corporate clients are looking to improve the international reach of their Web sites, why be left behind?

The code shown in Listing 0.3 causes a simple shape to be displayed with text in either English or French, depending on the user's language settings. Unfortunately, at the time this book was written, the Adobe SVG Viewer did not yet support this code.

Listing 0.3 (IntroInternational01.svg)

```
<?xml version="1.0" standalone="no"?>
<!DOCTYPE svg PUBLIC "-//W3C//DTD SVG 1.0//EN"
     "http://www.w3.org/TR/2001/PR-SVG-20010719/
     DTD/svg10.dtd">
<svg>
<rect x="50" y="50" rx="5" ry="5" width="200"
height="100" style="fill:#CCCCFF;
stroke:#000099"/>
<switch>
<text x="55" y="90" style="stroke:#000099;
fill:#000099; font-size:24;"
systemLanguage="en">
Hello!
</text>
<text x="55" y="90" style="stroke:#000099;
fill:#000099; font-size:24;"
systemLanguage="fr">
Bonjour!
</text>
<text x="55" y="90" style="stroke:#000099;
fill:#000099; font-size:24;">
It failed!
</text>
</switch>
</svg>
```

You can see in Figure 00.05 the displayed result when the language is set to English (en), and in Figure 00.06 the result when the language is set to French (fr).

SVG was also designed to be created using a simple text editor and using server-side scripts or programs. In other words, SVG was designed to be open to creation or implementation by programmers, or at least by those who can think like programmers. Of course, it can also be created using vector graphics drawing tools that are likely to be familiar to you. Those tools are described in Chapter 1, "The Basic SVG Tool Set."

Figure 00.05

The simple graphic that is displayed when the language settings are for English (en).

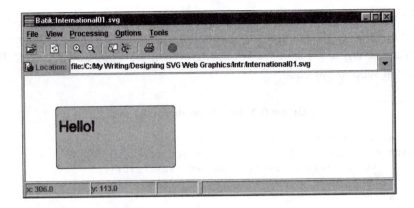

Figure 00.06

The same simple SVG graphic that is displayed when the language settings are for French (fr).

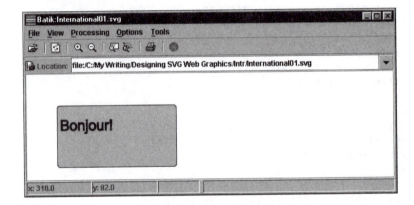

A potentially important SVG capability is that you can produce a complete Web site using only SVG. For Web authoring, you can use SVG as a "one-stop shop"—create your SVG Web graphics and embed them within SVG Web pages if you choose. You do not need to use HTML or XHTML. Of course, because SVG is XML, you can also combine it with other XML technologies to produce more sophisticated XML-based Web pages.

These characteristics of SVG are likely to change the world of graphics forever. I discuss the issue of SVG Web pages again in Chapter 12, "Creating a Simple SVG Web Site," because it is generating quite a bit of feeling in some quarters.

W3C

I have mentioned that W3C produced the SVG specification. In case you are not already familiar with W3C, I will explain a little about it here.

W3C, an acronym for the *World Wide Web Consortium*, is a cross-industry body whose members include giants like Microsoft, Sun, IBM, and Adobe, whose declared aim is to "Take the Web to its full potential." W3C has done work with graphics in the past. For example, it produced the Portable Network Graphics, or PNG, graphics format (see http://www.w3.org/TR/REC-png) in 1996.

However, W3C is best known for its work in the development of HTML and, more recently, XML and its associated family of technologies, including XHTML, XLink, and XSLT.

W3C produces specification documents, called "Recommendations," that carry great influence in the Web and e-business communities. That's not surprising because IBM, Adobe, Sun, Microsoft, and a host of other software companies who are W3C members have to vote on any proposal before it is finalized as a Recommendation. W3C Recommendations are not imposed on the Web industry; they are chosen by the industry.

W3C does not, technically speaking, produce standards, but the fact that the major players in the software scene are all members of the W3C means that its Recommendations generally carry great weight. Perhaps the most visible exception to this statement is Microsoft, which explicitly reserves the right to decide for itself which standards it adopts and, on occasion, takes its own line with regard to standards. However, even Microsoft is responsive to technology trends, exemplified in its abandonment of its preemptive version of "XSL" and subsequent adoption of W3C XSLT. I expect to see a similar move by Microsoft in relation to its own Vector Markup Language, VML, and its adoption of SVG.

XML

I want to say two things about XML. First, it is immensely important to the future of the Web. Second, a significant amount that has been written about it in the past couple of years is hype and is plain wrong, possibly because those who were writing about it didn't fully understand the topic!

XML is not a language in any normal sense. It is a meta-language (and might have better been called XMML), which means that it is designed to create a variety of what you would normally think of as languages, of which SVG is one example. Because these different languages are all built on the same syntax contained in the XML meta-language, powerful new possibilities exist for interchanging information (including graphical information) between computer applications because the structure of XML documents is predictable. Also, powerful new opportunities exist for using XML as the basis for dynamically generated Web pages. That XML processors can process any XML-based language is a good foundation for mixing different XML-based languages, including SVG, in one Web application.

On the Web, you have seen little of the additional power that XML brings to the table. In a few big sites, XML is used on the back end, but it is still HTML or XHTML that is presented on the client browser. That is in part because the main browsers—Internet Explorer, Netscape 6, and Opera— are all quite a bit off the pace in terms of implementing XML (as well as being off the pace, of course, in implementing other Web technologies, such as CSS).

During the lifetime of this book, I would expect to see that situation change significantly. Prototypes of new XML-based browsers are appearing, such as the X-Smiles browser described in Chapter 1, that make mixing SVG with other XML-based languages possible today.

One factor that has held XML back on the Web is the absence of an XML-compliant linking technology. The XML Linking Language (XLink) is now a full W3C Recommendation, and early browser implementations of XLinks are appearing; for example, in the Netscape 6 browser. Internet Explorer is now lagging behind in this respect. SVG viewers, including the Adobe SVG Viewer and the Batik viewer, implement XLink simple-type links. These subjects are discussed further in Chapter 5, "Creating Navigation Bars."

You can expect to see traditional browsers improve their XML capabilities. Also expect to see some exciting developments with multilanguage, XML-oriented browsers that prominently include SVG display facilities. One browser, X-Smiles (described in Chapter 1), can already display SVG with other XML-based languages, such as XSL-FO (Extensible Stylesheet Language Formatting Objects), XForms, and SMIL (Synchronized Multimedia Integration Language). You can create multimedia Web pages all based on XML and including SVG in a prominent place. Exciting, if demanding, times lie ahead with the growing use of SVG graphics in SMIL-based multimedia.

How Is SVG Different?

One important aspect of SVG you need to consider in a little more detail is how it differs from traditional Web graphics formats, both bitmap and vector. Before you go on to consider the detailed characteristics of SVG, step aside to look at some fundamental aspects of bitmap graphics.

Bitmap graphics

Bitmap graphics formats, such as GIF and JPEG, have been enormous practical successes on the Web. They were, and are, by no means perfect, as I mentioned earlier, but they were good enough for the early days of the Web. I have good reason to think—and this was an explicit aim of the SVG Working Group at W3C—that SVG will replace many uses of bitmap graphics.

As economic and time pressures build on all Web-facing businesses, the need for efficiency and cost containment is clear. And bitmap graphics can be (let me be honest) expensive commodities—expensive in terms of time and expensive in terms of money. One reason that they are expensive, from a business point of view, is that they are used in a closed, binary, non-editable format. To alter a bitmap graphic, you need to go back into your favorite graphics package and work again with the original version of your graphic (assuming that you saved it and can still find it!). That takes time and costs money.

The move from a monolingual Web using only English to a truly multi-lingual, genuinely worldwide Web is also exposing some of the weak-nesses of bitmap graphics. Suppose that you want to have a Web site in ten languages. If you want to do that with bitmap graphics, you need, in all likelihood, ten different bitmap graphics. If you want to edit them, you likely need to go back and find ten separate original files.

Then suppose that your company or client wants to change the color scheme for such an international, multilanguage Web site. You might have dozens of different graphics in the site that need to have their colors changed. And, of course, if your site is the ten-language version, you need to multiply that number by ten. To make any site-wide change for a multilingual international business is costly, in time and money.

What international businesses want is a graphics format that facilitates maintenance and change; a graphics format that is always easily editable; a graphics format that has internationalized capabilities built in.

Enter Scalable Vector Graphics! It is always editable. It is built on XML, which was designed to be used internationally. As I showed you in Figures 00.05 and 00.06, creating multilingual SVG graphics is straightforward.

In addition, you can use SVG with Cascading Style Sheets, including exter-nal Style sheets, to control the appearance of SVG graphics on a site-wide basis. After all, SVG is simply XML, and CSS can be used to style any XML. Do you see why I mentioned earlier that you might have to approach SVG with a new mindset?

From a business point of view, you can gain significant potential savings by using SVG both when creating graphics for a major Web site and when updating the design or carrying out other maintenance tasks. Corporations will look for graphic designers skilled in SVG. Your choice is to be among those who have actively acquired SVG skills and who are a sought-after commodity or to be among the group who become increasingly sidelined. The world of business on the Web is not a forgiving one. You need to be on the pace!

You might be getting a little worried at this point if you are a professional bitmap-oriented graphics designer. Part of your income, or perhaps much of it, comes from carrying out those changes to bitmap graphics I have just mentioned. They are, from a business point of view, highly inefficient. Graphics designers who can offer a graphics package that is XML based *and* potentially more efficient are likely to have a significant commercial advantage. If you don't acknowledge the forces that are operating on Web-based businesses, you are, in my view, likely to find your business increasingly squeezed. You need to adapt to the new Web graphics.

Enough of this business planning! Let's turn back to the technical issues relating to SVG and take a closer look at a number of aspects of SVG that, taken together, distinguish it from other existing graphics formats.

Text-based graphics

You might find it quite an odd concept to think of having a text description of a graphic that is sufficient to allow a graphic to be re-created. More than that, the graphic is stored in that text-based format, downloaded from the server to the client machine in that text-based format, and rendered by the SVG viewer and rendering engine only at the time when the graphic is to be viewed.

Because the various vector objects are downloaded as text, the source code (maybe that in itself is a strange thought) is available for inspection on the client machine.

SVG has the potential to open up graphics design in a way that is similar to the open way in which the use of HTML exploded because it was possible to right-click and choose View Source. As I see it, you have two choices: Stand on the sidelines and moan about "graphics thieves," or realize the creative potential of SVG, get aboard, and keep your eye on the future.

You might find the idea of anyone seeing exactly how your SVG graphic is structured profoundly threatening. At one level, you might be indignant that someone could learn from or borrow from (steal?) your work. But when you were learning about HTML, did you ever take a peek at how the experts did it?

Perhaps the kind of thought going through your mind is that you are "safe" with bitmap graphics or a proprietary vector format. But are you safe? This sort of opening up of technology is similar to what happened to the linotype operators a decade or two ago when desktop publishing (DTP) software systems arrived. A whole class of perceived highly skilled and relatively highly paid individuals were rendered almost superfluous by the arrival of DTP software. Does that mean that nobody makes a living today from participating in producing printed matter? Of course not! But the spectrum of skills in demand today is radically different from that of the heyday of linotype machines.

The kinds of skills base or knowledge base needed by successful Web graphics designers will, I believe, change fundamentally. You will no longer be able to rely on closed formats to protect your work. I am sure that linotype operators 20 years ago thought that their future was secure because their skills were not easily acquired. Their skills were quite simply bypassed.

The kinds of changes that are likely are a greater need for programmer-type thought patterns, awareness of customer needs, and skills in the internationalization of Web sites.

XML-based graphics

My purpose is not to provide you with a detailed primer of XML, and a detailed knowledge of XML isn't necessary for your initial exploration of SVG. In this section, I touch on some basic notions that help you begin to get a grip on the basics of what is now a huge and rapidly growing field of knowledge.

The source code for SVG graphics is not held in any arbitrary text format, but an SVG image (or an SVG document) is a "well-formed" XML document. That phrase means that the elements within an SVG image or document conform to the syntax required by the XML 1.0 Recommendation from the W3C. A well-formed SVG document might have (it isn't compulsory) an XML declaration as its first line, which could look like this:

```
<?xml version="1.0" standalone="no"?>
```

Following that might be a DOCTYPE declaration that provides information to the SVG rendering engine about what structure to expect in the SVG document. An SVG image that conforms to the November 2000 Candidate Recommendation would have the following DOCTYPE declaration:

```
<!DOCTYPE svg PUBLIC "-//W3C//DTD
        SVG 20001102//EN"
      "http://www.w3.org/TR/2000/
        CR-SVG-20001102/DTD/svg-20001102.dtd">
```

More specifically, an SVG document also must be "valid." In XML terminology, that means that the SVG image must be structured in the way demanded by the Document Type Definition (DTD) for the SVG language.

In the DOCTYPE declaration (which is confusingly similar in name to the DTD), you see a URL similar to

```
http://www.w3.org/TR/2000/CR-SVG-20001102/DTD/svg-20001102.dtd
```

That is the URL for the file that defines the allowable structure of an SVG document; in this case, one that conforms to the November 2000 SVG Candidate Recommendation. The SVG rendering engine (also called an SVG viewer) needs to process an SVG document with appropriate, predictable structure, and the DTD helps that process proceed smoothly.

You can look on the DOCTYPE declaration as stating where the DTD is to be found. The DTD defines what the allowed structure of the XML document—in this case, an SVG document—actually is. XML also allows part of the DTD to be embedded in the DOCTYPE declaration, but because I don't use that option in this book, after this paragraph, you can ignore that possible variant.

One of the powerful features of XML (and, by inference, SVG) is that it facilitates the interchange of information. Another is that XML-based languages can be used together in powerful and flexible ways. In Chapter 1, I briefly mention an XML processor that can display SVG with SMIL (Synchronized Multimedia Integration Language) and XSL-FO (Extensible Stylesheet Language Formatting Objects). So SVG is ideal both for integration with multimedia and with document layout formats. Although the focus of this book is on the use of SVG on the Web, SVG isn't limited to the Web.

You might be aware that XML includes the concept of *namespaces*, in which you can mix code from a variety of XML-based languages within one Web page. Each element is identified as belonging to a particular XML-based language, and each language has its own namespace prefix when used within that document, so the XML processor knows which elements are SVG and which are some other type of XML. In addition, you can use a scripting language, such as ECMAScript (JavaScript) to manipulate attributes or properties within more than one namespace (for example, to manipulate both an SVG graphic and the XHTML page that contains it). This mixing of XML-based languages opens up powerful, if daunting, creative possibilities.

If you find hints of the big and complex XML jigsaw puzzle a little over-whelming, don't worry because I don't bombard you with XML alphabet soup in this book. You need to learn new concepts if you are to make progress toward understanding SVG, but I explain it pretty much step-by-step as we go along.

Now move back from a brief perspective on the big picture, and take a closer look at the characteristics of SVG.

More SVG Capabilities

The reason that you are reading this book is probably that you want to find out *what* SVG can do and *how* you can make SVG do that for you. In this section, I discuss the display capabilities of SVG. Much of the remainder of this book focuses on how you use SVG.

Static graphics

The SVG specification provides a range of useful preset graphics shapes. If the shape you want isn't available, and you have the drawing skills, simply create it in your favorite vector drawing package. The current versions of Corel Draw, Adobe Illustrator, and Jasc WebDraw can all provide, at minimum, SVG export facilities. As I have already mentioned, libraries of vector graphics shapes are already available. If you can't draw the shape you want, a graphics library might have it or something close to it. Import the shape into Illustrator, for example, and save it as SVG, and you have an SVG visual component ready to modify or animate or have interactivity added to it.

SVG provides linear and radial gradients as well as an extensive range of filters that produce effects that, until recently, you would have expected only from specialized bitmap painting packages.

If your static shapes are too, well, static, have no doubt that SVG will let you bring them to life.

Animated graphics

SVG is capable of animating almost any part of an SVG image. You want to change the color of part of an image? It's simple: Just edit the stroke or fill properties. You want part of an image to become transparent or more opaque? Simply manipulate the opacity property. You want to move part of your image? Left or right? Change the x attribute. Up or down? Change the y attribute. Along a path? You can do that too.

SVG can also be combined with multimedia technologies. It has a close relationship with parts of the XML-based Synchronized Multimedia Integration Language (SMIL). Animation within SVG—specifically, the declarative type of animation—is based on the SMIL Animation specification and is discussed in Chapter 8, "Animation: SVG and SMIL Animation." SMIL animation is part of a larger SMIL 2.0 specification that offers powerful XML-based multimedia facilities.

For a glimpse of what is possible, take a look at http://www.x-smiles.org and download the demo files.

Interactive graphics

One of the fundamental requirements of a Web page is that it must be able to navigate, at user request, from page to page. Such interactive capabilities are routinely built in to HTML and XHTML Web pages and their Web graphics. You won't be surprised to learn that SVG has a full armory of interactivity functionality.

SVG offers a huge range of useful interactivity built in. Of course, you can create buttons that allow you to navigate from page to page. You can control animations of SVG elements by the way you click and move your mouse, for example.

No longer do you need to use JavaScript when you are creating rollovers for buttons or other navigation features. SVG provides a range of built-in events and event handlers that allow interactivity, like rollovers, to be created solely within SVG. But JavaScript capabilities are there to be used too, if you want to use them. The animation elements of SVG are powerful. For some uses, JavaScript is the icing on the cake.

You can still add additional types of interactivity by using JavaScript to manipulate the Document Object Model (DOM) of the SVG document or image.

Text layout

Many images, including buttons and logos, require the incorporation of text with graphic elements. SVG, of course, provides the ability to combine such parts of an image with the continuing advantage that all parts of the image remain editable.

SVG also has functionality that can allow you to lay out larger areas of text, including full SVG Web pages. If you want to look at an early experiment of what is possible here, visit http://www.svgspider.com/default.svg.

The range of possibilities as you piece together SVG visual components is enormous. Creating "furniture" for your Web page, such as buttons and logos, is straightforward. Rollovers? No problem, using the SVG animation elements or JavaScript. The limit to what you can create is likely to be your imagination and your detailed knowledge of SVG. This book is intended to help you understand SVG so that you can release your creative potential.

Millions of colors—on the Web!

One of the limiting factors of using GIFs on the Web has been that they are limited to the display of 256 (or 216) colors, usually of the "Web-safe" palette. The palette is calculated using a 6 x 6 x 6 color cube, giving a total of 216 colors. By contrast, SVG can use 16.7 million colors (24 bit) if your monitor and software support that setting.

The SVG rendering engine (also known as an SVG viewer) can make full use of whatever range of colors (up to 24 bit) that your graphics card and monitor are capable of displaying. The SVG reaches your computer as text-based source code, which is then rendered on the client side.

An SVG rendering engine (SVG viewer) interprets the source code and interpolates the true color needed in a gradient or other complex color transition, thus providing high-quality, true-to-life (or true-to-code) color.

SVG filters: Vector graphics that look like bitmaps

If you regularly use vector drawing packages, such as Corel Draw or Adobe Illustrator, you are familiar with the gradients and other subtle visual effects that can now be incorporated in vector graphics. SVG implements many of these in *filters*.

Many graphics that to the human eye have subtle and complex shading are possible to replicate by relatively simple mathematical formulae. You already know that because that is what your favorite bitmap editing package does for you routinely. When using SVG, you don't have to understand all the math, but you do need to have some concept of the properties of a particular visual appearance and how altering the values of certain inputs on an SVG element has an effect on the visual display.

One of the aspects of SVG with a great deal of potential for creative application are the filters provided within a conforming SVG rendering engine. These filters can provide many of the visual appearances usually associated with modern vector drawing packages or bitmap graphics applications, like Photoshop or Paint Shop Pro.

In addition, because SVG maintains the information that defines these filters as attributes of individual SVG elements, those attributes can have their value altered over time, which produces what you see as animations. So, not only do you have a useful and powerful range of SVG filters, but you can also animate their color, transparency, and position, for example, over time. The creative potential is huge.

Here's an important difference between "animated" GIFs and animated SVG images. An animated GIF is actually a miniature slide show. Each bitmap image has to be created individually, which is sometimes a time-consuming and costly process. If you want to produce a slow, smooth transition, you need many, many images embedded in the animated GIF. The file is big, therefore, and takes longer to download. In practice, most animated GIFs use rapid transitions and motion because those are more economical with file size and download time. With SVG, you can animate fast or slow with negligible differences in file size. Why? It is only a matter of a byte or two to alter the value of an SVG attribute, which is one reason that SVG graphics can provide sophisticated animation and still be downloaded quickly.

SVG gradients: Vector graphics that look like bitmaps

Conforming SVG rendering engines can render linear and radial gradients as they interpret and render SVG source code. Vector source code can produce an enormous range of bitmap linear and radial gradients.

You can combine these gradients with animations to produce attractive visual effects. Whether you want to produce startling quick-fire transitions (such as the onscreen appearance shown in Figure 00.02) or subtle, flowing changes depends on how you use your graphics.

Restyle Your Graphics or Web Site Using CSS

You might be shocked to realize that an SVG image can be styled using Cascading Style Sheets in the same way that an XHTML or HTML Web page can be styled. Of course, after you realize that an SVG image is held as a text document with start and end tags and is XML compliant, the fact that it can be styled with CSS is obvious. SVG elements (or *tags*) have style attributes that correspond to CSS2 properties. By creating CSS rules using appropriate CSS selectors, external Style sheets can be created that control the visual appearance of an SVG image onscreen.

Of course, because these CSS properties can also be animated within an SVG image, lots of interesting things are possible.

Combined with the fact that SVG graphics remain editable at all times, the entire look of a Web page, including its graphics, can be changed by simply changing the relevant style sheet. The business benefits of improving maintainability should be obvious. You want a new look for your Web site? Easy! Amend the stylesheet, and you have a new-look Web site. Depending on how your site is structured, the change can affect all language sites.

Of course, the downside for Web-oriented graphics designers is that repeat business for at least some types of site redesigns might simply dry up or generate substantially less income. Wiser Web designers won't look on this situation as primarily a threat (although in a sense it is one), but rather as an opportunity to improve efficiency or focus on the message and achieve a competitive edge.

SVG As Visual Components

The concept of Scalable Vector Graphics as "visual components" is, I believe, one of the most exciting and yet most radical concepts that SVG brings to the domain of the graphic designer.

SVG has visual components at many levels. You can combine and reuse these pieces of SVG code or functionality to make the creation of SVG images more efficient and quicker. SVG visual components are either provided by the rendering engine or created by you or another graphics designer. An SVG filter is created by using one or more visual components called *filter primitives*. You can create an animation visual component that you can reuse or adapt for use in many of your SVG drawings.

If your reaction to the idea of visual components is one of disdain because it is too mechanical and not sufficiently creative, just pause for a moment. This reuse of visual components by designers has been going on for centuries. And, if you are a Web graphics designer, you are almost 100 percent certain to already have been routinely using visual components in your bitmap images. But you might not have looked on them that way.

First, look at the historical use of visual components. Arguably, the first use of visual components took place at the time when the printing press was invented. Visual components, the printing plates, were created and used over and over again. The creative ability of someone with talent who crafted the printing plates was used time and time again. Of course, those who made their living by hand-writing manuscripts might have felt threatened. Similarly, when movable type was invented, the capacity for combining type in different ways added new flexibility that wasn't possible previously. Monks or other scribes might have felt deeply threatened at the times that the printing press and movable type were invented. The benefit for society was a marked improvement in the flow of information with consequent societal benefits.

Each time you create a graphic that uses type, you are making use of graphical shapes with particular meaning. Those shapes possibly were created by a specialist in that particular skill. Imagine how much slower expressing text in Web pages or Web graphics would be if you were unable to use fonts that someone else had created.

Your use of visual components is not limited to text. In all likelihood, whether you use bitmap or vector graphics software, you have made use of preset graphics objects. You can adjust properties on those objects, of course—changing the color, size, and position, for example—but you are actually reusing visual components created by the graphics software company. Imagine how tedious your task would be if you had to create from scratch each curve you use. Think of the time you would have to spend—and the mathematics you would have to master—to create smooth curves, for example. Worse still, imagine if you had to somehow adjust by hand the individual pixels in a photograph rather than make use of the premade visual components, such as the effects provided by Photoshop and similar programs.

Do you still think that you don't already make use of visual components? I hope now that you accept that you already do this—and on a daily basis.

So what does SVG bring to the table that makes awareness of SVG as visual components so powerful and so potentially important?

The difference that SVG makes is that you have detailed control over each property of each component and those properties remain totally editable at all times. If you want to put it simply, you can slot together parts of a graphic, including animations, a little bit like the way a child pushes together plastic bricks.

You might ask whether this process is just painting by numbers. In a way, it is, but so is all computer-based graphics work. It all depends on where the numbers are and how easily you can manipulate them.

In addition to allowing control over each property and attribute, the SVG specification allows for `<svg>` elements—one of which is the containing, or root, element of each SVG document or image—to be nested within each other. In other words, you can fit one SVG document or document fragment within another, in a way that has some similarities to the way Lego bricks are used together or the way in which complex e-commerce programs are constructed. Of course, the process with SVG is more complex and subtle than putting a child's plastic bricks together, but because you must follow rules for how this process is done, the visual components can be used together in synergy in ways that can be predicted to work.

More powerful still, an SVG document can import or include a separate SVG file to make up a composite image, in ways that are similar to the assembly of a frameset in HTML. You can assemble any SVG file—a visual component, if you like—with the other visual components in the importing file. If fact, you can also embed bitmap images within an SVG image and use that too as a visual component that can be animated.

By bringing together visual components in this way, graphics designers can use visual components (or objects) in a way that is very similar to what programmers use and have found to be effective in rapidly creating quality, reliable object-based software.

Don't throw your work away—reuse it!

Assembling an SVG document does not have to be done in only one setting. That same SVG document or image might, if appropriately designed, be capable of reuse in more than one way or in more than one project.

With careful planning, you can create (or will eventually be able to buy) SVG components that you can plug together to produce new and attractive SVG graphics. If you use vector graphics drawing tools, you might already know of or use some of the available libraries of shapes. If you use Photoshop or Paint Shop Pro, you might make use of plug-ins. Each of them can also be applied, in principle, to SVG. You might buy ready-made vector graphics shapes. Or, you might purchase additional filters that can piggyback on an SVG viewer to provide even more visual possibilities.

Part of the power of such libraries or plug-ins applied to SVG is that they are always editable. Any aspect you don't like, you can—if you have the relevant understanding of SVG—adapt precisely to your needs.

If you have an attractive SVG graphic, but are dissatisfied that it is static, simply add an animation visual component. You want it to move on the screen? No problem. You want it to change color or size while it moves? That too can be handled by SVG visual components.

When you assemble visual components, you can use techniques as simple as cutting and pasting relevant bits of source code.

Suppose that you have some static text like the following contained in an SVG image, and you want to change it and animate it:

```
<text x="50" y="50"
style="font-family:Arial, sans-serif; font-size:24;">
I am stuck in a bitmap rut!
</text>
```

Simply add an animation component that might look like this:

```
<animate attributeName="x" begin="2s" dur="10s"
from="50" to="500" fill="freeze"/>
```

and edit your text appropriately so that your SVG source code looks like this:

Listing 0.4 (AnimText.svg)

```
<?xml version="1.0" standalone="no"?>
<!DOCTYPE svg PUBLIC "-//W3C//DTD SVG 1.0//EN"
     "http://www.w3.org/TR/2001/PR-SVG-20010719/
      DTD/svg10.dtd">
<svg>
<text x="50" y="50"
style="font-family:Arial, sans-serif; font-size:24;">
<animate attributeName="x" begin="2s" dur="10s"
from="50" to="500" fill="freeze"/>
I am on the move with SVG!
</text>
</svg>
```

You have your first animated SVG image with a clear message, as shown in Figure 00.07.

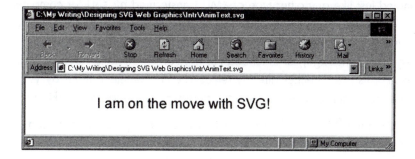

Figure 00.07

A simple and expressive text animation.

Just as you can adapt SVG visual components by adding animations, you can adapt for future use any SVG images created and debugged in earlier projects.

Don't worry, when I get into the meat of creating SVG images I take you through the necessary syntax and explain each aspect as I go. I simply want to show you how easy it is to plug together pieces of SVG—the visual components.

However, you are not limited to using only SVG as visual components.

Use bitmap graphics as visual components

The SVG specification allows for the import of bitmap images—specifically, JPEG and PNG—into SVG documents. That opens up a whole raft of creative possibilities. Animate photographs or bitmap buttons or other screen furniture around the screen by using the SVG built-in animation facilities, or augment those by adding JavaScript animation or interactivity.

Don't throw away your bitmap graphics skills. You can use selected bitmaps in new ways within SVG images. The possibilities are almost limitless.

Synergy with Other XML Technologies

One of the strategic strengths of SVG is that it is XML based. SVG can be handled just like any other type of XML, transformed by XSLT, or combined with other XML vocabularies, such as XHTML, XSL-FO (Extensible Stylesheet Language Formatting Objects), SMIL (the Synchronized Multimedia Integration Language), or Extended Form (XForms). XHTML, XSL-FO, SMIL, and XForms are all either already released as Recommendations by W3C or are under active development with prototypes around and working.

Don't be put off by the alphabet soup. The creative potential here can make your eyes bulge—and not only because you might have to spend long hours in front of the computer screen getting up to speed on all these technologies.

Synergy with XHTML

Perhaps the most obvious, practical use of SVG images now is as embedded images within HTML or XHTML Web pages. I describe those techniques in Chapter 10, "Embedding SVG in HTML or XHTML Pages." Depending on whether you want to use static or animated SVG, you can use SVG to replace GIFs, JPEGs, or Flash movies.

SVG also allows SVG and XHTML to be combined in the opposite way (by embedding HTML or XHTML within SVG Web pages). This can provide within an SVG Web page such facilities as interactive HTML or XHTML forms, which can't readily be provided within SVG itself.

Synergy with XSL-FO

Perhaps you are unfamiliar with the Extensible Stylesheet Language Formatting Objects, or XSL-FO. XSL-FO is an XML-based page layout (or, more precisely, document layout) language that can be displayed either on paper or on the Web.

XSL-FO Web pages are experimental at the moment, but do offer some facilities that HTML doesn't. SVG images can be embedded in XSL-FO pages in a straightforward way.

Synergy with XForms

When you are looking at the huge potential SVG synergy with other XML-based technologies, you are in danger of becoming overwhelmed in the alphabet soup of acronyms beginning with the letter *X*. The XForms specification being developed at the W3C aims to provide functionality that can be provided by HTML or XHTML forms only when scripted using JavaScript, for example.

Using SVG with XForms, you can provide an enormous range of XML-based Web functionality. SVG can provide graphics capabilities (and in SVG, Web pages can provide all the necessary text layout too). Watch this space! I can see that combination taking off.

SVG Limitations

I hope in the earlier parts of this introduction that I have transmitted something of my enthusiasm for SVG and have given you an impression of what it can do. If you are going to invest time and effort in learning SVG—and perhaps even bet the future of your business on it—you also want, and need, a realistic appraisal of its limitations.

Can SVG do everything? Of course not! Part of its limitation is the range of the SVG specification. For now, graphics designers are only beginning to get up to speed with the enormous potential that SVG offers. So, while you are still developing your skills in using SVG, you also need to be aware of the limitations of SVG itself and the tools now available to display it.

How fast is SVG?

Much depends on what aspect you are asking about, and much depends on how complex you want to make your SVG images. Also, the answer to specific questions about speed are changing all the time, as CPU speeds change and as those who are developing SVG rendering engines are learning how best to optimize them for speed in different settings.

Download times for SVG images (or "furniture") should be significantly faster than for equivalent bitmap images. Adding animations to SVG images does not, other than for complex animations, significantly increase download time.

Download times are only one part of the equation, though. How fast are SVG images displayed on the page? I have to be honest: SVG documents can be written that can bring an SVG processor to its knees, if the code hasn't been written particularly well or from trying to be too ambitious. You know that SVG can produce that exciting effect on your 1.5GHz machine, but you might forget that the 200MHz CPU that many users might still be using to access your image across the Web will struggle to cope with updating the display. SVG can be an intensive user of CPU cycles, particularly if many images are embedded in one page and several have continuing repeated animations.

Speed issues might arise partly because SVG viewers are still being written and refined. Certainly, significant speed improvements occurred between version 1 and version 2 of the Adobe SVG Viewer. Given the improvements in speed so far, I expect further performance improvements in future versions.

In parallel with improving SVG rendering engine speeds, SVG authors and designers are learning how better to write or tweak SVG to improve performance. CPU speeds are increasing steadily, and, as the experts will tell you, can be expected to increase for several years. I wonder whether trying to exploit fully the capabilities of SVG will be one reason that people will upgrade their computers.

The question that might well be in the front of your mind is how SVG will compare with Flash. Will you be subject to those interminable `Loading` messages, just as you are when you are visiting Flash Web sites? You needn't be. SVG can produce fast-loading Web pages, such as those accessible at http://www.svgspider.com/default.svg.

What happens when SVG animations become increasingly complex? Will download times increase? They will, but careful planning will, I expect, keep download times at acceptable levels. Will complex SVG animations be displayed on old computers with really slow processor speeds? I know of some SVG developers who are producing SVG on 166MHz machines, but I wouldn't recommend that as a routine.

Are SVG images high quality?

SVG images are intrinsically of higher quality than bitmap images, if by that one means that they can be zoomed and yet preserve image quality with no or minimal presence of the dreaded "jaggies." Take another look at Figures 00.03 and 00.04. Compare the close-up of the SVG text highly magnified with what a bitmap looks like when it is similarly magnified! In my view, there is no comparison.

Magnifying text shows that SVG images can be zoomed. But what use is that? Imagine using SVG to create a city map. You drive to the locality you want, and then you need to see more detail. No problem—just zoom in on the part of the SVG map for the locality where you need to go, and get a better look at street level.

Now you are almost there, but you need to see individual buildings. No problem—just zoom again.

This situation might work well on a desktop browser in your office, but what if you want that kind of functionality on the go? Remember that SVG was designed to be displayed on mobile devices as well as on traditional desktop machines. A viewer is available for the Pocket PC. I don't know of one for an in-car system yet, but you can probably expect to see them in a couple of years.

In addition to creating SVG images for Web pages, or complete Web pages, you can use SVG now for creating games or for maps on CD-ROM.

The future for SVG is exciting. If you grasp the basic techniques in this book and apply them fully and use them as a vehicle for your creative talents, you will have taken an important step toward being an active and successful participant in the SVG Web graphics revolution.

Don't be left behind!

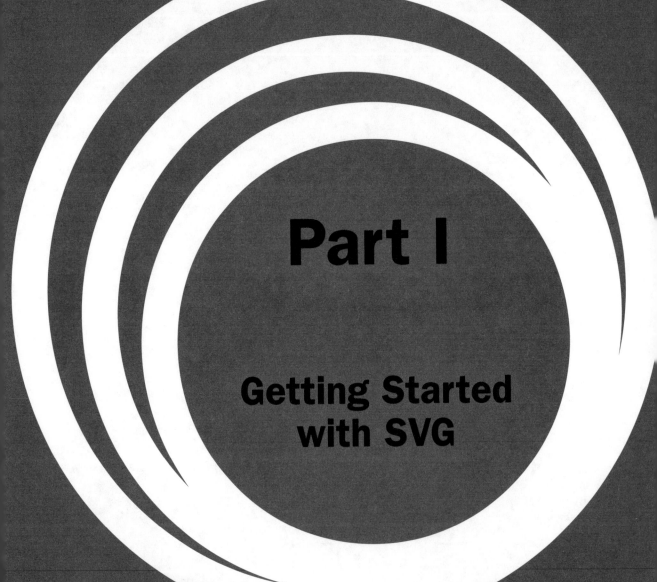

Part I

Getting Started with SVG

1

The Basic SVG
Tool Set

Creating and Editing SVG

To get started creating and viewing Scalable Vector Graphics images, you need two types of tools—something to create SVG with and something that allows you to view SVG onscreen.

You can, when you understand SVG syntax, create SVG documents or images with a text editor. An alternative way to produce SVG images, and perhaps the one you will initially find more convenient, is to use a vector graphics drawing package capable of handling SVG. Throughout this book, I use hand coding because that technique helps me bring out the techniques or points I want you to understand and that help you build up a range of knowledge and skills in SVG.

In this chapter, I describe for you the tools you need in order to create SVG and the software you need to install to view SVG.

Text Editors

Thinking that you can use a simple text editor to create sophisticated, animated, and interactive SVG graphics may be something of a shock to you. But, if you sufficiently understand the syntax of SVG, a text editor may be all you need. All the SVG in this book was hand coded. You could even use Windows Notepad, if you want.

You can use a simple text editor, but you can realize some advantages from using a text editor that has some awareness of XML and its need for being well formed, which is a requirement for all languages created using XML syntax. Scalable Vector Graphics, or SVG, is one of those languages. If your code is not well formed, an SVG viewer is not likely to render it properly—and perhaps not at all.

The following simple SVG document is also a complete description of a simple SVG image. The text-based markup completely describes the image that results when the SVG source code is rendered by an SVG viewer.

Listing 1.1 (SimpleRect.svg)

```
<?xml version="1.0" standalone="no"?>
<!DOCTYPE svg PUBLIC "-//W3C//DTD SVG 1.0//EN"
     "http://www.w3.org/TR/2001/PR-SVG-20010719/
        DTD/svg10.dtd">
<svg>
<rect
  x="10"
  y="20"
  width="100"
  height="100"
  style="fill:none; stroke:#000099; stroke-width:4;"/>
</svg>
```

I hope that you can see the similarity in editing HTML or XHTML source code. Perhaps the fact that you can describe graphics in this way is a little surprising. If you can visualize the final graphic, editing the source code can be fairly straightforward. The ability to visualize the resulting graphic, including animations, is something I found difficult initially, but, with increasing practice on my part, simple graphics or animations are not a problem. For complex animations, some planning and a diagram or two are helpful.

In case you have not already guessed, the SVG image is of a square with a deep blue outline and a totally transparent interior. (Yes, SVG has transparency that can be adjusted from totally transparent to totally opaque—or anywhere in between.) The square onscreen looks pretty much like Figure 01.01.

If you plan to use a text editor, you may be asking which one you should use.

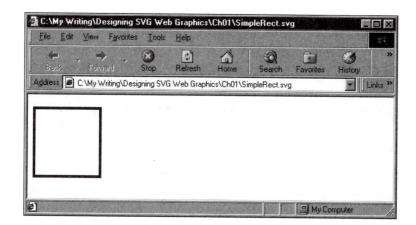

Figure 01.01

A simple SVG square with a transparent interior.

XML Writer

Many XML editors are on the market. One that I have used for some time is XML Writer, now at version 1.2.1. Further information about XML Writer is available at http://www.xmlwriter.com/. You can download a 30-day, fully functional evaluation copy of XML Writer from http://www.xmlwriter.com/download.shtml. I am not saying that XML Writer is better than any other product, but it has color coding of the code, can check for "well-formedness" (ensuring that the XML syntax is correct), works well for a beginner, is fairly cheap, and just doesn't "get in the way." From my point of view, it does a good job on small- to medium-size documents.

An important advantage of an XML editor like XML Writer is the color coding it can provide. This feature is useful when you are trying to locate where you have made some minor typing mistake or other syntax error. If you miss a quotation mark around the value of an attribute or make another simple syntax error within an SVG element, XML Writer is likely to produce an unusual color pattern onscreen that, if you focus on where the odd colors start, can help you find where the error is situated.

In addition, XML Writer can check your SVG document or image for well-formedness and to see whether it complies with the DOCTYPE declaration at the beginning of a piece of SVG code:

```
<!DOCTYPE svg PUBLIC "-//W3C//DTD SVG 1.0//EN"
    "http://www.w3.org/TR/2001/PR-SVG-20010719/
    DTD/svg10.dtd">
```

Many other XML editors are now available. Some, like XML Writer, are relatively cheap. Some are free. Some are expensive. In Appendix A, I list some useful Web sites where you can access further information on XML and XML tools.

When the SVG image is a simple one, spotting any mistake you have made is often easy. When an SVG image includes complex or sophisticated nested SVG elements with perhaps several animations in each SVG fragment, however, spotting well-formedness problems with the naked eye can become difficult. I cover this type of debugging issue in Chapter 14, "When Things Go Wrong."

Many, but not all, syntax errors in an SVG image are likely to cause the specific SVG element not to be displayed. Also, not all the other, later, SVG elements in the SVG document may be displayed. A simple syntax error at the beginning of a document can cause a total failure of the display of your carefully crafted image.

Vector Drawing Packages

A number of vector graphics packages are already available that can be used to produce sophisticated SVG images. Some have simply added a facility to export or save SVG created in the normal way. Others have the ability to both open and save SVG images. At least one allows you to see both the image you have drawn and the corresponding SVG source code with changes that are made in either the drawing or the code reflected in the other in real-time. When you are trying to learn the details of SVG, the latter approach has real advantages. In practice, the drawing program you use to produce SVG may well be influenced by the one you already own.

Adobe Illustrator is arguably one of the Big Three vector drawing packages. Of the other two major packages, Corel Draw 10 has useful SVG functionality (see the following section), whereas Macromedia Freehand seems, at least for the moment, to lack SVG functionality.

First, take a look at a new SVG-dedicated package, Jasc WebDraw, that lets you draw in the traditional way as well as tweak the SVG source code as you go along.

Jasc WebDraw

Jasc is perhaps best known for its inexpensive bitmap editor, Paint Shop Pro. Paint Shop Pro, although it is a bitmap package, has significant vector drawing capabilities. Jasc has harnessed its understanding of vector drawing to produce a dedicated SVG-oriented vector drawing package named WebDraw (now in Preview Release version 4b, see Figure 01.02). I won't be surprised if the WebDraw final release adds significant support for SVG animations.

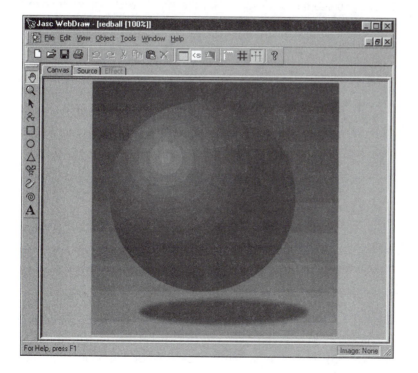

Figure 01.02

Jasc WebDraw (Preview Release) shows one of its sample SVG images. Note the tabs for Canvas and Source.

Further information on Jasc WebDraw is available at http://www.jasc.com/ webdraw.asp?. (Yes, the URL has a question mark at the end.) You can download an evaluation copy of WebDraw, which at the time this chapter was written was a preview release, from http://www.jasc.com/ wdrawdl.asp. Although WebDraw is in preview release form, it has been stable, in my experience. However, when using any preview release software, think carefully about whether you have any data that is important to back up.

You can use WebDraw as you would use any other vector drawing package. For example, to create a simple rectangle in the preview release, click on the rectangle tool, choose the properties of the rectangle in the Tool Options palette, click on the canvas to define the upper-left corner of your rectangle, and then drag outward to define its lower-right corner. User interface changes are likely in a final release.

So far, nothing is new. However, if you click on the Source tab within WebDraw, you see the SVG source for the simple rectangle you have just created. It looks something like this:

Listing 1.2 (WebDrawRect.svg)

```
<?xml version="1.0" standalone="no"?>
<!DOCTYPE svg PUBLIC "-//W3C//DTD SVG 1.0//EN"
        "http://www.w3.org/TR/2001/PR-SVG-20010719/
        DTD/svg10.dtd">
<svg width="500" height="500">
        <rect x="192" y="93" width="142" height="78"
        rx="0" ry="0" style="stroke-miterlimit:4;
        stroke-linejoin:miter;stroke-width:3;
        stroke-opacity:1;stroke:rgb(0,204,255);
                fill-opacity:1;fill:rgb(204,204,204);
                opacity:1"/>
</svg>
<!-- Generated by Jasc WebDraw PR4(tm) on 04/03/01
11:31:54 -->
```

In WebDraw, you can alter the image on the Canvas tab by either drawing on the canvas or altering the SVG source code in the Source tab (as shown in Figure 01.03). The code, which is accessible on the Source tab, has some color coding to assist you in editing it.

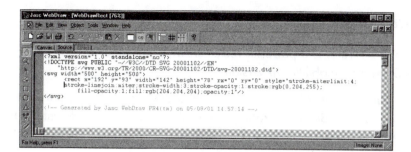

Figure 01.03

The source tab in Jasc WebDraw shows the source code for Listing 1.2.

You may notice that when Listing 1.2 was reloaded, WebDraw changed the date on which the file was generated and reformatted the code. This change can be irritating because if you have carefully formatted your SVG source, WebDraw unceremoniously mangles it. However, the facility to swap from the Canvas tab to the Source tab is useful. I understand that Jasc hopes to have addressed this problem in the final release so that when you load code, you can have what I call round-trip SVG.

If you want to give your rectangle a psychedelic yellow-green stroke rather than a pale blue one, you would, on the Source tab, change the `stroke` property of the `style` attribute from

```
stroke:rgb(0,204,255);
```

to

```
stroke:rgb(204,255,0);
```

If you then click on the Canvas tab, you see the color change for the stroke (outline) of the rectangle rendered as a striking (or horrible) yellow-green color.

When you have made your minor change to the source code, you can return to the Canvas tab to see the change reflected onscreen.

WebDraw has many more useful features already in place, and others are hinted at for a final release. The likely SVG animation functionality will doubtlessly attract lots of interest. It is already a competent SVG drawing and editing tool.

Adobe Illustrator

Adobe Illustrator is a powerful vector drawing package that has added SVG export capabilities in version 9.

You can find further information on Adobe Illustrator at http://www.adobe.com/products/illustrator/main.html. You can usually download from the Adobe site an evaluation copy of Illustrator (with, unfortunately, all SVG functionality disabled and also globally save-disabled).

The Adobe Web site, http://www.adobe.com/svg/, has a significant number of nice demos of using Illustrator to produce SVG. For example, to see some SVG animations that can be created using Illustrator, take a look at http://www.adobe.com/svg/illustrator/interactivity_palette/index2.html.

Corel Draw

Corel Draw is a powerful vector graphics drawing package that introduced an SVG export filter in version 9. If you are using Corel Draw 9, be aware that the SVG export filter for it is based on the March 2000 Working Draft of SVG and that a few pieces of syntax have changed since then. Corel Draw 10 has the capability to "round-trip" SVG (it can export SVG *and* open SVG files).

Historically, Corel Draw has been, at least in my opinion, a bit slow to adopt the mindset of design for the Web. However, the implementation of SVG functionality, together with changes in workflow within the application, make Corel Draw 10 a useful and powerful SVG drawing package.

Mayura Draw

The Mayura Draw shareware package, available for download from http://www.mayura.com, is a fairly basic vector drawing package. To create SVG using Mayura Draw, you must export the graphic. SVG is one of several graphics file formats available as export options.

This program does not achieve the functionality of the Canvas and Source tabs in Jasc WebDraw. Mayura Draw can save images as SVG files, but is unable to open or insert SVG files. Mayura Draw is therefore a vehicle to create simple SVG cheaply; because it does not have any round-trip functionality, I cannot recommend it for serious work.

Macromedia Freehand

I mention Freehand for two reasons. First, it is one of the major vector drawing packages. Second, at the time this chapter was written, Freehand offered *no* SVG functionality. One can only speculate whether that situation relates to Macromedia ownership of the Flash vector drawing environment. Because Flash is probably a significant part of the Macromedia revenue stream, the company, quite understandably, may not want to acknowledge the existence of a competing—and arguably, superior—vector drawing standard.

It does seem shortsighted for Macromedia to fail to support such an important standard as SVG.

SVG Viewers

Full SVG support hasn't been built-in yet to the standard editions of any of the main Web browsers (Internet Explorer 5.x, Netscape 6, and Opera 5). Limited native SVG support is in the development versions of the Mozilla browser (get further information at http://www.mozilla.org/projects/svg/), but none is in the released version of Netscape 6.0. To view SVG using any of the major HTML browsers, you need to download an SVG viewer. A number of SVG viewers are available.

The available SVG viewer downloads are significantly larger in size than, for example, the Flash viewer download. That statement isn't too surprising because SVG has more functionality than Flash does.

In addition to the plug-in for HTML browsers, a number of stand-alone SVG viewers are available, some focused only on SVG and others with exciting capabilities to display combinations of SVG with XSL-FO, SMIL, or XForms. In the short term, SVG images may be embedded in primarily HTML or XHTML Web pages. However, in the not-too-distant future, multi-namespace

XML browsers with SVG display functionality may open up display possibilities that HTML and XHTML browsers find difficult to match. In addition, SVG Web pages can be produced and then viewed in HTML Web browsers with the Adobe plug-in.

Adobe SVG Viewer

The Adobe SVG Viewer has the best overall functionality in displaying SVG. Adobe SVG Viewer version 2 provides good display functionality for the basic SVG graphic shapes (see Chapter 3, "Creating Static Graphic Elements"), SVG text (see Chapter 4, "Using Text in SVG"), gradients (see Chapter 6, "Creating SVG Gradients"), filters (see Chapter 7, "Using SVG Filters"), and animation (see Chapter 8, "Animation: SVG and SMIL Animation"). The Adobe Viewer is an excellent SVG viewer, but does have a few important limitations. Because of a bizarre (in my opinion) design decision, scroll bars were omitted from the SVG viewer; in stand-alone large SVG images, therefore, no scroll bars are displayed in the browser window. You can circumvent the problem by embedding the SVG image in an HTML shell, as explained in Chapter 10, "Embedding SVG in HTML or XHTML Pages." In response to user pressure, Adobe has promised to look seriously at the possibility of adding scroll bars in a future release. In addition, among other features in the SVG specification yet to be implemented is the ability to import other freestanding SVG images using the `<image>` element and the ability to include other types of content using the `<foreignObject>` element. Both those facilities would provide enormous scope for facilitating visual components in SVG.

I have not listed the current deficiencies of the Adobe SVG viewer because I think that the Adobe Viewer is poor but only because it still has farther to go. I think that it is already excellent, but its already impressive facilities have whetted my appetite, and that of other interested users, to see even more of the exciting capabilities of SVG.

You can download the Adobe viewer by visiting http://www. adobe.com/svg. From that page, a link may enable you to download the current version of the SVG viewer. Quite sensibly, Adobe has decided to focus, in this initial phase, on Internet Explorer and Netscape 4 browsers on the Windows and Macintosh platforms. Check this URL to find out whether further support has been added. Adobe also provides download-able documentation that describes in detail which features of SVG a partic-ular version of the SVG viewer supports.

> *You can install the Adobe SVG Viewer if you use the Netscape 6 or Opera 5 browsers, although neither of those browsers is officially supported. However, to do that, you need either Internet Explorer or Netscape 4 installed. Install the Adobe SVG Viewer for either of the supported browsers, and then copy the following files (for the current version) to the plug-ins directory of Netscape 6 or Opera 5, as appropriate: SVGViewer.zip, SVGView.dll, and NPSVGVw.dll. Netscape 6.01 seems to have a problem using the Adobe plug-in, although it works well with Netscape 6.0.*

If you want to get full enjoyment from this book and you have a suitable browser installed on your machine, be sure to use the Adobe SVG Viewer and enjoy the images and animations to their full potential.

CSIRO SVG Viewer

The CSIRO SVG Viewer is a Java-based SVG viewer that can be used on operating systems on which the Adobe SVG Viewer is not now supported. You can find information on the CSIRO SVG Toolkit at http://sis.cmis.csiro.au/svg/.

The CSIRO SVG Toolkit now has a more limited implementation of SVG than does the Adobe SVG Viewer. Unless you want to explore the parts of the CSIRO SVG Toolkit other than the viewer for desktop machines, there-fore, you should focus on the Adobe Viewer.

CSIRO also has an SVG viewer under development for the Pocket PC. Information on that topic is available on the CSIRO Web site.

X-Smiles viewer

The X-Smiles viewer is probably the most experimental of the SVG viewers listed here, but is also one of the most exciting. In fact, the X-Smiles viewer is not simply an SVG viewer; it can display SVG and can also display XSL-

FO, SMIL, and XForms, thus opening up a glimpse of new avenues for the use of SVG with other XML-based technologies. The kind of capability that X-Smiles is now capable of delivering is something that you will quite likely take for granted in the future.

Get further information on the X-Smiles viewer from http://www. x-smiles.org/. You can download the X-Smiles viewer from http://www. x-smiles.org/download.html. X-Smiles is now available as Preview Release version 0.33.

The X-Smiles viewer, a Java-based application, is in development, so check the X-Smiles site for any changes to the following installation instructions. Download the zipped Java executable to a suitable temporary directory. If you have WinZip (http://www.winzip.com/)or a similar program, unzip X-Smiles into a suitable directory, such as c:\XSmiles. When you are unzipping, make sure that the Use Folder Names option is checked. If you unzip without creating the appropriate folder hierarchy, X-Smiles doesn't run—the folder hierarchy is essential.

To run X-Smiles, you need to have a Java Virtual Machine (JVM) installed on your computer, version 1.2 or higher. If you do not already have a Java SDK or JRE installed, visit http://java.sun.com and look for Java SDK Standard Edition. Either version 1.2 or 1.3 works with X-Smiles.

If you have a suitable JVM installed, your CLASSPATH set up correctly, and the X-Smiles executable unzipped, you are ready to run the X-Smiles viewer (see Figure 01.04).

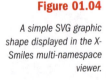

Figure 01.04

A simple SVG graphic shape displayed in the X-Smiles multi-namespace viewer.

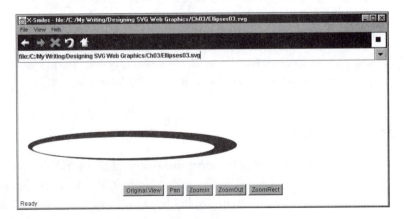

Batik

The Batik Java-based SVG viewer is part of the many XML-related projects under the auspices of the Apache Foundation (see Figure 01.05). General information on Batik is available at http://xml.apache.org/batik/index.html. You can download the Batik SVG Toolkit, of which the Batik SVG viewer is a part, from http://xml.apache.org/batik/dist/. The current version is Batik 1.0. Check this URL for the latest version if you want to use it. Installation instructions for Batik are available at http://xml.apache.org/batik/install.html.

CSIRO SVG Viewer for Pocket PCs

If you are interested in getting a glimpse of the potential of SVG on various browser platforms, not simply on the traditional desktop PC, take a peek at the SVG viewer for Pocket PCs, now under development at CSIRO. Further information is available at http://www.cmis.csiro.au/sis/SVGpocket.htm.

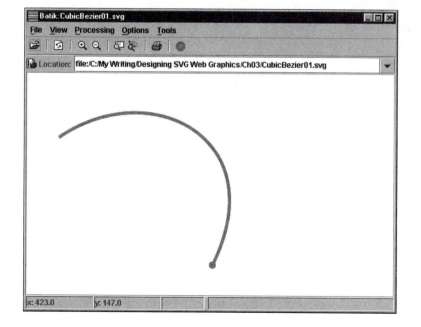

Figure 01.05

A cubic Bezier curve displayed in the Batik SVG viewer.

IBM SVGView

IBM developed an SVG viewer that appears not to have been updated to reflect the developments in the SVG specification. Information is available at http://www.alphaworks.ibm.com/tech/svgview.

Amaya

W3C produces the Amaya Web browser and authoring environment. Amaya has limited SVG display facilities. I have tried the Amaya browser and authoring environment on several occasions, only some related to SVG, and have always been disappointed. I know that others are enthusiastic about the potential of Amaya, but my own opinion is that it is not easy to use. I hope that, in time, some of its claimed potential will be realized. Until then, I mention Amaya only for completeness, but can't recommend it now as a useful SVG viewer. To check on further progress of Amaya, visit http://www.w3.org/Amaya/. Amaya version 5 has improved SVG support.

In summary, I recommend that you download and install the Adobe SVG Viewer, assuming that you are using a Windows or Mac platform. The implementations of SVG in Batik and X-Smiles are generally less complete than the implementation in the Adobe viewer.

So what will the serious players in the vector graphics market do as they jostle for position?

My guess is that Macromedia will try, for as long as possible, to publicly ignore SVG as a serious vector technology. By doing that, the company may hope to minimize awareness of SVG within the Flash community. Because SVG is, I believe, a superior technology to Flash—particularly for a Web that is increasingly XML based—Flash may in some future version provide at least a minimum of SVG export and run on a slogan that exclaims, "Use the authoring tool you know to produce exciting, new XML-based SVG graphics."

Adobe has perhaps the greatest investment in seeing SVG succeed. SVG provides a potentially powerful competitor to Flash as *the* Web vector technology. I would expect Adobe to improve SVG authoring and round-trip support for SVG in Illustrator and provide powerful SVG animation authoring in LiveMotion. Just as Adobe had two separate products in Photoshop and ImageReady, which are now closely integrated, the company may make a similar move to provide static and animated SVG functionality with Illustrator and LiveMotion, respectively.

Don't overlook Jasc WebDraw, which is already a competent SVG vector drawing tool. With the likely addition of SVG animations, WebDraw could become a useful tool indeed.

The superiority of SVG over Flash isn't the only issue. The usability of Illustrator and LiveMotion (or some new secret SVG product?) and WebDraw will have an impact on the penetration of SVG into the graphics market. It is too early to tell who the winners will be, but these three companies are all worth watching in the SVG space.

2

SVG Document Overview

In this chapter:

Syntax

This chapter looks at how the source code of an SVG image is structured. All SVG images, which are also SVG documents or document fragments, are also XML-compliant documents.

If you don't understand how XML syntax—and, therefore, SVG syntax—works, you can end up with endless frustration because an SVG viewer may not display any (or only parts) of your SVG image, if it isn't properly structured. That isn't surprising. Suppose that you are reading the instructions for the construction or configuration of a new gadget and you read, "Diggle the windlejump so that it is lineared upside the kindlespan." What do you do, apart from uttering some bad words or throwing the gadget out the window? You are probably stuck. If you don't structure your SVG documents properly, an SVG viewer has much the same problem: It stops. (It usually doesn't swear, though it may provide a helpful error message.) The worst message an SVG viewer has returned to me is "Junk after the document element," which I took to mean that I had made a major error (and I had).

Structure of an SVG Image (Document)

Let's begin to delve into SVG jargon and thought patterns. If you are not familiar with XML or HTML syntax and are not used to the notion of an image that is also code, it isn't always easy, but in time it all becomes second nature. Just as a concert pianist becomes free to express music with virtuoso power by becoming the master of many basic techniques, so it is with SVG.

The Preliminaries of an SVG Document

An SVG image can be completely described in an SVG document (or document fragment). The source code that describes the image is the input to an SVG rendering engine (an SVG viewer).

If you were going to draw a picture, you would want to know the kind of medium you were going to use, the tools you had available, and the size of the paper. The preliminaries of an SVG document provide much the same basic information to the SVG viewer. The XML declaration confirms what type of *medium* (syntax) will be used. The DOCTYPE declaration defines the allowed elements (tools, if you like). The `<svg>` element, called the *document element*, has attributes that define the size of the SVG canvas (or at least the size of the part of it on which this image will be rendered). With those three pieces of information available, an SVG viewer then has the basic information to be able to render an SVG image onscreen. Let's take a closer look at how these elements are used in practice.

All Scalable Vector Graphics documents (images) are applications of the syntax of the XML 1.0 Recommendation from the World Wide Web Consortium, or W3C. An SVG viewer should be told that the SVG document complies with XML syntax, which is done through the XML declaration. Including an XML declaration within each SVG image or document is advisable, although not compulsory. An XML declaration, at its simplest, looks like this:

```
<?xml version="1.0" ?>
```

Although the XML declaration is optional, when you do include it, the version attribute is compulsory. Also, the XML declaration has to be on the first line of the document with no characters, not even a space, in front of it and no spaces within the `<?xml` part. An XML declaration can have other attributes, such as the standalone or encoding attributes, which I don't describe further just now. Your favorite vector drawing package possibly adds one or more attributes automatically, as in this declaration from Jasc WebDraw:

```
<?xml version="1.0" standalone="no"?>
```

You don't need to add additional attributes, as long as you remember to include the version attribute. If you are working on a single platform in English, you don't need to worry too much about the other attributes. If you want to produce SVG graphics for a cross-platform, international, or multi-lingual audience, however, a fuller understanding of the encoding attribute, for example, is important.

The next thing in many SVG documents is typically the DOCTYPE declaration. This bit of XML terminology describes the location of the document that defines what structure the document should conform to.

> *The XML syntax rules define how the elements of an XML, or SVG, document are put together, but doesn't say what those elements or their attributes should be. The DOCTYPE declaration links to a related document, called a Document Type Definition, which specifies exactly which elements are allowed and what attributes they are allowed to have. Slight differences exist between the versions of SVG.*

If you view SVG documents on the Web, you may—for some time, at least—find a number of different DOCTYPE declarations.

If the SVG image was created to correspond to the March 2000 SVG Working Draft (the version used for the Adobe SVG Viewer version 1.0), the DOCTYPE declaration looks like this:

```
<!DOCTYPE svg PUBLIC "-//W3C//DTD SVG 20000303
Stylable//EN"
"http://www.w3.org/TR/2000/03/WD-SVG-20000303/
DTD/svg-20000303-stylable.dtd">
```

Many early SVG images placed on the Web used this DOCTYPE declaration (the SVG filter for Corel Draw 9 still does) because it was the SVG version on which the first release of the Adobe SVG Viewer was based and many early users of SVG initially wrote their code for that version.

If you see an image using the March 2000 type, be aware that the linking mechanism had an error, so don't just copy code to use in buttons, for example. It may not work in all current SVG viewers, although some viewers—such as the Adobe SVG Viewer—do, for reasons of backward compatibility, allow links to operate using incorrect syntax.

If an SVG document was written to correspond to the August 2000 Candidate Recommendation, it looks like this:

```
<!DOCTYPE svg PUBLIC "-//W3C//DTD SVG 20000802//EN"
"http://www.w3.org/TR/2000/CR-SVG-20000802/
DTD/svg-20000802.dtd">
```

SVG images using the November 2000 Candidate Recommendation use this DOCTYPE declaration:

```
<!DOCTYPE svg PUBLIC "-//W3C//DTD SVG 20001102//EN"
"http://www.w3.org/TR/2000/CR-SVG-20001102/
DTD/svg-20001102.dtd">
```

If you see these lines in the source code of an SVG image you are trying to understand, remember that some slight syntax changes have taken place over the intervening period and a few details will have changed. Particularly if you are using a new version of an SVG viewer, you may find that occasionally such images aren't displayed properly.

In time, the DOCTYPE declaration from the full SVG 1.0 Recommendation supplants all those shown previously.

What a DOCTYPE declaration does is to tell the SVG rendering engine (or viewer) the location of the Document Type Definition (DTD)—the document that defines the structure the SVG document should have. For the July 2001 Candidate Recommendation, the details of the correct structure are defined at http://www.w3.org/TR/2001/PR-SVG-20010719/DTD/svg10.dtd. An SVG viewer may have a local copy of the DTD (which defines the correct structure) built in, but if you are using general-purpose XML tools, such as XML Writer, you may need to be online before it can check whether your SVG image's structure is *valid* (or correct in structure, according to the DTD).

The DOCTYPE declaration tells the SVG viewer what structure of document is being used, but you may also want to use an external style sheet to control appearance. If your SVG image is using an external Cascading Style Sheet (CSS), you might find this instruction early in an SVG image:

```
<?xml-stylesheet href="MyStylesheet.css"
  type="text/css" ?>
```

This code is an XML *processing instruction*. It tells the SVG viewer that it should load a file named MyStylesheet.css. Stored in the same directory as the SVG image, this text file containing CSS should use that CSS file to define the style on appropriate elements in the SVG image. A more detailed discussion of the use of CSS with SVG is in Chapter 13, "Designing Your SVG for Use with CSS."

You can, and often it is a good idea, to insert comments that describe the purpose of the document. SVG provides a specific element for descriptions, the `<desc>` element that is discussed later in this chapter, but SVG can also use ordinary XML comments that have the same syntax as HTML/XHTML comments:

```
<!-- This is a comment. -->
```

Let's move on to look at the structure of the visible part of an SVG image.

The <svg> Element

Each SVG document or document fragment must have as its containing element the *element root*, a `<svg>` element. The `<svg>` element usually contains width and height *attributes*, which define the width and height of the SVG image. If no width or height is specified, the width and height are both assumed to be 100 percent of the available browser window.

> *The area defined by the `<svg>` element is the SVG initial viewport. Conceptually, it is a rectangular area through which you can view what is displayed on an area of the infinite SVG canvas. The width and height attributes define its dimensions. On an outer `<svg>` element, the default values of the x and y attributes (which define the position of the upper-left corner of the viewport) are both zero.*

NOTE

If you want to create a simple SVG graphic that is 300 pixels wide by 200 pixels high, you can start with something like the following, by either hand-coding it or having a drawing tool like Jasc WebDraw create it for you:

```
<?xml version="1.0" standalone="no"?>
<!DOCTYPE svg PUBLIC "-//W3C//DTD SVG 1.0//EN"
     "http://www.w3.org/TR/2001/PR-SVG-20010719/
     DTD/svg10.dtd">
<svg width="300" height="200"/>
<!-- Generated by Jasc WebDraw PR4(tm) on 04/03/01
 10:55:39 -->
```

The following syntax indicates that the `<svg>` element is empty:

```
<svg width="300" height="200"/>
```

The syntax for an empty element is a forward slash at the end of the element name (as in `<svg/>`, or, when attributes are present, the syntax can look like what you have read about in the text. This syntax is simply shorthand for `<svg></svg>`. You are likely to use empty elements quite often in your SVG images, such as when you use a rectangle, which is written as `<rect/>`.

If you are using WebDraw, adding any image component on the canvas tab inserts SVG elements correctly. If you are coding by hand, you need to split the `<svg>` element into starting (`<svg>`) and ending (`</svg>`) tags, like this:

```
<svg width="300" height="200">
</svg>
```

The correct place to insert other SVG elements is between these starting and ending tags.

If you are hand-crafting your SVG, I suggest that you save a template that looks something like this:

```
<?xml version="1.0" ?>
<!DOCTYPE svg PUBLIC "-//W3C//DTD SVG 1.0//EN"
     "http://www.w3.org/TR/2001/PR-SVG-20010719/
     DTD/svg10.dtd">
<svg width="" height="">
<!-- You would insert other SVG elements here,
nested within the <svg> element. -->
</svg>
```

This template saves you from typing the DOCTYPE declaration and reminds you that you need to decide on a size for the display area.

So the SVG viewer now knows that what it is being presented with is intended to be a valid SVG document.

As you have just read, the width and height attributes of the <svg> element define the size of the area on which the SVG is rendered. SVG element and attribute names are case sensitive. Therefore, the name of the <svg> element must be in all lowercase letters. Also, the names of the width and height attributes also must all be in lowercase letters.

In addition to getting the correct syntax for element tags, you need to know how to write the attribute names that occur on many SVG elements. Thus, when you write the following:

```
<svg width="300" height="200"/>
```

you have two attributes: width and height. An attribute on any SVG element takes this form:

```
attribute="value"
```

or

```
attribute='value'
```

Although you can use either single or double quotes, unlike in HTML, the quotes are compulsory in SVG. Because you also must use quotes in pairs, if you start with an apostrophe, for example, you must finish the attribute value with an apostrophe.

Within a <svg> element, all the other content describing the SVG image is nested:

```
<svg >
<!-- The other elements in the SVG document are
nested within the containing <svg> element -->
</svg>
```

A <svg> element can contain a single graphics element, which in this case displays a pale bluish rectangle in the upper-left corner of the screen:

```
<?xml version="1.0" standalone="no"?>
<!DOCTYPE svg PUBLIC "-//W3C//DTD SVG 1.0//EN"
```

```
        "http://www.w3.org/TR/2001/PR-SVG-20010719/
         DTD/svg10.dtd">
<svg width="300" height="200">
<rect x="0" y="0" width="20" height="40" style="fill:#CCCCFF;
 stroke:none;"/>
</svg>
```

Alternatively, a `<svg>` element can contain several, even dozens, of other SVG elements, some of which might themselves also contain a variety of nested SVG elements.

Nested SVG Elements

A `<svg>` element is like other SVG elements in that it can be nested within a `<svg>` element containing the SVG document. For example, to nest a `<svg>` element that is 100 x 100 pixels inside a `<svg>` element that is 400 pixels wide x 300 pixels high, you could use this code:

Listing 2.1 (NestedSVG.svg)

```
<?xml version="1.0" standalone="no"?>
<!DOCTYPE svg PUBLIC "-//W3C//DTD SVG 1.0//EN"
      "http://www.w3.org/TR/2001/PR-SVG-20010719/
       DTD/svg10.dtd">
<svg width="500" height="400">
<svg x="100" y="100" width="300" height="200">
<rect x="1" y="1" width="298" height="198"
style="stroke:red; stroke-width:2;
fill:none;"/>
<rect x="50" y="50" width="200" height="100"
style="fill:#EEEEEE;
stroke:blue;"/>
</svg> <!-- The end tag of the nested <svg> element -->
</svg> <!-- The end tag of the outer <svg> element -->
```

The first `<rect>` element, to be described in Chapter 3, "Creating Basic Static Graphic Elements," simply displays a rectangle to show where the outer boundary of the nested `<svg>` element is positioned onscreen, as shown in Figure 02.01.

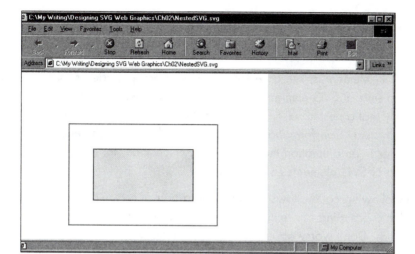

Figure 02.01

A nested <svg> element whose outer boundary is indicated by the outer rectangle outline.

When used in this way, the nested `<svg>` element can be used as the container for an SVG visual component, which can be made up of many SVG elements, including animated elements.

The advantage of grouping SVG elements within a nested `<svg>` element is that all the coordinates and positioning of the grouped elements refer to the upper-left corner of the nested SVG element. Within the nested `<svg>` element, the positioning of the other SVG elements is maintained relative to each other. So, to move all the elements that make up the component, you simply alter the x and y coordinates of the nested `<svg>` element. The whole group relocates within the containing `<svg>` element with the relative positions of the elements within the nested `<svg>` element preserved.

A nested `<svg>` element can be created directly within another `<svg>` element, as you have just read. SVG also has an `<image>` element that allows separately written and saved SVG document fragments (what I call *visual components*) to be inserted or imported into another SVG document. At the time this book was written, the Adobe SVG Viewer (version 2.0) does not yet allow the importing of SVG document fragments in this way.

A nested `<svg>` element is a useful container element to group other SVG elements. Another option is the grouping `<g>` element.

The <g> Element

The `<g>` element is, like a nested `<svg>` element, provided so that you can group several SVG elements within it. A `<g>` element has one important facility that a nested `<svg>` element does not have: A `<g>` element can be transformed. *Transformation* is a powerful tool in SVG whereby either statically or in an animation the shape, size, or position, for example, of a group of SVG elements can be changed.

The following code allows you to rotate a pair of rectangles contained within a grouping `<g>` element through 360 degrees over a period of ten seconds. Don't worry about how the animation works; this subject is discussed in Chapter 8, "Animation: SVG and SMIL Animation." Figure 02.02 shows the animation part completed. If the rectangles were created within a `<svg>` element, transforming them in this or any other way would not be possible. Thus, if you want to rotate, skew, or otherwise transform a group of SVG elements, you likely need to use the grouping `<g>` element.

Listing 2.2 (GExample01.svg)

```
<?xml version="1.0" standalone="no"?>
<!DOCTYPE svg PUBLIC "-//W3C//DTD SVG 1.0//EN"
    "http://www.w3.org/TR/2001/PR-SVG-20010719/
      DTD/svg10.dtd">
<svg width="500" height="400">
<g>
<animateTransform attributeName="transform"
type="rotate" values="0 150 100; 360 150 100"
begin="0s" dur="10s" />
<rect x="1" y="1" width="298" height="198"
style="stroke:red; stroke-width:2;
fill:none;"/>
<rect x="50" y="50" width="200" height="100"
style="fill:#EEEEEE;
stroke:blue;"/>
</g>
</svg>
```

Like `<svg>` elements, `<g>` elements can have associated `<desc>` and `<title>` elements (see the sections on the `<desc>` and `<title>` elements later in this chapter). These elements provide information that can be useful

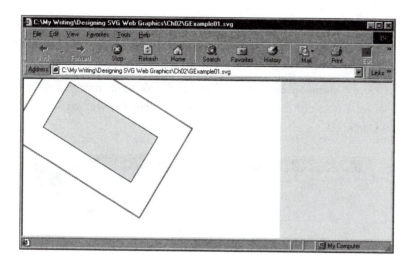

Figure 02.02

The grouped rectangles, nested in a <g> element, are partway through a `rotate` *transformation.*

when any later amendments are made to the code and also can be used to promote Web accessibility.

A `<g>` element can have an ID attribute to uniquely identify it within an SVG image. The `<desc>` element can be used to provide descriptive information about the purpose of the `<g>` element and its content, as in the following simple example of two groups of circles, each with transparent fill:

Listing 2.3 (idGs01.svg)

```
<?xml version="1.0" standalone="no"?>
<!DOCTYPE svg PUBLIC "-//W3C//DTD SVG 1.0//EN"
    "http://www.w3.org/TR/2001/PR-SVG-20010719/
     DTD/svg10.dtd">
<svg width="500" height="400">
<desc>Two groups each of which contains two circles
</desc>
<g id="RedGroup" style="fill:none; stroke:red;
stroke-width:4;">
<circle cx="100" cy="100" r="50" />
<circle cx="200" cy="100" r="50" />
</g>
<g id="BlueGroup" style="fill:none; stroke:blue;
stroke-width:4;">
<circle cx="100" cy="250" r="50" />
<circle cx="200" cy="250" r="50" />
</g>
</svg>
```

The ID attribute also can be used as the identifier for the target of an animation. Note in Figure 02.03 that the style information on the `<g>` element is applied to its child `<circle>` elements.

Just as `<svg>` elements can have other `<svg>` elements nested within them, `<g>` elements also can be nested within each other (as well as within `<svg>` elements).

Figure 02.03

Two pairs of circles, each nested in a <g> element, inherit their style properties from the parent <g> element.

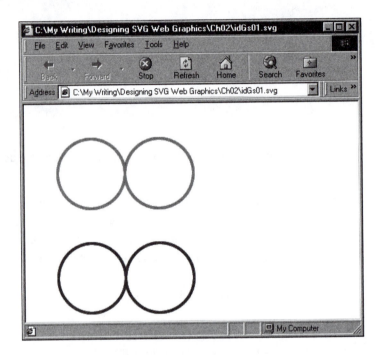

Some Basic SVG Elements

Chapter 3 describes the SVG elements that define basic graphical shapes—such as a rectangle and circle, as shown in previous examples—that directly create a visual appearance onscreen. First, this section describes a number of other SVG elements that are not necessarily immediately visible onscreen but that are useful nonetheless.

The SVG `<a>` element, which functions similarly to the HTML/XHTML `<a>` element, is considered in Chapter 5, "Creating Navigation Bars."

The <desc> element

SVG container or graphics elements can contain a text-only description contained within a <desc> element. This description provides the opportunity to document a whole SVG document or image, or part of it, thus facilitating maintenance.

A <desc> element, when it is the child of the outer <svg> element, should precede any other child elements except for the <title> or <metadata> elements. This is suggested because future versions of SVG may impose stricter rules on element content than does the current DTD, presumably by using W3C XML Schema (although that is not stated in the SVG specification). Ordering of the <title>, <desc>, and <metadata> elements appears to be not of importance for rendering or accessibility.

Listing 2.4 shows how you might use the <desc> element to describe the rectangle you read about in Chapter 1, "The Basic SVG Tool Set."

Listing 2.4 (DescExample.svg)

```
<?xml version="1.0" standalone="no"?>
<!DOCTYPE svg PUBLIC "-//W3C//DTD SVG 1.0//EN"
     "http://www.w3.org/TR/2001/PR-SVG-20010719/
     DTD/svg10.dtd">
<svg>
<desc>This image contains a simple square with a
transparent fill which will later
form the basis for an animated logo.
</desc>
<rect
  x="10"
  y="20"
  width="100"
  height="100"
  style="fill:none; stroke:#000099; stroke-width:4;"/>
</svg>
```

The <title> element

SVG container or graphics elements can contain a text-only title for the document or graphics object contained within a <title> element. This provides the opportunity to display information about the whole or part of an SVG document or image. An SVG viewer is not obliged to render the content of the `<title>` element but can do so; for example, as a tooltip or, as in the case of version 1 of the Batik viewer, in the title bar of the viewer. The Adobe Viewer does not yet display the content of the `<title>` element.

A `<title>` element, when it is the child of the outer `<svg>` element, should precede any other child elements other than `<desc>` or `<metadata>` elements. Ordering of the `<title>`, `<desc>`, and `<metadata>` elements appears to be not of importance for rendering or accessibility.

The <defs> element

The SVG specification encourages the reuse of code within individual SVG images or documents. This reuse is made possible by creating a definition of some element, or group of elements, within a `<defs>` element and then referencing that definition from another element in the main part of the SVG document.

Figure 02.04 shows an example of a linear gradient defined within the `<defs>` element, specifically within a `<linearGradient>` element (which is described further in Chapter 6, "Creating SVG Gradients"). The gradient is referenced using a bare names XPointer from a `<rect>` element.

Figure 02.04

An SVG linear gradient displayed by means of the `<defs>` element.

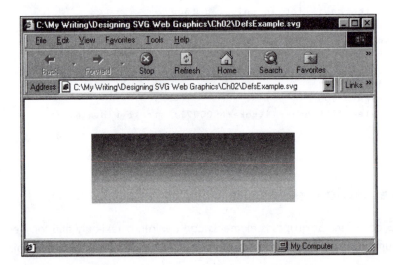

The code to render such an image is shown here.

Listing 2.5 (DefsExample.svg)

```
<?xml version='1.0'?>
<!DOCTYPE svg PUBLIC "-//W3C//DTD SVG 1.0//EN"
    "http://www.w3.org/TR/2001/PR-SVG-20010719/
    DTD/svg10.dtd">
<svg width="800" height="600">
<desc>A simple use of the &lt;defs&gt; element to
 contain the definition of a linear gradient.</desc>
<defs>
<linearGradient id="Gradient01" x1="0" x2="0" y1="0"
y2="150" gradientUnits="userSpaceOnUse">
<stop offset="20%" style="stop-color:#3300FF"/>
<stop offset="80%" style="stop-color:#CCCCFF"/>
</linearGradient>
</defs>
<rect x="100" y="50" width="300" height="100"
style="fill:url(#Gradient01)" />
</svg>
```

Many other uses of the `<defs>` element are defined in the SVG specification. For example, SVG filters are defined within a `<defs>` element and then referenced using the filter property on an element that occurs later in the document. (This topic is described further in Chapter 7, "Using SVG Filters.") Many other SVG elements can be used singly or in combination, including linear or radial gradients, SVG filters and animations, and the linking `<a>` element. When combinations of elements are used to define a sophisticated shape nested within the `<defs>` element, the shape can be reused elsewhere in the document, thus reducing overall file size.

The <symbol> element

The `<symbol>` element can be used to create graphical template objects that can be used more than once in an SVG image by employing the `<use>` element (see the next section, "The `<use>` element"). A `<symbol>` element is similar to a `<g>` element except that a `<symbol>` element is not rendered, but instances of the `<symbol>` element created by a `<use>` element are rendered.

A `<symbol>` element possesses `viewBox` and `preserveAspectRatio` attributes to allow the graphic defined by the `<symbol>` element to scale to fit the rectangular space defined by the referencing `<use>` element.

The <use> element

The `<use>` element can reference a `<symbol>`, `<svg>`, `<g>`, `<rect>`, `<line>`, or other element to reuse the referenced element within an SVG image (the `<rect>` and `<line>` elements are discussed in Chapter 3). Typically, the ID attribute of the referenced element, whether it is a single graphics object or a container object, is the means by which the `<use>` object achieves an unambiguous reference.

One important difference between the `<use>` element and the `<image>` element (see the next section, "The <image> element") is that the image element can reference a whole external file, whereas a `<use>` element cannot.

I mentioned earlier that SVG provides several ways of supporting the componentization of SVG so that you can think of parts of an SVG image as visual components.

In this section, you look at how you can make repeated use of simple, or not-so-simple, shapes within an SVG document. This example reuses a triangle defined within an SVG `<path>` element (which you meet in Chapter 3) contained within the `<defs>` element.

The triangle is defined in the `<path>` element in the following code, with the `<path>` element nested within a `<defs>` element:

```
<defs>
<path id="MyTriangle" d="M200 100 L300 300 100
300 Z" style="fill:#EEEEEE; stroke:red;" />
</defs>
```

The triangle has a red outline and a pale gray fill. To go on to reuse that triangle shape you simply display three similar triangles—one half-size, one normal-size, and one double-size—by using the SVG `<use>` element three times but scaling each use by, respectively, 0.5, 1.0 and 2.0. This arrangement produces the half-size, normal-size, and double-size triangles. Don't worry about the detail of scaling at this stage; concentrate on the idea of code reuse.

The code for the half-size triangle looks like this:

```
<g id="HalfSize" transform="scale(0.5) translate(0,0)">
<use xlink:href="#MyTriangle"/>
</g>
```

Use the grouping `<g>` element to contain the `<use>` element because the `<g>` element can be transformed. In this case, you simply scale the triangle by a factor of 0.5. The `translate(0,0)` is included so that you can see that you don't move the triangle at all, although when you look at Figure 02.05, you may think that you have. What has happened is that in the scaling by 0.5, the values of the points within the `<path>` element have also been multiplied by 0.5 and are therefore half as far from the origin of the coordinate system for the SVG image.

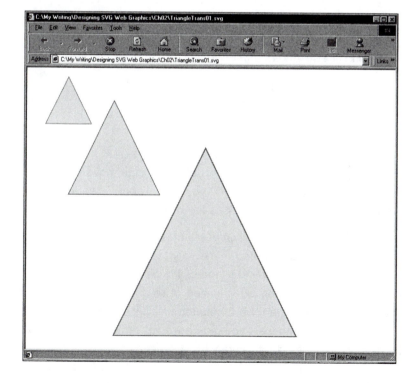

Figure 02.05

Three triangles, defined in the <defs> element and used in a <use> element, but scaled differently each time.

Listing 2.6 (TriangleTrans01.svg)

```
<?xml version="1.0" standalone="no"?>
<!DOCTYPE svg PUBLIC "-//W3C//DTD SVG 1.0//EN"
    "http://www.w3.org/TR/2001/PR-SVG-20010719/
    DTD/svg10.dtd">
<svg>
<defs>
<path id="MyTriangle" d="M200 100 L300 300 100
300 Z" style="fill:#EEEEEE; stroke:red;" />
</defs>
<!--By specifying the ID, I can reference this graphic
later with the "use" element-->
<g id="HalfSize" transform="scale(0.5) translate(0,0)">
<use xlink:href="#MyTriangle"/>
</g>
<!--Here I have referenced My triangle by referring to
its ID in the xlink:href attribute. In the XLinks
section in Chapter 5, I describe this further. -->
<g id="NormalSize" transform="scale(1.0)
translate(0,0)">
<use xlink:href="#MyTriangle"/>
</g>
<g id="DoubleSize" transform="scale(2.0)
translate(0,0)">
<use xlink:href="#MyTriangle"/>
</g>
<!--In all three of the above groups, I have
transformed the same triangle by scaling it.
This allows for smaller file sizes.-->
</svg>
```

Notice in Figure 02.05 that all aspects of the triangle have been scaled. In the double-size triangle, for example, you can probably see that the width of the outline is also twice as thick as the outline on the full-size triangle.

The <use> element, conceptually, causes a separate Document Object Model (DOM) tree to be created in memory. Because this element is not part of the DOM tree for the main part of the SVG image, access to parts of the element being referenced is limited. Also, functionality that can be achieved using SVG declarative animation or ECMAScript scripting is thus limited. In such circumstances, you may have to create separate instances of the element that would be referenced in order to create the desired animation or other effect. Thus, at least version 1.0 of the SVG specification has unfortunate limits on the reuse of elements for certain purposes.

The <image> element

The presence of the `<image>` element in an SVG document indicates that the content of an external file will be rendered into a rectangular area within the coordinate system of the referencing SVG image.

The `<image>` element can reference bitmap graphics files, such as PNG, GIF, or JPEG files. In addition, an important factor for the concept of visual components discussed throughout this book is that the `<image>` element also allows the importing of graphics files with the content type `text/xml+svg` (another SVG document or document fragment). Thus, a visual component created and saved in a file can be imported when needed.

An `<image>` element has x, y, width, and height attributes that define a rectangular area in which the bitmap or SVG image will be rendered. When an SVG file is being referenced, a new viewport is created with the boundaries of that viewport being defined by the x, y, width, and height attributes. The x and y attributes define the position of the upper-left corner of the viewport, and the width and height attributes define the dimensions within which the image is displayed. When an SVG file is being referenced, a separate DOM tree is created and properties from the referencing SVG image are not inherited by the referenced SVG image.

> At the time this book was written, the `<image>` element has been implemented in the Adobe SVG Viewer version 2.0 with respect to bitmap graphics, but not yet with respect to SVG images. This situation limits the scope for a significant aspect of SVG visual components, but you may not have to wait long before SVG files can also be accessed using the `<image>` element.

The `<image>` element is used with syntax such as the syntax used in the following code. Note the need for the x, y, width, and height attributes before the imported image can be appropriately rendered.

Listing 2.7 (ImageExample.svg)

```
<?xml version="1.0" standalone="no"?>
<!DOCTYPE svg PUBLIC "-//W3C//DTD SVG 1.0//EN"
    "http://www.w3.org/TR/2001/PR-SVG-20010719/
    DTD/svg10.dtd">
```

```
<svg width="800" height="600">
<desc>This graphic links to an external JPEG image
</desc>
<image x="200" y="200" width="200px" height="150px"
xlink:href="NiceImage.jpg">
<title>A nice JPEG image.</title>
</image>
</svg>
```

The <switch> element

The SVG `<switch>` element provides alternative rendering options if an SVG viewer is unable to render some aspect of content. When a `<switch>` element is activated, only one of the elements (or groups of elements) defined by the `<switch>` element is rendered. The `<switch>` element is particularly relevant if you employ SVG in a multinamespace context or using the `<foreignObject>` element because implementation is variable for the latter.

The `<switch>` element can also be used in multilingual SVG images or documents to control the text that is displayed according to the user's browser language settings, as you have read in Chapter 1. That use is described more fully in Chapter 17, "The Future of SVG".

Painter's Model

One of the important concepts about SVG that determines what you and your customers see onscreen is the rendering order for elements within an SVG image. The SVG term for this concept is the *painter's model*, in which the final rendering of an SVG image broadly resembles the way in which an oil painting is created. Just as when you apply oil paint to a canvas and cover up what is below it, you can obliterate (sometimes intentionally, sometimes not) other SVG elements rendered further back.

Typically, an element contained early in an SVG document is rendered toward the back and therefore is covered by paint applied as defined by later elements in the document.

Listing 2.8 illustrates how the painter's model works. The first `<rect>` element, which is pale bluish, is completely covered by the second `<rect>` element, which is red. However, because the third `<rect>` element is semi-transparent, with an opacity of 0.5, some of the red color of the second `<rect>` element can be seen as in Figure 02.06.

Listing 2.8 (PaintersModel.svg)

```
<?xml version="1.0" standalone="no"?>
<!DOCTYPE svg PUBLIC "-//W3C//DTD SVG 1.0//EN"
     "http://www.w3.org/TR/2001/PR-SVG-20010719/
      DTD/svg10.dtd">
<svg width="300" height="400">
<rect x="30" y="30" width="100" height="100"
style="fill:#CCCCFF; stroke:none;"/>
<rect x="80" y="80" width="100" height="100"
style="fill:#FF0000; stroke:none;"/>
<rect x="130" y="130" width="100" height="100"
style="fill:#0000FF; stroke:none; opacity:0.5"/>
</svg>
```

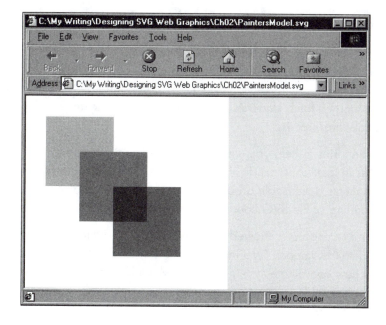

Figure 02.06

Three rectangles illustrating the SVG painter's model. A rectangle later in a document covers the one preceding it. However, the lower-right rectangle is partly transparent, and some of the color of the middle rectangle shows through.

In practice, if you are using a program such as WebDraw or Illustrator to create your SVG graphics and you bring an object to the front, that action causes it to be placed later in the SVG source code and thus rendered toward the front of the SVG painter's model.

When you use grouping elements, such as the `<g>` element, it is as though you have created a separate canvas for rendering the group, and the result of that rendering is then applied to the parent canvas. This situation can have some subtleties, but for many practical purposes your drawing package takes care of the details.

SVG shapes can be painted along their outline, typically represented by a stroke property, or paint can be applied to the interior of a shape (it is filled), and the corresponding property is the fill property.

The SVG painter's model is considerably more complex than just described, but this short description suffices for most purposes in this book.

SVG Coordinate Systems

The coordinate system used in SVG is potentially complicated. You may want to skim or skip this section on your first read through the book and return to study it later. Understanding SVG coordinate systems isn't a straightforward process.

This section tries to help you understand some key points, which you use in examples in later chapters. If you want to make maximum use of SVG visual components as reusable graphics components, you need at least some understanding of the SVG coordinate system.

Earlier in this chapter, I showed you a nested `<svg>` element but didn't discuss in detail its impact. One implication is that a nested `<svg>` element opens a new coordinate system within it, which is responsible for the useful effect of being able to move whole graphics around while preserving their relative positions.

First, look at some of the jargon. SVG graphics are painted on the SVG *canvas*, which is potentially infinite in size. In practice, you or other users see only a finite rectangular portion of the SVG canvas, which is the SVG *viewport*.

Lengths in SVG can be expressed without specific units and are then said to be expressed in *user units*. Alternatively, a variety of units can be used with a value of any length, as shown in Table 2.1.

SVG allows a variety of transformations—including rotation, skewing, translation, and scaling—that alter the coordinate system at the relevant part of an SVG document (or document fragment).

Table 2.1 Units of Measurement

Abbreviation	Meaning
em	The current font's font size
ex	The current font's x-height
px	Pixel
pt	Point
pc	Pica
cm	Centimeter
mm	Millimeter
in	Inch
%	Percentage

Establishing a new coordinate system

SVG allows for new coordinate systems to be established. Typically, that may be when a `<svg>` element is nested within an SVG document or document fragment. Suppose that you again have a simple rectangle nested within a `<svg>` element, which itself is positioned within another SVG element. Your source code might look like this (refer to Figure 2.1 for a visual reference):

Listing 2.9 (NestedSVG.svg)

```
<?xml version="1.0" standalone="no"?>
<!DOCTYPE svg PUBLIC "-//W3C//DTD SVG 1.0//EN"
    "http://www.w3.org/TR/2001/PR-SVG-20010719/
        DTD/svg10.dtd">
<svg width="500" height="400">
<svg x="100" y="100" width="300" height="200">
<rect x="1" y="1" width="298" height="198"
style="stroke:red; stroke-width:2; fill:none;"/>
<rect x="50" y="50" width="200" height="100"
style="fill:#EEEEEE; stroke:blue;"/>
</svg>
</svg>
```

The purpose of the red outline, represented by the first `<rect>` element, is simply to show the boundaries of the nested `<svg>` element. The second rectangle is to demonstrate the coordinate system within the nested `<svg>` element.

The red (outer) rectangle is positioned in the middle of the screen, yet because it has an x attribute of 1 and a y attribute of 1, you would expect it to be placed right at the edge. And it is. But it is placed at the edge of the new coordinate system created in the nested `<svg>` element that contains it so that the rectangle with the red outline shows in effect the position of the boundaries of the new coordinate system in the nested `<svg>` element. In that new coordinate system, the point (0,0) is in the upper-left corner of the red outline.

I use this technique of nesting `<svg>` elements frequently in this book. If you create a complex SVG graphic, with the relative positions of various SVG elements being important, you can preserve the relative positions of the elements and yet move the whole graphic around by simply altering the x and y attributes of the `<svg>` element within which you nest them.

If a transformation, such as a rotation, of the grouped graphic *must* be carried out, a `<svg>` element is not suitable—you have to use a `<g>` element instead.

The viewBox attribute

Now move on to take a look at the `viewBox` attribute of the `<svg>` element. The SVG *canvas* is potentially infinite in size, and the view box gives you a window into that infinitely sized canvas. Often, you create graphics that are wholly displayed in the view box, but you can create SVG graphics anywhere on the canvas. If you are looking at a map created in SVG and want to travel east, for example, you would find that you need to see a part of the "infinite" map further to the right. You could do that by altering the SVG view box and looking at a part of the map further to the right. Look at the basics of how that concept works.

To illustrate how the `viewBox` attribute works, I adapt the nested SVG example from the preceding section. Note the `viewBox` attribute on the outer `<svg>` element in Listing 2.10.

Listing 2.10 (ViewBox01.svg)

```
<?xml version="1.0" standalone="no"?>
<!DOCTYPE svg PUBLIC "-//W3C//DTD SVG 1.0//EN"
     "http://www.w3.org/TR/2001/PR-SVG-20010719/
        DTD/svg10.dtd">
<svg width="500" height="400" viewBox=" -70 -70
430 330">
<svg x="100" y="100" width="300" height="200">
<rect x="1" y="1" width="298" height="198"
style="stroke:red; stroke-width:2;
fill:none;"/>
<rect x="50" y="50" width="200" height="100"
style="fill:#EEEEEE;
stroke:blue;"/>
</svg>
</svg>
```

The following line shows four values for the `viewBox` attribute:

```
<svg width="500" height="400"
viewBox=" -70 -70 430 330">
```

The first pair of numbers represents the x and y coordinates of the upper-left corner of the view box. The second pair of numbers represents the x and y coordinates of the lower-right corner of the view box. Thus, the lower-right corner of the view box shown in Figure 02.07 is (430,330).

You can check whether you have this calculation correct by counting out the values of the coordinates for the lower-right corner of the rectangle with the blue outline (the gray fill). The starting x is -70; the nested `<svg>` element is offset to 100; within that element, the x attribute is 50; and the width of that `<rect>` element is 200. Adding those numbers (70 + 100+ 50 + 200), you find that the lower-right corner of the blue outline rectangle has an x coordinate at 420. Similarly, the y attribute is at 70 + 100 + 50 + 100 = 320. Thus, the lower-right corner of the blue outline rectangle should be 10 pixels from the lower-right corner of the view box, which corresponds to what is shown in Figure 02.07.

Figure 02.07

The view box is altered so that the upper-left corner is at coordinates (-70, -70) and the lower-right corner is at (430,330).

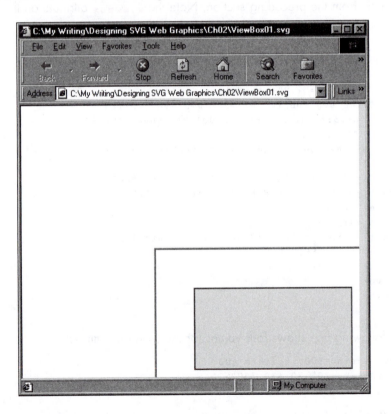

With me, so far? It might help if I create an animation of the view box here so that you can look at it working. Here is the code:

Listing 2.11 (ViewBox02.svg)

```
<?xml version="1.0" standalone="no"?>
<!DOCTYPE svg PUBLIC "-//W3C//DTD SVG 1.0//EN"
    "http://www.w3.org/TR/2001/PR-SVG-20010719/
    DTD/svg10.dtd">
<svg width="500" height="400" viewBox=" -120 -120
480 380">
<animate attributeName="viewBox" from="0 0 500 400"
to="-120 -120 480 380" begin="0s" fill="freeze"
dur="10s"/>
<svg x="100" y="100" width="300" height="200">
<rect x="1" y="1" width="298" height="198"
style="stroke:red; stroke-width:2;
fill:none;"/>
<rect x="50" y="50" width="200" height="100"
style="fill:#EEEEEE;
stroke:blue;"/>
</svg>
</svg>
```

To fully appreciate what is happening, you need to run the code onscreen. The animation represents the transition from the original position of the nested <svg> to the one shown in Listing 2.11. It looks as though you have cut out a window in a playing card and are looking through it at the two rectangles. Then, you move the card with the window in it up and to the left, giving the appearance that the rectangles are moving down and to the right, although the rectangles are stationary. The window, or view box, is what is moving.

If you don't grasp the information in this section immediately, don't worry about it. You don't need to understand it to move on to later chapters, but you may need to understand it when you begin creating some of your own, more advanced, SVG images.

Stretch to fit

SVG provides the means for you to create images that stretch to fit the available space.

First, I show you the use of percentages as the size of SVG elements within an SVG image. Figure 02.08 shows an example.

Figure 02.08

Each of the four rectangles shown is 50 percent of the size of the SVG view box. When the view box is resized, so is each rectangle.

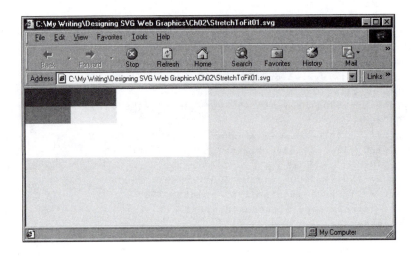

Here is the code that produced the figure:

Listing 2.12 (StretchToFit01.svg)

```
<?xml version="1.0" standalone="no"?>
<!DOCTYPE svg PUBLIC "-//W3C//DTD SVG 1.0//EN"
    "http://www.w3.org/TR/2001/PR-SVG-20010719/
    DTD/svg10.dtd">
<svg width="50%" height="50%">
    <rect x="0%" y="0%" width="25%" height="25%"
style="fill:blue"/>
    <rect x="25%" y="0%" width="25%" height="25%"
style="fill:green"/>
    <rect x="0%" y="25%" width="25%" height="25%"
style="fill:red"/>
    <rect x="25%" y="25%" width="25%" height="25%"
style="fill:yellow"/>
</svg>
```

Notice that the values of all the x, y, width, and height attributes are defined as percentages. The `<svg>` element is always half the height and width of the browser window. Similarly, each colored rectangle is always half the width and height of the SVG view box and is therefore a quarter of the width and height of the browser window. To see this effect in action, you need to experiment with the browser window size and watch the dimensions of the rectangles change.

This technique can be useful when you are creating, for example, entire SVG Web pages (see Chapter 12, "Creating a Simple SVG Web Site"). If you set the width and height of the `<svg>` element to 100 percent and create a `<rect>` element as the first element with width and height attributes of 100 percent, you have a uniform colored background that is resized as you resize the browser window.

SVG provides a technique that is useful when you don't know or don't control the size of the space in which an SVG image will be displayed.

Now, I use the `viewBox` attribute from the preceding section in a different way.

When you set `preserveAspectRatio` to `none`, you may find that the stretch-to-fit feature produces unacceptable distortion of your original image.

Listing 2.13 (StretchToFit02.svg)

```
<?xml version="1.0" standalone="no"?>
<!DOCTYPE svg PUBLIC "-//W3C//DTD SVG 1.0//EN"
    "http://www.w3.org/TR/2001/PR-SVG-20010719/
     DTD/svg10.dtd">
<svg width="300px" height="200px"
viewBox="0 0 600 400" preserveAspectRatio="none" >
<desc>This example uses the viewBox
attribute to automatically create an initial user
coordinate system which causes the graphic to scale
to fit into the viewport no matter what size the
viewport is.</desc>
<rect x="0" y="0" width="600" height="400"
style="fill:#990066" />
<circle cx="300" cy="200" r="150" style="fill:white;
stroke:red;
stroke-width:6;"/>
<text x="200" y="200" style="font-size:30;
font-family:Verdana">
Stretch to fit
</text>
</svg>
```

The code produces the appearance shown in Figure 02.09.

Figure 02.09

The SVG image fits the view box by virtue of the viewBox *attribute. If the view box is redimensioned, the image changes its dimensions to fit.*

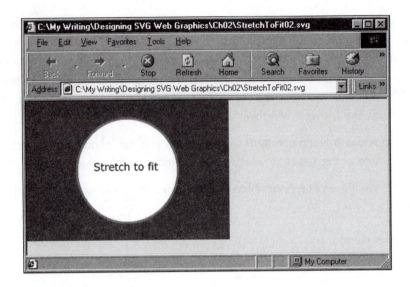

Try changing the width and height attributes of the `<svg>` element to 600px (pixels) and 400px, respectively, without changing anything else in the code. The circle and text resize to fill the defined space.

In Listing 2.13, you set the `preserveAspectRatio` attribute to a value of `none`. Whatever the dimensions of the width and height of the `<svg>` element, the contents then fill it. If you choose a shape with a lesser height, it is still resized, but the shape is distorted. If the code is as shown in Listing 2.14, you get the appearance shown in Figure 02.10.

Listing 2.14 (StretchToFit03.svg)

```
<?xml version="1.0" standalone="no"?>
<!DOCTYPE svg PUBLIC "-//W3C//DTD SVG 1.0//EN"
    "http://www.w3.org/TR/2001/PR-SVG-20010719/
    DTD/svg10.dtd">
<svg width="600px" height="100px"
viewBox="0 0 600 400" preserveAspectRatio="none" >
<rect x="0" y="0" width="600" height="400"
style="fill:#990066" />
<circle cx="300" cy="200" r="150" style="fill:white;
stroke:red; stroke-width:6;"/>
<text x="200" y="200" style="font-size:30;
font-family:Verdana">
Stretch to fit
</text>
</svg>
```

Figure 02.10

The circle and text are resized to completely fill the allowed space because the preserveAspectRatio *attribute is set to* none.

However, if you want for some reason to preserve the relative dimensions, or aspect ratio, of the SVG image, you can choose from a large number of options. Listing 2.15 preserves the aspect ratio and aligns the graphic with the left edge of the view box.

Listing 2.15 (StretchToFit04.svg)

```
<?xml version="1.0" standalone="no"?>
<!DOCTYPE svg PUBLIC "-//W3C//DTD SVG 1.0//EN"
      "http://www.w3.org/TR/2001/PR-SVG-20010719/
        DTD/svg10.dtd">
<svg width="600px" height="100px"
viewBox="0 0 600 400"
preserveAspectRatio="xMinYMax meet" >
<rect x="0" y="0" width="600" height="400"
style="fill:#990066" />
<circle cx="300" cy="200" r="150" style="fill:white;
stroke:red; stroke-width:6;"/>
<text x="200" y="200" style="font-size:30;
font-family:Verdana">
Stretch to fit
</text>
</svg>
```

As you can see in Figure 02.11, the aspect ratio is preserved, but much of the available space is not used.

The entire SVG coordinate system has a considerable number of complexities, other than as described in the preceding short summary. However, it suffices for the purposes of this book. If you need more detailed information, a full description is in Chapter 7 of the SVG specification.

Figure 02.11

The preserve-
AspectRatio *attribute
is used to preserve the
relative dimensions of a
resizable image and to
align it with the left edge
of the available space.
The many other possible
values for the* pre-
serveAspectRatio
*attribute are listed and
described in Chapter 7 of
the SVG specification.*

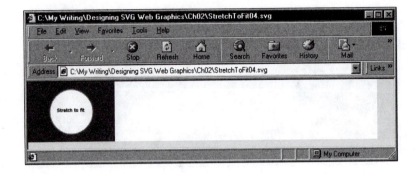

Fonts

SVG can be used for the presentation of both free-standing blocks of text (which are displayed similarly to HTML text) and text that partly forms graphics. In both types of uses, the graphic designer *must* have control over the appearance of the text onscreen.

For these types of situations, a designer needs to know that the chosen font, or something similar to it, is available to create the desired visual appearance whether or not that font has been installed on the user's computer. One option is to use the font-family property to specify a list of fonts, in the order of most desirable first, which the SVG viewer should use to render the applicable text.

However, on some occasions, particularly if a specific artistic appearance is sought, the display of a particular font may be particularly important .

To achieve such a predictable appearance, SVG makes use of the *WebFonts* facility, defined in the Cascading Style Sheets, Level 2 Recommendation from the W3C. For full information, see the CSS2 Recommendation at http://www.w3.org/TR/1998/REC-CSS2-19980512.

WebFonts

In one possible scenario, an SVG authoring tool may generate the parts of the WebFont relevant to the characters used within an SVG document. When used in a Web site, the file is likely to be stored in some suitable directory relative to the page being viewed.

However, a common problem with several aspects of CSS is that implementation is either patchy or inconsistent between available user agents (Web browsers or other viewing devices). To overcome the likely display inconsistencies that are possible when using WebFonts, the SVG specification defines SVG fonts that all conforming SVG viewers must support.

SVG Fonts

At its simplest, an *SVG font* is a font defined using an SVG `<font>` element. SVG fonts are designed to be used in display-only environments. In part, this approach seems designed to protect the intellectual property and, therefore, the income stream of companies that create fonts. If the font is legitimately installed on the authoring machine, the SVG font can be displayed to all who view the SVG image. However, the SVG font system doesn't allow editing of the SVG document on another machine if the font is not legitimately installed on it.

SVG fonts, either a full character set or a selective set including only those used in a particular SVG document or image, can be created automatically. For example, you can use the program `svgfont` to convert TrueType fonts to SVG fonts. Access further information and a download at http://www.steadystate.co.uk/svg/.

Delving deeper into fonts requires understanding a little more of the jargon. A glyph is the way a character is presented onscreen. Much of the time, a one-to-one mapping occurs from a character to the corresponding glyph. For example, the uppercase form of the first character of the English alphabet in the font being used on this page looks like this: A. However, that same character can be displayed using a range of serif or nonserif or cursive fonts. The display appearance then changes, but the same character is referred to.

Why tell you about glyphs? A font is a collection of glyphs that typically share some common visual features. They may all lack a serif (a short stroke at the bottom of certain letters, like l or i), or the relevant letters may all possess a serif. Well-known sans serif fonts (those that lack a serif) are Arial and Helvetica. Commonly used serif fonts include Times Roman and Times New Roman.

In this chapter, I have introduced you to some of the basic structure of an SVG document, to provide you with a foundation for understanding the framework of an SVG image. Move on to Chapter 3 and take a look at the basic SVG graphic shapes.

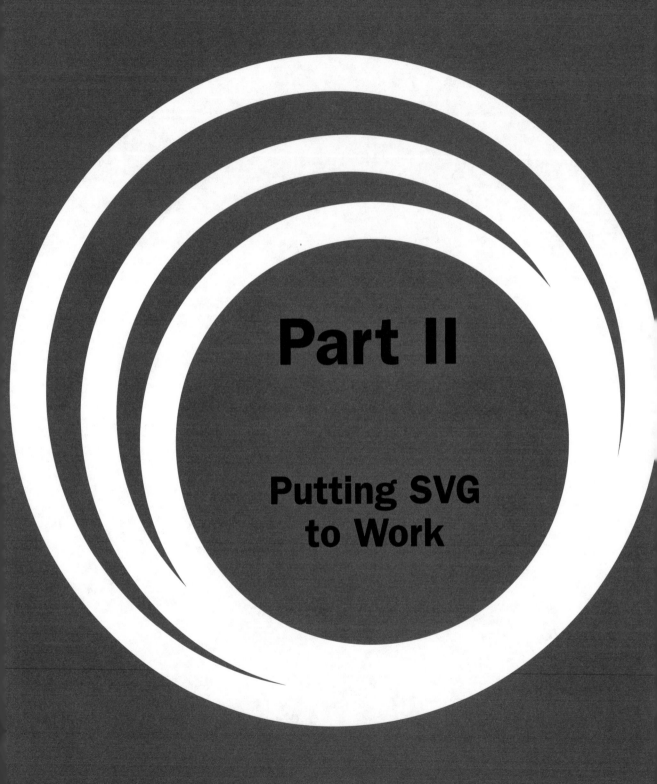

Part II

Putting SVG to Work

3

Creating Static
Graphics Elements

In this chapter:

Essential Building Blocks

This chapter introduces the basic elements that SVG provides to allow you to fully define the parts of an SVG image. You do want to have full control over how your image looks, don't you? Then you need to understand how to control these basic SVG elements.

These basic graphic elements are not visually exciting—they are, for want of a better term, just basic. However, you should understand and master them. Just as an artistic masterpiece, perhaps the Mona Lisa, is made up of hundreds and hundreds of basic brush strokes, sophisticated SVG images—whether they are static or include animation or interaction—are composed of several or dozens or even hundreds of SVG elements. If the image is deficient in some respect, you need to understand how to tweak it to produce just the effect you want.

The elements described in this chapter are essential building blocks of those exciting SVG images. The SVG elements you look at are the `<rect>` element, which represents a rectangle, and the `<circle>`, `<ellipse>`, `<line>`, `<polyline>`, `<polygon>`, and `<path>` elements.

Parts of this chapter may seem to you like a lesson in geometry. That isn't surprising because a computer screen is basically a grid of pixels. Or, if you prefer, the screen is like a sheet of graph paper with *very* small squares.

The simplest way to create SVG graphic shapes is to draw them in an SVG-enabled vector drawing package, such as Jasc WebDraw, Adobe Illustrator 9, or Corel Draw 10. Most vector drawing packages have preset primitives for rectangles, lines, and polygons, for example. However, if you use only vector drawing packages and don't understand the SVG underlying the image that is produced, you inevitably will be limited to some degree in the ways you can tweak the image or design an SVG image as a visual component for reuse.

In this chapter, I hand-craft much of the code to help you understand how the SVG elements work. In a production setting, you can choose which technique you prefer or combine the techniques to suit your knowledge and the characteristics of the image you are trying to create. However, read the following section to find out how to create your first SVG graphic using one of the available SVG-enabled vector drawing tools.

The <rect> Element

The SVG `<rect>` element, when rendered, causes a rectangle to be painted on the SVG canvas. When you drag out a rectangle using Jasc WebDraw or your favorite SVG-enabled vector drawing tool, you produce a simple SVG document that looks something like this:

Listing 3.1 (03WebDraw.svg)

```
<?xml version="1.0" standalone="no"?>
<!DOCTYPE svg PUBLIC "-//W3C//DTD SVG 1.0//EN"
     "http://www.w3.org/TR/2001/PR-SVG-20010719/
      DTD/svg10.dtd">
<svg width="500" height="500">
        <rect x="192" y="93" width="142" height="78"
rx="0" ry="0" style="stroke-miterlimit:4;
stroke-linejoin:miter; stroke-width:3; stroke-opacity:1;
stroke:rgb(0,204,255);
fill-opacity:1;fill:rgb(204,204,204);
opacity:1"/>
</svg>
<!-- Generated by Jasc WebDraw PR4(tm)
on 04/03/01 10:20:08 -->
```

Take a closer look at the `<rect>` element produced by WebDraw, with the code reformatted to aid readability:

```
<rect
  x="192"
  y="93"
  width="142"
  height="78"
  rx="0"
  ry="0"
  style="stroke-miterlimit:4;
         stroke-linejoin:miter;
         stroke-width:3;
         stroke-opacity:1;
         stroke:rgb(0,204,255);
         fill-opacity:1;
         fill:rgb(204,204,204);
         opacity:1"/>
```

As you can see, WebDraw automatically creates several SVG attributes for even a simple rectangle.

The x and y attributes of the `<rect>` element describe the location of the upper-left corner of the rectangle. The x attribute has a value of 0 toward the left side of the screen and increases as you move toward the right side. The y coordinate has a value of zero at the top of the screen and *increases* as you move down. After you have also defined the values of the width and height attributes of the rectangle, you know the coordinates of all four corners of the rectangle relative to the `<svg>` element within which it is contained. If only one `<svg>` element is in the document, its upper-left corner is at (0,0).

In the rectangle I drew, the corners are square, as shown by

```
rx="0"  ry="0"
```

which means that the radius of the corner is zero. To make the corners of a rectangle rounded, you simply give the `rx` or `ry` attributes positive integer values.

SVG allows you to simply create rounded corners for any rectangle. Those rounded corners need not be circular because SVG provides both an `rx` attribute to describe the x radius and an `ry` attribute to describe the y radius. Of course, when the values of the `rx` and `ry` attributes are equal, the corners are circular rather than elliptical.

The style attribute of the `<rect>` element has within it several Cascading Style Sheet, or CSS, properties.

Look first at the `stroke` property. It defines the color of the outline of the rectangle, which has a greenish blue stroke. The example shows one of three alternative syntaxes to describe the greenish blue color. The syntax used is `stroke:rgb(0,204,255)`, although it could also have been expressed as `stroke:#00CCFF`. For certain colors, SVG provides named colors. So if you have a red stroke for a rectangle, you can express it in three ways: `stroke:#FF0000`, `stroke:rgb(255,0,0)`, or `stroke:red`.

The `stroke-width` property defines the width of the stroke. The outline of a rectangle, and other SVG shapes, is assumed to have zero width. Therefore, when a stroke has a width of three (pixels), half is painted within the outline and half outside. When you are seeking precision placement, you need to be aware that thick strokes slightly increase the size of an SVG graphical element. Thus, the width onscreen of the rectangle is 145 pixels rather than the 142 stated in the width attribute (1.5 pixels overlap on one side and 1.5 overlap on the other, making a total increase of 3 pixels).

The `stroke-opacity` property has a value of 1, which means that it is fully opaque. The `stroke-opacity` property takes values from zero (totally transparent) to 1 (totally opaque). You may set any value you want between 0 and 1.

The `stroke-linejoin` property is defined as `miter`. The `stroke-miterlimit` attribute limits the width of the join of the sides to the top or bottom of the outline of the rectangle.

The fill property, like the stroke property described earlier in this chapter, can be expressed in two ways—or, in the case of named colors, in three ways. The `fill-opacity` property of the rectangle has a value of one, meaning that it is fully opaque.

As with the `stroke-opacity` property, the `fill-opacity` property can take values from zero (fully transparent) to one (fully opaque).

The `rx` and `ry` attributes allow the corners of a rectangle to be rounded. Typically, the `rx` and `ry` attributes are equal, although there is no need for them to be. If, for example, the `rx` attribute is significantly greater than the `ry` attribute, as shown in the following listing, you can produce a lozenge shape, as you can see in Figure 03.01:

Listing 3.2 (RectRndCorners01.svg)

```
<?xml version="1.0" standalone="no"?>
<!DOCTYPE svg PUBLIC "-//W3C//DTD SVG 1.0//EN"
      "http://www.w3.org/TR/2001/PR-SVG-20010719/
        DTD/svg10.dtd">
<svg width="400" height="300">
<rect x="100" y="100" width="150" height="75" rx="30" ry="15"
style="stroke:#000099;fill:#CCCCCC;stroke-width:4;"/>
</svg>
```

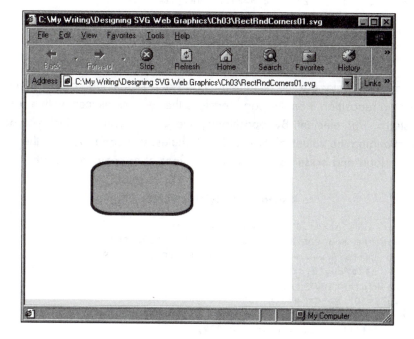

Figure 03.01

A rectangle that has rounded corners but unequal `rx` and `ry` attributes.

A Simple Square

Now create a simple square in SVG, which you use in a number of examples later on. A *square* is simply a rectangle with its width equal to its height, so you can use the `<rect>` element here.

What I want you to create is a simple static logo that at this stage uses only SVG `<rect>` elements and the `<svg>` element you learned about in Chapter 2, "SVG Image/Document Technical Overview."

First, create in Listing 3.3 an image with a single rectangle.

Listing 3.3 (SingleRect.svg)

```
<?xml version="1.0" standalone="no"?>
<!DOCTYPE svg PUBLIC "-//W3C//DTD SVG 1.0//EN"
    "http://www.w3.org/TR/2001/PR-SVG-20010719/
    DTD/svg10.dtd">
<svg width="400" height="500">
<rect x="10" y="20" width="100" height="100"
style="fill:none; stroke:#000099;
stroke-width:4;"/>
</svg>
```

Because you later use the rectangle as part of a simple logo and you may want to reposition it on the page, enclose the `<rect>` element within a nested `<svg>` element. By repositioning the `<svg>` element, which you do by changing the values of its x and y attributes, you can reposition the whole logo and preserve the relative positions of its component parts.

Listing 3.4 (SingleRectinSVG.svg)

```
<?xml version="1.0" standalone="no"?>
<!DOCTYPE svg PUBLIC "-//W3C//DTD SVG 1.0//EN"
    "http://www.w3.org/TR/2001/PR-SVG-20010719/
    DTD/svg10.dtd">
<svg width="400" height="500">
<svg x="0" y="0" width="300" height="400">
<rect x="10" y="20" width="100" height="100"
style="fill:none; stroke:#000099;
stroke-width:4;"/>
</svg>
</svg>
```

Both Listing 3.3 and Listing 3.4 produce the same visual appearance onscreen and are represented in Figure 03.02.

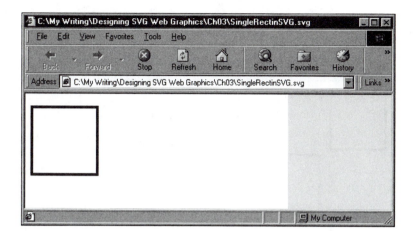

Figure 03.02

A simple rectangle with transparent fill, contained in a nested <svg> element, to allow later repositioning.

As part of the simple logo I have in mind to add another two `<rect>` elements, which are also nested within the `<svg>` element. When you add the two further `<rect>` elements one is directly below the first and the other is offset a little to the right.

Listing 3.5 (ThreeRectsinSVG.svg)

```
<?xml version="1.0" standalone="no"?>
<!DOCTYPE svg PUBLIC "-//W3C//DTD SVG 1.0//EN"
      "http://www.w3.org/TR/2001/PR-SVG-20010719/
      DTD/svg10.dtd">
<svg width="400" height="500">
<svg x="0" y="0" width="300" height="400">
<rect x="10" y="20" width="100" height="100"
style="fill:none; stroke:#000099;
stroke-width:4;"/>
<rect x="130" y="130" width="100" height="100"
style="fill:none;
stroke:#000099; stroke-width:4;"/>
<rect x="10" y="240" width="100" height="100"
style="fill:none; stroke:#000099;
stroke-width:4;"/>
</svg>
</svg>
```

Visually, this code is pretty simple. You still don't know yet about how to add text or other necessary parts of the logo. Onscreen, the code is shown in Figure 03.03.

Figure 03.03

*Three identical rec-
tangles with trans-
parent fill, which you
use in an animation
in Chapter 8,
"Animation: SVG and
SMIL Animation."*

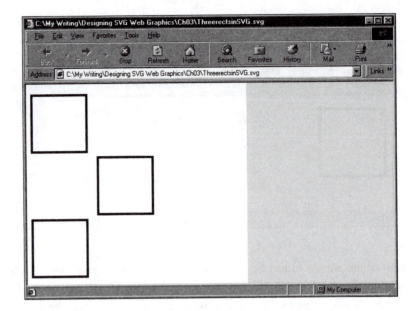

Now you can go on to learn a little about the SVG `<line>` element so that you can add a couple of lines to the logo to provide a little more visual interest.

The <line> Element

The SVG `<line>` element defines a straight line. A *line* has starting coordinates and ending coordinates. In addition, a line can have `stroke`, `stroke-width`, and `stroke-opacity` properties.

Thus, you can completely define a line in SVG like this, which defines a line running diagonally from the upper-left corner of an SVG image toward the lower-right corner. I have also included a second line whose `stroke-opacity` property is 0.5 as shown in Figure 03.04. (The line is semitransparent, so you can see how that setting affects the rendering of the line.)

Listing 3.6 (Line01.svg)

```
<?xml version="1.0" standalone="no"?>
<!DOCTYPE svg PUBLIC "-//W3C//DTD SVG 1.0//EN"
     "http://www.w3.org/TR/2001/PR-SVG-20010719/
      DTD/svg10.dtd">
<svg>
<line x1="50" y1="50" x2="300" y2="300"
style="stroke:#FF0000; stroke-width:4;
stroke-opacity:0.3;"/>
<line x1="50" y1="100" x2="300" y2="350"
style="stroke:#FF0000; stroke-width:4;
stroke-opacity:1;"/>
</svg>
```

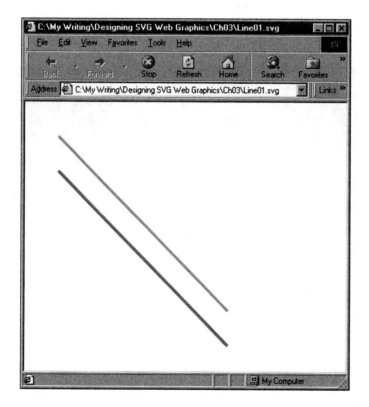

Figure 03.04

Two lines created using the SVG <line> element.

That concept is basic, so now go on and create part of a logo that you use later; you simply use two `<line>` elements and a `<rect>` element. See the appearance shown in Figure 03.05.

Listing 3.7 (WhiteRect.svg)

```
<?xml version="1.0" standalone="no"?>
<!DOCTYPE svg PUBLIC "-//W3C//DTD SVG 1.0//EN"
     "http://www.w3.org/TR/2001/PR-SVG-20010719/
        DTD/svg10.dtd">
<svg width="300" height="300">
<line x1="35" y1="135" x2="110" y2="180"
style="stroke-width:5;
stroke:#000099"/>
<line x1="35" y1="225" x2="110" y2="180"
style="stroke-width:5;
stroke:#000099"/>
<rect x="18" y="130" width="100" height="100"
style="fill:none; stroke:white;
stroke-width:16;"/>
</svg>
```

Figure 03.05

A right-pointing arrow created using two <line> elements and a <rect> element with a white outline.

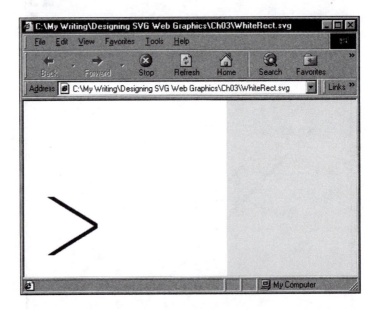

What this code does is to create a right-pointing arrowhead, whose edge shape is defined by the stroke of the <rect> element. Notice that the <rect> element occurs later in the document, so the white outline is painted on top of the two lines. If you put it together with the foundation of the three-rectangles logo, you have this code:

Listing 3.8 (ThreerectsPlusArrow.svg)

```
<?xml version="1.0" standalone="no"?>
<!DOCTYPE svg PUBLIC "-//W3C//DTD SVG 1.0//EN"
     "http://www.w3.org/TR/2001/PR-SVG-20010719/
      DTD/svg10.dtd">
<svg width="400" height="500">
<svg x="0" y="0" width="300" height="400">
<rect x="10" y="20" width="100" height="100"
style="fill:none; stroke:#000099;
stroke-width:4;"/>
<rect x="130" y="130" width="100" height="100"
style="fill:none;
stroke:#000099; stroke-width:4;"/>
<rect x="10" y="240" width="100" height="100"
style="fill:none; stroke:#000099;
stroke-width:4;"/>
<line x1="35" y1="135" x2="110" y2="180"
style="stroke-width:5;
stroke:#000099"/>
<line x1="35" y1="225" x2="110" y2="180"
style="stroke-width:5;
stroke:#000099"/>
<rect x="18" y="130" width="100" height="100"
style="fill:none; stroke:white;
stroke-width:16;"/>
</svg>
</svg>
```

The code looks like Figure 03.06 onscreen. You add text and animation to the logo in later chapters.

Now go on to create a scale using several SVG `<line>` elements. These can be useful visual components and can be reused in graphics or, typically, as in Flash movies, be animated. This chapter looks at creating a static scale.

I create the scale as a series of `<line>` elements nested within a grouping `<g>` element, which is itself nested within a `<defs>` element. If you read through the following code, you should be able to follow the construction of the scale. The first `<line>` element is the long horizontal line; and then follows the series of the longer of the two sizes of vertical scale marks; and then come the shorter, vertical scale marks. Following the `<defs>` element

Figure 03.06

A simple skeleton of a logo created using <rect> and <line> elements, which are developed further in later chapters.

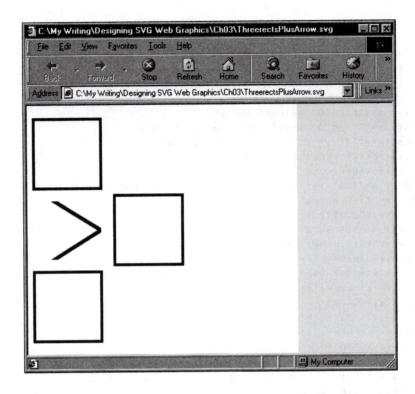

Figure 03.06

A simple skeleton of a logo created using <rect> and <line> elements, which are developed further in later chapters.

is a `<rect>` element to create the background color for the scale and a `<use>` element that uses an `xlink:href` attribute to reference the group `<g>` with an ID of `MyScale,` which you created in the `<defs>` element.

Listing 3.9 (Scale01.svg)

```
<?xml version="1.0" standalone="no"?>
<!DOCTYPE svg PUBLIC "-//W3C//DTD SVG 1.0//EN"
    "http://www.w3.org/TR/2001/PR-SVG-20010719/
    DTD/svg10.dtd">
<svg width="800" height="100">
<defs>
<g id="MyScale">
<line x1="50" y1="20" x2="750" y2="20"
style="stroke:white; fill:white;"/>
<line x1="50" y1="20" x2="50" y2="30"
style="stroke:white; fill:white;"/>
<line x1="150" y1="20" x2="150" y2="30"
```

```
style="stroke:white; fill:white;"/>
<line x1="250" y1="20" x2="250" y2="30"
style="stroke:white; fill:white;"/>
<line x1="350" y1="20" x2="350" y2="30"
style="stroke:white; fill:white;"/>
<line x1="450" y1="20" x2="450" y2="30"
style="stroke:white; fill:white;"/>
<line x1="550" y1="20" x2="550" y2="30"
style="stroke:white; fill:white;"/>
<line x1="650" y1="20" x2="650" y2="30"
style="stroke:white; fill:white;"/>
<line x1="750" y1="20" x2="750" y2="30"
style="stroke:white; fill:white;"/>
<line x1="300" y1="20" x2="300" y2="25"
style="stroke:white; fill:white;"/>
<line x1="400" y1="20" x2="400" y2="25"
style="stroke:white; fill:white;"/>
<line x1="500" y1="20" x2="500" y2="25"
style="stroke:white; fill:white;"/>
<line x1="600" y1="20" x2="600" y2="25"
style="stroke:white; fill:white;"/>
<line x1="700" y1="20" x2="700" y2="25"
style="stroke:white; fill:white;"/>
</g>
</defs>
<rect x="0" y="0" width="800" height="100"
style="fill:#CCCC99; stroke:none;"/>
<use y1="20" y2="20" xlink:href="#MyScale" />
</svg>
```

You may be asking why I went to the additional trouble of placing the `<g>` element in the definitions. Suppose that your client suggests to you that he wants the scale the other way up. Of course, you could make all the necessary individual changes to the x1, x2, y1, and y2 attributes, but, with the way I created this example, you don't need to. Simply alter one line of code, the `<use>` element, to read like this:

```
<use y1="20" y2="20" xlink:href="#MyScale"
transform="rotate(180 400 50)"/>
```

You can then rotate your scale through 180 degrees around the coordinates `(400,50)`, which turns the scale line upside down, as shown in Figure 03.07.

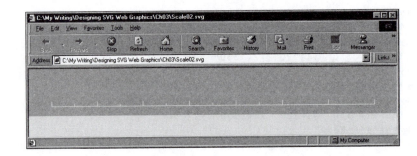

Figure 03.07

The scale rotated through 180 degrees by means of a trans-form on the <use> element.

If you want to preserve the same vertical position, you can rotate the scale around (400,20) by using this code:

```
<use y1="20" y2="20" xlink:href="#MyScale"
transform="rotate(180 400 20)"/>
```

It's done!

You can also create Web page furniture using <rect> and <line> elements, as shown in this example:

Listing 3.10 (RectWithLines01.svg)

```
<?xml version="1.0" standalone="no"?>
<!DOCTYPE svg PUBLIC "-//W3C//DTD SVG 1.0//EN"
      "http://www.w3.org/TR/2001/PR-SVG-20010719/
        DTD/svg10.dtd">
<svg xmlns:xlink="http://www.w3.org/1999/xlink">
<defs>
<line id="MyLine" x1="0" x2="300" y1="0" y2="0"
style="fill:#000099;
stroke:#000099; stroke-width:1;"/>
</defs>
<g>
<rect x="0" y="0" width="300" height="68"
style="fill:#DDDDFF; stroke:none"/>
<line x1="0" x2="300" y1="2" y2="2"
xlink:href="#MyLine"/>
<line x1="0" x2="300" y1="4" y2="4"
xlink:href="#MyLine" />
<line x1="0" x2="300" y1="6" y2="6"
xlink:href="#MyLine"/>
<use transform="translate(0,8)"
xlink:href="#MyLine"/>
<use transform="translate(0,12)"
```

```
xlink:href="#MyLine"/>
</g>
</svg>
```

Because I planned to use a `<line>` element possibly multiple times, I created a definition of a `<line>` element with an ID attribute of value `MyLine` so that I could reuse that same `<line>` element multiple times in the image.

Notice that I also used three `<line>` elements at the top of the image, in a way that gives (at least in the Adobe SVG Viewer) very fine lines, which are useful in creating patterns for Web page furniture. These fine lines can be used creatively with lines of differing stroke widths. Figure 03.08 shows the code in Listing 3.10. Listing 3.11 adapts that code.

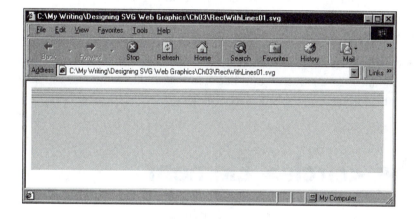

Figure 03.08

A rectangle with a pattern created using repeated lines.

Listing 3.11 (RectWithLines02.svg)

```
<?xml version="1.0" standalone="no"?>
<!DOCTYPE svg PUBLIC "-//W3C//DTD SVG 1.0//EN"
    "http://www.w3.org/TR/2001/PR-SVG-20010719/
    DTD/svg10.dtd">
<svg xmlns:xlink="http://www.w3.org/1999/xlink">
<defs>
<line id="MyLine" x1="0" x2="300" y1="0" y2="0"
style="fill:#000099;
stroke:#000099; stroke-width:0.05;"/>
</defs>
<g>
<rect x="0" y="0" width="300" height="68"
style="fill:#DDDDFF; stroke:none"/>
<line x1="0" x2="300" y1="2" y2="2"
```

```
xlink:href="#MyLine"/>
<line x1="0" x2="300" y1="4" y2="4"
xlink:href="#MyLine" style="fill:red;"/>
<line x1="0" x2="300" y1="6" y2="6"
xlink:href="#MyLine"/>
<use transform="translate(0,8)"
xlink:href="#MyLine"/>
<use transform="translate(0,12)"
xlink:href="#MyLine"/>
</g>
</svg>
```

You can create similarly fine lines within the lines created by the `<use>` element if the line is defined as having a stroke-width of 0.05 in the original definition (within a `<line>` element that is nested in a `<defs>` element), as shown in the preceding code. Note that even when using the `<use>` element, you can specify a modified style property.

So far, you have been looking at static SVG shapes, which involve only straight lines. Let's move on and begin to look at the graphical shapes provided by SVG that represent curved shapes.

The <circle> Element

A *circle*, at least in geometry, is completely described by its radius and the coordinates of its center. In SVG too, those are the most important attributes of a `<circle>` element. In addition, of course, it has a style attribute with various CSS properties you can use.

Listing 3.12 (ThreeCircles.svg)

```
<?xml version="1.0" standalone="no"?>
<!DOCTYPE svg PUBLIC "-//W3C//DTD SVG 1.0//EN"
     "http://www.w3.org/TR/2001/PR-SVG-20010719/
       DTD/svg10.dtd">
<svg width="300" height="200">
<circle cx="50" cy="100" r="40"
style="fill:#000099; stroke:#FF0099;
fill-opacity:0.1;"/>
<circle cx="150" cy="100" r="40"
```

```
style="fill:#000099; stroke:#FF0099;
fill-opacity:0.5;"/>
<circle cx="250" cy="100" r="40"
style="fill:#000099; stroke:#FF0099;
fill-opacity:1;"/>
</svg>
```

In the preceding code, I have created three circles, which differ only in their `cx` coordinates and the value of the `fill-opacity` property. The position of each circle is determined by the `cx` and `cy` attributes, which define, respectively, the x and y coordinates of the center of the circle.

Each circle has the same fill color, a deep blue, but the value of the `fill-opacity` property varies from 0.1 in the left circle to 1 (fully opaque) in the right one. The opacity must be in the range 0 (fully transparent) to 1 (fully opaque). The effect of varying the opacity of the fill is shown in Figure 03.09.

The `<circle>` element has many similarities to the `<ellipse>` element, which is discussed next.

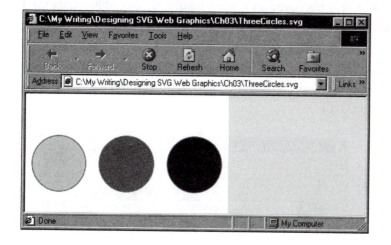

Figure 03.09

Three circles with varying opacities of fill: 0.1, 0.5, and 1.

The <ellipse> Element

An ellipse, geometrically speaking, is simply a circle where the radius in the x direction and the radius in the y direction differ. If the radii are the same, the curved graphic element is a circle. In SVG, you can represent a circle by using either a `<circle>` element or an `<ellipse>` element with the x and y radii being equal.

A simple ellipse shape would have SVG source code like this:

Listing 3.13 (SimpleEllipse01.svg)

```
<?xml version="1.0" standalone="no"?>
<!DOCTYPE svg PUBLIC "-//W3C//DTD SVG 1.0//EN"
    "http://www.w3.org/TR/2001/PR-SVG-20010719/
    DTD/svg10.dtd">
<svg width="250" height="150">
<ellipse cx="80" cy="70" rx="35" ry="10"
style="stroke:red; fill:#CCCCCC"/>
</svg>
```

The `cx` and `cy` attributes define the position of the center of the ellipse. However, an ellipse has two radii, not one, as the `<circle>` element had. The `rx` attribute defines the radius in the horizontal direction, and the `ry` attribute defines the radius in the vertical direction.

Onscreen, it is displayed as a small ellipse, as shown in Figure 03.10. Note that the edges of the ellipse, which have a red stroke against a white background, do show significant *jaggies* at parts of the circumference.

However, the jaggies behave quite differently from jaggies on a bitmap graphic, as you can see when you zoom in close on the ellipse, as shown in Figure 03.11.

Figure 03.10

An `<ellipse>` element showing jaggies.

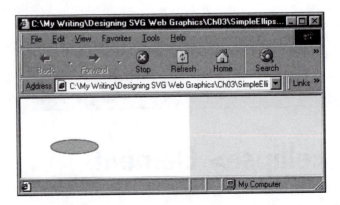

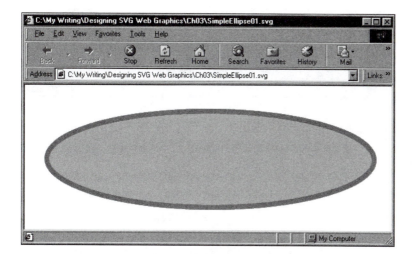

Figure 03.11

The ellipse shown in Figure 03.10 is zoomed. Note that the jaggies are less obvious than in the original image.

Combining Ellipses

You likely know that by combining two ellipses that differ only slightly in size and shape, you can obtain a variety of interesting and attractive curved shapes. For example, with the following code:

Listing 3.14 (Ellipses02.svg)

```
<?xml version="1.0" standalone="no"?>
<!DOCTYPE svg PUBLIC "-//W3C//DTD SVG 1.0//EN"
     "http://www.w3.org/TR/2001/PR-SVG-20010719/
      DTD/svg10.dtd">
<svg>
<ellipse cx="80" cy="170" rx="350" ry="100"
style="stroke:none; fill:red"/>
<ellipse cx="50" cy="172" rx="360" ry="110"
style="stroke:none; fill:white"/>
</svg>
```

you can produce the curve shown in Figure 03.12, which hints at dynamism and other positive attributes. You probably have seen many online logos created by combining ellipses in similar ways.

Figure 03.12

*The curved shape
produced by Listing
3.14 is zoomed.*

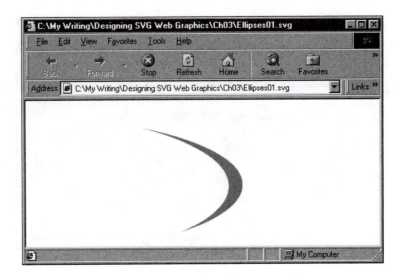

The figure shows the curve zoomed in, but you can produce a similar
appearance, as shown in the following code:

Similarly, by adjusting relative x and y axis radii, by means of changing
the values of the **rx** and **ry** attributes, you can create pseudo-3D ellipses
using simple vector shapes, as shown in the following code and seen in
Figure 03.13:

Listing 3.15 (Ellipses03.svg)

```
<?xml version="1.0" standalone="no"?>
<!DOCTYPE svg PUBLIC "-//W3C//DTD SVG 1.0//EN"
    "http://www.w3.org/TR/2001/PR-SVG-20010719/
    DTD/svg10.dtd">
<svg>
<g>
<ellipse cx="240" cy="170" rx="220" ry="30"
style="stroke:none; fill:#000099"/>
<ellipse cx="221" cy="174" rx="192" ry="22"
style="stroke:none; fill:white"/>
</g>
</svg>
```

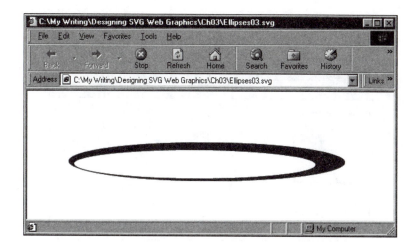

Figure 03.13

A pseudo-3D shape created using two <ellipse> elements.

In later chapters, you use these types of ellipses shapes to create simple static or animated logos.

The <polyline> Element

A `<polyline>` element can create any shape that consists of only straight lines drawn sequentially. The following simple example draws three sides of the rectangle you created in an earlier example. If you omit any mention of the `fill` property, a black and fully opaque fill is inserted. In this example (illustrated in Figure 03.14), I have created an almost transparent fill of the same color as the stroke.

Listing 3.16 (Polyline01.svg)

```
<?xml version="1.0" standalone="no"?>
<!DOCTYPE svg PUBLIC "-//W3C//DTD SVG 1.0//EN"
    "http://www.w3.org/TR/2001/PR-SVG-20010719/
    DTD/svg10.dtd">
<svg width="300" height="200">
<polyline style="stroke:#000099; stroke-width:4;
fill:#000099; fill-opacity:0.1"
 points="10,20 110,20 110,120 10,120"/>
</svg>
```

Figure 03.14

*A <polyline>
element that creates
three sides of a
square and has a fill
that is 90 percent
transparent.*

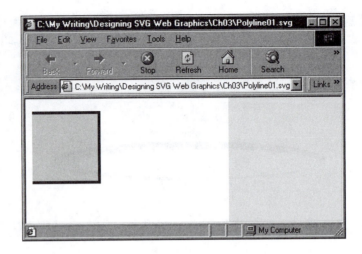

The <polygon> Element

The <polygon> element is used for a shape with multiple (at least three) straight sides. Figure 03.15 and the following example show a hexagon with a red stroke and a gray fill.

Listing 3.17 (Polygon01.svg)

```
<?xml version="1.0" standalone="no"?>
<!DOCTYPE svg PUBLIC "-//W3C//DTD SVG 1.0//EN"
    "http://www.w3.org/TR/2001/PR-SVG-20010719/
    DTD/svg10.dtd">
<svg width="400" height="500" >
<polygon style="fill:#CCC; stroke:red; stroke-width:3"
points="150,75 258,137.5 258,262.5
150,325 42,262.5 42,137.5" />
</svg>
```

If you were so inclined, you could create a rectangle or square using the <polygon> element, but the <rect> element is usually more convenient.

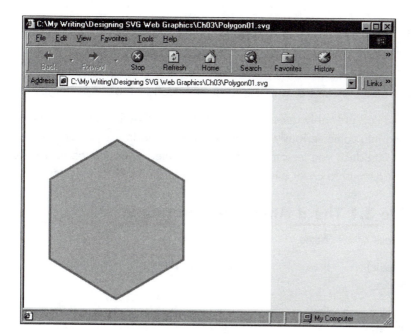

Figure 03.15

A hexagon created using the <poly-gon> *element.*

The <path> Element

The <path> element is probably the most important SVG shape, at least in the sense that it is the most versatile. Any 2-dimensional shape that you can draw, an SVG <path> element can describe. Except for the simplest shapes, however, you would be well advised to let a vector drawing package automatically create the code for you.

The following is an example of a <path> element:

```
<path d="M10,20 L110,20 110,120 10,120"
style="fill:#000099; fill-opacity:0.1;
stroke:#000099; stroke-width:4"/>
```

The d attribute of the <path> element describes several types of drawing action. The M10,20 means to move to coordinates (10,20). The L110,20 means to draw a line from the preceding point to coordinates (110,20). The 110,120 means the same as L110, 120 would. When the action (in this case, drawing a line) is the same as the preceding action, the letter can be omitted. The final part of the value of the `d` attribute, `10,120`, means to draw a line to (10,120).

The `d` attribute can be complex, as summarized in Table 3.1.

As you can probably guess from the abbreviated definitions, you may be getting into some seriously serious geometry here. In the sections that follow, I introduce you to some of the syntax hinted at by the table, although I don't attempt to cover everything relating to the `<path>` element.

Table 3.1 The d Attribute Commands

Command	Name	Description
M (absolute) m (relative)	moveto	Moves to described point without drawing
L (absolute) l (relative)	lineto	Draws a line from the current point to the point defined
H (absolute) h (relative)	horizontal lineto	Draws a horizontal line from the current point to the point defined
V (absolute) v (relative)	vertical lineto	Draws a vertical line from the current point to the point defined
C (absolute) c (relative)	curveto	Draws a cubic Bezier curve from the current point
S (absolute) s (relative)	shorthand/ smooth curveto	Draws a cubic Bezier curve from the current point
Q (absolute) q (relative)	quadratic Bezier curveto	Draws a quadratic Bezier curve from the current point
T (absolute) t (relative)	shorthand/ smooth quadratic Bezier curveto	Draws a quadratic Bezier curve from the current point
A (absolute) a (relative)	elliptical arc	Draws an arc from the current point
Z or z	closepath	Closes the path by drawing a line to the first point of the path

Creating open shapes using straight lines

You can create lines and shapes created by one or multiple lines by using the `<path>` element. For example, the shape you created earlier using the `<polyline>` element can also be created using the `<path>` element, as shown in the following listing. The visual appearance is identical to the one shown in Figure 03.14.

Listing 3.18 (Path01.svg)

```
<?xml version="1.0" standalone="no"?>
<!DOCTYPE svg PUBLIC "-//W3C//DTD SVG 1.0//EN"
     "http://www.w3.org/TR/2001/PR-SVG-20010719/
      DTD/svg10.dtd">
<svg width="300" height="200">
<path d="M10,20 L110,20 110,120 10,120"
style="fill:#000099; fill-opacity:0.1;
stroke:#000099; stroke-width:4"/>
</svg>
```

You can see that the `<path>` element uses a much more cryptic syntax than, for example, the `<line>` element. In a moment, you examine that syntax in more detail. The reason for the cryptic syntax is that the `<path>` element can be used to create immensely complex shapes. Because each drawing action to create these types of shapes has to be incorporated in the path data, the path data attribute can become very long. By using a cryptic, abbreviated syntax, the size of the SVG file containing such shapes is minimized, and download times are therefore kept from being unnecessarily long. A black, fully opaque fill is created for a `<path>` element unless a fill is specified. To create an outline without any fill, you must specify the fill property to have a value of `none`.

Look more closely at the syntax of the `d` attribute of the `<path>` element. The `d` attribute represents the path data. It may help you to visualise the values in the `d` attribute as a series of instructions for drawing on a sheet of graph paper. `M10,20` indicates a move to (10,20) with the pen raised from the paper so that that no visual representation of that movement occurs. `L110,20` means to draw a line from the current point (10,20) to the point defined after the `L` (110 along and 20 down, or (110,20). The next part of the path data is `110,120`. The absence of a leading letter doesn't mean that I have forgotten how to write `L110,120`; the SVG specification assumes, however, if the preceding command was to draw a straight line, that you keep on drawing straight lines until another type of instruction is given. Similarly, the final part of the path data, `10,120`, means to draw a straight line to (10,120). The values of the `stroke`, `stroke-width`, and `stroke-opacity` properties (defaults to 1, fully opaque) define the visual appearance along the lines that are drawn.

Each part of the path data in the preceding example is described as a series of points with the absolute x and y coordinates. The `<path>` element has an alternative syntax that uses relative coordinates and for which the lowercase equivalent letter is used. For example, to draw a straight line using relative coordinates rather than absolute ones, you use the lowercase of *L* as the initial letter. The following example produces the same visual appearance as the preceding example, but uses relative movements to express the drawing of the line.

Listing 3.19 (Path02.svg)

```
<?xml version="1.0" standalone="no"?>
<!DOCTYPE svg PUBLIC "-//W3C//DTD SVG 1.0//EN"
    "http://www.w3.org/TR/2001/PR-SVG-20010719/
      DTD/svg10.dtd">
<svg width="300" height="200">
<path d="M10,20 l100,0 0,100 -100,0"
style="fill:#000099; fill-opacity:0.1;
stroke:#000099; stroke-width:4"/>
</svg>
```

The preceding path data indicates, "Move to (10,20) absolute, draw a straight line to a point 100 pixels to the right, then draw a straight line to a point 100 pixels down, and, finally, draw a straight line to a point 100 pixels to the left."

Creating closed shapes using straight lines

Just as you can create open shapes using straight lines, so can you create closed shapes. The following code describes the creation of a triangle that has a red stroke and a gray fill. The `<rect>` element simply provides a border for the SVG image, as you can see in Figure 03.16.

Listing 3.20 (ClosedPath.svg)

```
<?xml version="1.0" standalone="no"?>
<!DOCTYPE svg PUBLIC "-//W3C//DTD SVG 1.0//EN"
    "http://www.w3.org/TR/2001/PR-SVG-20010719/
    DTD/svg10.dtd">
<svg width="400" height="400" viewBox="0 0 400 400">
<desc>A simple path that draws a triangle</desc>
<rect x="1" y="1" width="398" height="398"
style="fill:none; stroke:red"/>
<path d="M 200 100 L 300 300 L 100 300 z"
style="fill:#CCCCCC; stroke:red; stroke-width:3"/>
</svg>
```

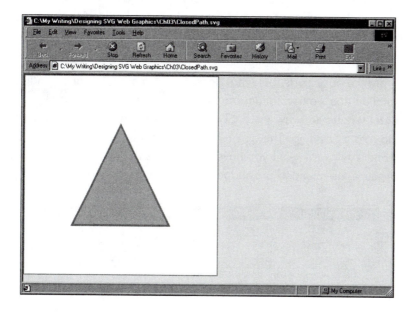

Figure 03.16

A triangle created using the <path> element.

Creating arcs

Take a look now at creating an elliptical arc. In the following example, I was trying to draw an arc from the extreme left side of an ellipse to its highest point.

Listing 3.21 (ArcPath02.svg)

```
<?xml version="1.0" standalone="no"?>
<!DOCTYPE svg PUBLIC "-//W3C//DTD SVG 1.0//EN"
    "http://www.w3.org/TR/2001/PR-SVG-20010719/
    DTD/svg10.dtd">
```

```
<svg width="300" height="200">
<ellipse cx="150" cy="100" rx="60" ry="40"
style="fill:none; stroke:#999999; stroke-width:1;"/>
<path style="fill:none; stroke:#990000;
stroke-width:3;"
        d="M90,100 A60,40 0 0,1 150,60 " />
</svg>
```

Consider the content of the `d` attribute step by step. The `M90,100` is a move command similar to those you have read about earlier in this chapter. The point you move to is on the outline of the `<ellipse>` element. The `A60,40` means to draw an arc with x radius of 60 and y radius of 40. The final part of the syntax, `150,60`, defines where the final point of the arc is located—at a point with coordinates (150,60), which is the highest point on the arc.

Those are the easy parts, but what does `0  0,1` mean? The first `0` indicates any rotation, the x-axis-rotation, from the current coordinate system. Because I wanted to draw the arc along the outline of the ellipse, I didn't want to rotate anything. The `0,1` refers, respectively, to the `large-arc-flag` and `sweep-flag`. If you have `x-axis-rotation` set at zero, you can produce the intended arc shape, as you can see in Figure 03.17.

Figure 03.17

An arc drawn along part of the circumference of an ellipse.

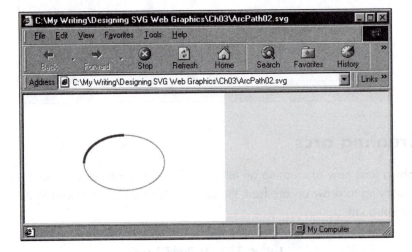

Creating a quadratic Bezier curve

My purpose here is not to describe the mathematics of quadratic Bezier curves. I want to show you a simple example and discuss the syntax within the data path `d` attribute. In the following example, I show you two quadratic Bezier curves.

Listing 3.22 (QuadraticBezier02.svg)

```
<?xml version="1.0" standalone="no"?>
<!DOCTYPE svg PUBLIC "-//W3C//DTD SVG 1.0//EN"
     "http://www.w3.org/TR/2001/PR-SVG-20010719/
      DTD/svg10.dtd">
<svg>
<path d="M50,100 Q200,0 300,300"
style="fill:none; stroke:red; stroke-width:5" />
<circle cx="300" cy="300" r="5" style="fill:red; stroke:red;"/>
<path d="M50,100 Q200,0 200,200 T500,200"
style="fill:none; stroke:blue; stroke-width:2" />
<circle cx="200" cy="200" r="5" style="fill:blue;
stroke:blue;"/>
</svg>
```

The starting point of the thicker curve is defined by the command `M50,100`, so you know that the curve starts at (50,100). The syntax `Q200,0` defines the location of a control point, which influences the shape of the curve. The data `300,300` defines where the curve finishes, as you can see by the presence of the small circle at the end of the thicker (red) curved line.

In the second, thinner (blue) curve, you find, as before, that the first part of the path data is `M50,100`, which is a move command defining the starting point of the curve. The final part of the path data, `T500,200`, defines the location of the other end of the curve. The `Q200,0` again defines the control point. The data `200,200` defines the "end," if you like, of the first part of the curve (as shown by the small circle on the thinner line). This curve is shown in Figure 03.18.

Mastery of the control of Bezier curves takes time. If you have experience in controlling the shape of Bezier curves in a vector drawing package, making progress with this process is likely to be easier.

Figure 03.18

A quadratic Bezier curve.

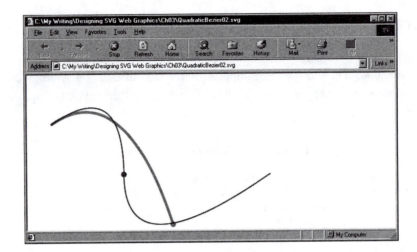

Creating cubic Bezier curves

A *cubic* Bezier curve is similar to a quadratic Bezier, but has control points at both ends of the curve.

Listing 3.23 (CubicBezier01.svg)

```
<?xml version="1.0" standalone="no"?>
<!DOCTYPE svg PUBLIC "-//W3C//DTD SVG 1.0//EN"
     "http://www.w3.org/TR/2001/PR-SVG-20010719/
       DTD/svg10.dtd">
<svg>
<path d="M50,100 C200,0 400,100 300,300"
style="fill:none; stroke:red; stroke-width:5" />
<circle cx="300" cy="300" r="5" style="fill:red;
stroke:red;"/>
</svg>
```

Look at the content of the path data d attribute, which produces the appearance shown in Figure 03.19. The first part of the data defines the starting point of the curve at (50,100). The two pairs of data in C200,0 400,0 define the coordinates for the control points for the start of the curve, at (50,100), and the end of the curve, at (300,300), respectively. As I have done previously, I have included a small circle in the figure so that you can verify the end point of the curve.

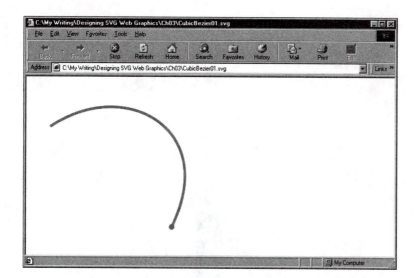

Figure 03.19

A cubic Bezier curve.

Notice that, as before, the fill property is set to a value of `none`. If the fill property is omitted, the curve has a solid, opaque black fill.

The examples of the quadratic and cubic Bezier curves show open curves. If you want to close any of the curves, you can add a `z closepath` command to the end of the values contained in the path data `d` attribute of the `<path>` element.

Having looked at the graphics shapes of SVG, you examine, in Chapter 4, "Using Text in SVG," the use of text in SVG.

4

Using Text in SVG

In this chapter:

Text Basics

SVG, clearly, has to be able to display and lay out text. Many Web graphics—for example, company logos—make significant use of text. Similarly, various types of artistic text can add design benefits to a range of graphics contained in Web pages. SVG text can have many SVG effects applied to it, such as gradients, animations, and patterns. All SVG graphics designers should understand how to manipulate text in SVG.

In addition to the use of individual characters or short sequences of characters in logos, for example, SVG offers the potential to lay out significant amounts of text, even to the extent of creating complete SVG Web pages (see Chapter 12, "Creating a Simple SVG Web Site"). In that setting, understanding the functionality for controlling the display and layout of text that SVG provides is particularly important. The ability of SVG to lay out significant amounts of text is not surprising because SVG draws heavily on the Adobe Precision Graphics Markup Language, which draws significantly on PostScript—the page-layout language *par excellence*.

SVG holds text as character data within `<text>` elements in an XML-compliant source file. The rendering of that character data onscreen is, at the point of display, a bitmap (as is the case for HTML text and all other text). The human eye reads back into that bitmap the characters and words and reads the meaning into those. It is quite a complex process.

The SVG source code for the rendered text always remains as character data and is therefore accessible to suitable XML-capable search engines, for example.

Also, if the SVG image or document is being created dynamically, the characters to be displayed can similarly be *dynamically* updated. For example, you may want to update the current stock price of your company, hold it in a database that is updated on an ongoing basis, and then access that data at the time the SVG graphic (or Web page) is being constructed.

First, let's examine in more detail how text behaves and is controlled in SVG.

Text in SVG

Text to be displayed in SVG is held as character data. All text is contained within `<text>` elements, but can be further nested within `<tspan>` elements.

When text is displayed, the font defined in the style attribute of the `<text>` or `<tspan>` element or in an external CSS style sheet is associated with font tables that define how individual characters are to be displayed in that font. The font tables associate a character with its visual representation—a glyph.

Listing 4.1 illustrates the difference between a glyph and a character. Each of the five glyphs shown in Figure 04.01 represents the uppercase version of a character—in this case, the first letter in the English alphabet, the letter *A*. Yet each glyph has a different appearance. In each of the font tables for a font family specified in a style attribute on a `<tspan>` element is a glyph for an uppercase *A*, and it is displayed onscreen. Depending on which fonts you have installed, the appearance on your own machine may differ from that shown in Figure 04.01.

Listing 4.1 (Glyphs01.svg)

```
<?xml version="1.0" standalone="no"?>
<!DOCTYPE svg PUBLIC "-//W3C//DTD SVG 1.0//EN"
    "http://www.w3.org/TR/2001/PR-SVG-20010719/
    DTD/svg10.dtd">
<svg>
<text>
<tspan x="20" y="20" style="font-family:Arial;
font-size:18; fill:red; stroke:red;">A </tspan>
<tspan x="40" y="20" style="font-family:'Times New
```

```
Roman'; font-size:18; fill:red; stroke:red;">A </tspan>
<tspan x="60" y="20" style="font-family:'Courier New';
font-size:18; fill:red; stroke:red;">A </tspan>
<tspan x="80" y="20" style="font-family:'Brush Script';
font-size:18; fill:red; stroke:red;">A </tspan>
<tspan x="100" y="20" style="font-family:fantasy;
font-size:18; fill:red; stroke:red;">A </tspan>
</text>
</svg>
```

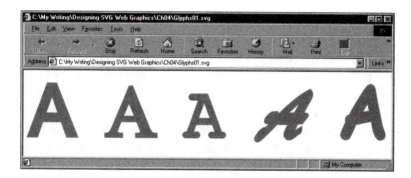

Figure 04.01

Five different glyphs from five distinct font families, each of which represents the uppercase character A (zoomed to enlarge the glyphs to aid comparison).

The visual appearance of the glyph depends on the font you have chosen. If you choose a serif font, like Times New Roman, you expect all relevant characters to be displayed with serifs. If you choose a sans serif font, like Arial, you expect no visible serifs on any glyphs in that font. Similarly, if you choose a fancy font, the visual appearance may be markedly different although the characters being represented remain the same.

The position at which text is rendered onscreen depends on the value of the x and y attributes of the `<text>` element. If you want to place text further to the right and then increase the value of the x attribute. If you want it further down the page, increase the value of the y attribute. However, placement of text is not quite the same as the onscreen placement of a rectangle, for example, as the following example shows:

Listing 4.2 (TextRectCoords.svg)

```
<?xml version="1.0" standalone="no"?>
<!DOCTYPE svg PUBLIC "-//W3C//DTD SVG 1.0//EN"
     "http://www.w3.org/TR/2001/PR-SVG-20010719/
     DTD/svg10.dtd">
<svg width="300" height="200">
```

```
<rect x="50" y="50" width="200" height="50"
style="fill:none; stroke:red;"/>
<text x="50" y="50" style="font-family:Arial,
sans-serif; font-size:14;">
This text is also placed at (50,50)
</text>
<text x="50" y="65" style="font-family:Arial,
sans-serif; font-size:14;">
This text is placed at (50,65)
</text>
</svg>
```

The x and y attributes of text refer to the lower-left corner of the invisible box that contains the text, whereas the x and y attributes of a rectangle refer to the position of its upper-left corner. As you can see in Figure 04.02, the x and y attributes of the `<text>` element must be adjusted in order to place text "within" a rectangle—you can't simply assume that if the rectangle is at (50,50) you can use the same coordinates for text you want to display within the rectangle.

SVG gives you the ability to lay out text not only in space onscreen but also in time. You can therefore create a different, more dynamic exposure of text, whether it is part of some preset SVG animation or you create some interactive SVG applications (see the text animations in Chapter 8, "Animation: SVG and SMIL Animation").

Figure 04.02

The placement of x and y attributes of `<text>` and `<rect>` elements differs.

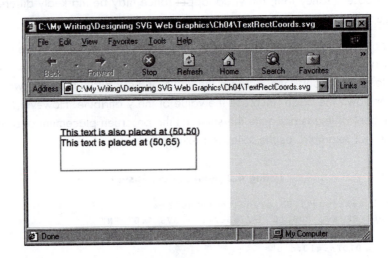

Internationalization

SVG is an application language of XML and therefore uses the Unicode standard, which effectively provides a potentially universal character set. Thus, for most practical purposes, the character set of any language can be expressed in SVG.

The direction in which text is displayed varies from one language to another. Text can be displayed from left to right, as in English; from right to left, as in Arabic; or vertically, as in a number of Asian languages. SVG supports each of these languages.

In addition, SVG provides features that support the selective display of text in a multilingual Web environment, using the `systemLanguage` attribute (discussed in more detail in Chapter 17, "The Future of SVG").

Comparing text in SVG to bitmap graphics

If you create text in a bitmap graphics package, the text is likely, depending on the package and version, to remain editable while it is within the editing package. However, after you export the graphic as a GIF or JPEG image, the text (and indeed, all the graphic) is no longer editable—what you perceive as text is now simply a bitmap pattern of pixels with no intrinsic meaning. Of course, when the human eye sees the bitmap pattern, it can make that complex interpretive leap that attaches meaning to the bitmap pattern. To a computer, however—a search engine, for example—all connection between that bitmap pattern and the character data it represents has been lost.

In SVG, however, the text remains searchable or editable at all times. The source code for an SVG image is all text, including the string that is to be rendered as text in the SVG image.

Suppose that you want to locate important slogans about Web graphics formats and your bitmap graphic includes the slogan "Join us in a rut with bitmap graphics." Then, perhaps to your relief, a search engine wouldn't be able to find it. On the other hand, if you include in your SVG logo the slogan "Graphics come alive with SVG," an XML-capable search engine could search for it and find all occurrences.

Comparing SVG text to HTML/XHTML

Two important differences between HTML text and SVG text are discussed here.

First, HTML has a major advantage in that paragraph text can simply be inserted within an HTML `<p>` element with no thought or planning about line length or word wrap, for example. The HTML browser takes care of all that. If the browser window is resized, the word wrapping is adjusted to create appropriate new line lengths.

In contrast, SVG—perhaps because of its roots in the page description language PostScript, which is designed for static media—does not, at least in version 1.0, allow automatic word wrapping. A fixed line length must be decided upon, which means making some explicit decisions about the likely screen resolution to be used by visitors to your site.

The SVG `<foreignObject>` element may allow HTML, perhaps with automatic word wrapping, to be embedded within SVG images or Web pages.

Second, SVG has no elements equivalent to elements such as the `<b>` and `<i>` elements in HTML. All styling of text in SVG takes place in style attributes or individual attributes equivalent to CSS2 properties or in internal style sheets in a `<style>` element or in an external CSS style sheet.

Consider in detail the three text-related elements in SVG: the `<text>`, `<tspan>`, and `<tref>` elements. All text in SVG is contained, directly or indirectly, within `<text>` elements, so look first at that topic.

The <text> Element

Looked at as SVG, text is simply another part of the source code to be rendered by an SVG viewer. Therefore, all the manipulations that are possible with other graphics can also be carried out with text. You can transform text or alter its opacity or animate it. In one sense, text in SVG is just another type of graphic to be displayed.

A `<text>` element contains information about the screen position of the text in x and y attributes, and the styling information may be contained in a style attribute or in individual attributes corresponding to CSS2 style properties.

Styling SVG text

To apply style to SVG text, you can use either of two syntaxes. Either use a style attribute and then add the desired range of CSS properties as a list of values separated by semicolons within the style attribute, or specify each CSS property as a separate SVG attribute.

My preference is to use the style attribute and—except for this section—that is the only syntax you see in this book. Why do I prefer that method? Perhaps the reason is that I see style as a visual component so that if I cut and paste the "style visual component," I can do so knowing that I can reproduce a visual appearance I created previously and liked. Using the other technique, I may miss copying the font attribute or another non-style attribute may be inserted within the various attributes on a particular element.

Another advantage of using the style attribute is that when you break out the styling into a separate CSS style sheet (see Chapter 13, "Designing Your SVG for Use with CSS"), the syntax is almost correct for an external style sheet. Simply remove `style='` and the closing quotes and you have syntax that is already correct for use in a free-standing style sheet. Simply add the selector and the opening and closing curly brackets in the correct place, and that part of your work is done. If you use separate font and stroke attributes, for example, when you begin to want to create an external CSS style sheet, you have much more deleting, cutting, and pasting to do. Because I believe that using external CSS style sheets is a powerful tool to reduce the burden of maintenance on a Web site, the choice of using the style attribute is, at least for me, an obvious one.

The first `<text>` element in Listing 4.3 contains all the styling information within a single style attribute. The second `<text>` element contains the styling information in a range of individual attributes, such as `font-family` and `font-size`. The two approaches are visually equivalent, as you can see in Figure 04.03.

Listing 4.3 (TextStyle01.svg)

```
<?xml version="1.0" standalone="no"?>
<!DOCTYPE svg PUBLIC "-//W3C//DTD SVG 1.0//EN"
     "http://www.w3.org/TR/2001/PR-SVG-20010719/
        DTD/svg10.dtd">
<svg>
<text x="50" y="50"
  style="font-family:Arial, sans-serif; font-size:24;
fill:#000066; stroke:#000066;
  font-style:italics; font-stretch:normal;">
Some SVG text
</text>
<text x="50" y="80"
  font-family="Arial, sans-serif"
  font-size="24"
  fill="#000066"
  stroke="#000066"
  font-style="italics"
  font-stretch="normal">
Some SVG text
</text>
</svg>
```

Figure 04.03

Two strings of SVG text, the first styled using a single style attribute and the second styled by individual attributes.

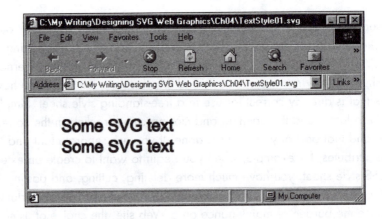

Laying out SVG text

The essentials of the display and layout of text in SVG are straightforward: They have to be contained in `<text>` elements. You can optionally use `<tspan>` or `<tref>` elements within `<text>` elements.

The simplest approach, although not necessarily the most flexible or useful for larger bodies of text, is to simply enclose the required text within SVG `<text>` elements within whose attributes the style information for the text is contained.

Let me first highlight the potential problem and then later discuss techniques to accommodate the way SVG lays out text. To display a simple greeting in SVG, you write code like the following:

Listing 4.4 (HelloSVGWorld2.svg)

```
<?xml version="1.0" standalone="no"?>
<!DOCTYPE svg PUBLIC "-//W3C//DTD SVG 1.0//EN"
      "http://www.w3.org/TR/2001/PR-SVG-20010719/
      DTD/svg10.dtd">
<svg width="800" height="600">
<text x="0" y="40" style="stroke:#000099; fill:#CCCCFF;
  font-family:Arial; font-size:36;">
Hello World! Welcome to the future of Internet
Graphics - SVG!
</text>
</svg>
```

You can see that the attributes of the `<text>` element are not much different from those of the `<rect>` element you have read about in Chapter 3, "Creating Static Graphics Elements." You position the `<text>` element relative to the upper-left corner of the containing `<svg>` element within the SVG graphic by using the x and y attributes. The style of the displayed text is controlled by the style attribute and its attendant CSS properties. You chose a deep blue outline for the text and pale blue fill. The font family is Arial, and the font size is 36.

Let's see what this looks like onscreen (see Figure 04.04).

Figure 04.04

SVG text illustrating the absence of automatic word wrapping of text.

Right away, you can see the problem. Unlike an `<h1>` header element in HTML or XHTML, an SVG `<text>` element does not automatically word-wrap within the size of the browser window. Worse, if you maximize the browser window, you find that the SVG text doesn't even word-wrap at the end of the dimensions of the `<svg>` element. The SVG viewer, unlike an HTML browser, doesn't lay out text for you. You need to provide the planning necessary to achieve the appearance you want.

You have to decide the positioning of SVG text onscreen by writing the code to start each new line and positioning that new line onscreen. To get the greeting fitted in the available width, you need to split it on two lines. Even then, the second line only just squeezes into the `<svg>` element, see Figure 04.05.

Listing 4.5 (HelloSVGWorld3.svg)

```
<?xml version="1.0" standalone="no"?>
<!DOCTYPE svg PUBLIC "-//W3C//DTD SVG 1.0//EN"
    "http://www.w3.org/TR/2001/PR-SVG-20010719/
    DTD/svg10.dtd">
<svg width="800" height="600">
<text x="0" y="40" style="stroke:#000099; fill:#CCCCFF;
font-family:Arial;
font-size:36;">
Hello World!
</text>
<text x="0" y="80" style="stroke:#000099; fill:#CCCCFF;
font-family:Arial; font-size:36;">
Welcome to the future of Internet Graphics - SVG!
</text>
</svg>
```

Figure 04.05

Splitting SVG text on two lines to fit it into the available screen space.

I admit it—I designed the previous examples so that the SVG text layout would look bad. I wanted to share with you the sense of horror I felt as I first realized that I would have to do some of the layout work myself in order to use text extensively in SVG. In practice, laying out the text has not been nearly as bad as I first expected. If you take a look at the preceding code, you see that the start tag of each of the `<text>` elements is identical, with the exception of the value of the y attribute. So, if you want to use repeating `<text>` elements like this, simply copy a `<text>` start tag and paste it where you start each new line.

I also recommend keeping the start tag of the `<text>` element, the actual text to be displayed, and the end tag `</text>` on separate lines. That way, you can visually scan to see where the text should be broken on each line. It varies according to font size and other factors, but if you lay out text more than occasionally with SVG, the whole process soon becomes second nature.

If you get the line length worked out for your first line of text, all the others are pretty easy after that. Then, just paste in the `<text>` element after the preceding `</text>` tag, start a new line for the following text, and continue typing. The process soon becomes second nature. However, you do need to do the planning of content better than you may have done when creating text for HTML—adding a few words in SVG can be a bit tedious, so plan ahead.

If you lay out a verse of an ancient (17th century) Scottish melody, you can see the use of multiple `<text>` elements.

Listing 4.6 (Psalm23.svg)

```
<?xml version="1.0" standalone="no"?>
<!DOCTYPE svg PUBLIC "-//W3C//DTD SVG 1.0//EN"
     "http://www.w3.org/TR/2001/PR-SVG-20010719/
       DTD/svg10.dtd">
<svg width="500" height="400">
<text x="20" y="30" style="font-size:24;
font-family:Arial, sans-serif; fill:red; stroke:red;">
Psalm 23
</text>
<text x="20" y="60" style="font-size:16;
font-family:'Times Roman', serif; fill:red;
stroke:red;">
```

```
The Lord's my Shepherd
</text>
<text x="20" y="80" style="font-size:16; font-family:
 'Times Roman', serif; fill:red; stroke:red;">
I'll not want
</text>
<text x="20" y="100" style="font-size:16; font-family:
 'Times Roman', serif; fill:red; stroke:red;">
He makes me down to lie
</text>
<text x="20" y="120" style="font-size:16; font-family:
 'Times Roman', serif; fill:red; stroke:red;">
In pastures green He leadeth me
</text>
<text x="20" y="140" style="font-size:16; font-family:
 'Times Roman', serif; fill:red; stroke:red;">
The quiet waters by
</text>
</svg>
```

Figure 04.06 shows the output from Listing 4.6.

Figure 04.06

Text laid out using multiple <text> elements.

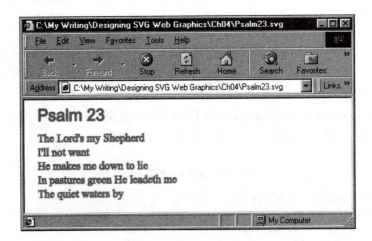

One of the benefits of SVG text, compared to bitmap graphics, is that it can be copied and pasted from an SVG image of a Web page.

However, if you display the output of Listing 4.6 and try to copy the verse, a problem arises. You can copy only a line at a time. A similar problem arises if you want to make the text available to certain accessibility applications for the visually impaired—you obscure the fact that the unit of information here is the verse rather than the line. The SVG `<tspan>` element, described later in this chapter, helps you get around this problem.

Fine-tuning the appearance of text

SVG gives you independent control of the stroke and fill properties of any font you choose to use. This situation has both potential advantages and disadvantages, which, at least in some settings, you need to think about carefully.

When you are using SVG `<text>` elements (alone or with nested `<tspan>` elements) to lay out substantial amounts of text—for example, on an SVG Web page—the impact of the width of the stroke can significantly impair text legibility. The adverse impact of the stroke varies considerably depending on, for example, the font size, whether the stroke and fill are the same color, the text colors (stroke and fill), and the background against which they are displayed. The following example, displayed in Figure 04.07, demonstrates how increasing the stroke width can adversely affect readability.

Listing 4.7 (StrokeWidth01.svg)

```
<?xml version="1.0" standalone="no"?>
<!DOCTYPE svg PUBLIC "-//W3C//DTD SVG 1.0//EN"
     "http://www.w3.org/TR/2001/PR-SVG-20010719/
      DTD/svg10.dtd">
<svg width="300" height="200">
<text x="50" y="50" style="font-family:Arial,
sans-serif; font-size:14; stroke:none;">
This has no stroke
</text>
<text x="50" y="75" style="font-family:Arial,
sans-serif; font-size:14; stroke:black;
stroke-width:1;">
Stroke width is 1.
</text>
<text x="50" y="100" style="font-family:Arial,
sans-serif; font-size:14; stroke:black;
stroke-width:2;">
Stroke width is 2.
</text>
<text x="50" y="125" style="font-family:Arial,
```

```
sans-serif; font-size:14; stroke:black;
stroke-width:3;">
Stroke width is 3.
</text>
</svg>
```

Figure 04.07

The effect of no stroke and increasing stroke width on the readability of SVG text.

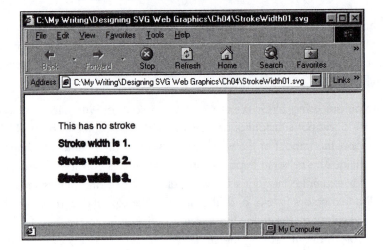

For this font size with the chosen background and text colors, either a `stroke` property of `none` or a `stroke-width` of 1 gives the best readability, in my view.

When you begin to use substantially larger text sizes, the problem of readability is not prominent, although the overall effect of the visual appearance is. Take a look at Figure 04.08.

The first line shows what the fill looks like at 72 pixels. However, when you apply stroke attributes to such big fonts, you run into the practical issue that half the stroke is painted outside the outline and half inside. So if, as shown in the third line in Figure 04.08, you want a stroke width of 2 outside the fill, you also get the likely unwanted effect of a similar stroke width overlapping the fill.

However, remember from Chapter 2 that SVG has a painter's model. An element that appears later in the document, as long as it has 100 percent opacity, covers up any element that occurs earlier in the document at the same coordinates. This situation gives you the solution to the problem of half the stroke's being painted over the fill. To create text with a stroke

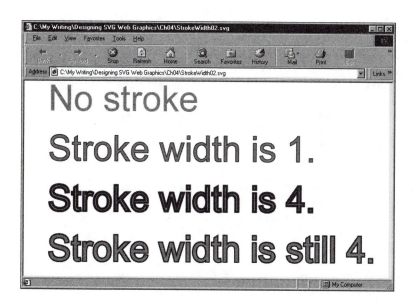

Figure 04.08

Stroke width and the double use of text to remove overlap of the stroke into the fill of large font text.

width of 2 without the fill, you need two copies of the text. The first copy is created using a `stroke-width` property with the value 4. At this stage, you have a `stroke-width` of 2 inside the outline and covering part of the fill. If you add another text element with all identical attributes but with a `stroke` property of `none`, it covers over the fill that has the intrusion of the stroke and gives you a string of text that has the fill displayed as you intended for that font size and with the stroke wholly outside the fill. That is how the final line of text in Figure 04.08 was created.

Of course, by doing so, you slightly increase the file size because you have essentially two descriptions of the same text. Adding a few dozen bytes to the file size seems to me to be a good trade-off for this type of situation. Notice too that I have used a grouping `<g>` element in the code because these two `<text>` elements need to be kept together to maintain the desired effect.

Listing 4.8 (StrokeWidth02.svg)

```
<?xml version="1.0" standalone="no"?>
<!DOCTYPE svg PUBLIC "-//W3C//DTD SVG 1.0//EN"
    "http://www.w3.org/TR/2001/PR-SVG-20010719/
    DTD/svg10.dtd">
```

```
<svg width="750" height="400">
<text x="50" y="60" style="font-family:Arial,
sans-serif; font-size:72;
stroke:none; fill:red;">
No stroke
</text>
<text x="50" y="160" style="font-family:Arial,
sans-serif; font-size:72;
fill:red; stroke:black; stroke-width:1;">
Stroke width is 1.
</text>
<text x="50" y="260" style="font-family:Arial,
sans-serif; font-size:72;
fill:red; stroke:black; stroke-width:4;">
Stroke width is 4.
</text>
<g>
<text x="50" y="360" style="font-family:Arial,
sans-serif; font-size:72;
fill:red; stroke:black; stroke-width:4;">
Stroke width is still 4.
</text>
<text x="50" y="360" style="font-family:Arial,
sans-serif; font-size:72;
fill:red; stroke:none; stroke-width:4;">
Stroke width is still 4.
</text>
</g>
</svg>
```

Kerning

Kerning refers to the spacing between individual character glyphs. If letters are spaced too far apart, readers wonder whether a stray space character has been left behind; if the glyphs are too close together, the visual appearance simply looks cluttered.

Kerning tables are provided with many fonts. These tables indicate (most likely in the opinion of the creator of the font) what amount of space should exist between given pairs of glyphs when that particular font is in use. If you do not specify any information about kerning when defining the style attribute of a `<text>` element, an SVG processor "assumes" that the value for the kerning property has been set to `auto`.

SVG also gives you the opportunity to turn kerning off, by specifying a number that describes the space between individual glyphs. If you want to disable the use of the kerning tables but do not want to add additional space between glyphs, you set the value of the kerning property to 0. Here is an example using auto kerning and three manual settings:

Listing 4.9 (Kerning01.svg)

```
<?xml version="1.0" standalone="no"?>
<!DOCTYPE svg PUBLIC "-//W3C//DTD SVG 1.0//EN"
     "http://www.w3.org/TR/2001/PR-SVG-20010719/
     DTD/svg10.dtd">
<svg width="300" height="200">
<text x="50" y="50" style="font-family:Arial,
sans-serif; font-size:14;
stroke:black; stroke-width:1; kerning:auto;">
Auto kerning
</text>
<text x="50" y="75" style="font-family:Arial,
sans-serif; font-size:14;
stroke:black; stroke-width:1; kerning:0;">
Manual kerning, value 0.
</text>
<text x="50" y="100" style="font-family:Arial,
sans-serif; font-size:14;
stroke:black; stroke-width:1; kerning:1;">
Manual kerning, value 1.
</text>
<text x="50" y="125" style="font-family:Arial,
sans-serif; font-size:14;
stroke:black; stroke-width:1; kerning:3;">
Manual kerning, value 3.
</text>
</svg>
```

In Figure 04.09, you can see the effect of auto kerning and those manually set kerning values. The effect on the legibility of kerning is evident.

The use or avoidance of `stroke` attributes on glyphs also has a distinct impact on desirable kerning values. If you remove the stroke from glyphs and leave the kerning unchanged, the visual effect is distinctly different.

Figure 04.09

Auto kerning and three manual settings of kerning on SVG text.

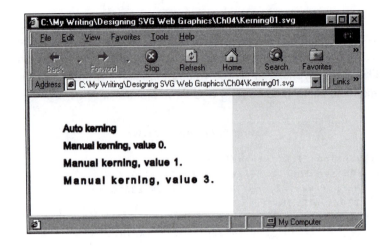

Listing 4.10 (Kerning02.svg)

```
<?xml version="1.0" standalone="no"?>
<!DOCTYPE svg PUBLIC "-//W3C//DTD SVG 1.0//EN"
      "http://www.w3.org/TR/2001/PR-SVG-20010719/
      DTD/svg10.dtd">
<svg width="300" height="200">
<text x="50" y="50" style="font-family:Arial,
sans-serif; font-size:14;
stroke:none; kerning:auto;">
Auto kerning
</text>
<text x="50" y="75" style="font-family:Arial,
sans-serif; font-size:14;
stroke:none; kerning:0;">
Manual kerning, value 0.
</text>
<text x="50" y="100" style="font-family:Arial,
sans-serif; font-size:14;
stroke:none; kerning:1;">
Manual kerning, value 1.
</text>
<text x="50" y="125" style="font-family:Arial,
sans-serif; font-size:14;
stroke:none; kerning:3;">
Manual kerning, value 3.
</text>
</svg>
```

In the text shown in Figure 04.10, I have removed the `stroke` attributes from all glyphs and left the four kerning settings as shown in Figure 04.09. As I hope you can appreciate, the visual impression of individual kerning settings varies depending on the presence or absence of a stroke on an individual glyph.

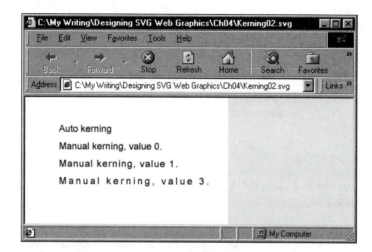

Figure 04.10

The visual effect of the kerning settings shown in Figure 04.09 on text with no stroke.

Letter spacing

Whether or not you use auto kerning or set it manually, you also can add space between glyphs by making use of the `letter-spacing` property. You can use this property with or without explicitly expressed units. If you want to relate the spacing between glyphs to the em size, for example, you can specify that the value of the `letter-spacing` property is `0.5em`. In the following example, I have not used units.

Listing 4.11 (LetterSpacing01.svg)

```
<?xml version="1.0" standalone="no"?>
<!DOCTYPE svg PUBLIC "-//W3C//DTD SVG 1.0//EN"
     "http://www.w3.org/TR/2001/PR-SVG-20010719/
       DTD/svg10.dtd">
<svg width="400" height="200">
<text x="20" y="50" style="font-family:Arial,
sans-serif; font-size:14;
stroke:none; kerning:auto;">
Auto kerning, no letter spacing
```

```
</text>
<text x="20" y="75" style="font-family:Arial,
sans-serif; font-size:14;
stroke:none; kerning:auto; letter-spacing:1;">
Auto kerning, letter spacing of 1.
</text>
<text x="20" y="100" style="font-family:Arial,
sans-serif; font-size:14;
stroke:none; kerning:auto; letter-spacing:2;">
Auto kerning, letter spacing of 2.
</text>
<text x="20" y="125" style="font-family:Arial,
sans-serif; font-size:14;
stroke:none; kerning:auto; letter-spacing:3;">
Auto kerning, letter spacing of 3.
</text>
</svg>
```

As you can see in Figure 04.11, letter spacing can have a significant impact on the visual impression your text creates.

Figure 04.11

The effect of letter spacing on text.

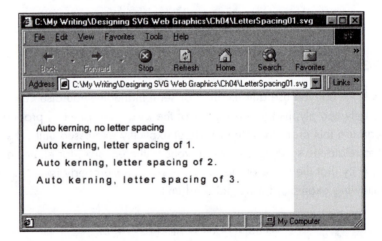

The <tspan> Element

The `<tspan>` element doesn't help you get around the need to calculate where line breaks should be, but it does help you with the copying of text by the user and the accessibility issues I mentioned earlier. This element also allows you to place text on the page by using a relative positioning mechanism rather than an absolute position, as is used with `<text>` elements. To see how this is done, take another look at Psalm 23, this time using both `<text>` and `<tspan>` elements.

Listing 4.12 (Psalm23tspan.svg)

```
<?xml version="1.0" standalone="no"?>
<!DOCTYPE svg PUBLIC "-//W3C//DTD SVG 1.0//EN"
     "http://www.w3.org/TR/2001/PR-SVG-20010719/
      DTD/svg10.dtd">
<svg width="500" height="400">
<text x="20" y="30" style="font-size:24;
font-family:Arial, sans-serif; fill:red; stroke:red;">
Psalm 23
</text>
<text>
<tspan x="20" y="60" style="font-size:16;
font-family:'Times Roman', serif; fill:red;
stroke:red;">
The Lord's my Shepherd
</tspan>
<tspan x="20" dy="1em" style="font-size:16;
font-family: 'Times Roman', serif; fill:red;
stroke:red;">
I'll not want
</tspan>
<tspan x="20" dy="1em" style="font-size:16;
font-family: 'Times Roman', serif; fill:red;
stroke:red;">
He makes me down to lie
</tspan>
<tspan x="20" dy="1em" style="font-size:16;
font-family: 'Times Roman', serif; fill:red;
stroke:red;">
In pastures green He leadeth me
</tspan>
<tspan x="20" dy="1em" style="font-size:16;
font-family: 'Times Roman', serif; fill:red;
stroke:red;">
The quiet waters by
</tspan>
</text>
</svg>
```

I left the header, `Psalm 23`, within its separate `<text>` element. However, the verse is contained in one `<text>` element now, rather than in five, as in the preceding version. Each line is now contained in a `<tspan>` element rather than in a `<text>` element. If you attempt to select the whole verse, displayed in a browser for copying, you find that you can now do so. Similarly accessibility tools for the visually impaired can treat the verse as a unit.

Notice too that I have used two different ways of describing where a `<tspan>` element will be placed. For the first line, I used absolute positioning, like this:

```
<tspan x="20" y="60" style="font-size:16;
font-family:'Times Roman', serif; fill:red;
stroke:red;">
The Lord's my Shepherd
</tspan>
```

whereas for each of the other `<tspan>` elements, I used relative positioning for the vertical position using the `dy` attribute. The `dy` attribute basically specifies how far down from the preceding line the line contained in the `<tspan>` element should be positioned.

The use of relative positioning with `<tspan>` elements can make the task of adding text or repositioning a block of text significantly simpler than when you use absolute positioning. Suppose that you want to reposition all the text 20 pixels farther down the page. You simply need to change the y attribute in the first `<tspan>` element to

```
<tspan x="20" y="80" style="font-size:16;
font-family:'Times Roman', serif; fill:red;
stroke:red;">
The Lord's my Shepherd
</tspan>
```

The relatively positioned remaining `<tspan>` elements would maintain their position relative to that first one. Of course, you need to keep in mind whether the space into which the `<tspan>` elements may be moving is already occupied and, if so, whether or how you need to reposition the existing occupants of that space.

You can use this technique of relative positioning in a number of Web graphics situations. Let me show you how to create the framework for a simple scrolling window, which is displayed like some Java applets, to express a little bit of pro-SVG propaganda. You create the text here so that you have a simple rectangular window. In Chapter 8, you add the animation to create the scrolling window.

Here is the code to create the window. As you read through it, you will hopefully notice a couple of things that are not strictly necessary to create a static window like this one but that help you with the animation and later, when you place the animated window on an HTML or SVG Web page.

Listing 4.13 (TextWindow.svg)

```
<?xml version="1.0" standalone="no"?>
<!DOCTYPE svg PUBLIC "-//W3C//DTD SVG 1.0//EN"
    "http://www.w3.org/TR/2001/PR-SVG-20010719/
    DTD/svg10.dtd">
<svg width="200" height="200">
<svg x="0" y="0" width="200" height="200">
<rect x="0" y="0" width="200" height="200"
style="stroke:#990066; fill:none;"/>
<text>
<tspan x="5" y="25" style="font-size:14;
font-family:Arial, sans-serif; stroke:#990066;
fill:#990066">
Scalable Vector Graphics
</tspan>
<tspan x="5" dy="2em" style="font-size:10;
font-family:Arial, sans-serif;">
The World Wide Web Consortium has
</tspan>
<tspan x="5" dy="1em" style="font-size:10;
font-family:Arial, sans-serif;">
announced the availability of its
</tspan>
<tspan x="5" dy="1em" style="font-size:10;
font-family:Arial, sans-serif;">
exciting new XML-based graphics
</tspan>
<tspan x="5" dy="1em" style="font-size:10;
font-family:Arial, sans-serif;">
format, SVG, for the display
</tspan>
<tspan x="5" dy="1em" style="font-size:10;
```

```
font-family:Arial, sans-serif;">
of 2D graphics, text and bitmap
</tspan>
<tspan x="5" dy="1em" style="font-size:10;
font-family:Arial, sans-serif;">
graphics.
</tspan>
<tspan x="5" dy="2em" style="font-size:10;
font-family:Arial, sans-serif;">
Further information is available
</tspan>
<tspan x="5" dy="1em" style="font-size:10;
font-family:Arial, sans-serif;">
at the W3C web site,
</tspan>
<tspan x="5" dy="2em" style="font-size:10;
font-family:Arial, sans-serif; fill:blue; stroke:blue">
http://www.w3.org/
</tspan>
</text>
</svg>
</svg>
```

First, notice that I have created a separate `<svg>` element to contain the scrolling window.

```
<svg width="200" height="200">
<svg x="0" y="0" width="200" height="200">
<rect x="0" y="0" width="200" height="200"
style="stroke:#990066; fill:none;"/>
```

The existence of the inner `<svg>` element means that you can use the whole thing as a visual component and drop it into a page wherever you want. The only things you need to change are the x and y attributes of the inner `<svg>` element. Everything else is positioned relative to the upper-left corner of that nested `<svg>` element so that relative positioning is maintained.

Second, notice how I have used absolute positioning for the first `<tspan>` element (as shown in Figure 04.12). All other `<tspan>` elements are positioned relative to that one. Has the possibility crossed your mind that if I can animate the first `<tspan>` element, all the others will follow?

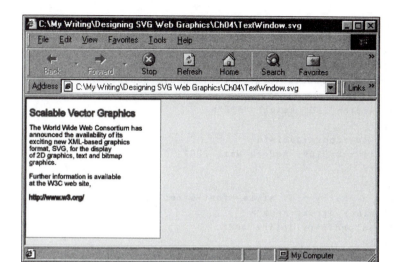

Figure 04.12

A text window to which you add scrolling functionality in Chapter 8.

If you use a `<tspan>` *element without specifying* x, y, dx, *or* dy *attributes, the tagged text is positioned immediately after the text preceding the* `<tspan>` *tag.*

Okay, I admit it. It doesn't scroll. Not yet, anyway. You add the scrolling functionality in Chapter 8, where you learn about SVG animation. For the moment, think of your code as a static visual component to which you can add a range of animations, including your declared ambition of creating an applet-like scrolling window.

The <tref> Element

The use of the `<tref>` element has many similarities to the way the `<use>` element works. The text to be inserted is created in a `<text>` element nested within the `<defs>` element toward the beginning of an SVG document. The referenced `<text>` element has an ID attribute that the referencing `<tref>` element makes use of by means of the `xlink:href` attribute.

In this simple example, copyright information is defined in a `<text>` element whose ID is `CopyrightInfo`. That element is then referenced by the `<tref>` element later in the SVG document.

Listing 4.14 (tref01.svg)

```
<?xml version="1.0" standalone="no"?>
<!DOCTYPE svg PUBLIC "-//W3C//DTD SVG 1.0//EN"
     "http://www.w3.org/TR/2001/PR-SVG-20010719/
       DTD/svg10.dtd">
<svg width="600" height="300">
<defs>
<text id="CopyrightInfo">
Copyright &#0169; Andrew Watt 2001
</text>
</defs>
<text x="50" y="30" style="font-size:14;
fill:blue; stroke:none">
This is ordinary inline text.
</text>
<text x="50" y="50" style="font-size:14;
fill:blue; stroke:none">
The following text was created using the
&lt;tref&gt; element.
</text>
<text x="50" y="80" style="font-size:14;
fill:red; stroke:none;">
<tref xlink:href="#CopyrightInfo"/>
</text>
</svg>
```

The output is shown in Figure 04.13.

Figure 04.13

Text displayed onscreen by means of the <tref> element.

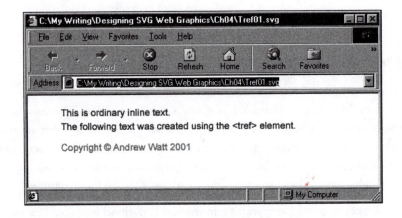

Displaying Text on a Path

I described in Chapter 3, "Creating Basic Static Graphic Elements," how the SVG `<path>` element is created. The `<path>` element can be used in combination with the `<text>` element and the `<textPath>` element to display text on a path.

Listing 4.15 (TextonPath01.svg)

```
<?xml version="1.0" standalone="no"?>
<!DOCTYPE svg PUBLIC "-//W3C//DTD SVG 1.0//EN"
      "http://www.w3.org/TR/2001/PR-SVG-20010719/
      DTD/svg10.dtd">
<svg width="1000" height="300">
<defs>
<path id="MyCurve"
d="M 100 250
C 200 100 300 0 400 80
C 500 150 600 300 700 200
C 800 100 900 0 1000 100" />
</defs>
<use xlink:href="#MyCurve" style="fill:none;
stroke:white" />
<text style="font-family:Arial, sans-serif;
font-size:18; fill:blue">
<textPath xlink:href="#MyCurve">
Scalable Vector Graphics allows you to place
text on a path. You can use the &lt;path&gt;,
&lt;text&gt;  and  &lt;textPath&gt;
elements.
</textPath>
</text>
</svg>
```

The `<use>` element references the `<path>` element contained in the `<defs>` element. The `<text>` element defines the style of the text to be displayed, and the nested `<textPath>` element references the same `<path>` element over which the text is fitted.

Figure 04.14 shows the text of Listing 4.15 displayed on a path.

Figure 04.14

*SVG text displayed
on a path.*

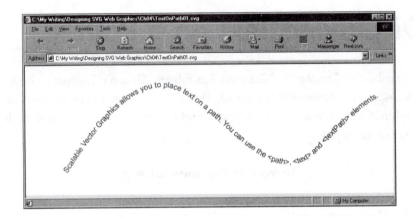

Now that you have looked in this and the previous two chapters at the structure of an SVG document, static SVG graphic shapes, and text handling in SVG, you are ready to go on to Chapter 5, "Creating Navigation Bars," to create some useful SVG images—navigation bars.

5

Creating
Navigation Bars

In this chapter:

Navigation Bars

The requirements document for the SVG specification states explicitly that SVG was intended to replace "many uses" of bitmap graphics. One of the most common uses for bitmap and, to a degree, binary vector graphics on the Web has been for the creation of navigation graphics, whether it is simple text, buttons, 3D buttons, or something a little more sophisticated. Needless to say, any of the commonly used types of navigation graphics can be created straightforwardly using SVG. In this chapter, I show you how to create a variety of SVG navigation graphics for Web pages, to familiarize you with the relevant techniques.

The most interesting types of navigation "furniture" incorporate additional SVG visual components, such as animations, gradients, and interactions. Look at the graphics you create in this chapter as visual components you can add to those other types of visual components later to produce the graphics you want.

Before you can use any type of SVG graphic to navigate from page to page, you need to know how to create Web links in SVG from one Web page to another. After you have done that, you learn how to construct various pieces of Web page furniture to which you can apply your links.

Navigation around SVG images or Web pages is further discussed in Chapter 12, "Creating a Simple SVG Web Site," which discusses the creation of SVG Web pages.

In addition, to use any but the most basic Web page navigation, you also want to be able to add rollover effects to your SVG elements. I introduce simple mouseover and mouseout interactivity in this chapter and apply it to navigation graphics. Interactivity in SVG is discussed more fully in Chapter 11, "Creating Interactive SVG Graphics."

So let's move on and look at linking Web pages in SVG.

Linking Web Pages Using SVG

SVG provides two mechanisms for linking that operate in slightly different ways: the `<a>` element and XLinks.

To use SVG for navigating between Web pages, whether those are standard HTML or XHTML Web pages or SVG Web pages (as described in Chapter 12), you typically use the SVG `<a>` element.

The `<a>` element

Functionally, the SVG `<a>` element closely resembles an HTML or XTHML `<a>` element. The graphic or text that defines the link is nested within the `<a>` element, like this:

Listing 5.1 (SimpleA01.svg)

```
<?xml version="1.0" standalone="no"?>
<!DOCTYPE svg PUBLIC "-//W3C//DTD SVG 1.0//EN"
    "http://www.w3.org/TR/2001/PR-SVG-20010719/
    DTD/svg10.dtd">
<svg>
<a xlink:href="PageToGoTo.html">
<text x="20" y="20" style="fill:blue; stroke:blue;
font-size:14;">
Click Here!
</text>
</a>
</svg>
```

You click on the graphic or text that denotes the link defined by the `<a>` element and, if the target of the link is the same browser window (which is the default behavior), the content of the browser window is replaced by the content of the Web page, whether it is HTML/XHTML or an SVG Web page to which the `<a>` element links.

With the preceding code, you have a functioning link, as you can see in Figure 05.01. Note the pointing-hand cursor onscreen and the target for the link, PageToGoTo.html, in the status bar of the browser window.

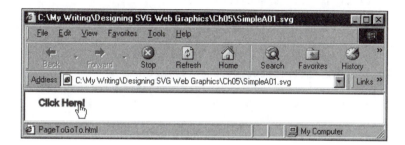

Figure 05.01

A simple text link using the SVG `<a>` element. Note the pointing-hand cursor because the mouse is over the content of the `<a>` element.

Notice the difference between the locator `xlink:href` attribute in the SVG `<a>` element and that with which you are probably familiar in HTML or XHTML. You must use an `xlink:href` attribute rather than the `href` attribute you use in HTML. The value of the `xlink:href` attribute is simply a typical URL (Uniform Resource Locator). In the example, the link is made to the URL http://www.svgspider.com/default.svg. Because no indication exists otherwise, the default behavior of an SVG `<a>` element is that the target Web page is opened in the same browser window.

The following example shows how to create a simple button using a `<rect>` element with rounded corners that is nested within an SVG `<a>` element. The resulting graphic is shown in Figure 05.02.

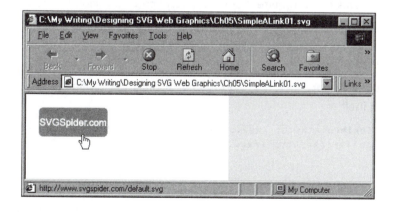

Figure 05.02

A simple SVG navigation graphic nested within an `<a>` element.

Notice that as with a bitmap graphic used in HTML or XHTML, the SVG graphic also produces a pointing-hand cursor when the mouse hovers over the graphic to indicate that the graphic is a hyperlink.

Listing 5.2 (SimpleALink01.svg)

```
<?xml version="1.0" standalone="no"?>
<!DOCTYPE svg PUBLIC "-//W3C//DTD SVG 1.0//EN"
    "http://www.w3.org/TR/2001/PR-SVG-20010719/
     DTD/svg10.dtd">
<svg width="300" height="200"
  xmlns:xlink="http://www.w3.org/1999/xlink" >
<a xlink:href="http://www.svgspider.com/default.svg">
<rect x="20" y="20" width="100" height="40" rx="5"
ry="5" style="fill:red; stroke:red;"/>
<text x="20" y="45" style="fill:white; stroke:white;
font-size:14;">
SVGSpider.com
</text>
</a>
</svg>
```

In the start tag of the `<svg>` element is a namespace declaration I included for the XLink namespace:

```
xmlns:xlink="http://www.w3.org/1999/xlink"
```

Any processor application is then aware that when it encounters in your SVG document an attribute with an `xlink` prefix, the attribute belongs to the XLink namespace. An XLink-aware processor, such as an SVG viewer, then interprets the meaning of the attribute correctly. The Adobe SVG Viewer seems not to require that the namespace declaration be made, but being explicit about the namespace URI http://www.w3.org/1999/xlink, which is being referred to when the namespace prefix `xlink` is being used, is good practice.

An alternative approach is to add the namespace declaration to the `<a>` element itself:

```
<a xlink:href="http://www.svgspider.com/default.svg"
   xmlns:xlink="http://www.w3.org/1999/xlink">
```

All parts of the graphic that are to act as the hyperlink need to be nested within the `<a>` element. For example, the following code does not produce the desired result of linking because the `<text>` element lies outside the `<a>` element:

Listing 5.3 (SimpleALink02.svg)

```
<?xml version="1.0" standalone="no"?>
<!DOCTYPE svg PUBLIC "-//W3C//DTD SVG 1.0//EN"
    "http://www.w3.org/TR/2001/PR-SVG-20010719/
     DTD/svg10.dtd">
<svg width="300" height="200">
<a xlink:href="http://www.svgspider.com/default.svg">
<rect x="20" y="20" width="100" height="40" rx="5"
ry="5" style="fill:red; stroke:red;"/>
</a>
<!-- The text is not nested within the <a> element
as it should be. -->
<text x="20" y="45" style="fill:white; stroke:white;
font-size:14;">
SVGSpider.com
</text>
</svg>
```

The `<text>` element is not nested within the `<a>` element and is placed in front of the `<rect>` element. However, if you attempt to click on the link when the mouse is over the text rather than over the rectangle, no linking behavior results. That isn't surprising because the `<text>` element isn't nested correctly within the linking `<a>` element. One hint that something is wrong is that if you mouse over the graphic, the pointing-hand cursor that is present when you mouse over the rectangle changes to an I-bar-type cursor when you move it over the text. The cure is simple: Nest the text properly within the `<a>` element.

In HTML, you can open a link in a new window by setting the `target` attribute of the `<a>` element to `_blank`. In SVG, you set the `xlink:show` attribute of the SVG `<a>` element to `new` to achieve the same effect. In Internet Explorer 5.5, you can also use a `target` attribute with the value `_blank`, as you can in HTML. (See Listing 5.4, which uses the `target` attribute that works with Internet Explorer in the absence of support for the `xlink:show` attribute in the Adobe SVG Viewer.)

Listing 5.4 (SimpleALink03.svg)

```
<?xml version="1.0" standalone="no"?>
<!DOCTYPE svg PUBLIC "-//W3C//DTD SVG 1.0//EN"
    "http://www.w3.org/TR/2001/PR-SVG-20010719/
    DTD/svg10.dtd">
<svg width="300" height="200">
<a xlink:href="http://www.svgspider.com/default.svg"
target="new">
<rect x="20" y="20" width="100" height="40" rx="5"
ry="5" style="fill:red; stroke:red;"/>
<text x="20" y="45" style="fill:white; stroke:white;
font-size:14;">
SVGSpider.com
</text>
</a>
</svg>
```

In the preceding code, I used the `target` attribute. The SVG specification recommends the use of `xlink:show` with a value of `new` to achieve the same effect.

Figure 05.03 shows the linked page opened in a new window. The page being linked from is shown in the rear window. The linked page, `http://www.svgspider.com/default.svg`, is opened in a new browser window.

Thus, by using the SVG `<a>` element, you can either replace the content of the current window or, if the `target` attribute is given a value of `_blank`, you can open a new window.

mailto links

Strictly speaking, mailto links are not part of a navigation bar, but because they are based on the SVG `<a>` element, I describe them here.

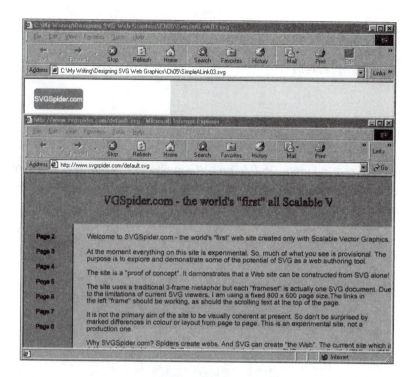

Figure 05.03

The `target` *attribute on the* `<a>` *element when set to a value of* `new` *causes a new window to be opened in Internet Explorer to display the page or image referenced by the* `xlink:href` *attribute.*

Suppose that on the AndrewWatt.com Web site page on consulting services, you want to add a mailto link. The link is part of an SVG header for a particular Web page that includes other links. Your SVG code looks something like this:

Listing 5.5 (MailTo.svg)

```
<?xml version="1.0" standalone="no"?>
<!DOCTYPE svg PUBLIC "-//W3C//DTD SVG 1.0//EN"
      "http://www.w3.org/TR/2001/PR-SVG-20010719/
      DTD/svg10.dtd">
<svg width="800" height="150">
<svg x="0" y="0" width="800" height="150">
<rect x="0" y="0" width="800" height="150"
style="fill:black; stroke:none;"/>
<text x="30" y="30" style="font-family:Arial,
sans-serif; font-size:36; stroke:#CCFF00;
fill:#CCFF00;">
AndrewWatt.com
</text>
<a xlink:href="mailto:Consulting@AndrewWatt.com">
```

```
<text x="30" y="60" style="font-family:Arial,
sans-serif; font-size:16; stroke:#3333FF;
fill:#3333FF;">
Consulting Services
</text>
</a>
</svg>
</svg>
```

As you can see in Figure 05.04, an SVG mailto link, when properly written, causes the cursor to change to a hand, and in the Adobe SVG Viewer the link is displayed in the browser status bar.

Figure 05.04

Clicking on a mailto link in an SVG element causes the relevant mailing application to open a new email form, appropriately addressed. Here, the functionality is shown in AOL 6.0.

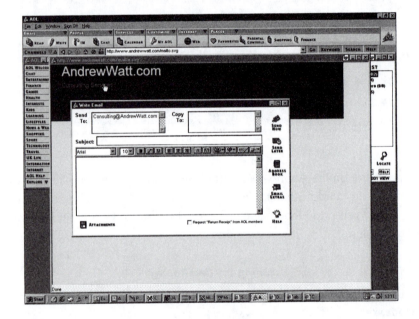

If you attempt to create a mailto link and find that the hand cursor is present but the link text is absent from the browser status bar, you may have written

```
<a href="mailto:Consulting@AndrewWatt.com">
```

using an `href` attribute (incorrect in SVG) rather than what you need to write, which is

```
<a xlink:href="mailto:Consulting@AndrewWatt.com">
```

using the `xlink:href` attribute.

Remember that because SVG is XML, it uses the XLink linking mechanism, not the HTML one. The syntax is similar but not identical.

Having introduced you to the SVG `<a>` element, I now describe the XLink functionality provided in SVG.

XLinks

As you have read in the preceding section, SVG provides in its `<a>` element linking capabilities that are similar to those in HTML and XHTML but using the `xlink:href` attribute. However, the `xlink:href` attribute is only one of several XLink linking attributes supported in the SVG specification. First, let's take a look at what XLinks are about.

XLink has no elements; rather, it has *global attributes*. XLink attributes can be associated with any SVG element—indeed, with any XML element—by simply adding the XLink namespace declaration in the appropriate place and using the available XLink linking attributes. SVG implements only simple-type XLinks, which broadly correspond to familiar hyperlinking functionality in HTML and XHTML.

In addition to the `xlink:href` attribute, which you read about earlier, SVG also supports `xlink:type`, `xlink:role`, `xlink:arcrole`, `xlink:title`, `xlink:show`, and `xlink:actuate` global attributes.

The `<a>` element functionality is equivalent to the following XLink linking attributes placed on a `<rect>` element.

Listing 5.6 (XLink02.svg)

```
<?xml version="1.0" standalone="no"?>
<!DOCTYPE svg PUBLIC "-//W3C//DTD SVG 1.0//EN"
     "http://www.w3.org/TR/2001/PR-SVG-20010719/
        DTD/svg10.dtd">
<svg width="300" height="200">
<rect
  xmlns:xlink="http://www.w3.org/1999/xlink"
  xlink:type="simple"
  xlink:href="Replacement.svg"
  xlink:show="replace"
  xlink:actuate="onRequest"
  x="20" y="20" width="100" height="40" rx="5"
```

```
ry="5" style="fill:red;
stroke:red;"/>
<text x="20" y="45" style="fill:white;
stroke:white; font-size:14;">
Click to link
</text>
</svg>
```

The XLink functionality lies in the following code:

```
<rect
  xmlns:xlink="http://www.w3.org/1999/xlink"
  xlink:type="simple"
  xlink:href="Replacement.svg"
  xlink:show="replace"
  xlink:actuate="onRequest"
  x="20" y="20" width="100" height="40" rx="5"
ry="5" style="fill:red;
stroke:red;"/>
```

The XLink namespace is declared on the `<rect>` element. The meaning of `xlink:href` is as you saw previously—it specifies the URL being linked to. The `xlink:show` attribute defines where the linked page or image will be displayed. In this case, the value of the `xlink:show` attribute is `replace`, which means that it is displayed in the current window. The `xlink:actuate` attribute has the value `onRequest`, which means that the link is activated when the containing element, the `<rect>` element, is clicked.

To use the XLink syntax to open a new window on request, you use this syntax:

```
<rect
  xmlns:xlink="http://www.w3.org/1999/xlink"
  xlink:type="simple"
  xlink:href="Replacement.svg"
  xlink:show="new"
  xlink:actuate="onRequest"
  x="20" y="20" width="100" height="40" rx="5"
ry="5" style="fill:red;
stroke:red;"/>
```

To open a new window when a page loads—for example, to provide instructions for using a program or to make known details of a special offer from an e-store—you set `xlink:show` to `new` and `xlink:actuate` to `onLoad`, as shown in the following example:

```
<rect
  xmlns:xlink="http://www.w3.org/1999/xlink"
  xlink:type="simple"
  xlink:href="Replacement.svg"
  xlink:show="new"
  xlink:actuate="onLoad"
  x="20" y="20" width="100" height="40" rx="5"
ry="5" style="fill:red;
stroke:red;"/>
```

None of the XLink attributes can be animated, although you can animate SVG elements on which the XLink attributes are present.

The full XLink linking functionality is not now supported in the Adobe SVG Viewer. Hopefully, by the time you read this chapter, one or more of the SVG viewers will have fully implemented XLink functionality and you can then try out the preceding code.

Adding Mouseover Effects

I talk about interactivity in SVG in greater detail in Chapter 11. In this chapter, I look only at mouseover and mouseout, which enable you to implement rollovers using SVG declarative syntax.

Rollover effects can be achieved in several ways, using SVG declarative animation. In Listing 5.7, the `<set>` element is used to create an animation that begins when the text is moused and ends when the mouse is removed. Notice that the `<set>` element is nested within the `<text>` element whose font-size property is being animated.

Listing 5.7 (MouseEvents01.svg)

```
<?xml version="1.0" standalone="no"?>
<!DOCTYPE svg PUBLIC "-//W3C//DTD SVG 1.0//EN"
    "http://www.w3.org/TR/2001/PR-SVG-20010719/
    DTD/svg10.dtd">
```

```
<svg width="800" height="200">
<text x="50" y="50" style="font-size:24;
font-family:Arial, sans-serif;
stroke:red; fill:red;">
<set attributeName="font-size" begin="mouseover"
end="mouseout" to="36" />
This text will enlarge when moused.
</text>
<text x="50" y="100" style="font-size:24;
font-family:Arial, sans-serif;
stroke:red; fill:red;">
<set attributeName="font-size" begin="mouseover"
end="mouseout" to="36" />
This text will enlarge when moused.
</text>
</svg>
```

Figure 05.05 shows the text when the lower text is moused. As you can see, the font size has increased. The font size increases from 24 to 36 while the mouse is over the text.

Figure 05.05

The lower text is moused, and its font size has increased.

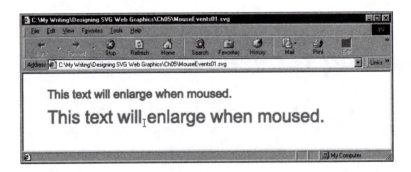

No `<a>` element is present in the code, so the pointing-hand cursor is not present. As you can see, an I-bar cursor appears when the mouse is over the text.

The `<set>` element creates step-wise transition from one value of an attribute or property to another. You may want to create a more subtle rollover effect that would require using one of the other SVG animation elements. For example, you may want text to expand its font size and then shrink back slightly. You could achieve that effect by using the `<animate>` element. However, you then would need to use two `<animate>` elements—

one to create the mouseover animation and the second to create the mouseout animation.

Listing 5.8 (MouseEvents02.svg)

```
<?xml version="1.0" standalone="no"?>
<!DOCTYPE svg PUBLIC "-//W3C//DTD SVG 1.0//EN"
     "http://www.w3.org/TR/2001/PR-SVG-20010719/
      DTD/svg10.dtd">
<svg width="1000" height="200">
<text x="50" y="50" style="font-size:24;
font-family:Arial, sans-serif;
stroke:red; fill:red;">
<animate attributeName="font-size" begin="mouseover"
dur="1s" values="24; 36; 32" fill="freeze" />
<animate attributeName="font-size" begin="mouseout"
dur="0.5s" values="32; 33; 24" fill="freeze" />
This text will enlarge then shrink slightly
when moused.
</text>
</svg>
```

The mouseover animation lasts 1 second, and the mouseout animation lasts 0.5 seconds. In practice, you may want something a little faster than that. Similarly, you almost certainly will choose smaller font sizes; the large font sizes chosen here help you to see what is happening. During the first half-second of the mouseover event, the font size increases from 24 to 36, and then it shrinks back to 32 over the final half-second.

In the earlier examples of hyperlinking in SVG, two or more elements were nested within a single <a> element. When it comes to creating rollover effects on multiple elements, you need to make sure that you apply an appropriate animation to all the elements within the <a> element you want to animate.

I show you how to create a rollover that adapts the code shown in Listing 5.8. The rollover effect you create changes the white text to red (which involves animating both its fill and stroke properties) and the fill of the rectangle to white, leaving the stroke of the rectangle red. The appearance when the button is not moused is shown in Figure 05.06; the way it looks when it is moused is shown in Figure 05.07.

Figure 05.06

A mouseover effect where the fill and stroke of the text and the fill of the rectangle all change when the button is moused. In this figure, the button is not moused.

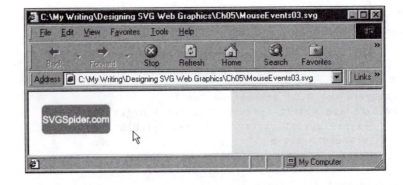

Figure 05.07

The same button when moused. The fill and stroke of the `<text>` element and the fill of the `<rect>` element all change color.

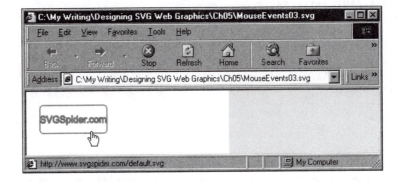

In Listing 5.9, I show you the code that achieves the desired rollover effect.

Listing 5.9 (MouseEvents03.svg)

```
<?xml version="1.0" standalone="no"?>
<!DOCTYPE svg PUBLIC "-//W3C//DTD SVG 1.0//EN"
    "http://www.w3.org/TR/2001/PR-SVG-20010719/
    DTD/svg10.dtd">
<svg width="300" height="200">
<a xlink:href="http://www.svgspider.com/default.svg"
target="new" id="MouseTest">
<rect x="20" y="20" width="100" height="40" rx="5"
ry="5" style="fill:red;
stroke:red;">
<animate begin="MouseTest.mouseover" dur="0.1s"
attributeName="fill" from="red" to="white"
fill="freeze"/>
<animate begin="MouseTest.mouseout" dur="0.1s"
attributeName="fill" from="white" to="red"
```

```
fill="freeze"/>
</rect>
<text x="20" y="45" style="fill:white;
stroke:white; font-size:14;" pointer-events="none">
<animate begin="MouseTest.mouseover" dur="0.1s"
attributeName="fill" from="white" to="red"
fill="freeze"/>
<animate begin="MouseTest.mouseout" dur="0.1s"
attributeName="fill" from="red" to="white"
fill="freeze"/>
<animate begin="MouseTest.mouseover" dur="0.1s"
attributeName="stroke" from="white" to="red"
fill="freeze"/>
<animate begin="MouseTest.mouseout" dur="0.1s"
attributeName="stroke" from="red" to="white"
fill="freeze"/>
SVGSpider.com
</text>
</a>
</svg>
```

To achieve the desired effect, the mouseover must apply when anything within the `<a>` element is moused. Just add an `id` attribute to the `<a>` element (in this case, `MouseTest`), and use that `id` attribute as part of the value of the `begin` attribute for all mouseover effects. Thus, the following syntax means that when anything within the `<a>` element is moused, the mouseover effect begins:

```
begin='MouseTest.mouseover'
```

To achieve different color changes on the text and on the rectangle, you need separate animations nested within the `<text>` and `<rect>` elements, respectively. The first pair of `<animate>` elements within the `<text>` element changes the fill from white to red (and back again on mouseout); the second pair of `<animate>` elements changes the stroke property. The `<animate>` element nested within the `<rect>` element changes its fill property on mouseover and changes it back on mouseout.

You could have used the `<set>` animation element in a way similar to what you read about earlier for achieving a similar effect.

These animations are very simple. You can combine color changes like these with slight changes in font size or opacity, replace a solid fill with a graduated one, or even create an animated graduated fill. The possibilities are legion, but these simple effects are sufficient to allow you to move on and look at the creation of some Web page navigation furniture.

Simple Navigation Bars

In this section, I describe how to create simple navigation bars. The navigation furniture that is produced is not necessarily of a type you use in a production Web page, but the techniques I show you are useful in many settings. As with so many other aspects of SVG, what I am showing you are visual components you can use with other SVG visual components to produce your own SVG graphics.

The navigation bars I show you how to create in this section are typically in their own nested `<svg>` elements to allow you to reposition the navigation bar as a unit on the Web page while preserving the relative positions of its parts.

If you want to test these bars embedded within HTML and XHTML Web pages, see Chapter 10, "Embedding SVG in HTML or XHTML Pages," for the syntax required to do that.

Text Navigation Bars

A text navigation bar has just about the simplest design you can create. The code for a three-page text navigation bar is shown in Listing 5.10. The purpose of the deep blue rectangle is simply to show you the boundary of the navigation bar. The navigation bar is contained within a nested `<svg>` element. If you want to move the navigation bar slightly up or to the side (or even to the right side of the page), you can do that by changing only the x and y attributes of the nested `<svg>` element and maintaining the relative positioning of everything inside it.

Listing 5.10 (TextNavBar01.svg)

```
<?xml version="1.0" standalone="no"?>
<!DOCTYPE svg PUBLIC "-//W3C//DTD SVG 1.0//EN"
       "http://www.w3.org/TR/2001/PR-SVG-20010719/
        DTD/svg10.dtd">
<svg width="200" height="600">
<rect x="150" y="0" width="50" height="600"
style="fill:#000099"/>
<svg x="0" y="0">
<a xlink:href="Page02" id="Page02Link">
<text x="20" y="30" style="font-family: Arial,
sans-serif; font-size:12; fill:#000099;
stroke:#000099">
<set attributeName="stroke"
begin="Page02Link.mouseover" end="Page02Link.mouseout"
 to="#FF0066"/>
<set attributeName="fill" begin="Page02Link.mouseover"
 end="Page02Link.mouseout" to="#FF0066"/>
Page 02
</text>
</a>
<a xlink:href="Page03" id="Page03Link">
<text x="20" y="60" style="font-family: Arial,
sans-serif; font-size:12; fill:#000099;
stroke:#000099">
<set attributeName="stroke"
begin="Page03Link.mouseover" end="Page03Link.mouseout"
 to="#FF0066"/>
<set attributeName="fill" begin="Page03Link.mouseover"
 end="Page03Link.mouseout" to="#FF0066"/>
Page 03
</text>
</a>
<a xlink:href="Page04" id="Page04Link">
<text x="20" y="90" style="font-family: Arial,
sans-serif; font-size:12; fill:#000099;
stroke:#000099">
<set attributeName="stroke"
begin="Page04Link.mouseover" end="Page04Link.mouseout"
 to="#FF0066"/>
<set attributeName="fill" begin="Page04Link.mouseover"
 end="Page04Link.mouseout" to="#FF0066"/>
Page 04
</text>
</a>
</svg>
</svg>
```

Let's look in more detail at how the link and rollover effect for the link to Page 2 is constructed:

```
<a xlink:href="Page02" id="Page02Link">
<text x="20" y="30" style="font-family: Arial,
sans-serif; font-size:12; fill:#000099;
stroke:#000099">
<set attributeName="stroke"
begin="Page02Link.mouseover" end="Page02Link.mouseout"
 to="#FF0066"/>
<set attributeName="fill" begin="Page02Link.mouseover"
 end="Page02Link.mouseout" to="#FF0066"/>
Page 02
</text>
</a>
```

As before, the link is contained within an `<a>` element. The link is defined by the `xlink:href` attribute. Notice that the `<a>` element has an `id` attribute, which is used in defining the mouse effects. To create the rollover effect, you can use the `<set>` element because the changes you want are simple step-wise color changes from `#000099` to `#FF0066`.

To create the links for additional pages, you can use the preceding code as a simple visual component, copy it, and then adjust various attributes accordingly. In this case, you need to change the `id` attribute on the `<a>` element, the y attribute on the `<text>` element, the `begin` and `end` attributes on both `<set>` elements, and the text contained within the `<text>` element that describes the link.

Figure 05.08 shows the simple text navigation bar with one of the links being moused.

Figure 05.08

A simple text navigation bar with one of the links showing a change in color when moused.

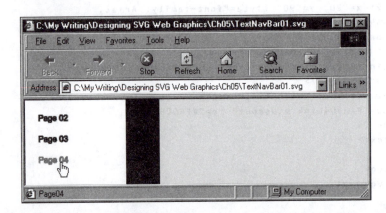

A simple horizontal text navigation bar is created similarly. Listing 5.11 provides you with code for that.

Listing 5.11 (TextNavBar02.svg)

```
<?xml version="1.0" standalone="no"?>
<!DOCTYPE svg PUBLIC "-//W3C//DTD SVG 1.0//EN"
    "http://www.w3.org/TR/2001/PR-SVG-20010719/
    DTD/svg10.dtd">
<svg width="800" height="200">
<svg x="0" y="0">
<a xlink:href="Page02" id="Page02Link">
<text x="20" y="30" style="font-family: Arial,
sans-serif; font-size:12; fill:#000099;
stroke:#000099">
<set attributeName="stroke"
begin="Page02Link.mouseover" end="Page02Link.mouseout"
 to="#FF0066"/>
<set attributeName="fill" begin="Page02Link.mouseover"
 end="Page02Link.mouseout" to="#FF0066"/>
Page 02
</text>
</a>
<text x="70" y="30" style="font-family: Arial,
sans-serif; font-size:12; fill:#999999;
stroke:#999999">
|
</text>
<a xlink:href="Page03" id="Page03Link">
<text x="80" y="30" style="font-family: Arial,
sans-serif; font-size:12; fill:#000099;
stroke:#000099">
<set attributeName="stroke"
begin="Page03Link.mouseover" end="Page03Link.mouseout"
 to="#FF0066"/>
<set attributeName="fill" begin="Page03Link.mouseover"
 end="Page03Link.mouseout" to="#FF0066"/>
Page 03
</text>
</a>
<text x="130" y="30" style="font-family: Arial,
sans-serif; font-size:12; fill:#999999;
stroke:#999999">
|
</text>
<a xlink:href="Page04" id="Page04Link">
```

```
<text x="140" y="30" style="font-family: Arial,
sans-serif; font-size:12; fill:#000099;
stroke:#000099">
<set attributeName="stroke"
begin="Page04Link.mouseover" end="Page04Link.mouseout"
 to="#FF0066"/>
<set attributeName="fill" begin="Page04Link.mouseover"
 end="Page04Link.mouseout" to="#FF0066"/>
Page 04
</text>
</a>
</svg>
</svg>
```

The horizontal navigation bar is shown in Figure 05.09. Note that I have added gray spacers between the linking elements. Be careful not to nest those within an `<a>` element because you are unlikely to want those to have either linking functionality or to show a rollover effect.

Figure 05.09

A horizontal naviga-tion bar with gray vertical spacers and rollover changes in text color.

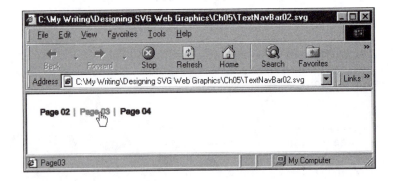

Tabbed Navigation Bars

One of the navigation graphics commonly used within some of the major e-commerce sites is the tabbed navigation bar. Take a look at Amazon.com or similar sites to find lots of tabbed navigation bars. Often, the tabbed navigation bar is combined with menu choices or drop-down menus (such as that shown in Chapter 11) in the space below the navigation tabs.

To demonstrate how to create a tabbed navigation bar in SVG, I show you how to create a possible navigation bar for S-V-G.com with links to a number of other SVG and XML technology-related sites. Figure 05.10 shows the finished product with one of the tabs moused.

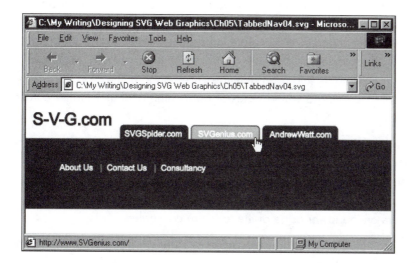

Figure 05.10

A tabbed navigation bar demonstrating a rollover effect on the tab being moused.

The first step is to create a basic layout with a `<rect>` element that is 100 percent of the browser window width, nested within a nested `<svg>` element. If you do happen to need to reposition the navigation bar, you simply alter the x or y attributes of the nested `<svg>` element, thus saving lots of work fiddling with multiple positioning attributes on individual elements.

Listing 5.12 (TabbedNav01.svg)

```
<?xml version="1.0" standalone="no"?>
<!DOCTYPE svg PUBLIC "-//W3C//DTD SVG 1.0//EN"
    "http://www.w3.org/TR/2001/PR-SVG-20010719/
      DTD/svg10.dtd">
<svg>
<svg width="100%" height="250" >
<text x="10" y="40" style="font-family:Arial,
sans-serif; font-size: 24; fill:#000066;
stroke:#000066">
S-V-G.com
</text>
<rect x="0" y="60" width="100%" height="100"
style="fill:#000099; stroke:#000099;"/>
</svg>
</svg>
```

The next step is to add the individual tabs and their text. At this stage, a little planning and careful sizing can save lots of time fiddling later. Decide, if possible, on the number of tabs you need. Then create each tab together with its associated text so that you finish (or so you hope) the creation of one tab before going on to create the next. One reason for doing that is that if you change, for example, the font size of the text on the tabs or swap a long name into a tab intended for a short name, you have to start manually adjusting a whole series of positioning attributes further across the page.

Be sure to place the `<rect>` elements for each tab earlier in the document order than the `<rect>` element that forms the dark blue bar across the screen. Suppose that you want to create rounded corners on the top of the tabs. By placing the `<rect>` elements behind the large bar, the rounded corners on the lower edge of the tabs are concealed.

This example has only three added tabs, although in a production setting you may want to add a larger number. I now have a static tabbed bar. The code for it is shown in Listing 5.13.

Listing 5.13 (TabbedNav02.svg)

```
<?xml version="1.0" standalone="no"?>
<!DOCTYPE svg PUBLIC "-//W3C//DTD SVG 1.0//EN"
    "http://www.w3.org/TR/2001/PR-SVG-20010719/
        DTD/svg10.dtd">
<svg>
<svg width="100%" height="250" >
<text x="10" y="40" style="font-family:Arial,
sans-serif; font-size: 24; fill:#000066;
stroke:#000066">
S-V-G.com
</text>
<rect x="140" y="40" width="100" height="25" rx="5"
ry="5" style="fill:#000099; stroke:#000099"/>
<text x="146" y="56" style="fill:white; stroke:white;">
SVGSpider.com
</text>
<rect x="245" y="40" width="100" height="25" rx="5"
ry="5" style="fill:#000099; stroke:#000099"/>
<text x="255" y="56" style="fill:white; stroke:white;">
SVGenius.com
</text>
```

```
<rect x="350" y="40" width="110" height="25" rx="5"
ry="5" style="fill:#000099; stroke:#000099"/>
<text x="360" y="56" style="fill:white; stroke:white;">
AndrewWatt.com
</text>
<rect x="0" y="60" width="100%" height="100"
style="fill:#000099; stroke:#000099;"/>
</svg>
```
```
</svg>
```

Next, I have added an `<a>` element to each tab. While coding, I find it helpful to create gaps between blocks of work, such as each tab. That strategy makes it less likely that I inadvertently insert code in the wrong place, and I avoid debugging time. Because I plan to create a mouseover effect for each tab, I add an `id` attribute to each `<a>` element, to be used in the `begin` and `end` attributes of a `<set>` element. Because I also want each link to open in a new window, I set the `target` attribute of each `<a>` element to a value of `new`.

I use a `<set>` element to create the rollover effect on each tab. The rollover effect I have chosen is of the fill property of the tab. It changes from a deep blue, #000099, to a pale bluish color, #CCCCFF. I had considered also adding a rollover of the text color to a deep blue, but decided that the rollover effect on the rectangle fill alone was satisfactory.

Following the addition of the `<a>` elements and the rollover effects, the code looks like that shown in Listing 5.14.

Listing 5.14 (TabbedNav03.svg)

```
<?xml version="1.0" standalone="no"?>
<!DOCTYPE svg PUBLIC "-//W3C//DTD SVG 1.0//EN"
      "http://www.w3.org/TR/2001/PR-SVG-20010719/
       DTD/svg10.dtd">
<svg>
<svg width="100%" height="250" >
<text x="10" y="40" style="font-family:Arial,
sans-serif; font-size: 24; fill:#000066;
stroke:#000066">
S-V-G.com
</text>
<a xlink:href="http://www.svgspider.com/default.svg"
  target="new" id="SVGSpiderLink">
```

```
<rect x="140" y="40" width="100" height="25" rx="5"
ry="5" style="fill:#000099; stroke:#000099">
<set begin="SVGSpiderLink.mouseover"
end="SVGSpiderLink.mouseout" attributeName="fill"
to="#CCCCFF"/>
</rect>
<text x="146" y="56" style="fill:white; stroke:white;">
SVGSpider.com
</text>
</a>
<a xlink:href="http://www.SVGenius.com/" target="new"
 id="SVGeniusLink">
<rect x="245" y="40" width="100" height="25" rx="5"
ry="5" style="fill:#000099; stroke:#000099">
<set begin="SVGeniusLink.mouseover"
end="SVGeniusLink.mouseout" attributeName="fill"
to="#CCCCFF"/>
</rect>
<text x="255" y="56" style="fill:white; stroke:white;">
SVGenius.com
</text>
</a>
<a xlink:href="http://www.AndrewWatt.com/"
target="new" id="AWLink">
<rect x="350" y="40" width="110" height="25" rx="5"
ry="5" style="fill:#000099; stroke:#000099">
<set begin="AWLink.mouseover" end="AWLink.mouseout"
attributeName="fill" to="#CCCCFF"/>
</rect>
<text x="360" y="56" style="fill:white; stroke:white;">
AndrewWatt.com
</text>
</a>
<rect x="0" y="60" width="100%" height="100"
style="fill:#000099; stroke:#000099;"/>
</svg>
</svg>
```

In Figure 05.11, you can see the rollover effect working on one of the tabs.

As a final step in this example, I add a simple horizontal text navigation bar for the About Us, Contact Us, and Consultancy pages. I firmly believe in the notion of visual components, and the code in Listing 5.11 is this type of visual component. It already has the functionality you need for a horizontal navigation bar for this example, and it is nested in its own `<svg>`

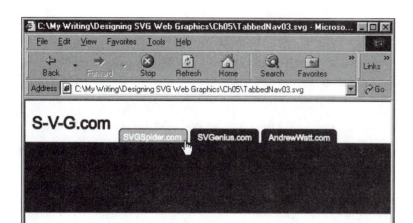

Figure 05.11

A tabbed navigation bar with functioning rollover effect.

element so that you can reposition the horizontal text navigation bar as a whole. Of course, I needed to make a number of adjustments to various attributes, including the x and y attributes on the `<svg>` element, which contains the horizontal text navigation bar. The link text, `xlink:href` attributes, text fill, and stroke also needed to be tweaked to correspond to their new use. Despite those changes, the reuse of the horizontal text navigation bar saved time in adding code to the tabbed navigation bar.

When reusing code, be careful to paste it in the correct place. Failure to do so can cause major problems with the display of SVG. Also, particularly in your early attempts at reusing code, make sure that you change only one thing or a couple of obviously connected things at a time. Then, resave (with a new filename so that you can go back to a previous working version), and view the SVG again in an SVG viewer.

If you are careful and methodical in making these types of changes, you should minimize the likelihood of making a series of changes, making a mistake while carrying them out, and then not knowing which of the changes you made is causing your problem.

Listing 5.15 (TabbedNav04.svg)

```
<?xml version="1.0" standalone="no"?>
<!DOCTYPE svg PUBLIC "-//W3C//DTD SVG 1.0//EN"
    "http://www.w3.org/TR/2001/PR-SVG-20010719/
    DTD/svg10.dtd">
```

```
<svg>
<svg width="100%" height="250" >
<text x="10" y="40" style="font-family:Arial,
sans-serif; font-size: 24; fill:#000066;
stroke:#000066">
S-V-G.com
</text>
<a xlink:href="http://www.svgspider.com/default.svg"
 target="new" id="SVGSpiderLink">
<rect x="140" y="40" width="100" height="25" rx="5"
ry="5" style="fill:#000099; stroke:#000099">
<set begin="SVGSpiderLink.mouseover"
end="SVGSpiderLink.mouseout" attributeName="fill"
to="#CCCCFF"/>
</rect>
<text x="146" y="56" style="fill:white; stroke:white;">
SVGSpider.com
</text>
</a>
<a xlink:href="http://www.SVGenius.com/" target="new"
 id="SVGeniusLink">
<rect x="245" y="40" width="100" height="25" rx="5"
ry="5" style="fill:#000099; stroke:#000099">
<set begin="SVGeniusLink.mouseover"
end="SVGeniusLink.mouseout" attributeName="fill"
to="#CCCCFF"/>
</rect>
<text x="255" y="56" style="fill:white; stroke:white;">
SVGenius.com
</text>
</a>
<a xlink:href="http://www.AndrewWatt.com/" target="new"
 id="AWLink">
<rect x="350" y="40" width="110" height="25" rx="5"
ry="5" style="fill:#000099; stroke:#000099">
<set begin="AWLink.mouseover" end="AWLink.mouseout"
attributeName="fill" to="#CCCCFF"/>
</rect>
<text x="360" y="56" style="fill:white; stroke:white;">
AndrewWatt.com
</text>
</a>
<rect x="0" y="60" width="100%" height="100"
style="fill:#000099; stroke:#000099;"/>
```

```
<svg x="30" y="75" width="800" height="100">
<a xlink:href="AboutUs.html" id="AboutUsLink">
<text x="20" y="30" style="font-family: Arial,
sans-serif; font-size:12; fill:white; stroke:white;">
<set attributeName="stroke"
begin="AboutUsLink.mouseover"
end="AboutUsLink.mouseout"
  to="#FF0066"/>
<set attributeName="fill" begin="AboutUsLink.mouseover"
  end="AboutUsLink.mouseout" to="#FF0066"/>
About Us
</text>
</a>
<text x="80" y="30" style="font-family: Arial,
sans-serif; font-size:12; fill:#999999;
stroke:#999999">
|
</text>
<a xlink:href="ContactUs.html" id="ContactLink">
<text x="90" y="30" style="font-family: Arial,
sans-serif; font-size:12; fill:white; stroke:white;">
<set attributeName="stroke"
begin="ContactLink.mouseover"
end="ContactLink.mouseout" to="#FF0066"/>
<set attributeName="fill" begin="ContactLink.mouseover"
  end="ContactLink.mouseout" to="#FF0066"/>
Contact Us
</text>
</a>
<text x="160" y="30" style="font-family: Arial,
sans-serif; font-size:12; fill:#999999;
stroke:#999999">
|
</text>
<a xlink:href="Consultancy.html" id="ConsultancyLink">
<text x="170" y="30" style="font-family: Arial,
sans-serif; font-size:12; fill:white; stroke:white">
<set attributeName="stroke"
begin="ConsultancyLink.mouseover"
end="ConsultancyLink.mouseout" to="#FF0066"/>
<set attributeName="fill"
begin="ConsultancyLink.mouseover"
end="ConsultancyLink.mouseout" to="#FF0066"/>
Consultancy
</text>
</a>
</svg> <!-- This is the end of the re-used
```

```
horizontal text nav bar. -->
</svg> <!-- This is the end of the deep blue bar we
created early in this example. -->
</svg> <!-- This is the end of the document
<svg> element. -->
```

Notice the three `</svg>` end tags in this code. A horizontal text navigation bar (contained in its own `<svg>` element) is nested within the `<svg>` element, which contains the deep blue bar that formed the basis for the tabbed navigation bar, which is itself nested within the document `<svg>` element.

Figure 05.12 shows the finished tabbed navigation bar with one of the choices in the reused horizontal text navigation bar moused.

Figure 05.12

The completed tabbed navigation bar with rollover effects accessible on the tabs and on the link choices in the reused horizontal text navigation bar.

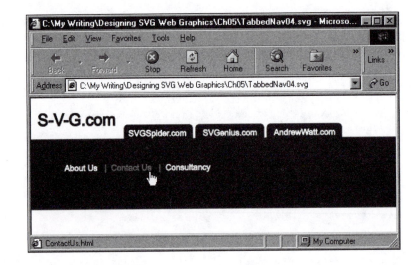

You can, of course, make many further refinements to such a tabbed navigation bar. One that comes to mind is to set each part of the link text of the horizontal text navigation bar against a self-colored rectangle, with or without an outline, and to create additional rollover effects on the fill or the stroke of the rectangle.

Using <svg> Elements to Aid Positioning

Back in Chapter 2, "SVG Document Overview," I mentioned that you could nest one `<svg>` element inside another and that you could use the nested `<svg>` element as a container for an SVG component. Creating navigation bars, as you have seen in the examples in this chapter, can be a useful application of that technique.

A navigation bar can consist of many individual components, including graphical shapes and text. If you nest within a `<svg>` element all the SVG elements that make up the navigation bar, all the positioning of the elements within a group relative to each other remains fixed. By altering the values of the x and y attributes of the nested `<svg>` element, the whole navigation bar and its component parts or other visual components can be moved around without disturbing the carefully crafted relative positioning of its parts. This makes the reuse of SVG code much easier and saves you from lots of time writing new code (and thus saves time debugging it), making the whole operational use of SVG more pleasant, more fun, and more efficient.

With the techniques in this chapter, your repertoire of knowledge about SVG is growing to the point where you can begin to produce useful SVG graphics. Chapter 6, "Creating SVG Gradients," examines the use of gradients to allow you to produce more subtle and sophisticated visual effects than with the solid fills you have seen in the examples so far.

6

Creating SVG Gradients

What Are Gradients?

One of the visually attractive features of many bitmap graphics on the Web is the use of gradients to add a subtle or sophisticated appearance to an image. Similar effects are available in proprietary vector formats. SVG too provides gradients that can be used to good effect throughout SVG images.

A *gradient* is a smooth transition from one color to another along a vector. Several color transitions can be applied along the same vector and can be combined to provide complex, subtle, and sometimes very attractive color transitions. In addition to allowing color transitions, SVG provides for transitions in opacity.

In SVG jargon, *gradients* are simply a special type of "paint server." To apply the paint from a paint server, you simply reference the paint server using a URL and specify whether the paint server should be applied to the stroke or the fill of an element.

The types of gradient available in SVG version 1.0 are a linear gradient and a radial gradient, respectively controlled by the `<linearGradient>` and `<radialGradient>` elements. Aspects of the SVG linear and radial gradients can be animated. This chapter looks at only the construction of non-animated gradients. I introduce you to animated gradients in Chapter 8, "Animation: SVG and SMIL Animation."

Both linear and radial gradients are created and used in a similar way. The gradient is best defined using either a `<linearGradient>` or `<radialGradient>` element, as appropriate, nested within the `<defs>` element of an SVG document.

The definition of the gradient is then accessed by another SVG element using a URL within the `style` attribute of the referencing graphics element. The following simple example shows a linear gradient being referenced by the `fill` property of a `<rect>` element.

Listing 6.1 (BasicLinGradient.svg)

```
<?xml version="1.0" standalone="no"?>
<!DOCTYPE svg PUBLIC "-//W3C//DTD SVG 1.0//EN"
     "http://www.w3.org/TR/2001/PR-SVG-20010719/
        DTD/svg10.dtd">
<svg width="500" height="300">
<defs>
<linearGradient id="MyFirstGradient">
<stop offset="5%" style="stop-color:#FF6600"/>
<stop offset="95%" style="stop-color:#FFFFCC"/>
</linearGradient>
</defs>
<rect style="fill:none; stroke:red"
x="1" y="1" width="498" height="298"/>
<rect x="50" y="50" width="300" height="100"
style="fill:url(#MyFirstGradient); stroke:none"/>
</svg>
```

The definition of the gradient takes place here:

```
<defs>
<linearGradient id="MyFirstGradient">
<stop offset="5%" style="stop-color:#FF6600"/>
<stop offset="95%" style="stop-color:#FFFFCC"/>
</linearGradient>
</defs>
```

and that definition is accessed by the following code within the second `<rect>` element:

```
style="fill:url(#MyFirstGradient); stroke:none"
```

The `fill` property is defined to refer to a URL, `#MyFirstGradient`. The syntax `#MyFirstGradient` is a "bare name" XPointer that behaves similarly to the similar syntax in HTML you may be familiar with.

The output of Listing 6.1 is shown in Figure 06.01.

Take a closer look at creating linear gradients.

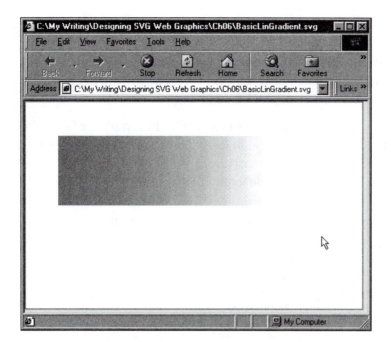

Figure 06.01

A basic linear gradient with the color transition taking place along a horizontal vector.

The <linearGradient> Element

Linear gradients in SVG can be defined as horizontal gradients, vertical gradients, or diagonally at any angle between the horizontal and vertical. A horizontal gradient is created when the values of the y1 and y2 attributes of the <linearGradient> element are the same and the x1 and x2 attributes differ. A vertical gradient results when the x1 and x2 attributes or the <linearGradient> element are the same and the y1 and y2 attributes differ. A diagonal gradient results when both pairs of attributes differ.

A linear gradient can have two colors or many colors. Each color used in a gradient is specified using a <stop> element, which has stop-color and stop-opacity attributes. SVG also allows you to vary individually the opacity of the "stop colors" that are present within a linear gradient, allowing a large range of subtle visual effects to be achieved.

Creating a banner using a linear gradient

Use what you have learned about linear gradients to create a banner that uses a linear gradient and could be a banner on an HTML or XHTML Web page or even on an SVG Web page.

You want to produce a gradient that starts at deep blue at the top and shades down to pale blue in its lower part. To produce such a vertical linear gradient, the x1 and x2 attributes of the `<linearGradient>` element need to be same. Your code looks like this:

Listing 6.2 (RectGradient0.svg)

```
<?xml version='1.0'?>
<!DOCTYPE svg PUBLIC "-//W3C//DTD SVG 1.0//EN"
    "http://www.w3.org/TR/2001/PR-SVG-20010719/
    DTD/svg10.dtd">
<svg width="800" height="600">
<defs>
<linearGradient id="MyBlueGradient"
gradientUnits="userSpaceOnUse" x1="0"
y1="0" x2="0" y2="120" >
<stop offset="10%" style="stop-color:#000066"/>
<stop offset="75%" style="stop-color:#EEEEFF"/>
</linearGradient>
</defs>
<rect x="0" y="0" width="800" height="100"
style="fill:url(#MyBlueGradient);"/>
</svg>
```

Note the use of the `<defs>` element to contain the definition of the `<linearGradient>` element. The linear gradient is used as the fill of the `<rect>` element and is accessed by this syntax:

```
style="fill:url(#MyBlueGradient);"
```

The `url()` function makes use of a bare-names XPointer, which is similar to the fragment identifier in HTML and XHTML. The syntax

```
#MyBlueGradient
```

refers to the element in the current document that has an `id` attribute with a value of `MyBlueGradient`, which in this case is present on the `<linearGradient>` element nested within the `<defs>` element.

The linear gradient has two colors—a deep blue with a 10 percent offset and a pale blue with a 75 percent offset. The appearance that is produced is shown in Figure 06.02.

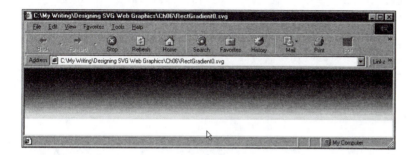

Figure 06.02

A vertical linear gradient that could be used as the basis for a banner in a Web page.

Using linear gradients within text

So far, you have seen linear gradients used within graphic shapes, but SVG also allows you to use linear gradients within text. Both vertical and horizontal gradients are possible within text.

In practice, to achieve useful vertical gradients within a glyph or block of text, you need to choose a fairly large font size. To use a vertical linear gradient, you define it as before within the `<defs>` element using a `<linearGradient>` element (see Figure 06.03).

Listing 6.3 (GradientInText01.svg)

```
<?xml version='1.0'?>
<!DOCTYPE svg PUBLIC "-//W3C//DTD SVG 1.0//EN"
    "http://www.w3.org/TR/2001/PR-SVG-20010719/
     DTD/svg10.dtd">
<svg width="800" height="600">
<defs>
<linearGradient id="MyBlueGradient"
gradientUnits="userSpaceOnUse" x1="0"
y1="0" x2="0" y2="100" >
<stop offset="10%" style="stop-color:#000066"/>
<stop offset="75%" style="stop-color:#AAAADD"/>
</linearGradient>
<linearGradient id="MyBrightGradient"
gradientUnits="userSpaceOnUse" x1="0" y1="100"
x2="0" y2="200">
<stop offset="10%" style="stop-color:#FF0000"/>
```

```
<stop offset="90%" style="stop-color:#FFFF00"/>
</linearGradient>
</defs>

<text x="50" y="70" style="font-family:Times,
serif; font-size:72; fill:url(#MyBlueGradient);">
Hello SVG!
</text>
<text x="50" y="170" style="font-family:Times,
serif; font-size:72; fill:url(#MyBrightGradient);">
Hello bright SVG!
</text>
</svg>
```

Figure 06.03

Two strings of text containing vertical linear gradients.

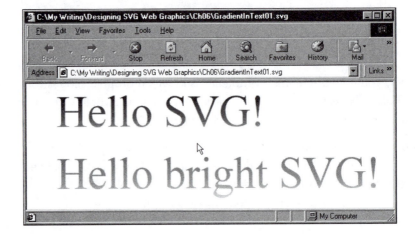

The visual appearance of gradients in text can change markedly, depending on the color of the background against which they are set. Listing 6.4 and Figure 06.04 show the difference in appearance by changing the background from white to black.

Listing 6.4 (GradientInText02.svg)

```
<?xml version='1.0'?>
<!DOCTYPE svg PUBLIC "-//W3C//DTD SVG 1.0//EN"
      "http://www.w3.org/TR/2001/PR-SVG-20010719/
      DTD/svg10.dtd">
<svg width="800" height="600">
<defs>
<linearGradient id="MyBlueGradient"
gradientUnits="userSpaceOnUse" x1="0"
```

```
 y1="0"  x2="0"  y2="100" >
<stop offset="10%"  style="stop-color:#000066"/>
<stop offset="75%"  style="stop-color:#AAAADD"/>
</linearGradient>
<linearGradient id="MyBrightGradient"
gradientUnits="userSpaceOnUse"  x1="0"
y1="100"
x2="0"  y2="200">
<stop offset="10%"  style="stop-color:#FF0000"/>
<stop offset="90%"  style="stop-color:#FFFF00"/>
</linearGradient>
</defs>
<rect x="0"  y="0"  width="800"  height="600" />
<text x="50"  y="70"  style="font-family:Times,
serif; font-size:72;
fill:url(#MyBlueGradient);">
Hello SVG!
</text>
<text x="50"  y="170"  style="font-family:Times,
serif; font-size:72;
fill:url(#MyBrightGradient);">
Hello bright SVG!
</text>
</svg>
```

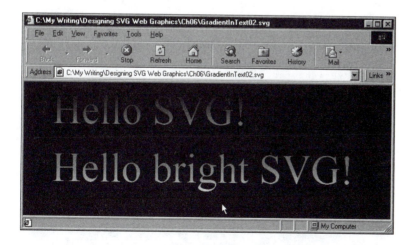

Figure 06.04

Vertical gradient in text against a black background.

If you want to create a horizontal gradient, you do not have to use large-size fonts, although you can do it as shown in Listing 6.5, as you can see in Figure 06.05. In this further example, I have used a vertical gradient on the first `<text>` element and a horizontal gradient, with three stops, on the second.

Listing 6.5 (GradientInTextHoriz.svg)

```
<?xml version='1.0'?>
<!DOCTYPE svg PUBLIC "-//W3C//DTD SVG 1.0//EN"
    "http://www.w3.org/TR/2001/PR-SVG-20010719/
    DTD/svg10.dtd">
<svg width="800" height="600">
<defs>
<linearGradient id="MyBlueGradient"
gradientUnits="userSpaceOnUse" x1="0"
y1="0" x2="0" y2="100" >
<stop offset="10%" style="stop-color:#000066"/>
<stop offset="75%" style="stop-color:#AAAADD"/>
</linearGradient>
<linearGradient id="MyBrightGradient"
gradientUnits="userSpaceOnUse" x1="0" y1="100"
x2="600" y2="100">
<stop offset="10%" style="stop-color:#FF0000"/>
<stop offset="60%" style="stop-color:#FFFF00"/>
<stop offset="90%" style="stop-color:#00FF00"/>
</linearGradient>
</defs>
<rect x="0" y="0" width="800" height="600" />
<text x="50" y="70" style="font-family:Arial,
sans-serif; font-size:36; fill:url(#MyBlueGradient);">
SVGenius.com
</text>
<text x="50" y="100" style="font-family:Arial,
sans-serif; font-size:24;
fill:url(#MyBrightGradient);">
Expressing the creative genius of SVG!
</text>
</svg>
```

Figure 06.05

A horizontal linear gradient within the lower text.

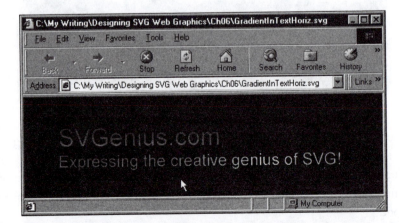

Creating a vertical gradient

In the introduction to this chapter, I defined a gradient as a color transition along a vector. Most of the examples I have shown you are graduated along a horizontal vector. To create a vertical gradient, you simply alter the direction of the vector. Instead of the value of x1 and x2 being different, you keep x1 and x2 the same and make y1 and y2 different.

Rotating a gradient

You have seen in this chapter how SVG provides two basic vectors— horizontal and vertical—along which a gradient is painted. If you want a gradient that is implemented on a diagonal, you have more than one option.

One option is simply to rotate the object containing the gradient, using a transform attribute on a containing grouping <g> element, like this:

Listing 6.6 (RotatedGradient01.svg)

```
<?xml version="1.0" standalone="no"?>
<!DOCTYPE svg PUBLIC "-//W3C//DTD SVG 1.0//EN"
     "http://www.w3.org/TR/2001/PR-SVG-20010719/
     DTD/svg10.dtd">
<svg width="500" height="400">
<defs>
<linearGradient id="MyRotatedGradient">
<stop offset="5%" style="stop-color:#FF6600"/>
<stop offset="95%" style="stop-color:#FFFFCC"/>
</linearGradient>
</defs>
<rect x="1" y="1" width="498" height="398"
style="fill:none; stroke:red;"/>
<g transform="rotate(40 150 50)translate(100,50)">
<rect x="50" y="50" width="300" height="100"
style="fill:url(#MyRotatedGradient); stroke:none"/>
</g>
</svg>
```

I have used a rectangle to show that both the <rect> element and the con- tained gradient rotate, as you can see in Figure 06.06.

Figure 06.06

*A rotated gradient
produced by using a
rotate transformation
on a <g> element.*

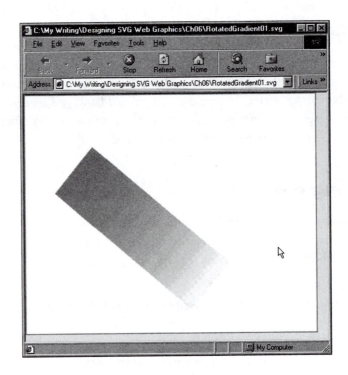

A more general solution is to rotate the gradient itself or, more precisely, to
create a diagonal gradient. To create a diagonal vector, you simply have
to make sure that the x1 and x2 attributes differ and that the y1 and y2
attributes also differ. If you use only undefined user units for the dimensions
in your SVG image, you also need to set the gradientUnits attribute to
a value of userSpaceOnUse:

```
<linearGradient id="MyDiagonalGradient"
x1="50" y1="50" x2="400" y2="200"
gradientUnits="userSpaceOnUse">
```

as shown in this example:

Listing 6.7 (DiagonalLinGradient.svg)

```
<?xml version="1.0" standalone="no"?>
<!DOCTYPE svg PUBLIC "-//W3C//DTD SVG 1.0//EN"
     "http://www.w3.org/TR/2001/PR-SVG-20010719/
      DTD/svg10.dtd">
```

```
<svg width="500" height="300">
<defs>
<linearGradient id="MyDiagonalGradient" x1="50"
y1="50" x2="400" y2="200"
gradientUnits="userSpaceOnUse">
<stop offset="20%" style="stop-color:#FF6600"/>
<stop offset="80%" style="stop-color:#FFFFCC"/>
</linearGradient>
</defs>
<!-- Outline the drawing area in red. -->
<rect style="fill:none; stroke:red"
x="1" y="1" width="498" height="298"/>
<rect x="50" y="50" width="300" height="100"
style="fill:url(#MyDiagonalGradient); stroke:none"/>
</svg>
```

In Figure 06.07, you can see the visual appearance produced by Listing 6.7. You may notice that the red color tends to dominate the gradient and that the diagonal part of the color transition is not striking.

As you can see if you display this graphic onscreen, it graduates from a reddish hue in the upper-left corner of the rectangle to a pale, creamy yellow in the lower right.

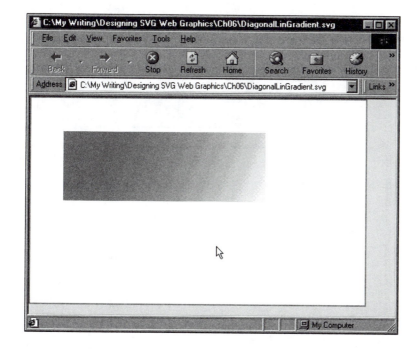

Figure 06.07

In this diagonal gradient, notice that the lower-right corner is paler than the upper-right corner.

Applying a gradient to an outline

An SVG gradient can be applied to an outline in much the same way as it is applied to a fill. Here is a simple example:

Listing 6.8 (LinGradientStroke.svg)

```
<?xml version="1.0" standalone="no"?>
<!DOCTYPE svg PUBLIC "-//W3C//DTD SVG 1.0//EN"
    "http://www.w3.org/TR/2001/PR-SVG-20010719/
    DTD/svg10.dtd">
<svg width="400" height="200">
<defs>
<linearGradient id="MyFirstGradient">
<stop offset="5%" style="stop-color:#990066"/>
<stop offset="95%" style="stop-color:#FFFF00"/>
</linearGradient>
</defs>
<rect style="fill:none; stroke:#990066"
x="1" y="1" width="398" height="198"/>
<rect x="50" y="50" width="300" height="100"
style="stroke:url(#MyFirstGradient);
stroke-width:3; fill:none"/>
</svg>
```

The visual appearance is shown in Figure 06.08.

Figure 06.08

A horizontal linear gradient applied to the outline of a rectangle.

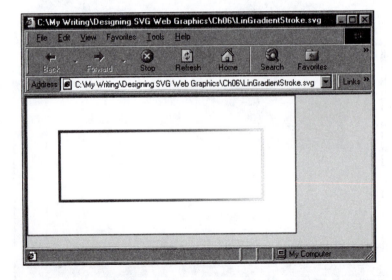

The key change is to define the stroke by referencing a previously defined gradient:

```
style="stroke:url(#MyFirstGradient);
stroke-width:3; fill:none"
```

Varying the opacity within a gradient

As I mentioned earlier, you can also define a stop-opacity property for each stop-color property in a linear gradient. In the following example, I have defined three rectangles that are identical in all color respects except for the opacity of the #FF6600 stop-color property on the left side of each gradient.

Listing 6.9 (LinGradientOpacity01.svg)

```
<?xml version="1.0" standalone="no"?>
<!DOCTYPE svg PUBLIC "-//W3C//DTD SVG 1.0//EN"
     "http://www.w3.org/TR/2001/PR-SVG-20010719/
      DTD/svg10.dtd">
<svg width="500" height="400">
<defs>
<linearGradient id="MyFirstGradient">
<stop offset="5%" style="stop-color:#FF6600"/>
<stop offset="95%" style="stop-color:#FFFFCC"/>
</linearGradient>
<linearGradient id="MyFirstOpacityGradient">
<stop offset="5%" style="stop-color:#FF6600;
stop-opacity:0.5;"/>
<stop offset="95%" style="stop-color:#FFFFCC"/>
</linearGradient>
<linearGradient id="MySecondOpacityGradient">
<stop offset="5%" style="stop-color:#FF6600;
stop-opacity:0.1;"/>
<stop offset="95%" style="stop-color:#FFFFCC"/>
</linearGradient>
</defs>
<rect style="fill:none; stroke:red"
x="1" y="1" width="498" height="298"/>
<rect x="50" y="20" width="300" height="50"
style="fill:url(#MyFirstGradient); stroke:none"/>
<rect x="50" y="95" width="300" height="50"
style="fill:url(#MyFirstOpacityGradient);
```

```
stroke:none"/>
<rect x="50" y="170" width="300" height="50"
style="fill:url(#MySecondOpacityGradient);
stroke:none"/>
</svg>
```

In Figure 06.09, you can see how varying the `stop-opacity` of the left color (red) alters the visual appearance of the left side of the gradient.

Figure 06.09

The left end of three horizontal linear gradients, which show a stop opacity (from top to bottom) of 1, 0.5, and 0.1, respectively.

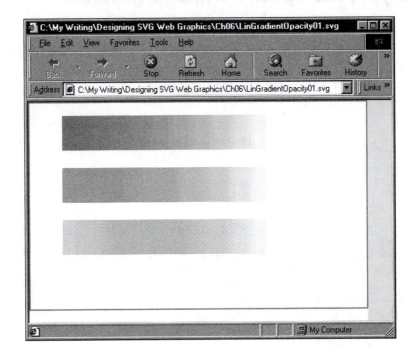

Repeating gradients

In the examples you have seen in this chapter, if the gradient is completed inside the outline of a graphics element, the color is simply "padded" out to the edge of the graphics element. This padding implicitly uses the default setting of the `spreadMethod` attribute, which has the value `pad`. However, the `spreadMethod` attribute has two other possible values that allow you to repeat gradients, but in two distinct ways.

You can also repeat SVG gradients. For example, in the following listing, you create two rectangles containing linear gradients which shows two ways in which a gradient can be repeated. In the first rectangle, you use the following code to cause the gradient to repeat:

```
<linearGradient id="MyRepeatingGradient"
x1="50" y1="50" x2="100" y2="200"
gradientUnits="userSpaceOnUse" spreadMethod="repeat">
```

If you study the following figure or, better, run the code, you see that the gradient makes a smooth transition from a reddish hue to pale yellow and then suddenly, step-wise, starts at the reddish hue again. Thus, the gradient is repeating in a direction from upper left to lower right.

However, in the lower rectangle, you reflect the gradient using this code:

```
<linearGradient id="MyReflectingGradient" x1="50"
  y1="250" x2="200" y2="300"
gradientUnits="userSpaceOnUse" spreadMethod="reflect">
```

so that the gradient changes smoothly to a pale metallic pink color and then smoothly changes back to a dark maroon. Both changes are smooth because the second change is the mirror image of the first (see Figure 06.10).

Figure 06.10

Two rectangles show-ing different spread methods. The top shows a repeat method, and the bottom shows a reflect method.

Listing 6.10 (RepeatingGradient.svg)

```
<?xml version="1.0" standalone="no"?>
<!DOCTYPE svg PUBLIC "-//W3C//DTD SVG 1.0//EN"
     "http://www.w3.org/TR/2001/PR-SVG-20010719/
       DTD/svg10.dtd">
<svg width="500" height="400">
<defs>
<linearGradient id="MyRepeatingGradient"
x1="50" y1="50" x2="100" y2="200"
gradientUnits="userSpaceOnUse" spreadMethod="repeat">
<stop offset="20%" style="stop-color:#FF6600"/>
<stop offset="40%" style="stop-color:#FFFFCC"/>
</linearGradient>
<linearGradient id="MyReflectingGradient" x1="50"
y1="250" x2="200" y2="300"
gradientUnits="userSpaceOnUse" spreadMethod="reflect">
<stop offset="20%" style="stop-color:#990066"/>
<stop offset="40%" style="stop-color:#FFCCFF"/>
</linearGradient>
</defs>
<rect style="fill:none; stroke:red"
x="1" y="1" width="498" height="398"/>
<rect x="50" y="50" width="300" height="100"
style="fill:url(#MyRepeatingGradient); stroke:none"/>
<rect x="50" y="250" width="300" height="100"
style="fill:url(#MyReflectingGradient); stroke:none"/>
</svg>
```

You can also see the difference between repeated and reflected gradients when you are using three color gradients, as shown in Listing 6.11.

Listing 6.11 (3ColorGradients.svg)

```
<?xml version="1.0" standalone="no"?>
<!DOCTYPE svg PUBLIC "-//W3C//DTD SVG 1.0//EN"
     "http://www.w3.org/TR/2001/PR-SVG-20010719/
      DTD/svg10.dtd">
<svg width="600" height="400">
    <linearGradient id="reflected" x1="0%" y1="0%"
x2="50%" y2="0%"
spreadMethod="reflect"
gradientUnits="objectBoundingBox">
        <stop offset="10%"
style="stop-color:rgb(255,0,0)"/>
        <stop offset="50%"
style="stop-color:rgb(255,255,0)"/>
        <stop offset="90%"
style="stop-color:rgb(0,0,255)"/>
    </linearGradient>
    <linearGradient id="repeated" x1="0%"
y1="0%" x2="50%" y2="0%"
spreadMethod="repeat"
gradientUnits="objectBoundingBox">
        <stop offset="10%"
style="stop-color:rgb(255,0,0)"/>
        <stop offset="50%"
style="stop-color:rgb(255,255,0)"/>
        <stop offset="90%"
style="stop-color:rgb(0,0,255)"/>
    </linearGradient>
    <rect x="98" y="30" width="408"
height="140" rx="0" ry="0"
style="stroke:none;fill:url(#repeated)"/>
    <rect x="98" y="220" width="408"
height="140" rx="0" ry="0"
style="stroke:none;fill:url(#reflected)"/>
</svg>
```

In Figure 06.11, you can see a repeated gradient in the top rectangle and a reflected gradient in the bottom one.

Figure 06.11

Repeated gradient (top) and reflected gradient shown using three color gradients.

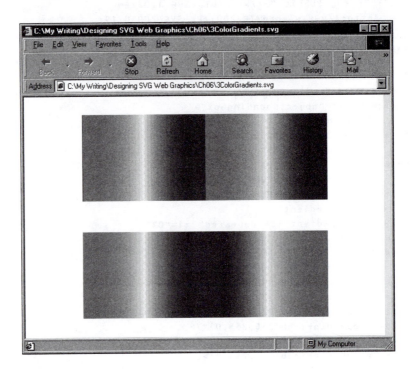

Gaining control over gradients

If you are creating gradients in Corel Draw 10 or a similar vector drawing package, the code for your SVG gradients is produced for you. But if you are serious about mastering SVG (and I suggest that you should be) and you try to create gradients by hand, establishing exactly where a gradient should be displayed relative to an SVG element can be quite difficult at times.

I suggest that you experiment with an SVG image like this one, which has a number of rectangles laid out in order to display different parts of a fairly elongated gradient:

Listing 6.12 (TestRects01.svg)

```
<?xml version="1.0" standalone="no"?>
<!DOCTYPE svg PUBLIC "-//W3C//DTD SVG 1.0//EN"
     "http://www.w3.org/TR/2001/PR-SVG-20010719/
     DTD/svg10.dtd">
<svg width="800" height="600">
<defs>
<linearGradient id="MyBlueGradient"
gradientUnits="userSpaceOnUse"
x1="0" y1="50" x2="800" y2="50" >
<stop offset="10%" style="stop-color:#FF0066"/>
<stop offset="75%" style="stop-color:#EEEEFF"/>
</linearGradient>
</defs>
<rect x="100" y="200" width="100"
height="100" style="fill:url(#MyBlueGradient)"/>
<rect x="200" y="100" width="100"
height="100" style="fill:url(#MyBlueGradient)"/>
<rect x="300" y="200" width="100"
height="100" style="fill:url(#MyBlueGradient)"/>
<rect x="400" y="100" width="100"
height="100" style="fill:url(#MyBlueGradient)"/>
<rect x="500" y="0" width="100"
height="100" style="fill:url(#MyBlueGradient)"/>
<rect x="600" y="100" width="100"
height="100" style="fill:url(#MyBlueGradient)"/>
</svg>
```

You can see in each of the displayed rectangles shown in Figure 06.12 how the gradient is affecting that part of the SVG viewport, assuming that the gradient will be made visible there. By experimenting with this type of test bed, you soon begin to get a feel for how an adjustment of one parameter of a gradient changes the visual appearance.

To see how the same issues pan out on a diagonal linear gradient, look at Figure 06.13 of the following code:

Figure 06.12

A test group of rectangles for visualizing the appearance of a linear gradient.

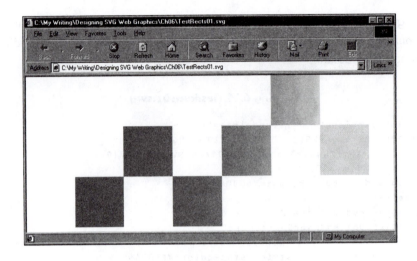

Listing 6.13 (FourCircles01.svg)

```
<?xml version="1.0" standalone="no"?>
<!DOCTYPE svg PUBLIC "-//W3C//DTD SVG 1.0//EN"
    "http://www.w3.org/TR/2001/PR-SVG-20010719/
    DTD/svg10.dtd">
<svg width="400" height="300">
<defs>
<linearGradient id="MyBlueGradient"
gradientUnits="userSpaceOnUse" x1="90"
y1="50" x2="150" y2="150" >
<stop offset="10%" style="stop-color:#FF0066"/>
<stop offset="75%" style="stop-color:#EEEEFF"/>
</linearGradient>
</defs>
<ellipse cx="100" cy="50" rx="50" ry="50"
style="fill:url(#MyBlueGradient)">
</ellipse>
<ellipse cx="100" cy="150" rx="50" ry="50"
style="fill:url(#MyBlueGradient)">
</ellipse>
<ellipse cx="200" cy="100" rx="50" ry="50"
style="fill:url(#MyBlueGradient)">
</ellipse>
<ellipse cx="300" cy="150" rx="50" ry="50"
style="fill:url(#MyBlueGradient)">
</ellipse>
</svg>
```

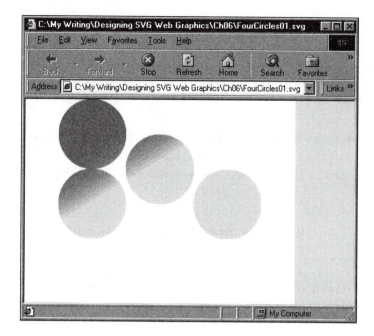

Figure 06.13

Visualizing a diagonal gradient using repeating circular shapes.

Notice that the upper-left circle is almost uniformly the deep pink color, with only a hint of the gradient in the lower-right area. Similarly, the lower-right circle is essentially a pale blue color. The gradient between deep pink and pale blue is present only on the diagonal on which the other two circles are placed. If you miscalculate the positioning of an element, you can find that it has a uniform color. If that happens, one cause is that you have placed the element in the wrong place to apply the rapidly graduating part of the gradient to the element.

The <radialGradient> Element

The second type of gradient provided in SVG is the radial gradient. It is defined within a `<radialGradient>` element nested within the `<defs>` element of an SVG document:

```
<radialGradient id="MyRadialGradient"
gradientUnits="userSpaceOnUse"
cx="100" cy="100" r="50" fx="100" fy="100">
<stop offset="20%" style="stop-color:#990066"/>
<stop offset="70%" style="stop-color:pink"/>
</radialGradient>
```

and is referenced by another SVG element occurring later in the document. The `<radialGradient>` element must have an `id` attribute to allow it to be referenced by any graphical element elsewhere in the SVG (see Figure 06.14).

Listing 6.14 (RadialGradientTwoStops.svg)

```
<?xml version="1.0" standalone="no"?>
<!DOCTYPE svg PUBLIC "-//W3C//DTD SVG 1.0//EN"
       "http://www.w3.org/TR/2001/PR-SVG-20010719/
       DTD/svg10.dtd">
<svg width="200" height="200">

<defs>
<radialGradient id="MyRadialGradient"
gradientUnits="userSpaceOnUse"
cx="100" cy="100" r="50" fx="100" fy="100">
```

Figure 06.14

A simple radial gradient with two stops.

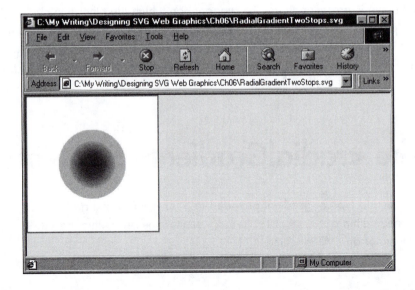

```
<stop offset="20%" style="stop-color:#990066"/>
<stop offset="70%" style="stop-color:pink"/>
</radialGradient>
</defs>
<rect style="fill:none; stroke:#990066"
x="1" y="1" width="198" height="198"/>
<circle style="fill:url(#MyRadialGradient);
stroke:none"
cx="100" cy="100" r="50"/>

</svg>
```

It is also possible to have more than two `<stop>` elements in a radial gradient, as shown in this example:

Listing 6.15 (RadialGradient01.svg)

```
<?xml version="1.0" standalone="no"?>
<!DOCTYPE svg PUBLIC "-//W3C//DTD SVG 1.0//EN"
    "http://www.w3.org/TR/2001/PR-SVG-20010719/
     DTD/svg10.dtd">
<svg width="200" height="200">
<g>
<defs>
<radialGradient id="MyRadialGradient"
gradientUnits="userSpaceOnUse"
cx="100" cy="100" r="50" fx="100" fy="100">
<stop offset="20%" style="stop-color:#990066"/>
<stop offset="70%" style="stop-color:pink"/>
<stop offset="100%" style="stop-color:#FFFF99"/>
</radialGradient>
</defs>
<rect style="fill:none; stroke:#990066"
x="1" y="1" width="198" height="198"/>
<circle style="fill:url(#MyRadialGradient);
stroke:none"
cx="100" cy="100" r="50"/>
</g>
</svg>
```

In Figure 06.15, you can see the effect of adding an additional stop to the preceding radial gradient.

Figure 06.15

A radial gradient with three stop colors.

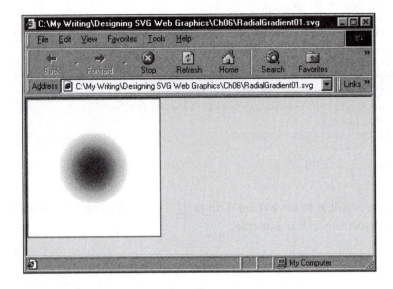

SVG Gradients

Gradients can produce some lovely visual effects, whether you are seeking subtle graduations of color or startling, vibrant—or even shocking—visual effects. To achieve the precise effect you are looking for, you need to understand how to control SVG gradients.

If you want to study how different stop color and stop opacities affect the visual appearance of SVG elements, one technique I find useful is to create linear (or, to a lesser extent, radial) gradients that encompass the whole screen. Then create a small SVG object—a rectangle or circle, perhaps—and animate it slowly across the gradient and study how the colors and opacities affect the SVG object. The gradient itself is invisible except where it impinges on the object. The slow movement of the object allows you to study how adjusting the parameters of the gradient—whether they are offset, stop-color, or stop-opacity properties—affects the visual appearance. By using that technique, you in effect isolate different parts of the gradient so that you can examine each one. The technique for animating an SVG object along a gradient is described in Chapter 8.

Multiple <stop> Elements

SVG allows you to add as many <stop> elements as you want to a <linearGradient> or <radialGradient> element. In addition, you can set the stop-opacity properties for each <stop> element independently, thus giving a huge range of potential visual appearances.

SVG Gradients at Work

Take a look now at how you can put SVG gradients to work, by creating a banner or a top frame using an SVG gradient.

Size your SVG viewport to be 800 pixels wide. You should aim to create a vertical gradient that shades from a deep pink at the top to a pale blue at the bottom.

The source code looks like this:

Listing 6.16 (BannerGradient.svg)

```
<?xml version='1.0'?>
<!DOCTYPE svg PUBLIC "-//W3C//DTD SVG 1.0//EN"
     "http://www.w3.org/TR/2001/PR-SVG-20010719/
      DTD/svg10.dtd">
<svg width="800" height="600">
<defs>
<linearGradient id="MyPinkGradient"
gradientUnits="userSpaceOnUse" x1="0"
y1="0" x2="0" y2="120" >
<stop offset="10%" style="stop-color:#FF0066"/>
<stop offset="75%" style="stop-color:#EEEEFF"/>
</linearGradient>
</defs>
<rect x="0" y="0" width="800" height="100"
style="fill:url(#MyPinkGradient);"/>
</svg>
```

The gradient appears as shown in Figure 06.16.

Figure 06.16

A simple banner gradient.

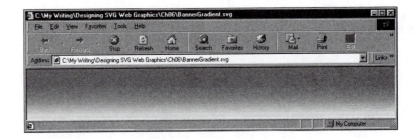

You can build on that simple start by adding some blue lines over the lower part of the gradient, which looks like Figure 06.17.

The code to produce Figure 06.17 looks like this:

Listing 6.17 (BannerGradient02.svg)

```
<?xml version='1.0'?>
<!DOCTYPE svg PUBLIC "-//W3C//DTD SVG 1.0//EN"
    "http://www.w3.org/TR/2001/PR-SVG-20010719/
    DTD/svg10.dtd">
<svg width="800" height="600">
<defs>
<linearGradient id="MyPinkGradient"
gradientUnits="userSpaceOnUse" x1="0"
y1="0" x2="0" y2="120" >
<stop offset="10%" style="stop-color:#FF0066"/>
<stop offset="75%" style="stop-color:#EEEEFF"/>
</linearGradient>
</defs>
<rect x="0" y="0" width="800" height="100"
style="fill:url(#MyPinkGradient);"/>
<g>
<rect x="0" y="82" width="800" height="1"
```

```
style="fill:#000066; stroke:#000066;
stroke-width:1"/>
<rect x="0" y="86" width="800" height="1"
style="fill:#000066; stroke:#000066;
stroke-width:1"/>
<rect x="0" y="90" width="800" height="1"
style="fill:#000066; stroke:#000066;
stroke-width:1"/>
<rect x="0" y="94" width="800" height="1"
style="fill:#000066; stroke:#000066;
stroke-width:1"/>
<rect x="0" y="98" width="800" height="1"
style="fill:#000066; stroke:#000066;
stroke-width:1"/>
</g>
</svg>
```

As it stands, this code would produce a pleasant-looking top frame. But suppose that you want to take things a stage further and use that gradient as a basis for a slightly unusual page layout, perhaps for a splash page, leaving space for an animation in the central part of the page.

You could reuse the logo you created in Chapter 3, "Creating Static Graphics Elements," and produce an SVG Web page that looks like the one shown in Figure 06.18.

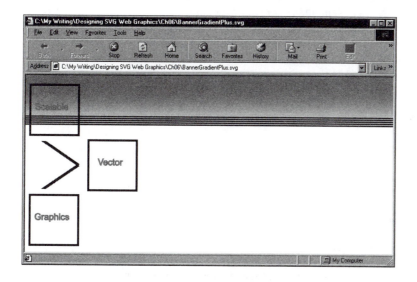

Figure 06.18

Combining the skeleton logo from Chapter 3 with the banner, which includes a linear gradient.

The code to produce Figure 06.18 looks like this:

Listing 6.18 (BannerGradientPlus.svg)

```
<?xml version='1.0'?>
<!DOCTYPE svg PUBLIC "-//W3C//DTD SVG 1.0//EN"
    "http://www.w3.org/TR/2001/PR-SVG-20010719/
     DTD/svg10.dtd">
<svg width="800" height="600">
<defs>
<linearGradient id="MyPinkGradient"
gradientUnits="userSpaceOnUse" x1="0"
y1="0" x2="0" y2="120" >
<stop offset="10%" style="stop-color:#FF0066"/>
<stop offset="75%" style="stop-color:#EEEEFF"/>
</linearGradient>
</defs>
<rect x="0" y="0" width="800" height="100"
style="fill:url(#MyPinkGradient);"/>
<g>
<rect x="0" y="82" width="800" height="1"
style="fill:#000066; stroke:#000066;
stroke-width:1"/>
<rect x="0" y="86" width="800" height="1"
style="fill:#000066; stroke:#000066;
stroke-width:1"/>
<rect x="0" y="90" width="800" height="1"
style="fill:#000066; stroke:#000066;
stroke-width:1"/>
<rect x="0" y="94" width="800" height="1"
style="fill:#000066; stroke:#000066;
stroke-width:1"/>
<rect x="0" y="98" width="800" height="1"
style="fill:#000066; stroke:#000066;
stroke-width:1"/>
</g>
<!-- The logo from an earlier chapter
is re-used here. -->
<svg x="0" y="0" width="400" height="500">
<rect x="10" y="20" width="100" height="100"
style="fill:none; stroke:#000099;
stroke-width:4;"/>
<rect x="130" y="130" width="100" height="100"
style="fill:none;
stroke:#000099; stroke-width:4;"/>
<rect x="10" y="240" width="100" height="100"
style="fill:none; stroke:#000099;
```

```
stroke-width:4;"/>
<line x1="35" y1="130" x2="110" y2="180"
style="stroke-width:5;
stroke:#000099"/>
<line x1="35" y1="230" x2="110" y2="180"
style="stroke-width:5;
stroke:#000099"/>
<rect x="20" y="130" width="100" height="100"
style="fill:none; stroke:white;
stroke-width:4;"/>
<text x="20" y="70" style="font-size:18;
stroke:#FF0066; fill:#FF0066;">
Scalable</text>
<text x="150" y="180" style="font-size:18;
stroke:#FF0066; fill:#FF0066;">
Vector</text>
<text x="20" y="290" style="font-size:18;
stroke:#FF0066; fill:#FF0066;">
Graphics</text>
</svg>
</svg>
```

SVG Patterns

SVG views plain color, gradients, and patterns as three types of paint servers that can be painted on an SVG canvas.

Listing 6.19 demonstrates a simple SVG pattern and Figure 06.19 illustrates it.

Listing 6.19 (Pattern01.svg)

```
<?xml version="1.0" standalone="no"?>
<!DOCTYPE svg PUBLIC "-//W3C//DTD SVG 1.0//EN"
      "http://www.w3.org/TR/2001/PR-SVG-20010719/
      DTD/svg10.dtd">
<svg width="6cm" height="4cm" viewBox="0 0 800 400">
<defs>
 <pattern id="CirclePattern"
patternUnits="userSpaceOnUse"
   x="0" y="0" width="100" height="100"
```

```
      viewBox="0 0 10 10" >
        <circle cx="5" cy="5" r="2"
style="stroke:pink; fill:green;"/>
  </pattern>
</defs>
<rect fill="none" stroke="blue" x="1" y="1"
width="798" height="398"/>
<rect fill="url(#CirclePattern)"
style="stroke:green; stroke-width:5;"
 x="40" y="40" width="700" height="250" />
</svg>
```

Figure 06.19

*A simple
SVG pattern.*

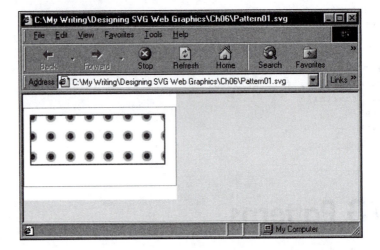

In this chapter, you added some understanding of SVG gradients to your skills in SVG. Chapter 7, "Using SVG Filters," moves on to examine the SVG filters that give you another series of visual effects you can apply.

7

Using SVG Filters

In this chapter:

Why Use Filters

The filters provided in the SVG specification give to SVG many of the features you might have associated in the past exclusively with bitmap graphics programs.

All graphics are presented onscreen as bitmaps. The only question is *when* a graphic is converted to bitmaps. In graphics programs like Adobe Photoshop or Jasc Paint Shop Pro, the rendering to bitmap is carried out within the graphics program and, when you are creating GIFs and JPEGs, for example, the generated gradients are saved and exported as bitmap graphics. With SVG, the instructions are retained in an editable format until the SVG elements are rendered on the client machine by the SVG viewer.

Not surprisingly, companies such as Adobe and Jasc, which have expertise in understanding rendering, have been active in the SVG area. An SVG viewer has rendering functions broadly similar to those contained in what you traditionally think of as bitmap graphics programs but does the rendering "live" on the user's computer at the time you want an image to be displayed.

The detail of the syntax for using SVG filters can become a little overwhelming at times, and I cannot cover everything in the available space in this book. I introduce you to the general principles that apply widely to using SVG filters and show you some examples that apply to a few of the SVG filters. First, look at how an SVG filter is constructed. You create a simple drop shadow, an effect that is widely used in Web graphics.

A full description of the SVG filters is in Chapter 15 of the SVG specification, at http://www.w3.org/TR/SVG/.

Using SVG Filters

An SVG filter is created from one or more *filter primitives;* for example, a Gaussian Blur. An SVG filter is made up of one or more filter primitives nested within a `<filter>` element. The skeleton for the source code of any SVG image that uses filters looks something like this:

Listing 7.1 (FilterSkeleton01.svg)

```
<?xml version="1.0" standalone="no"?>
<!DOCTYPE svg PUBLIC "-//W3C//DTD SVG 1.0//EN"
    "http://www.w3.org/TR/2001/PR-SVG-20010719/
    DTD/svg10.dtd">
<svg>
<defs>
<filter id="GetAHandle">
<!-- Filter primitives go here. -->
</filter>
</defs>
<!-- SVG text or graphics shapes go here. -->
</svg>
```

The definition of the filter is nested within a `<defs>` element. The filter itself is defined within a `<filter>` element that has, as a required attribute, an `id` attribute, which is how any graphical element within the SVG image gets a handle on the particular filter to be applied. For example, if you want a rectangle to use the preceding filter, it looks something like this:

```
<rect x="50" y="50" width="200" height="100"
style="filter:url(#GetAHandle)"/>
```

The `filter` property is used together with the "bare names" version of XPointer—the # character, in this case—to point to the filter to be used. If you are not familiar with XPointer, just think of the # character as a way of identifying a named part of the same SVG document (in this case, a named `<filter>` element). Remember that SVG is an application of XML, so the `id` attribute of the `filter` element is case sensitive. If you use the wrong case on one letter, the filter effect is not likely to be applied.

You add, nested within a `<filter>` element, any filter primitives you want.

You possibly already know that a drop shadow is typically created using a Gaussian Blur, which is then offset from the original image. Now apply the Gaussian Blur, which is defined in a moment, to the text `Hello SVG!`:

Listing 7.2 (FilterSkeleton02.svg)

```
<?xml version="1.0" standalone="no"?>
<!DOCTYPE svg PUBLIC "-//W3C//DTD SVG 1.0//EN"
    "http://www.w3.org/TR/2001/PR-SVG-20010719/
      DTD/svg10.dtd">
<svg>
<defs>
<filter>
<!-- Filter primitives go here. -->
</filter>
</defs>
<text x="50" y="50" style="font-family:Arial,
sans-serif; font-size:24;">
Hello SVG!</text>
</svg>
```

Now add the definition of the blur, which produces the drop shadow:

```
<defs>
<filter id="GetAHandle">
<feGaussianBlur in="SourceAlpha" stdDeviation="2">
</feGaussianBlur>
</filter>
</defs>
```

You add, nested within the `<filter>` element, the `<feGaussianBlur>` element. All SVG filter primitives are named in this way—the element name starts with `fe` (lowercase) and then the name of the filter primitive. Notice that `<feGaussianBlur>` has an `in` attribute whose value is `SourceAlpha`, which means that the source to which the blur is applied is the alpha channel of the relevant image. The `stdDeviation` attribute controls how blurred the resulting image is. For the size of text you will use, a stdDeviation of 2 is about right. If you use a stdDeviation of 1, the shadow is too hard (in my opinion).

You have a few things left to do. You need to link the text to the filter you have just created. Because you don't want to display only the blurred shadow, you need a sharp copy of the text too (which I create as deep blue text).

The final code for the text Hello SVG! with a drop shadow looks like this:

Listing 7.3 (FilterSkeleton03.svg)

```
<?xml version="1.0" standalone="no"?>
<!DOCTYPE svg PUBLIC "-//W3C//DTD SVG 1.0//EN"
    "http://www.w3.org/TR/2001/PR-SVG-20010719/
     DTD/svg10.dtd">
<svg>
<defs>
<filter id="GetAHandle">
<feGaussianBlur in="SourceAlpha" stdDeviation="2">
</feGaussianBlur>
</filter>
</defs>
<text x="53" y="53" style="font-family:Arial,
sans-serif; font-size:24; filter:url(#GetAHandle)">
Hello SVG!</text>
<text x="50" y="50" style="font-family:Arial,
sans-serif; font-size:24; stroke:#000099; fill:#000099">
Hello SVG!</text>
</svg>
```

You can see the text Hello SVG! onscreen with a reasonably presentable drop shadow, as shown in Figure 07.01.

So now you have seen how to create an SVG filter using a single filter primitive. To do that, you "cheated" in the sense that you created the blur from the content of a <text> element and then added another <text> element to display the text itself.

In most cases when you use SVG filters, you combine filter primitives using a technique similar to the one I am about to show you. First, add a result attribute to the <feGaussianBlur> element:

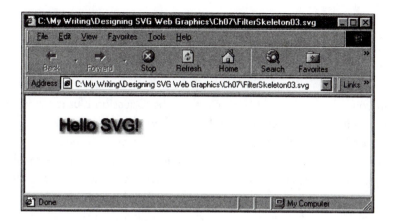

Figure 07.01

A simple drop shadow effect created using only the `<feGaussianBlur>` filter primitive plus an additional copy of the text.

Listing 7.4 (CombinedShadow01.svg)

```
<?xml version="1.0" standalone="no"?>
<!DOCTYPE svg PUBLIC "-//W3C//DTD SVG 1.0//EN"
    "http://www.w3.org/TR/2001/PR-SVG-20010719/
     DTD/svg10.dtd">
<svg>
<defs>
<filter id="CombinedDropShadow">
<feGaussianBlur in="SourceGraphic" stdDeviation="2"
 result="ShadowOut">
</feGaussianBlur>
</filter>
</defs>
<text x="50" y="50" style="font-family:Arial,
sans-serif; font-size:24;
filter:url(#CombinedDropShadow)">
Hello SVG!</text>
</svg>
```

You can use the value of the `result` attribute as the input to further filters. In this example, as you build the parts, you use the value of the `result` attribute of the `<feGaussianBlur>` element as the input to a `<feOffset>` element and then use the output of that as the input to a `<feMerge>` element. Your aim is to create, eventually, a combination filter that displays both the original text and the drop shadow without having to use two `<text>` elements, as you did in the preceding example:

```
<filter id="CombinedDropShadow">
<feGaussianBlur in="SourceGraphic" stdDeviation="2"
```

```
result="ShadowOut"/>
<feOffset in="ShadowOut" dx="3" dy="3"
result="ShadowOnly"/>
</filter>
```

When you add the `<feOffset>` element, the Gaussian blur is taken as the input, and then it is offset to the right and down by three pixels. The `dx` and `dy` attributes signify a difference in the value of the `x` and `y` attributes, respectively, from those in the source image, so it is moved three pixels to the right and down. At this stage, however, you have only the drop shadow to work with, not the original text, so you need to combine the original image and the drop shadow you have just created. You do this using the `<feMerge>` element, like this:

```
<feMerge>
 <feMergeNode in="ShadowOnly"/>
 <feMergeNode in="SourceGraphic"/>
</feMerge>
```

The `<feMerge>` element takes as input two things: the `ShadowOnly` output of the `<feOffset>` element and the source image (in this case, the content of the `<text>` element, which follows later in the document).

The source code for the finished text with a drop shadow looks like this:

Listing 7.5(CombinedShadow03.svg)

```
<?xml version="1.0" standalone="no"?>
<!DOCTYPE svg PUBLIC "-//W3C//DTD SVG 1.0//EN"
     "http://www.w3.org/TR/2001/PR-SVG-20010719/
      DTD/svg10.dtd">
<svg>
<defs>
<filter id="CombinedDropShadow">
<feGaussianBlur in="SourceGraphic" stdDeviation="2"
 result="ShadowOut"/>
<feOffset in="ShadowOut" dx="3" dy="3"
result="ShadowOnly"/>
<feMerge>
 <feMergeNode in="ShadowOnly"/>
 <feMergeNode in="SourceGraphic"/>
</feMerge>
</filter>
```

```
</defs>
<text x="50" y="50" style="font-family:Arial,
sans-serif; font-size:24; stroke:#000099; fill:#000099;
 filter:url(#CombinedDropShadow);">
Hello SVG!</text>
</svg>
```

The text with a drop shadow looks onscreen like Figure 07.02.

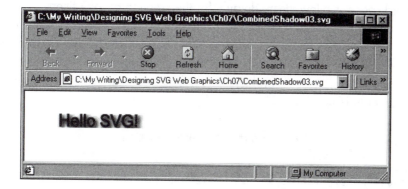

Figure 07.02

The text with a drop shadow created using the `<feGaussianBlur>`, `<feOffset>`, *and* `<feMerge>` *filter primitives.*

If you try zooming in on this image (by right-clicking in the Adobe SVG Viewer), as shown in Figure 07.03, notice how the quality of the image is maintained. Both the text and the drop shadow remain clear and with none of the "jaggies" you would expect when magnifying a bitmap, such as a GIF image.

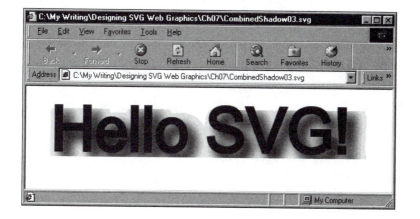

Figure 07.03

A zoomed view of the text and drop shadow produced by Listing 7.5. Notice that the shadow has a sharp, linear cutoff on both its top and bottom edges.

Notice that, using this technique, the drop shadow is a deep blue color, just like the text. In the preceding example, the drop shadow uses the alpha channel and is gray. If you want a gray shadow, simply change the value of the `in` attribute of the `<feGaussianBlur>` element from `SourceGraphic` to `SourceAlpha`.

In Figure 07.03, you can see a sharp edge, at both the bottom and top of the shadow, produced by the filter you created. The reason is that only a limited space is allowed, by default, for the creation of SVG filters. Because you have offset the shadow and blurred it, you need to have more space available to you if you want to achieve a full-size shadow with nice, fuzzy edges. To allow enough space for all the shadow, you need to insert and adjust the `width`, `y`, and `height` attributes on the `<filter>` element, as shown in Listing 7.6:

Listing 7.6 (CombinedShadow04.svg)

```
<?xml version="1.0" standalone="no"?>
<!DOCTYPE svg PUBLIC "-//W3C//DTD SVG 1.0//EN"
    "http://www.w3.org/TR/2001/PR-SVG-20010719/
    DTD/svg10.dtd">
<svg>
<defs>
<filter id="CombinedDropShadow" width="140%" y="-20%"
  height="200%">
<feGaussianBlur in="SourceGraphic" stdDeviation="2"
result="ShadowOut"/>
<feOffset in="ShadowOut" dx="3" dy="3"
result="ShadowOnly"/>
<feMerge>
  <feMergeNode in="SourceGraphic"/>
  <feMergeNode in="ShadowOnly"/>
</feMerge>
</filter>
</defs>
<text x="50" y="50" style="font-family:Arial,
sans-serif; font-size:24;
stroke:#000099; fill:#000099;
filter:url(#CombinedDropShadow);
line-height:28pt">
Hello SVG!</text>
</svg>
```

As you can see in Figure 07.04, the shadow is now displayed with a much softer edge, although there is still a hint of a linear edge at the top.

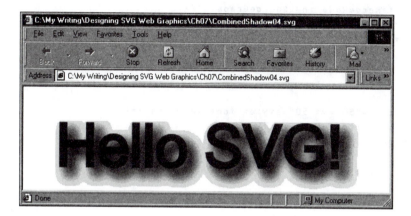

In addition to ensuring that you allow enough space for the drop shadow, you also need to be careful that you write the `<feMerge>` element in the way I just described rather than like this:

```
<feMerge>
  <feMergeNode in="SourceGraphic"/>
  <feMergeNode in="ShadowOnly"/>
</feMerge>
```

If the drop shadow is placed later in the document than the reference to the source graphic, the drop shadow is painted, according to the SVG Painter's model, in front of the graphic. This effect can be fairly noticeable if the text is fairly light colored, as shown here:

Listing 7.7 (CombinedShadow05.svg)

```
<?xml version="1.0" standalone="no"?>
<!DOCTYPE svg PUBLIC "-//W3C//DTD SVG 1.0//EN"
     "http://www.w3.org/TR/2001/PR-SVG-20010719/
     DTD/svg10.dtd">
<svg>
<defs>
<filter id="CombinedDropShadow" width="140%" y="-20%"
  height="200%">
<feGaussianBlur in="SourceAlpha" stdDeviation="2"
result="ShadowOut"/>
```

```
<feOffset in="ShadowOut" dx="3" dy="3"
result="ShadowOnly"/>
<feMerge>
  <feMergeNode in="SourceGraphic"/>
  <feMergeNode in="ShadowOnly"/>
  <!-- THIS IS WRONG. THE SHADOW IS IN FRONT OF
THE TEXT. -->
</feMerge>
</filter>
</defs>
<text x="50" y="50" style="font-family:Arial,
sans-serif; font-size:24;
stroke:#CC0099; fill:#CC0099;
filter:url(#CombinedDropShadow);">
Hello SVG!</text>
</svg>
```

Having looked at some basic techniques for using SVG filters, move on and look at the range of possibilities you can experiment with.

The Range of SVG Filters

With something as visually exciting and creative as the SVG filters, just listing them seems a shame, but I start this section by doing that. Strictly speaking, this list shows the filter primitives available in SVG:

feBlend

feColorMatrix

feComponentTransfer

feComposite

feConvolveMatrix

feDiffuseLighting

feDisplacementMap

feFlood

feGaussianBlur

feImage

feMerge

```
feMorphology
feOffset
feSpecularLighting
feTile
feTurbulence
```

These filter primitives can be used singly or in combination. Used singly, they can sometimes produce useful effects, but when they are used in combination, some unusual and visually arresting effects are possible.

I encourage you to experiment with using the filter primitives singly, applying them to both text and graphical shapes. In doing that, you gain a feel for what each filter primitive does and you begin to achieve a feeling that you are in control of the filters rather than their being in control of you. I don't pretend that you will quickly master all the filters because literally many thousands of permutations exist. However, if you practice and spend time studying the visual effects of changing the various attributes of the filter primitives, you will gradually find that you can more often anticipate the visual effect you will create by making any particular adjustment to an attribute.

Examples Using SVG Filters

In this section, I can only hope to give you a flavor of what is possible with SVG filters. However, I think that I've provided enough to whet your appetite to spend time experimenting with them. Certainly, some impressive visual effects are possible.

Gaussian Blur

The `<feGaussianBlur>` filter primitive defines in Listing 7.8 a generic filter you can use. In the first `<use>` element, you adjust the opacity of the Gaussian blur to 0.4:

Listing 7.8 (SimpleShadow.svg)

```
<?xml version="1.0" standalone="no"?>
<!DOCTYPE svg PUBLIC "-//W3C//DTD SVG 1.0//EN"
     "http://www.w3.org/TR/2001/PR-SVG-20010719/
     DTD/svg10.dtd">
<svg width="500" height="300">
<defs>
<filter id="MyGaussianFilter">
 <feGaussianBlur stdDeviation="1.5"/>
</filter>
<g id="SomeText">
 <text style="font-family:Arial, sans-serif;
font-size:24;">SVG</text>>
</g>
</defs>
<use x="30" y="40" xlink:href="#SomeText"
style="opacity:0.4; filter:url(#MyGaussianFilter)"/>
<use x="27" y="37" xlink:href="#SomeText"
style="opacity:1.0; font-face:bold; stroke:red;
fill:red;"/>
<use x="30" y="80" xlink:href="#SomeText"
style="opacity:1;
 filter:url(#MyGaussianFilter)"/>
<use x="27" y="77" xlink:href="#SomeText"
style="opacity:1.0; font-face:bold;
 stroke:red; fill:red;"/>
</svg>
```

As you can see in Figure 07.05, the opacity of the top shadow is significantly less than the lower one.

Turbulence—Static

One of the seemingly simple filter primitives is the `<feTurbulence>` element. Yet, despite its seeming simplicity, it offers lots of possibilities for some attractive visual effects.

First look at a simple static image generated by using the `<feTurbulence>` filter primitive. The source code looks like this:

Figure 07.05

Two Gaussian blurs used as drop shadows; the top has an opacity of 0.4 and the bottom an opacity of 1.

Listing 7.9 (Turbulence01.svg)

```
<?xml version="1.0" standalone="no"?>
<!DOCTYPE svg PUBLIC "-//W3C//DTD SVG 1.0//EN"
     "http://www.w3.org/TR/2001/PR-SVG-20010719/
      DTD/svg10.dtd">
<svg width="400" height="500">
<defs>
  <filter id="Turbulence1" in="SourceImage"
filterUnits="objectBoundingBox">
      <feTurbulence in="SourceAlpha" type="turbulence"
baseFrequency="0.01" numOctaves="1" seed="0" >
      </feTurbulence>
</filter>
</defs>
<rect x="0" y="0" width="400" height="500"
style="filter:url(#Turbulence1)"/>
</svg>
```

This simple code produces the attractive abstract pattern shown in Figure 07.06.

Figure 07.06

An abstract pattern produced using the `<feTurbulence>` filter primitive. For the code, see Listing 7.9.

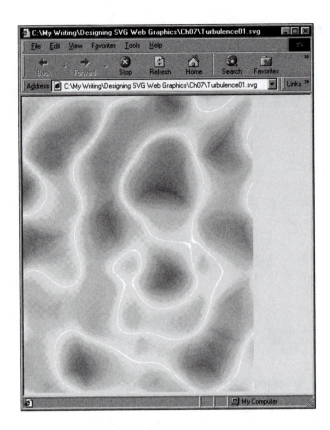

You can restrict the effect of a `<filter>` element to a defined rectangular area within an SVG element. For example, Listing 7.10 confines the `<feTurbulence>` filter primitive to a rectangle of the dimensions defined within the `<filter>` element:

Listing 7.10 (Turbulence02.svg)

```
<?xml version="1.0" standalone="no"?>
<!DOCTYPE svg PUBLIC "-//W3C//DTD SVG 1.0//EN"
    "http://www.w3.org/TR/2001/PR-SVG-20010719/
    DTD/svg10.dtd">
<svg width="400" height="500">
<defs>
   <filter id="Turbulence1" in="SourceImage"
filterUnits="userSpaceOnUse"
    x="200" y="150" width="100" height="50">
      <feTurbulence in="SourceAlpha" type="turbulence"
```

```
baseFrequency="0.01"
numOctaves="1" seed="0" >
        </feTurbulence>
</filter>
</defs>
<rect x="0" y="0" width="400" height="500"
style="filter:url(#Turbulence1)"/>
</svg>
```

In Figure 07.07, you can see how the filter effect is restricted.

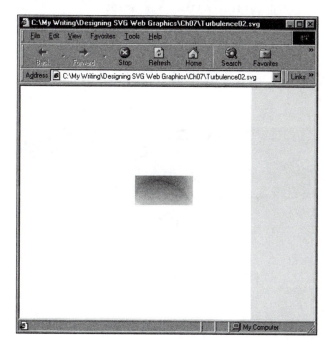

Figure 07.07

The
<feTurbulence>
filter is restricted to a
rectangular area of
the screen by means
of the x, y, width,
and height *attrib-*
utes on the contain-
ing <filter>
element.

If you increase the base frequency on the <feTurbulence> filter primitive, you can get, rather than attractive waves, a tiny, speckled effect, as with the code shown in Listing 7.11. However, if you zoom in to the maximum allowed by the Adobe Viewer, you see that the pattern is essentially the same, only much smaller:

Listing 7.11 (Turbulence03.svg)

```
<?xml version="1.0" standalone="no"?>
<!DOCTYPE svg PUBLIC "-//W3C//DTD SVG 1.0//EN"
    "http://www.w3.org/TR/2001/PR-SVG-20010719/
```

```
        DTD/svg10.dtd">
<svg width="400" height="500">
<defs>
 <filter id="Turbulence1" in="SourceImage"
filterUnits="userSpaceOnUse" >
  <feTurbulence in="sourceGraphic" type="turbulence"
baseFrequency="0.5"
     numOctaves="1" seed="0" >
  </feTurbulence>
</filter>
</defs>
<rect x="0" y="0" width="400" height="500"
style="fill:red; filter:url(#Turbulence1)"/>
</svg>
```

Figure 07.08 shows the speckling effect produced by the code shown in Listing 7.11.

Figure 07.08

A speckled effect produced by increasing the baseFrequency attribute on the <feTurbulence> filter.

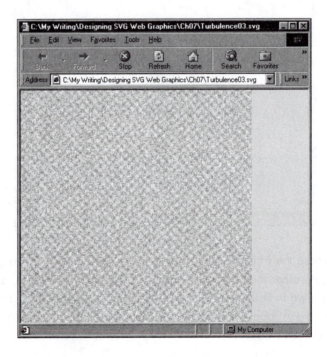

The `in` attribute of the `<feTurbulence>` filter can take a number of inputs. For example, if, as shown in Listing 7.12, a semitransparent green rectangle serves as the background, you can add a greenish cast to the image you see in Figure 07.09.

Listing 7.12 (Turbulence04.svg)

```
<?xml version="1.0" standalone="no"?>
<!DOCTYPE svg PUBLIC "-//W3C//DTD SVG 1.0//EN"
     "http://www.w3.org/TR/2001/PR-SVG-20010719/
       DTD/svg10.dtd">
<svg width="400" height="500">
<defs>
 <filter id="Turbulence1" in="SourceImage"
filterUnits="userSpaceOnUse" >
  <feTurbulence in="BackgroundImage" type="turbulence"
baseFrequency="0.01"
      numOctaves="1" seed="0" >
  </feTurbulence>
</filter>
</defs>
<rect  x="0" y="0" width="400" height="500"
style="fill:#99FF99; opacity:0.5;"/>
<rect x="0" y="0" width="400" height="500"
style="fill:red; filter:url(#Turbulence1)"/>
</svg>
```

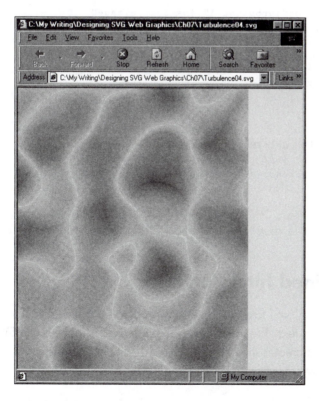

Figure 07.09

*A turbulence filter
that uses a source
image (a semi-
opaque green
rectangle).*

In the preceding example, I used a plain-colored background, but you can also use linear or radial gradients in all or part of the background image and use that as the input to the `<feTurbulence>` filter primitive, as in Listing 7.13 and shown in Figure 07.10.

Listing 7.13 (Turbulence05.svg)

```
<?xml version="1.0" standalone="no"?>
<!DOCTYPE svg PUBLIC "-//W3C//DTD SVG 1.0//EN"
     "http://www.w3.org/TR/2001/PR-SVG-20010719/
     DTD/svg10.dtd">
<svg width="400" height="500">
<defs>
<linearGradient id="MyBlueGradient"
gradientUnits="userSpaceOnUse" x1="90"
y1="50" x2="400" y2="500" >
<stop offset="10%" style="stop-color:#000066"/>
<stop offset="40%" style="stop-color:#FFFF00"/>
<stop offset="75%" style="stop-color:#9999FF"/>
</linearGradient>
  <filter id="Turbulence1" in="SourceImage"
filterUnits="userSpaceOnUse" >
   <feTurbulence in="BackgroundImage" type="turbulence"
baseFrequency="0.01"
     numOctaves="1" seed="0" >
   </feTurbulence>
</filter>
</defs>
<rect  x="0" y="0" width="400" height="500"
style="fill:url(#MyBlueGradient); opacity:0.8;"/>
<rect x="0" y="0" width="400" height="500"
style="fill:red; filter:url(#Turbulence1)"/>
</svg>
```

Many attractive visual effects are possible, so I encourage you to experiment.

Combined filters on text

In this section, you take a look at how you can produce some combined filter effects on text. The following example makes use of several SVG filter primitives. It creates the text `Hello SVG!` with an orange glow or shadow behind it, which you can see in Figure 07.11.

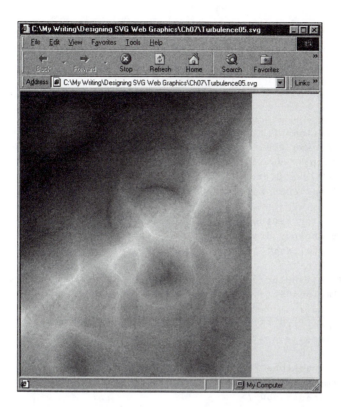

Figure 07.10

A turbulence filter using a linear gradient as the input source image.

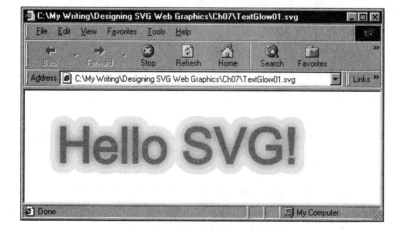

Figure 07.11

A combination of filter primitives applied to text.

The following code produces that appearance. The code uses several SVG filter primitives: `<feMorphology>`, `<feGaussianBlur>`, `<feFlood>` and `<feComposite>`:

Listing 7.14 (TextGlow01.svg)

```
<?xml version="1.0" standalone="no"?>
<!DOCTYPE svg PUBLIC "-//W3C//DTD SVG 1.0//EN"
      "http://www.w3.org/TR/2001/PR-SVG-20010719/
      DTD/svg10.dtd">
<svg width="600" height="600">
<defs>
 <filter id="MyGlow" y="-40%" height="180%">
  <feMorphology in="SourceAlpha" result="morphedAlpha"
operator="dilate"
radius="1"/>
  <feGaussianBlur in="morphedAlpha" result="blurredAlpha"
stdDeviation="3"/>
  <feFlood result="flooded" style="flood-color:#FF9900;
flood-opacity:0.75"/>
  <feComposite in="flooded" result="coloredShadow"
operator="in"
in2="blurredAlpha"/>
  <feComposite in="SourceGraphic" operator="over"
in2="coloredShadow"/>
 </filter>
</defs>
<text x="100" y="50"   style="fill:red; stroke:red;
filter:url(#MyGlow);
font-size:36;">
Hello SVG!
</text>
</svg>
```

The filter is created, as before, within a `<filter>` element, like this:

```
<filter id="MyGlow" y="-40%" height="180%">
```

The `<feMorphology>` element uses the alpha channel of the source image (the text `Hello SVG!`) as the input and uses the `operator` attribute, set to a value of `dilate`, to control the size of the image:

```
<feMorphology in="SourceAlpha" result="morphedAlpha"
operator="dilate"
radius="1"/>
```

Try experimenting with the value for the `radius` attribute to increase or decrease the size of the image. Using values such as 0.5, 2, or 3 gives you an impression of what the attribute does.

The result from the `<feMorphology>` primitive is used as the input to a `<feGaussianBlur>` primitive:

```
<feGaussianBlur in="morphedAlpha"
result="blurredAlpha" stdDeviation="3"/>
```

The `stdDeviation` attribute can be used again to vary the size of the resulting blur. Values in the range from 1 to 4 allow you to see the range of effects, although you can always explore more extreme values:

```
<feFlood result="flooded" style="flood-color:#FF9900;
flood-opacity:0.75"/>
   <feComposite in="flooded" result="coloredShadow"
operator="in"
in2="blurredAlpha"/>
```

Then you add an `<feFlood>` primitive. The `flood-color` property of the `style` attribute controls the color of the shadow you are creating. In the example, the `flood-color` property is set to #FF9900, an orange color. You can also vary the opacity by adjusting the value of the `flood-opacity` property; in this case, set at 0.75.

You then pull all those effect together using an `<feCompositive>` filter primitive.

You must include the `y` and `height` attributes because the default values don't give enough space for the full effect of the filter to be correctly applied. If you use only

```
<filter id="MyGlow">
```

without specifying values for `y` and `height` attributes, you find that the filter effect is truncated, as you can see in Figure 07.12.

Figure 07.12

A zoomed view of a truncated glow effect on text.

Creating filtered text shapes

In most of the examples of filters used with text, you have been placing a variety of filter effects behind the text and leaving the text itself in pristine condition. But you can alter the appearance of the text itself as well as create shadows, for example. Figure 07.13 shows one example, building on the `<feTurbulence>` primitive you saw earlier in this chapter.

Figure 07.13

An unusual filter effect on text.

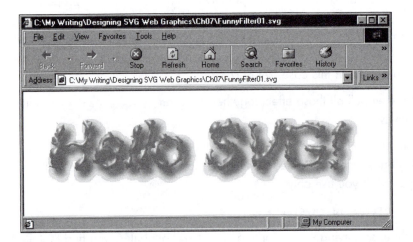

First, look at the code that produced that appearance, and then take a closer look at some aspects of the code:

Listing 7.15 (FunnyFilter01.svg)

```
<?xml version="1.0" standalone="no"?>
<!DOCTYPE svg PUBLIC "-//W3C//DTD SVG 1.0//EN"
     "http://www.w3.org/TR/2001/PR-SVG-20010719/
      DTD/svg10.dtd">
<svg>
<defs>
 <filter id="MyOddFilter" y="-30%" height="180%">
   <feTurbulence result="turb" baseFrequency="0.1"
numOctaves="2" seed="0" stitchTiles="noStitch"
type="turbulence"/>
   <feDisplacementMap in="SourceGraphic"
result="displacedSource" scale="10" xChannelSelector="R"
 yChannelSelector="G"
    in2="turb"/>
   <feGaussianBlur in="displacedSource" result="blur"
stdDeviation="2"/>
   <feOffset in="blur" result="offsetBlurredSource"
dx="4" dy="4"/>
   <feSpecularLighting result="specularOut" in="blur"
surfaceScale="5" specularConstant="1"
specularExponent="10" lighting-color="#FFFFFF">
   <fePointLight x="-5000" y="-10000" z="2000"/>
   </feSpecularLighting>
   <feComposite result="specularOut" in="specularOut"
operator="in" in2="displacedSource"/>
   <feComposite result="litPaint" in="displacedSource"
operator="arithmetic" k1="0" k2="1" k3="1" k4="0"
    in2="specularOut"/>
   <feComposite in="litPaint" operator="over"
in2="offsetBlurredSource"/>
 </filter>
</defs>
<text x="50" y="50"  style="fill:red; stroke:red;
font-style:italic; filter:url(#MyOddFilter);
font-size:48;">
Hello SVG!
</text>
</svg>
```

Having filters of this complexity can be a bit overwhelming. Trying to explain the effects of modifying each attribute is a lengthy process and is difficult to show in printed media, such as a book. So the best (and highly suggested) solution is for you to experiment. Let me focus on a couple of points in this example, however. If you modify the `lighting-color` attribute of the `<feSpecularLighting>` primitive, you can alter the color of the highlights on the text to which the filter has been applied. For example, if you change it to #00FF00, you can get interesting green highlights on the text.

You can also experiment with the position of the source for the `<fePointLight>` element. The following line

```
<fePointLight x="-5000" y="-10000" z="2000"/>
```

indicates that the source of the point light is 5,000 pixels to the left of the screen, 10,000 pixels above the top of the screen, and 2,000 pixels nearer to you than the screen is. I often prefer the appearance created by having the spotlight source a long way away from the text or other SVG object. However, for some purposes, you might find that you prefer the appearance (sometimes a little distorted) that closer light sources produce.

You can produce other interesting possibilities if you use two different colors for the fill and stroke properties of the `<text>` element. Note that applying text styling, such as italics, to the text is a straightforward process, as is applying this somewhat complex filter.

The field of SVG filters is enormous, and a discussion of this subject needs a book of its own. I hope that I have given you a flavor of what is possible with SVG filters and that you are encouraged to try experimenting with them on your own. Many interesting effects are waiting to be discovered.

8

Animation: SVG and SMIL Animation

In this chapter:

Basic Animations

One of the most visually attractive aspects of SVG is its potential for animation. Most parts of an SVG image can be animated—position onscreen, width, height, color, opacity, stop colors in a gradient, attributes of SVG filters. The visual effects are potentially legion. But before you get carried away or overwhelmed by the potential, look at how SVG animation is done.

SVG images can be animated by two methods: the use of declarative SVG elements (mostly using elements borrowed from SMIL Animation) or the use of ECMAScript (JavaScript) or another scripting language to manipulate the Document Object Model (DOM) of an SVG image. The two methods can be combined into one image.

This chapter focuses on declarative animation.

In practice, portraying in a book the visual appearances that SVG animation produces is difficult. Therefore, I strongly encourage you to experiment with the SVG code provided and view these animations on your own computer. A number of the animations presented in this chapter are accessible online on the Web site http://www.svgspider.com/default.svg.

SVG As an Animation Grammar

Animation is a time-based alteration in the characteristics of an image. During an SVG animation, the SVG rendering engine maintains two copies of the value to be animated. One is the original value (which is maintained in the DOM), and the other is the presentation value, the value that gives rise to the onscreen appearance during an animation.

Before I discuss and show you working SVG animations, I want to discuss the general way in which SVG animations are implemented and the various forms of syntax you can apply.

Basic Attributes of an Animation

To define an animation, you need to know what is to be animated, when the animation will begin, what is the starting value of the attribute to be animated, and what is the presentation value of that attribute at the end of the animation.

The attribute to be animated is specified by the value of the `attributeName` attribute. For example, if the `fill` attribute will be animated, you expect to see

```
attributeName="fill"
```

as an attribute on the animation element.

The timing of the beginning of an animation is determined by the value of the `begin` attribute. For example, if the animation will begin six seconds after the page loaded, you see this line in the code:

```
begin="6s"
```

SVG animations can be chained. If the animation will begin five seconds after the end of the `First` animation (identified by the `id` attribute of the former animation having the value of `First`), you see

```
begin="First.end+5s"
```

and, therefore, achieving the timing you want.

For many of the animations you use, you should define the duration, using the `dur` attribute. If the duration is not specified then, for most animations the SVG rendering engine will have insufficient information to implement the animation. To define the duration of an animation as being ten seconds, you use the `dur` attribute, like this:

```
dur="10s"
```

Several general methods exist for altering the values of an attribute. One uses both the `from` and `to` attributes so that for a color animation, you might see

```
from="red" to="blue"
```

Or, if you are altering the size of a rectangle in steps of ten pixels, you might use the `from` and `by` attributes, like this:

```
from="100px" by="10px"
```

which defines the change during the course of the animation. You can omit the `from` attribute if it is the same as the original value of the attribute defined in the `attributeName` and if it is contained in the Document Object Model (DOM). However, you should include the `from` attribute routinely because it acts as a reminder of the need to consider the beginning value of the attribute.

Finally, you can specify a variety of values to be displayed during the animation by using a `values` attribute. If you want to change the `x` attribute of an element successively from 5 to 10 to 30 to 5, you write something like this:

```
attributeName="x" values="5; 10; 30; 5"
```

I haven't yet discussed what happens at the end of the duration defined by the `dur` attribute. The default behavior is that the original value (the one maintained in the DOM) for the `target` attribute is again displayed. If you want instead to preserve the final version of the presentation attribute, you can do so like this:

```
fill="freeze"
```

which freezes the animation with the presentation value still on display.

Be careful not to confuse the fill *attribute on a simple SVG graphical shape, like the* <rect> *or* <circle> *elements, with the* fill *attribute of an animation element. The* fill *attribute of a graphical shape defines the paint to be applied within the outline of the shape. The* fill *attribute of an animation element defines whether the original value held in the DOM or the presentation value created during the animation is displayed after the animation is complete.*

The SMIL Animation facilities do not limit you to a one- off animation. They provide syntax to define an indefinitely repeating animation or an animation that repeats a defined number of times. To produce an animation that repeats exactly three times, you use

```
repeatCount="3"
```

Or, to produce an indefinitely repeating animation, you use

```
repeatCount="indefinite"
```

You see later in this chapter many examples of precisely how to use these methods. My purpose now is simply to show you the range of syntax available to the SVG designer.

Applying SVG Animation to SVG Static Elements

Before you go on to look in detail at the animation elements in SVG, look at how an animation can be added to a simple SVG shape.

Typically, if you have a simple graphical shape with no content, you express it as an empty element:

```
<rect x="100" y="100" width="10px" height="100px"
style="stroke:red; fill:rgb(0,0,0)"/>
```

However, when you want to add an animation to it, you need to nest the SVG animation element between the start tag and end tag of the element representing the graphical shape, like this:

```
<rect x="100" y="100" width="10px" height="100px"
style="stroke:red;
fill:rgb(0,0,0)">
<!-- The animation element goes in here. -->
</rect>
```

If you want to have an animation that changes both the `width` and `height` attributes of a simple rectangle over a period of ten seconds, therefore, you would have an SVG image whose source code looks like this:

Listing 8.1 (AnimRect.svg)

```
<?xml version='1.0'?>
<!DOCTYPE svg PUBLIC "-//W3C//DTD SVG 1.0//EN"
    "http://www.w3.org/TR/2001/PR-SVG-20010719/
    DTD/svg10.dtd">
<svg width="300" height="250">
<rect x="100" y="100" width="10px" height="100px"
style="stroke:red; fill:rgb(0,0,0)">
    <animate attributeName="width"  from="10px"
to="100px"
            begin="0s" dur="10s" repeatCount="1"
fill="freeze"/>
    <animate attributeName="height" from="100px"
to="10px"
            begin="0s" dur="10s" repeatCount="1"
fill="freeze"/>
</rect>
</svg>
```

By nesting the animation elements like this, you define the scope of the animation. Because, in this case, the `<animate>` element is nested immediately within the `<rect>` element, the attributes of the containing `<rect>` element are animated.

More Complex Animations

So far, the simple syntax you have looked at produces linear changes in an attribute smoothly over the duration of the animation. SVG, however, provides alternative methods to add other nonlinear or noninterpolated animations.

First, compare linear and discrete modes on a color animation. The top rectangle shown in Figure 08.01 changes slowly in color from white to yellow over 16 seconds. The lower rectangle stays white until the 16 seconds have passed and then changes step-wise from white to yellow. The discrete `calcMode` is needed particularly in situations where no interpolated values exist—for example, when you are changing the visibility attribute from `visible` to `hidden` or vice versa. Interpolation values exist for the `opacity` attribute, but the `visibility` attribute is a separate thing, with the only possible values being `hidden` or `visible`.

Figure 08.01

The rectangles are animated using linear and discrete calculation modes, respectively, with resulting significant differences in animation behavior. Partway through the animation, the top rectangle is pale yellow and the bottom rectangle is still white (before the step-wise change to yellow).

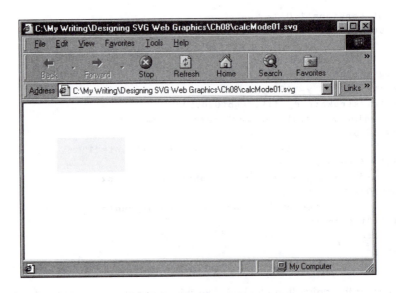

Listing 8.2 (calcMode01.svg)

```
<?xml version="1.0" standalone="no"?>
<!DOCTYPE svg PUBLIC "-//W3C//DTD SVG 1.0//EN"
    "http://www.w3.org/TR/2001/PR-SVG-20010719/
    DTD/svg10.dtd">
```

```
<svg>
<rect x="50" y="50" width="100" height="50"
style="fill:#FFFFFF">
<animate attributeName="fill" calcMode="linear"
from="#FFFFFF" to="#FFFF00" begin="2s" dur="16s"/>
</rect>
<rect x="50" y="150" width="100" height="50"
style="fill:#FFFFFF">
<animate attributeName="fill" calcMode="discrete"
from="#FFFFFF" to="#FFFF00" begin="2s" dur="16s"/>
</rect>
</svg>
```

Having looked at the difference between linear and discrete calculation modes, move on and look at paced calculation mode.

Figure 08.02 demonstrates the difference between linear calculation mode and paced calculation mode. The example shows two lines being animated by rotation using the `<animateTransform>` element. One animation uses linear calculation mode, and the other uses paced calculation mode.

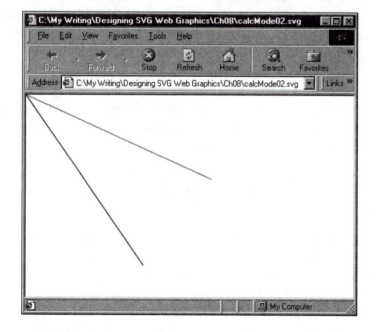

Figure 08.02

A moment, early in the animation, when the blue line is animating faster than the red.

Listing 8.3 (calcMode02.svg)

```
<?xml version="1.0" standalone="no"?>
<!DOCTYPE svg PUBLIC "-//W3C//DTD SVG 1.0//EN"
     "http://www.w3.org/TR/2001/PR-SVG-20010719/
        DTD/svg10.dtd">
<svg>
<line x1="0" y1="0" x2="300" y2="0" style="fill:red;
stroke:red;">
<animateTransform attributeName="transform"
calcMode="linear" type="rotate" values="0; 22; 45; 90;
 0; 90; 22; 45; 0" dur="16s"/>
</line>
<line x1="0" y1="0" x2="300" y2="0" style="fill:blue;
stroke:blue;">
<animateTransform attributeName="transform"
calcMode="paced" type="rotate" values="0; 22; 45; 90;
0; 90; 22; 45; 0" dur="16s"/>
</line>
</svg>
```

Paced mode evens out the rotations over the 16 seconds of the rotation shown in Figure 08.02. However, linear mode divides all the changes into equal periods, so in the first period, it moves 22 degrees (and therefore lags behind the blue paced `calcMode` line). In the next period, the red linear `calcMode` line is again slower, traveling 23 degrees. In the third period, it speeds up a little, traveling through 45 degrees. In the fourth period, it speeds up more, traveling through 90 degrees, overtaking during the fifth time interval the steadier-paced line (forgive the pun) the paced `calcMode` blue line shown in the example.

If you take time to run the code, these differences are much easier to appreciate than if you attempt to understand what is happening by simply reading this text.

You can produce additional permutations by combining the use of the `values` attribute, the `keyTimes` attribute, and the linear `calcMode`. In the following code, pay particular attention to the `keyTimes` and `values` attributes. At 0 seconds (the first key time), the width of the rectangle is 10 pixels. At the second key time (12 seconds), the width has increased to only 20 pixels (the animation is slow). However, by the third key time (16 seconds), the width has increased to 110 pixels. If you run the animation, you should see 12 seconds of slow animation followed by a distinct increase in speed at 12 seconds. Figure 08.03 shows a moment in the middle of this animation.

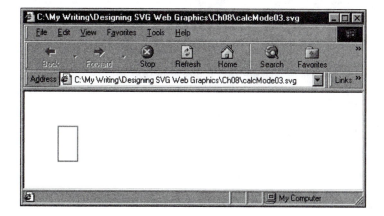

Figure 08.03

An animation of the rectangle width controlled by the keyTimes *attribute, partly completed.*

Listing 8.4 (calcMode03.svg)

```
<?xml version="1.0" standalone="no"?>
<!DOCTYPE svg PUBLIC "-//W3C//DTD SVG 1.0//EN"
     "http://www.w3.org/TR/2001/PR-SVG-20010719/
      DTD/svg10.dtd">
<svg>
<rect x="50" y="50" width="10" height="50" s
tyle="fill:none; stroke:red; stroke-width:1;">
<animate begin="0s" dur="16s" attributeName="width"
fill="freeze"
  keyTimes="0s; 12s; 16s"
  values = "10; 20; 110"/>
</rect>
</svg>
```

In addition, the `splines` calculation mode (which I don't use in the examples in this book) is used in conjunction with the `keyTimes` and `keyValues` attributes. This mode is described fully in the SVG and SMIL Animation specifications (see Appendix A for the URLs).

In SVG, you can alter the appearance of an image over time by changing the values of one or more attributes of SVG elements over time. More specifically, each SVG animation element alters the presentation value of an attribute of an SVG element. The original value of the attribute is preserved, for possible future use, in the Document Object Model (DOM) of the SVG image or document. An SVG animation element is typically a child of the parent element, the value of whose attribute is being manipulated. For example, to change the color of a rectangle, you nest the `<animateColor>` element (described in more detail later) within the `<rect>` element, like this (and shown in Figure 08.04):

Listing 8.5 (ColorAnim00.svg)

```
<?xml version="1.0" standalone="no"?>
<!DOCTYPE svg PUBLIC "-//W3C//DTD SVG 1.0//EN"
      "http://www.w3.org/TR/2001/PR-SVG-20010719/
         DTD/svg10.dtd">
<svg>
<rect x="20" y="20" width="100" height="50"
style="fill:white; stroke:black;">
<animateColor begin="5s" attributeName="fill"
from="white" to="red" dur="8s" fill="freeze"/>
</rect>
</svg>
```

Figure 08.04

The fill of the rectangle is partway from white to red.

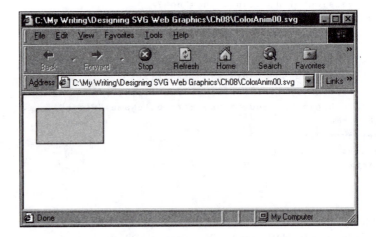

Don't worry about the detail at the moment; just notice that the `<animateColor>` element is a child of the `<rect>` element whose fill color it changes. You can animate attributes on SVG elements other than the parent of an animation element if the animation element possesses a `targetElement` or `href` attribute. The `href` attribute belongs to the XML Linking Language (Xlink) namespace. It is not an HTML or XHTML `href` attribute. In this chapter, you focus on the default behavior where an animation element manipulates with time the presentation value of an attribute on its parent element.

SVG allows you to animate many attributes of SVG elements. You can change the color of a graphic, change its position, change its transparency, or make part of an image visible or hidden, for example, all by using the declarative animation syntax. You can produce particularly attractive or subtle effects when SVG filters are animated over time.

SVG provides five animation elements:

```
<animate>
<set>
<animateColor>
<animateMotion>
<animateTransform>
```

The first four elements are derived directly from SMIL Animation. The fifth animation element, `<animateTransform>`, is an SVG-specific animation element.

The `<animate>` element allows changes to be made to scalar SVG (XML) attributes or to CSS properties over time. The `<set>` element is an alternative to the `<animate>` element in some situations, conveniently allowing nonnumeric values to be set. The `<animateColor>` element allows color to be changed over time. The `<animateMotion>` element allows part of an SVG image to be moved along some path over time.

The `<animateTransform>` element allows the animation of one or more of the SVG transformation attributes; for example, scale. SVG provides, in addition to the `<animateTransform>` element, four other extensions to the animation functionality in SMIL Animation. A `path` attribute permits the animation of SVG path data. You can use an `<mpath>` element as a child of an `<animateMotion>` element to provide access to path data. A `keyPoints` attribute has been added to the `<animateMotion>` element, compared to the SMIL Animation original, to provide additional control of the speed of motion animations. A `rotate` attribute has been added to the `<animateMotion>` element and determines whether an object being animated along a path changes its orientation to correspond to the direction of the path at a particular point. (Think of how a car turns as a road curves.)

SVG, SMIL Animation, and SMIL 2.0

As I indicate in the preceding section, SVG derives four of its five declarative animation elements from SMIL Animation. *SMIL*, by the way, is the Synchronized Multimedia Integration Language. A W3C Recommendation for SMIL 1.0 was issued on June 15, 1998, and is at http://www.w3.org/TR/REC-smil. The SMIL Animation specification is, at the time this book was written, still in the W3C Proposed Recommendation stage. The latest version is at http://www.w3.org/TR/smil-animation. Also under development is the SMIL 2.0 specification, also a Proposed Recommendation. The latest version is at http://www.w3.org/TR/smil20.

SMIL Animation is the most important of these three specifications as far as understanding SVG animations in isolation is concerned. However, SMIL 1.0 and SMIL 2.0 allow the integration of multimedia components within which static or animated SVG graphics can play a useful part. A discussion of those exciting possibilities of the multimedia use of SVG is beyond the scope of this book.

SMIL Animation provides a way of expressing animations using XML-compliant elements that describe an animation along a timeline. In addition, SMIL Animation—and, hence, SVG—allows individual animations to be combined in visually attractive ways. Many animations described in this chapter are fairly simple because you must understand how each animation component works. After you understand fully how each one works, you should be in a good position to combine animation elements to good visual effect.

To produce an SVG animation, you declare a `target` attribute on an SVG element. For example, if you want to change the width of a rectangle, you use the `width` attribute as the `target` attribute, something like this:

Listing 8.6 (ChangeWidth.svg)

```
<?xml version="1.0" standalone="no"?>
<!DOCTYPE svg PUBLIC "-//W3C//DTD SVG 1.0//EN"
    "http://www.w3.org/TR/2001/PR-SVG-20010719/
     DTD/svg10.dtd">
```

```
<svg width="400" height="300">
<rect x="50" y="100" width="10" height="10"
style="fill:red; stroke:black; stroke-width:3;">
<animate attributeName="width"  from="10"  to="100"
            begin="0s" dur="20s" />
</rect>
</svg>
```

When the rectangle is first displayed, it has a width of ten user units. The attributeName attribute of the <animate> element indicates that the target attribute is the width attribute of the <rect> element. The animation begins at 0s, which means 0 seconds (immediately) after the image is displayed. The duration of the animation, expressed by the dur attribute, is 20 seconds. During that time, the value of the width attribute changes from 10 to 100. Visually, what was initially a small square increases progressively in width over a period of 20 seconds:

```
<animate attributeName="width"  from="10"  to="100"
            begin="0s" dur="20s" />
```

You have not specified that the rectangle retains its animated shape; therefore, it snaps back to the appearance of a small square after the animation is complete. If I had wanted the rectangle to retain the shape it had at the end of the animation, I would have added this line:

```
fill="freeze"
```

The original value of the target attribute is always available to be displayed again. During the animation, a copy of the original target attribute is created, and its changing values contribute to the display you see. However, the original value of the attribute remains unchanged in the SVG document's Document Object Model (DOM).

The <animate> Element

I look at the <animate> element as a general-purpose SVG animation element because it can do some of everything. For some animations, the more specialized animation elements (<animateColor>, <animateTransform>, <animateMotion>, and <set>) provide additional control or convenience.

Animating motion

One straightforward type of animation that is possible using the `<animate>` element is linear animation, which can be done horizontally, vertically, or (by combining two animations) diagonally.

Animate a circle horizontally first:

Listing 8.7 (LinCircleAnim01.svg)

```
<?xml version="1.0" standalone="no"?>
<!DOCTYPE svg PUBLIC "-//W3C//DTD SVG 1.0//EN"
     "http://www.w3.org/TR/2001/PR-SVG-20010719/
        DTD/svg10.dtd">
<svg width="500" height="300">
<circle cx="50" cy="50" r="10" style="fill:#990066">
   <animate attributeName="cx" from="50" to="450"
begin="2s" dur="10s"
     repeatCount="indefinite"/>
</circle>
</svg>
```

Similarly, you can animate the circle vertically by animating the `cy` attribute rather than the `cx` attribute:

Listing 8.8 (LinCircleAnim02.svg)

```
<?xml version="1.0" standalone="no"?>
<!DOCTYPE svg PUBLIC "-//W3C//DTD SVG 1.0//EN"
     "http://www.w3.org/TR/2001/PR-SVG-20010719/
        DTD/svg10.dtd">
<svg width="500" height="300">
<circle cx="50" cy="50" r="10" style="fill:#990066">
   <animate attributeName="cy" from="50" to="250"
begin="2s" dur="10s"
     repeatCount="indefinite"/>
</circle>
</svg>
```

Or, by animating simultaneously the `cx` and `cy` attributes, you can move the circle diagonally across the screen:

Listing 8.9 (LinCircleAnim03.svg)

```
<?xml version="1.0" standalone="no"?>
<!DOCTYPE svg PUBLIC "-//W3C//DTD SVG 1.0//EN"
    "http://www.w3.org/TR/2001/PR-SVG-20010719/
    DTD/svg10.dtd">
<svg width="500" height="300">
<circle cx="50" cy="50" r="10" style="fill:#990066">
    <animate attributeName="cx" from="50" to="450"
begin="2s" dur="10s"
    repeatCount="indefinite"/>
  <animate attributeName="cy" from="50" to="250"
begin="2s" dur="10s"
    repeatCount="indefinite"/>
</circle>
</svg>
```

Animating size

You can use the `<animate>` element to animate the size of an SVG element. The example in Listing 8.10 shows indefinitely repeating animations of a row of squares that change size in response to an `<animate>` element.

Listing 8.10 (GrowingSquares01.svg)

```
<?xml version="1.0" standalone="no"?>
<!DOCTYPE svg PUBLIC "-//W3C//DTD SVG 1.0//EN"
    "http://www.w3.org/TR/2001/PR-SVG-20010719/
    DTD/svg10.dtd">
<svg width="150" height="100">
<rect x="10" y="20" width="0" height="0"
style="fill:none; stroke:red; stroke-width:1">
<animate begin="0s" attributeName="width" values="0;
10; 0; 10; 0;" dur="5s" repeatCount="indefinite"/>
<animate begin="0s" attributeName="height" values="0;
10; 0; 10; 0;" dur="5s" repeatCount="indefinite"/>
</rect>
<rect x="25" y="20" width="0" height="0"
style="fill:none; stroke:yellow; stroke-width:1">
<animate begin="1s" attributeName="width" values="0;
10; 0; 10; 0;" dur="5s" repeatCount="indefinite"/>
<animate begin="1s" attributeName="height" values="0;
10; 0; 10; 0;" dur="5s" repeatCount="indefinite"/>
</rect>
<rect x="40" y="20" width="0" height="0"
```

```
style="fill:none; stroke:blue; stroke-width:1">
<animate begin="2s" attributeName="width" values="0;
10; 0; 10; 0;" dur="5s" repeatCount="indefinite"/>
<animate begin="2s" attributeName="height" values="0;
10; 0; 10; 0;" dur="5s" repeatCount="indefinite"/>
</rect>
<rect x="55" y="20" width="0" height="0"
style="fill:none; stroke:#FF6600; stroke-width:1">
<animate begin="3s" attributeName="width" values="0;
10; 0; 10; 0;" dur="5s" repeatCount="indefinite"/>
<animate begin="3s" attributeName="height" values="0;
10; 0; 10; 0;" dur="5s" repeatCount="indefinite"/>
</rect>
<rect x="70" y="20" width="0" height="0"
style="fill:none; stroke:#00FF00; stroke-width:1">
<animate begin="4s" attributeName="width" values="0;
10; 0; 10; 0;" dur="5s" repeatCount="indefinite"/>
<animate begin="4s" attributeName="height" values="0;
10; 0; 10; 0;" dur="5s" repeatCount="indefinite"/>
</rect>
<rect x="85" y="20" width="0" height="0"
style="fill:none; stroke:#FF00FF; stroke-width:1">
<animate begin="5s" attributeName="width" values="0;
10; 0; 10; 0;" dur="5s" repeatCount="indefinite"/>
<animate begin="5s" attributeName="height" values="0;
10; 0; 10; 0;" dur="5s" repeatCount="indefinite"/>
</rect>
</svg>
```

With animations like this, I can never make up my mind whether they are a nice background piece of motion or an irritating irrelevance. Overall, I like this one.

Figure 08.05 shows one part of the animation.

The <set> Element

The `<set>` element provides a straightforward way of setting the value of an attribute or property to a particular value for a specified period. As with the other SMIL Animation and SVG animation elements, the `<set>` element sets the `presentation` attribute value, leaving the original value of the `target` attribute unchanged in the DOM.

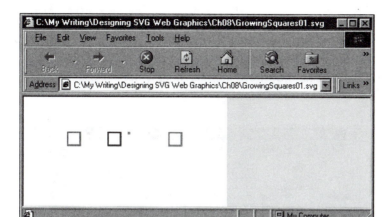

Figure 08.05

The animation of the size of the multiple squares at one point during the repeating animation.

You can use the `<set>` element to set the value of an attribute for which interpolated values make no sense; for example, the `visibility` attribute can have only the values `hidden` or `visible`. The additive or accumulative attributes are not permitted on a `<set>` element. Also, the `repeatCount` attribute does not cause the animation to be repeated, but simply extends the duration for which the animated presentation value is displayed.

For example, you can use the `<set>` element to control simple rollover effects, like this:

Listing 8.11 (Set01.svg)

```
<?xml version="1.0" standalone="no"?>
<!DOCTYPE svg PUBLIC "-//W3C//DTD SVG 1.0//EN"
     "http://www.w3.org/TR/2001/PR-SVG-20010719/
      DTD/svg10.dtd">
<svg>
<rect x="50" y="50" rx="5" ry="5" width="150"
height="50" style="fill:#000099; stroke:#000099;">
<set begin="mouseover" end="mouseout"
attributeName="fill" from="#000099" to="#CCCCFF"/>
</rect>
</svg>
```

When the mouse is moved over the rectangle, the fill changes to a sort of pale blue and remains like that until the mouse is moved away, ending the animation. This provides a more succinct syntax as an alternative to paired

`<animate>` elements to achieve mouseover and mouseout effects. Figure 08.06 shows the rectangle before it is moused, and Figure 08.07 shows the appearance of the rectangle while it is being moused. Note that no pointing hand is there because the rectangle is not enclosed within an `<a>` element.

Figure 08.06

The rectangle not moused.

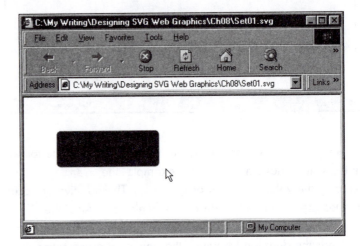

Figure 08.07

The rectangle showing the mouseover change in the fill.

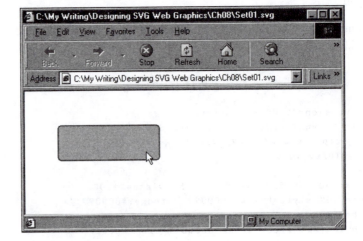

Animating visibility

SVG allows you, using the `<set>` element, to make an element or group of elements visible or hidden.

Suppose that you want to keep some text hidden for two seconds and make it visible for six seconds. Because the text is to be hidden initially, you set the `visibility` attribute in the `<text>` element to a value of `hidden`. The animation is controlled by a `<set>` element, which animates the `visibility` attribute from `hidden` to `visible`. The `begin` attribute indicates that the animation begins two seconds after the image is loaded, and the `dur` attribute indicates that the text is visible for six seconds. After that period, the original value of the visibility property is restored (the text is again hidden).

Listing 8.12 (AnimVisibility.svg)

```
<?xml version="1.0" standalone="no"?>
<!DOCTYPE svg PUBLIC "-//W3C//DTD SVG 1.0//EN"
      "http://www.w3.org/TR/2001/PR-SVG-20010719/
       DTD/svg10.dtd">
<svg>
<text id="TextElement" x="40" y="40"
style="font-family:Verdana, sans-serif; font-size:30;
 visibility:hidden; fill:#990066;stroke:#990066" >
And now you see me!
<set attributeName="visibility" attributeType="CSS"
 to="visible"
begin="2s" dur="6s"/>
</text>
</svg>
```

You can also make the text visible and keep it visible. To do that, you change the `<set>` element as follows:

```
<set attributeName="visibility" attributeType="CSS"
 to="visible"
begin="2s" fill="freeze"/>
```

Listing 8.12 is a time-based visibility animation. You can also create event-based visibility animations, such as in Listing 8.13, where mousing the rectangle causes the circle to become visible.

Listing 8.13 (Rollover01.svg)

```
<?xml version='1.0'?>
<!DOCTYPE svg PUBLIC "-//W3C//DTD SVG 1.0//EN"
```

```
          "http://www.w3.org/TR/2001/PR-SVG-20010719/
          DTD/svg10.dtd">
<svg width="300" height="200">
<g style="display:none">
<animate attributeName="display" from="none" to="block"
begin="Button.mouseover" dur="0.1s" fill="freeze" />
<animate attributeName="display" from="block" to="none"
begin="Button.mouseout"
dur="0.1s" fill="freeze" />
<circle cx="20" cy="25" r="10" style="fill:red;"/>
</g>
<rect id="Button" x="40" y="10" width="100" height="30"
rx="5" ry="5"
style="fill:red;">
<animateColor begin="mouseover" attributeName="fill"
from="red" to="blue"
dur="0.1s" fill="freeze" />
<animateColor begin="mouseout" attributeName="fill"
from="blue" to="red"
dur="0.1s" fill="freeze" />
</rect>
</svg>
```

In Listing 8.13, I have created a group `<g>` element to control visibility. When visibility is controlled within a `<g>` element, it depends on animating the `display` property rather than the `visibility` property used in Listing 8.12.

```
<g style="display:none">
<animate attributeName="display" from="none" to="block"
begin="Button.mouseover" dur="0.1s" fill="freeze" />
<animate attributeName="display" from="block" to="none"
begin="Button.mouseout"
dur="0.1s" fill="freeze" />
<circle cx="20" cy="25" r="10" style="fill:red;"/>
</g>
```

The `display` attribute begins with a value of `none`. The first `<animate>` element changes the value of the `display` attribute from `none` to `block`, which makes the circle (which is part of the content of the `<g>` element) visible on mouseover. On mouseout, the second `<animate>` element causes the value of the `display` attribute to return to `none`, so the circle disappears from the screen.

A rollover of similar visual appearance could have been achieved by using the `<circle>` element without a containing `<g>` element and creating and animating a `visibility` attribute on the `<circle>` element from `hidden` to `visible` as shown in Figure 08.08.

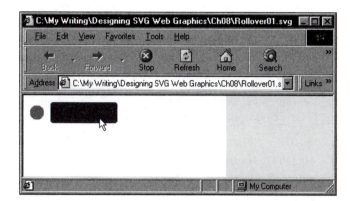

Figure 08.08

The circle becomes visible when the rectangle is moused and disappears when the mouse is removed from the rectangle.

Animating URIs

When an SVG fill is referenced, you make use of a URI that refers to the `id` attribute on the `<linearGradient>` or other element that defines the fill. That URI, like so many other SVG attributes, can be animated. Listing 8.14 contains a simple animation that puts this concept into practice and changes for a defined period the linear gradient used to fill one of the four circles (see Figure 08.09).

Listing 8.14 (CircleGradient02.svg)

```
<?xml version="1.0" standalone="no"?>
<!DOCTYPE svg PUBLIC "-//W3C//DTD SVG 1.0//EN"
    "http://www.w3.org/TR/2001/PR-SVG-20010719/
    DTD/svg10.dtd">

<svg width="400" height="300">
<defs>
<linearGradient id="MyBlueGradient"
gradientUnits="userSpaceOnUse" x1="90"
y1="50" x2="150" y2="150" >
<stop offset="10%" style="stop-color:#FF0066"/>
<stop offset="75%" style="stop-color:#EEEEFF"/>
</linearGradient>
```

```
<linearGradient id="MyGreenGradient"
gradientUnits="userSpaceOnUse" x1="60"
y1="50" x2="120" y2="150" >
<stop offset="10%" style="stop-color:#FF0066"/>
<stop offset="75%" style="stop-color:#CCFFCC"/>
</linearGradient>
</defs>

<ellipse cx="100" cy="50" rx="50" ry="50"
style="fill:url(#MyBlueGradient)">
</ellipse>

<ellipse cx="100" cy="150" rx="50" ry="50"
style="fill:url(#MyBlueGradient)">
</ellipse>

<ellipse cx="200" cy="100" rx="50" ry="50"
style="fill:url(#MyBlueGradient)">
</ellipse>

<ellipse cx="300" cy="150" rx="50" ry="50"
style="fill:url(#MyBlueGradient)">
<set attributeName="fill" from="url(#MyBlueGradient)"
to="url(#MyGreenGradient)"
  begin="3s" dur="5s" repeatCount="1"/>
</ellipse>

</svg>
```

Figure 08.09

The URI referenced by the fill of the lower-right circle has been altered by the `<set>` *element.*

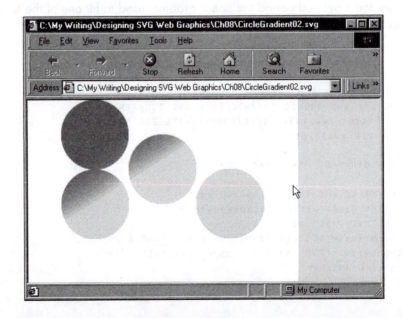

As you can see in the following code, the `from` attribute of the `<set>` element refers to the `<LinearGradient>` element with an `id` attribute of `MyBlueGradient` and then alters to `MyGreenGradient` the gradient being referenced. At the end of the animation, because no `fill` attribute is on the `<set>` element, the gradient used returns to the one described by the `fill` property of the `<ellipse>` element:

```
<ellipse cx="300" cy="150" rx="50" ry="50"
style="fill:url(#MyBlueGradient)">
<set attributeName="fill" from="url(#MyBlueGradient)"
to="url(#MyGreenGradient)"
  begin="3s" dur="5s" repeatCount="1"/>
</ellipse>
```

Chaining animations

So far, you have created animations that are either solitary or timed independently of each other. SMIL Animation—and, hence, SVG—also allows you to chain animations so that, if you have two animations, the second animation begins in a defined relationship to some aspect of the timing of the first animation. Look now at some examples of how animations can be chained.

In fact, all SVG animations are chained! Pause, and as you look at the following code, think for a moment what I mean:

Listing 8.15 (Chaining01.svg)

```
<?xml version="1.0" standalone="no"?>
<!DOCTYPE svg PUBLIC "-//W3C//DTD SVG 1.0//EN"
    "http://www.w3.org/TR/2001/PR-SVG-20010719/
    DTD/svg10.dtd">
<svg width="300" height="100">
<rect x="10" y="45" width="10" height="10"
style="fill:pink;">
<animate begin="2s" dur="10s"
attributeName="width" from="10" to="250"/>
</rect>
</svg>
```

The `begin` attribute has a value representing two seconds, but what does that two seconds refer to? It is timed relative to the end of document loading, so you have, even in that basic example, the chaining of events: The SVG document finishes loading, and the animation of the `width` attribute begins two seconds later. What you need to do is to understand the more general syntax to express the chaining of animations. Take a look at the following simple example, and you can see how this process works. I have added `id` attributes to the original `<rect>` element, the `<animate>` element, and the new `<rect>` so that you can be clear about exactly which part I am talking about.

Listing 8.16 (Chaining02.svg)

```
<?xml version="1.0" standalone="no"?>
<!DOCTYPE svg PUBLIC "-//W3C//DTD SVG 1.0//EN"
     "http://www.w3.org/TR/2001/PR-SVG-20010719/
     DTD/svg10.dtd">
<svg width="300" height="100">
<rect id="MaroonRect" x="10" y="15" width="10"
height="10" style="fill:#990066;">
<animate begin="PinkAnim.begin+2s" dur="10s"
attributeName="width" from="10" to="250"/>
</rect>
<rect id="PinkRect" x="10" y="45" width="10"
height="10" style="fill:pink;">
<animate id="PinkAnim" begin="2s" dur="10s"
attributeName="width" from="10" to="250"/>
</rect>
</svg>
```

The animation proceeds as follows: Two seconds after document loading is complete, the pink rectangle is animated because of this code:

```
<animate id="PinkAnim" begin="2s" dur="10s"
attributeName="width" from="10" to="250"/>
```

Notice that the animation has the `id` of `PinkAnim`. In the following line, another animation is linked to the beginning of that animation:

```
<animate begin="PinkAnim.begin+2s" dur="10s"
attributeName="width" from="10" to="250"/>
```

by the syntax

```
begin="PinkAnim.begin+2s"
```

meaning that the animation starts relative to the element identified by the id attribute of value PinkAnim—more specifically, two seconds after that animation begins. Figure 08.10 shows the animation part completed.

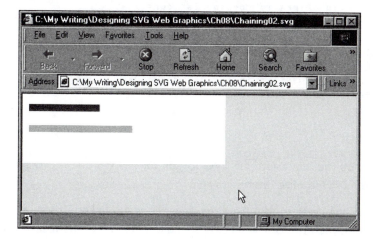

Figure 08.10

Because the animation of the top rectangle starts two seconds after the lower one begins, the top rectangle is smaller during much of the animation.

Similarly, you can add another animation that is started relative to the end of the PinkAnim animation, by using this code:

```
<rect id="YellowRect" x="10" y="75" width="10"
height="10" style="fill:#FFFF00;">
<animate begin="PinkAnim.end+2s" dur="10s"
attributeName="width" from="10" to="250"/>
</rect>
```

If you run the following listing, you see that the pink rectangle is animated two seconds after document loading is complete. Two seconds later, the maroon rectangle is animated; two seconds after that, the animation of the pink rectangle is completed, and two seconds after that the animation of the yellow rectangle begins.

Listing 8.17 (Chaining03.svg)

```
<?xml version="1.0" standalone="no"?>
<!DOCTYPE svg PUBLIC "-//W3C//DTD SVG 1.0//EN"
     "http://www.w3.org/TR/2001/PR-SVG-20010719/
       DTD/svg10.dtd">
```

```
<svg width="300" height="100">
<rect id="MaroonRect" x="10" y="15" width="10"
height="10" style="fill:#990066;">
<animate begin="PinkAnim.begin+2s" dur="10s"
attributeName="width" from="10" to="250"/>
</rect>
<rect id="PinkRect" x="10" y="45" width="10"
height="10" style="fill:pink;">
<animate id="PinkAnim" begin="2s" dur="10s"
attributeName="width" from="10" to="250"/>
</rect>
<rect id="YellowRect" x="10" y="75" width="10"
height="10" style="fill:#FFFF00;">
<animate begin="PinkAnim.end+2s" dur="10s"
attributeName="width" from="10" to="250"/>
</rect>
</svg>
```

In case you are interested, the SVG jargon for `PinkAnim.end` is syncbase, and the `2s` is the offset from it.

To modify the code so that the three animations are linked in sequence, you use as the syncbase for the second animation the end of the first one, and use as the syncbase for the third animation the end of the second. This process is implemented in the following code. I don't want you to get obsessed with the visual impact of changing the width of rectangles; rather, I want you to consider the power that is available if you chain animations in this way.

Listing 8.18 (Chaining04.svg)

```
<?xml version="1.0" standalone="no"?>
<!DOCTYPE svg PUBLIC "-//W3C//DTD SVG 1.0//EN"
     "http://www.w3.org/TR/2001/PR-SVG-20010719/
        DTD/svg10.dtd">
<svg width="300" height="100">
<rect id="MaroonRect" x="10" y="15" width="10"
height="10"
style="fill:#990066;">
<animate id="MaroonAnim" begin="PinkAnim.end"
dur="5s" attributeName="width" from="10"
to="250"/>
</rect>
<rect id="PinkRect" x="10" y="45" width="10"
height="10" style="fill:pink;">
```

```
<animate id="PinkAnim" begin="2s" dur="5s"
attributeName="width" from="10"
to="250"/>
</rect>
<rect id="YellowRect" x="10" y="75" width="10"
height="10"
style="fill:#FFFF00;">
<animate id="YellowAnim" begin="MaroonAnim.end"
dur="5s" attributeName="width" from="10"
to="250"/>
</rect>
</svg>
```

Look at how you can develop this idea further. Notice that the yellow rectangle has an `id` attribute on its nested `<animate>` element. To link a fourth animation to the chain is a straightforward process: Just reference `YellowAnim.end` as the syncbase. If that fourth animation has an `id` attribute, you can easily add a fifth.

Can you also see how you can use this concept to create and exploit animation visual components?

As far as the "fourth" animation is concerned, the only thing it sees is the end of the `YellowAnim` animation. What comes before that is immaterial. The three linked animations are essentially an animated visual component, as far as the fourth animation is concerned. At its simplest level, you can link a further animation, which can be simple or complex, into the end of the `YellowAnim` animation. But nothing stops you from linking it instead to the `MaroonAnim` animation, or to the `PinkAnim` animation. So your simple animation could have three different animation paths as spinoffs from this simple start.

Determining multiple times to begin an animation

So far, you have looked at just using one value for the `begin` attribute of an `<animate>` element. However, SVG allows you to use a list of them. Make use of that facility by modifying the code for the pink rectangle, like this:

```
<rect id="PinkRect" x="10" y="45" width="10"
height="10" style="fill:pink;">
<animate id="PinkAnim" begin="2s; YellowAnim.end"
dur="5s" attributeName="width" from="10"
to="250"/>
</rect>
```

Notice that the `begin` attribute of the `<animate>` element has a value of `2s; YellowAnim.end`. It contains a list of values. The first value indicates that the pink rectangle is animated two seconds after the document finishes loading. The second value indicates that the pink rectangle is animated when the yellow rectangle has finished its animation. You have therefore created a looping animation, by chaining the first animation to the end of the third.

The ordering of the individual values within the `values` attribute is immaterial. You can insert additional values that should occur early after other values without causing any error, always assuming that you remember to separate individual values by semicolons inserted in the correct place.

To put these two ideas together, you can create a sequence of three animations. At the end of any of the individual animations, you can spin off other animations. In addition, you can loop back to the beginning of the first animation, creating a looping animation. Whenever the animations are as simple as those with the rectangles, this process isn't spectacular; if you apply your creativity, however, to create more sophisticated animation, perhaps involving color changes or animated gradients, for example, you can begin to glimpse the potential creative power available to you.

You can add another dimension to this process. What if the start of the animations are triggered by user events? What if by mousing part of an SVG image or clicking on a particular part, you can create a cascade of chained animations—perhaps some of which loop too? Can you see the huge potential here? Don't worry if your brain is aching at the practical difficulties in visualizing, planning, and coding all that material—just allow yourself to take a look at the potential power of it.

In the final example in this section I have cheated a bit. Interaction isn't covered until Chapter 11, "Creating Interactive SVG Graphics," so I don't explain the code for the interactive animations here (although you should be able to work it out if you have been following this discussion). I simply describe what it does. I have removed the starting point at two seconds after the document loads. To start the chain reaction (forgive the pun), you need to either mouse over the maroon or yellow squares or click on the pink one (as in Figure 08.11. Before you do anything, the screen looks something like this:

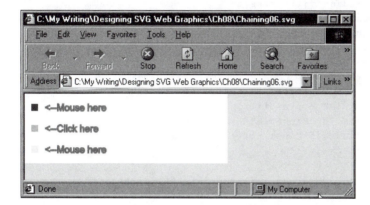

Figure 08.11

The appearance of Listing 8.19 before any of the small squares is activated by mousing or clicking.

Start by mousing or clicking a single square and following the chain of animations from one rectangle to another to convince yourself that, after they're started, they work as they previously did.

After you have done that, explore a little of how things have become more complex. If you mouse two squares with a little time between, you start two animations. In fact, you will have started four animations, including the two that hide the text <--Mouse here. The total animation you see depends on the relative times of when you mouse or click the relevant squares (see Figure 08.12).

Listing 8.19 (Chaining06.svg)

```
<?xml version="1.0" standalone="no"?>
<!DOCTYPE svg PUBLIC "-//W3C//DTD SVG 1.0//EN"
     "http://www.w3.org/TR/2001/PR-SVG-20010719/
      DTD/svg10.dtd">
<svg width="300" height="100">
<rect id="MaroonRect" x="10" y="15" width="10"
height="10"
style="fill:#990066;">
```

```
<animate id="MaroonAnim" begin="PinkAnim.end;
mouseover" dur="5s" attributeName="width" from="10"
to="250"/>
</rect>
<text x="30" y="25" style="fill:red; stroke:red;
font-size:14">
<animate begin="MaroonAnim.begin" dur="0.1s"
attributeName="visibility" from="visible"
to="hidden" fill="freeze"/>
<animate begin="MaroonAnim.end" dur="0.1s"
attributeName="visibility" from="hidden"
to="visible" fill="freeze"/>
&lt;--Mouse here
</text>
<rect id="PinkRect" x="10" y="45" width="10"
height="10" style="fill:pink;">
<animate id="PinkAnim" begin="YellowAnim.end;
click" dur="5s" attributeName="width" from="10"
to="250"/>
</rect>
<text x="30" y="55" style="fill:red; stroke:red;
font-size:14">
<animate begin="PinkAnim.begin" dur="0.1s"
attributeName="visibility" from="visible" to="hidden"
fill="freeze"/>
<animate begin="PinkAnim.end" dur="0.1s"
attributeName="visibility" from="hidden"
to="visible" fill="freeze"/>
&lt;--Click here
</text>
<rect id="YellowRect" x="10" y="75" width="10"
height="10"
style="fill:#FFFF00;">
<animate id="YellowAnim" begin="MaroonAnim.end;
mouseover" dur="5s" attributeName="width" from="10"
to="250"/>
</rect>
<text x="30" y="85" style="fill:red; stroke:red;
font-size:14">
<animate begin="YellowAnim.begin" dur="0.1s"
attributeName="visibility" from="visible" to="hidden"
fill="freeze"/>
<animate begin="YellowAnim.end" dur="0.1s"
attributeName="visibility" from="hidden" to="visible"
fill="freeze"/>
&lt;--Mouse here
</text>
</svg>
```

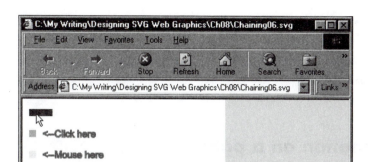

Figure 08.12

The animation shortly after the maroon (top) rectangle has been moused.

The more sensible or practical use is probably to allow, for example, multiple entry points into an animation. That could be a slide show, and, by mousing some visual cue for where you want to start, you can avoid repeating material you have already seen.

Or apply this in an SVG game? I leave creating that to you. You need to return from these flights of enjoyable creative fancy to consider some of the other SVG animation elements.

The <animateMotion> Element

The purpose of the `<animateMotion>` element is to create an animation along a path. The following code creates an animation where a circle traces the shape of a rectangle four times.

Listing 8.20 (AnimPath00.svg)

```
<?xml version="1.0" standalone="no"?>
<!DOCTYPE svg PUBLIC "-//W3C//DTD SVG 1.0//EN"
     "http://www.w3.org/TR/2001/PR-SVG-20010719/
      DTD/svg10.dtd">
<svg>
<circle cx="0" cy="0" r="5" style="fill:red;
stroke:red;">
```

```
<animateMotion path="M50,50 150,50 150,100 50,100 z"
dur="5s"
        repeatCount="4" />
</circle>
</svg>
```

Animation on a path

One of the most compelling types of animation is animation on a path. The path along which the animation can take place is any path that can be expressed in SVG, which leaves enormous scope for creativity.

Let's continue with a further example so that you can understand how to construct more visually exciting animations at a later stage. The animation whose source code is shown next is a small, red circle traveling along a semicircular path over a period of six seconds (see Figure 08.13).

Listing 8.21 (AnimPath01.svg)

```
<?xml version="1.0" standalone="no"?>
<!DOCTYPE svg PUBLIC "-//W3C//DTD SVG 1.0//EN"
        "http://www.w3.org/TR/2001/PR-SVG-20010719/
         DTD/svg10.dtd">
<svg width="500" height="300">
<path d="M100,250 C 100,50 400,50 400,250"
style="fill:none; stroke:#00FF00; stroke-width:5" />
<circle x="100" y="50" r="10" style="fill:red;">
<animateMotion dur="6s" repeatCount="indefinite"
path="M100,250 C 100,50 400,50 400,250" />
</circle>
</svg>
```

As you can see if you have loaded the code, the animation starts immediately after the SVG image is loaded. If I had wanted to delay the start of the animation, I could have added a `begin` attribute to the `<animateMotion>` element. Similarly, if you had wanted the animation to occur only once, you could have added to the `<animateMotion>` element a `fill` attribute with a value of `freeze`.

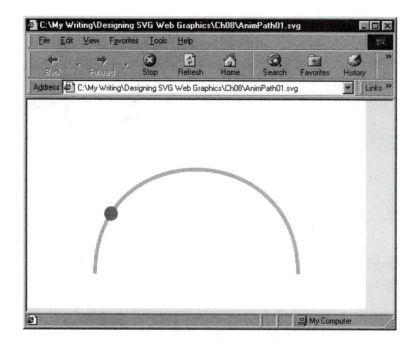

Figure 08.13

Animation of a circle along a path.

You can animate the circle, or any other SVG element or element grouping, along more complex paths. In the following example, the circle travels along a sinuous curve across the screen. The `<path>` element creates a visible red path that is drawn onscreen. The `path` attribute of the `<animateMotion>` element has the same values; therefore, the circle appears to travel along the curving red line (as shown in Figure 08.14).

Listing 8.22 (AnimPath02.svg)

```
<?xml version="1.0" standalone="no"?>
<!DOCTYPE svg PUBLIC "-//W3C//DTD SVG 1.0//EN"
     "http://www.w3.org/TR/2001/PR-SVG-20010719/
      DTD/svg10.dtd">
<svg width="1000" height="300">
<path d="M100,250
C200,100 300,0 400,80
C500,150 600,300 700,200
C800,100 900,0 1000,100"
style="stroke:red;fill:none;stroke-width:2;"/>
<circle x="100" y="250" r="10" style="fill:red;">
<animateMotion dur="10s" path="M100,250
C200,100 300,0 400,80
```

```
C500,150 600,300 700,200
C800,100 900,0 1000,100" repeatCount="indefinite"/>
</circle>
</svg>
```

Figure 08.14

A circle partway
through an animation
along a sinuous
path.

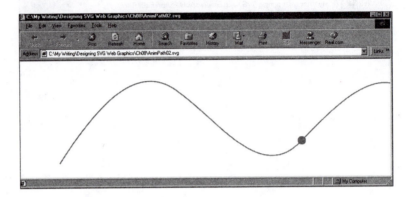

If you run the code and look carefully at the animation, you see that the circle is nicely centered on the curve, as you can see in Figure 08.14. However, if you alter the code so that a rectangle follows the same path:

Listing 8.23 (AnimPath03.svg)

```
<?xml version="1.0" standalone="no"?>
<!DOCTYPE svg PUBLIC "-//W3C//DTD SVG 1.0//EN"
    "http://www.w3.org/TR/2001/PR-SVG-20010719/
    DTD/svg10.dtd">
<svg width="1000" height="300">
<path d="M100,250
C200,100 300,0 400,80
C500,150 600,300 700,200
C800,100 900,0 1000,100"
style="stroke:red;fill:none;stroke-width:2;"/>
<rect x="0" y="0" width="20" height="20"
style="fill:red;">
<animateMotion dur="10s" path="M100,250
C200,100 300,0 400,80
C500,150 600,300 700,200
C800,100 900,0 1000,100" repeatCount="indefinite"/>
</rect>
</svg>
```

you find that it looks okay at some parts of the animation and that, at other points, the rectangle hangs off the curve rather untidily by its upper-left corner. The circle is placed symmetrically on the curve because the circle's center is the reference point for the cx and cy attributes. For the rectangle, on the other hand, the upper-left corner is referenced by the x and y attributes.

However, that problem is easily fixed. Simply change the x and y attributes to a negative number that is half the width and height, respectively:

```
<rect x="-10" y="-10" width="20" height="20"
style="fill:red;">
<animateMotion dur="10s" path="M100,250
C200,100 300,0 400,80
C500,150 600,300 700,200
C800,100 900,0 1000,100" repeatCount="indefinite"/>
</rect>
```

and the rectangle is then symmetrically displayed. The amended code is included in the listing as AnimPath04.svg.

When you want to create an animation along a path, however, you probably don't use something as symmetrical as a circle or rectangle. Also, you might want the SVG object being animated to "point" along the direction of a path. Suppose that you have plans to create a simulation of a fairground ride. The rectangle stays upright all the time, which doesn't look realistic with a vehicle to follow the track. You need to add a `rotate` attribute with the value of `auto`; then, you find that the rectangle follows the curve in a much more lifelike manner.

Listing 8.24 (AnimPath05.svg)

```
<?xml version="1.0" standalone="no"?>
<!DOCTYPE svg PUBLIC "-//W3C//DTD SVG 1.0//EN"
       "http://www.w3.org/TR/2001/PR-SVG-20010719/
       DTD/svg10.dtd">
<svg width="1000" height="300">
<path d="M100,250
C200,100 300,0 400,80
C500,150 600,300 700,200
C800,100 900,0 1000,100"
style="stroke:red;fill:none;stroke-width:2;"/>
<rect x="-20" y="-10" width="40" height="20"
style="fill:red;">
<animateMotion dur="10s" path="M100,250
```

```
c200,100 300,0 400,80
c500,150 600,300 700,200
c800,100 900,0 1000,100" repeatCount="indefinite"
rotate="auto"/>
</rect>
</svg>
```

You can use a similar technique when you are animating vehicles or a spacecraft or other creative mobile objects along a path.

Scrolling text using <animateMotion>

You can use the `<animateMotion>` element to create scrolling text. Look at an example I used in the SVGSpider.com Web site. If you look at Page03.svg on the site, you might recognize where this example was used.

The following code displays three separate text animations, each using `<animateMotion>` elements and each animated independently. Two of the pieces of text are animated from right to left, and the third is animated from left to right:

Listing 8.25 (MultiScrollingText.svg)

```
<?xml version='1.0'?>
<!DOCTYPE svg PUBLIC "-//W3C//DTD SVG 1.0//EN"
    "http://www.w3.org/TR/2001/PR-SVG-20010719/
    DTD/svg10.dtd">
<svg width="800" height="600" >
<rect x="0" y="0" width="800" height="100"
style="fill:#ccccff;"/>
<svg x="250" width="300" height="100"
zoomAndPan="disable">
<rect x="0" y="0" width="300" height="100"
style="fill:white;"/>
<text style="font-family:serif; stroke:red; fill:red;
font-size:16;">
Aren't Scalable Vector Graphics wonderful?
  <animateMotion path="M 400 90 L -300 90"
  begin="0s" dur="12s" repeatCount="indefinite" />
</text>
<text style="font-family:serif; stroke:green;
fill:green; font-size:36;
font-weight:bold;">
```

```
SVG
  <animateMotion begin="4s" path="M -300 70 L 400 70"
  dur="12s" repeatCount="indefinite"/>
</text>
<a xlink:href="http://www.svgenius.com/" target="new">
<text y="-5" style="font-family:sans-serif;
stroke:orange; fill:orange; font-size:20;">
Experimental SVG at SVGenius.com
  <animateMotion begin="2s" path="M 400 30 L -300 30"
  dur="12s" repeatCount="indefinite"/>
</text>
</a>
<rect height="300" width="50" x="0" y="0"
style="opacity:0.3; fill:white;
color:white;"/>
<rect height="300" width="50" x="250" y="0"
style="opacity:0.3; fill:white;
color:white;"/>
<rect x="0" y="0" width="300" height="100"
style="stroke:#000066;
stroke-width:2; fill:none;"/>
</svg>
<rect width="800" height="2" x="0" y="98"
style="stroke:#003399;fill:#003399"/>
</svg>
```

This code produces an animation onscreen, which is captured as shown in Figure 08.15.

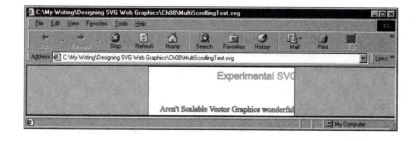

Figure 08.15

Two of the three lines of scrolling text are visible onscreen.

If you are wondering what the following lines in the code do, they add a slight masking effect to the early and late parts of the visual animation:

```
<rect height="300" width="50" x="0" y="0"
style="opacity:0.3; fill:white;
color:white;"/>
```

```
<rect height="300" width="50" x="250" y="0"
style="opacity:0.3; fill:white;
color:white;"/>
```

You can use colors other than white and vary the opacity to achieve a desirable effect:

```
<rect height="300" width="50" x="0" y="0"
style="opacity:0.4; fill:#9999FF;
color:white;"/>
<rect height="300" width="50" x="250" y="0"
style="opacity:0.4; fill:#9999FF;
color:white;"/>
```

Make sure to change the fill color of the background `<rect>` element to match. In these examples, I used a plain fill for these masking rectangles, but you could use a `<linearGradient>` element to create a graduated mask. Of course, you could use shapes other than a `<rect>` element.

The <animateColor> Element

The `<animateColor>` element allows you to change the color of an SVG element or element group over time.

Now create a simple color animation of the color of some text. The following code animates the fill of the text `Chameleon SVG` from red to black (see Figure 08.16). The animation starts two seconds after the image loads, takes six seconds for the color transition, and is frozen with the new color properties (both the fill and the stroke are black when the animation finishes).

Listing 8.26 (ChamText01.svg)

```
<?xml version="1.0" standalone="no"?>
<!DOCTYPE svg PUBLIC "-//W3C//DTD SVG 1.0//EN"
    "http://www.w3.org/TR/2001/PR-SVG-20010719/
    DTD/svg10.dtd">
<svg>
<text x="50" y="80" style="fill:red; stroke:black;
font-family:Arial, sans-serif; font-size:72;">
```

```
Chameleon SVG
<animateColor attributeName="fill" attributeType="CSS"
from="rgb(255,0,0)" to="rgb(0,0,0)"
begin="2s" dur="6s" fill="freeze" />
</text>
</svg>
```

Figure 08.16

The color animation of the fill of the text is completed.

The `<animateColor>` attribute uses the `from` and `to` attributes, which you saw earlier in this chapter. The values of the `fill` attribute of the `<text>` element that is being animated can be expressed as `rgb(255,0,0)` or as `#FF0000` or as a named color—red. Notice too the addition of the `attributeType` attribute in the `<animateColor>` element, which specifies that the property to be animated is a CSS property.

The <animateTransform> Element

In this section, I introduce you to the `<animateTransform>` element. SVG transformations are some of the most complex parts of SVG; in the space available in this chapter, I introduce you to some of the more commonly used animations.

When I first started using animated transformations, I sometimes had difficulty holding all the detail in my head, which would allow me to adequately visualize what any tweaking I did to my code would do. With practice, that feeling of lack of control fairly quickly disappears. Don't be surprised if, for one or two of these transformations, you don't pick it up immediately.

Rotation Using <animateTransform>

Take a look at a simple rotation, using a grouping `<g>` element you used in an example in Chapter 3, "Creating Static Graphics Elements." The rotation turns the rectangle through 360 degrees in a 9-second period, using its upper-left corner as the pivot point. The code for the transformation is shown here:

```
<animateTransform begin="1s" dur="10s" type="rotate"
from="0 150 150" to="360 150 150"
attributeName="transform"/>
```

You should be familiar with the meaning of the `begin` and `dur` attributes. You must specify the `attributeName` property (in this case, `transform`) and the `type` attribute (in this case, `rotate`). Notice that the `from` attribute contains three values, separated by spaces: `0 150 150`. The first number is the starting position in degrees, meaning that it has its normal upright position. The second number is the `x` coordinate of the pivot point for the rotation, and the third number is the `y` coordinate of the pivot point.

The `to` attribute, similarly, contains three figures. The first is the number, in degrees, for the position of the rectangle at the end of the animation. Of course, 360 degrees looks the same as 0 degrees; during the period of the animation, however, the rectangle is rotated smoothly through 360 degrees (from 0 degrees to 360 degrees) over a period of nine seconds. As with the `from` attribute, the second and third numbers of the `to` attribute describe, respectively, the `x` and `y` coordinates of the pivot point (se Figure 08.17).

If you take time to run the code, you see that the rotation is smooth and doesn't change in speed throughout the animation, similar to the second hand on a watch. Here is the full code:

Listing 8.27 (Rotation01.svg)

```
<?xml version="1.0" standalone="no"?>
<!DOCTYPE svg PUBLIC "-//W3C//DTD SVG 1.0//EN"
    "http://www.w3.org/TR/2001/PR-SVG-20010719/
    DTD/svg10.dtd">
```

```
<svg xmlns:xlink="http://www.w3.org/1999/xlink">
<g>
<animateTransform begin="1s" dur="10s" type="rotate"
from="0 150 150" to="360 150 150"
attributeName="transform"/>
<rect x="150" y="150" width="300" height="68"
style="fill:#DDDDFF; stroke:none">
</rect>
<line x1="150" x2="450" y1="152" y2="152"
xlink:href="#MyLine"/>
<line x1="150" x2="450" y1="154" y2="154"
xlink:href="#MyLine" style="fill:red;"/>
<line x1="150" x2="450" y1="156" y2="156"
xlink:href="#MyLine"/>
</g>
</svg>
```

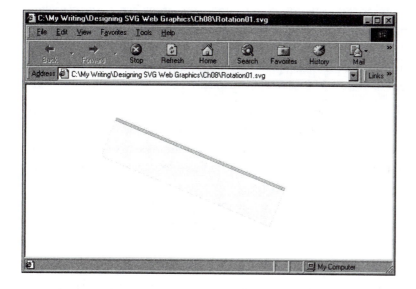

Figure 08.17

A rotate animation of a rectangle, early in the animation.

Now you move on to create a slightly more complex rotation transformation. Although I walk you through the code and describe in detail what is happening, if you are going to be able to figure all this out, you need to run the code.

You use a similar rectangle, but animate it in a more complex way. The most important part of the code is the `<animateTransform>` element, so first look at it in isolation:

```
<animateTransform begin="0s" dur="12s"
attributeName="transform" type="rotate"
values="0 150 150; -180 150 150; 180 150 150;
 360 150 150"
additive="sum" accumulate="none" calcMode="linear"
fill="remove" />
```

The begin and dur attributes should be familiar to you by now. The animation lasts 12 seconds. As shown in the preceding rotation, you have an attributeName attribute with a value of transform and a type attribute with a value of rotate. The values attribute at first sight looks complex, so let me break it down to make it easier to understand. The first three figures are the same as shown in the preceding example and describe the starting point of the animation—a rectangle that is right side up. The second group of three numbers represents the position of the rectangle at the end of four seconds (one-third of the way through the animation). At four seconds, the rectangle is rotated, anticlockwise, by 180 degrees, which is what the -180 means. The rotation is around the x and y coordinates of 150 and 150, respectively.

The next four seconds are defined by 180 150 150, which means that the rectangle at the end of eight seconds is again upside down (as it was after four seconds), but has traveled from -180 degrees to +180 degrees in those four seconds. In other words, in those four seconds, the rectangle rotates 360 degrees clockwise. At four seconds, you see the rectangle switch from an anticlockwise rotation to a clockwise rotation. In addition, you might notice that from four to eight seconds, the rotation is twice as fast as before.

The final set of figures, 0 150 150, tells you that at 12 seconds the rectangle is back where it started—upright. During the final 4 seconds, it rotates from 180 degrees to 0 degrees (clockwise), which is slower than the 360 degrees clockwise in the preceding 4 seconds. Just as the rectangle swings past the horizontal at 8 seconds, you should be able to see a distinct slowing in pace.

Maybe you are wondering how I could be sure that the contents in the values attribute refer to the positions at 0, 4, 8, and 12 seconds. I knew that because the calcMode attribute had a value of linear, which means that equal steps exist between the values in the values attribute.

If you add an extra set of three values to the `values` attribute, you see the positions at 0, 3, 6, 9, and 12 seconds.

Here is the full code:

Listing 8.28 (Rotation02.svg)

```
<?xml version="1.0" standalone="no"?>
<!DOCTYPE svg PUBLIC "-//W3C//DTD SVG 1.0//EN"
    "http://www.w3.org/TR/2001/PR-SVG-20010719/
    DTD/svg10.dtd">
<svg xmlns:xlink="http://www.w3.org/1999/xlink">
<defs>
<line id="MyLine" x1="150" x2="450" y1="150" y2="150"
style="fill:#000099;
stroke:#000099; stroke-width:0.05;"/>
</defs>
<g>
<animateTransform dur="12s" attributeName="transform"
type="rotate"
values="0 150 150; -180 150 150; 180 150 150; 360
150 150"
additive="sum" accumulate="none" calcMode="linear"
fill="remove" />
<rect x="150" y="150" width="300" height="68"
style="fill:#DDDDFF;
stroke:none"/>
<line x1="150" x2="450" y1="152" y2="152"
xlink:href="#MyLine"/>
<line x1="150" x2="450" y1="154" y2="154"
xlink:href="#MyLine"
style="fill:red;"/>
<line x1="150" x2="450" y1="156" y2="156"
xlink:href="#MyLine"/>
<use transform="translate(0,8)" xlink:href="#MyLine"/>
<use transform="translate(0,12)" xlink:href="#MyLine"
style="fill:red"/>
</g>
</svg>
```

If you want to create an endlessly repeating animation, you can modify the `<animateTransform>` element to look like this:

```
<animateTransform dur="12s" attributeName="transform"
type="rotate"
values="0 150 150; -180 150 150; 180 150 150; 360
150 150"
```

```
additive="sum" accumulate="none" calcMode="linear"
fill="remove" restart="always"
repeatCount="indefinite" />
<rect x="150" y="150" width="300" height="68"
style="fill:#DDDDFF;
stroke:none"/>
```

Note the addition of the `restart` and `repeatCount` attributes to the `<animateTransform>` element.

Simple Sample Animations

In this section, I show you a few examples of the ways in which you can apply SVG animations.

Animating gradients

Take a look again at the linear gradient you saw early in Chapter 6, "Creating SVG Gradients," and look at how you can animate it:

Listing 8.29 (AnimBasicLinGradient01.svg)

```
<?xml version="1.0" standalone="no"?>
<!DOCTYPE svg PUBLIC "-//W3C//DTD SVG 1.0//EN"
    "http://www.w3.org/TR/2001/PR-SVG-20010719/
    DTD/svg10.dtd">
<svg width="500" height="300">
<defs>
<linearGradient id="MyFirstGradient">
<stop offset="5%" style="stop-color:#FF6600"/>
<stop offset="95%" style="stop-color:#FFFFCC"/>
</linearGradient>
</defs>
<rect style="fill:none; stroke:red"
x="1" y="1" width="498" height="298"/>
<rect x="50" y="50" width="300" height="100"
style="fill:url(#MyFirstGradient); stroke:none"/>
</svg>
```

First, animate the pale yellow color that forms the right end of the gradient. To do that, you split the `<stop>` element into start and end tags and insert an `<animate>` element. You will choose to animate the color from pale yellow to deep blue, starting at three seconds, taking five seconds for the animation and allowing the animation to drop back to the original pale yellow color. You don't need to alter anything in the `<rect>` element because you are changing only the characteristics of the referenced fill:

```
<linearGradient id="MyFirstGradient">
<stop offset="5%" style="stop-color:#FF6600"/>
<stop offset="95%" style="stop-color:#FFFFCC">
<animate attributeName="stop-color" begin="3s"
dur="5s" from="#FFFFCC"
to="#000066"/>
</stop>
</linearGradient>
```

If you want to animate both ends of the gradient, you similarly add another `<animate>` element nested within the other `<stop>` element of the `<linearGradient>` element. In the following code, you alter the color from a reddish color to pale blue over the same period as the right end of the gradient is being animated (as shown in Figure 08.18).

Listing 8.30 (AnimBasicLinGradient02.svg)

```
<?xml version="1.0" standalone="no"?>
<!DOCTYPE svg PUBLIC "-//W3C//DTD SVG 1.0//EN"
    "http://www.w3.org/TR/2001/PR-SVG-20010719/
      DTD/svg10.dtd">
<svg width="500" height="300">
<defs>
<linearGradient id="MyFirstGradient">
<stop offset="5%" style="stop-color:#FF6600">
<animate attributeName="stop-color" begin="3s"
dur="5s" from="#FF6600" to="#CCCCFF"/>
</stop>
<stop offset="95%" style="stop-color:#FFFFCC">
<animate attributeName="stop-color" begin="3s"
dur="5s" from="#FFFFCC" to="#000066"/>
</stop>
</linearGradient>
</defs>
```

```
<rect style="fill:none; stroke:red"
x="1" y="1" width="498" height="298"/>
<rect x="50" y="50" width="300" height="100"
style="fill:url(#MyFirstGradient); stroke:none"/>
</svg>
```

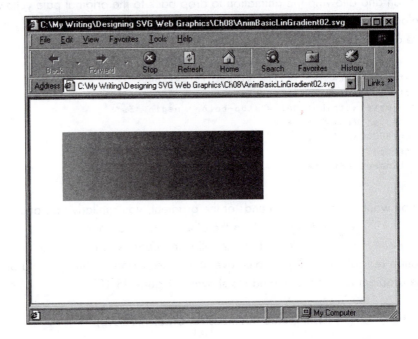

To see the effect of the animation, you need to run the code. By adjusting the relative timing of the two animations, you can create some interesting wave effects.

Animating across a gradient

In the preceding section, I showed you how to animate the gradient within a static SVG shape. You can also produce interesting color effects on an SVG shape if you animate it within a linear gradient. Run the following code, and watch how the color of the rectangle changes from deep pink to pale blue (as in Figure 08.19).

Listing 8.31 (AnimatedGradientRect01.svg)

```
<?xml version="1.0" standalone="no"?>
<!DOCTYPE svg PUBLIC "-//W3C//DTD SVG 1.0//EN"
    "http://www.w3.org/TR/2001/PR-SVG-20010719/
        DTD/svg10.dtd">
<svg width="800" height="600">
<defs>
<linearGradient id="MyBlueGradient"
gradientUnits="userSpaceOnUse"
x1="0" y1="50" x2="800" y2="50" >
<stop offset="10%" style="stop-color:#FF0066"/>
<stop offset="75%" style="stop-color:#EEEEFF"/>
</linearGradient>
</defs>
<rect x="0" y="200" width="100" height="100"
style="fill:url(#MyBlueGradient)">
<animate attributeName="x" begin="0s" dur="10s"
from="0" to="700" repeatCount="indefinite"/>
</rect>
</svg>
```

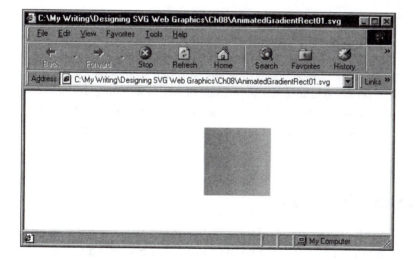

Figure 08.19

A rectangle partway through its animation across a gradient.

Against a white background, animating across a gradient can be an interesting effect, depending how you configure the gradient. Suppose that you modify the second stop color so that it is the same as the background color; you can obtain an interesting, dissolving animation using code like the following:

Listing 8.32 (AnimatedGradientRect02.svg)

```
<?xml version="1.0" standalone="no"?>
<!DOCTYPE svg PUBLIC "-//W3C//DTD SVG 1.0//EN"
     "http://www.w3.org/TR/2001/PR-SVG-20010719/
      DTD/svg10.dtd">
<svg width="800" height="600">
<defs>
<linearGradient id="MyBlueGradient"
gradientUnits="userSpaceOnUse"
x1="0" y1="50" x2="800" y2="50" >
<stop offset="10%" style="stop-color:#FF0066"/>
<stop offset="75%" style="stop-color:#EEEEFF"/>
</linearGradient>
</defs>
<rect x="0" y="0" width="100%" height="100%"
style="fill:#EEEEFF; stroke:#EEEEFF"/>
<rect x="0" y="200" width="100" height="100"
style="fill:url(#MyBlueGradient)">
<animate attributeName="x" begin="0s" dur="10s"
from="0" to="700" repeatCount="indefinite"/>
</rect>
</svg>
```

The important difference from the preceding code is that a background color in a `<rect>` element fills the whole space so that as the square animates, it seems to disappear into a veil of mist. Of course, by adjusting the `offset` attribute values of the `<stop>` elements or the values of the `stop-color` attributes, you can obtain more striking or more subtle effects to suit your needs.

Animating text

If you recall, in Chapter 4, "Using Text in SVG," you created a static box of text that I indicated would be used to display a scrolling text window. Now go on to create the scrolling text window by adding an appropriate animation visual component:

Listing 8.33 (TextWindowAnimation.svg)

```
<?xml version="1.0" standalone="no"?>
<!DOCTYPE svg PUBLIC "-//W3C//DTD SVG 1.0//EN"
```

```
      "http://www.w3.org/TR/2001/PR-SVG-20010719/
        DTD/svg10.dtd">
<svg width="200" height="200">
<svg x="0" y="0" width="200" height="200">
<rect x="0" y="0" width="200" height="200"
style="stroke:#990066; fill:none;"/>
<text>
<tspan x="5" y="25" style="font-size:14;
font-family:Arial, sans-serif; stroke:#990066; fill:#990066">
<animate attributeName="y" begin="2s" dur="20s"
from="225" to="-120" repeatCount="indefinite"/>
Scalable Vector Graphics
</tspan>
<tspan x="5" dy="2em" style="font-size:10;
font-family:Arial, sans-serif;">
The World Wide Web Consortium has
</tspan>
<tspan x="5" dy="1em" style="font-size:10;
font-family:Arial, sans-serif;">
announced the availability of its
</tspan>
<tspan x="5" dy="1em" style="font-size:10;
font-family:Arial, sans-serif;">
exciting new XML-based graphics
</tspan>
<tspan x="5" dy="1em" style="font-size:10;
font-family:Arial, sans-serif;">
format, SVG, for the display
</tspan>
<tspan x="5" dy="1em" style="font-size:10;
font-family:Arial, sans-serif;">
of 2D graphics, text and bitmap
</tspan>
<tspan x="5" dy="1em" style="font-size:10;
font-family:Arial, sans-serif;">
graphics.
</tspan>
<tspan x="5" dy="2em" style="font-size:10;
font-family:Arial, sans-serif;">
Further information is available
</tspan>
<tspan x="5" dy="1em" style="font-size:10;
font-family:Arial, sans-serif;">
at the W3C web site,
</tspan>
<tspan x="5" dy="2em" style="font-size:10;
font-family:Arial, sans-serif; fill:blue; stroke:blue">
```

```
http://www.w3.org/
</tspan>
</text>
</svg>
</svg>
```

Notice that only one `<animate>` element is in the code, although it has many lines of text. When the first `<tspan>` element is animated under control of the `<animate>` element, the subsequent `<tspan>` elements are repositioned because their vertical position is defined by the `dy` attribute. When the first `<tspan>` moves up, the following `<tspan>` elements also move up to keep the vertical separation at the correct distance. Figure 08.20 illustrates this.

Figure 08.20

Scrolling text in the text window.

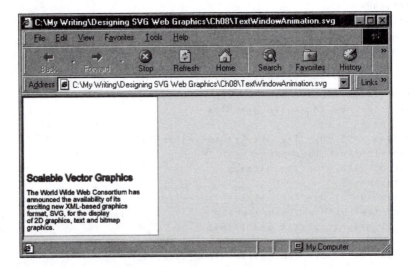

You have colored the text referring to http://www.w3.org `blue`, implying that you can link from the scrolling text. To add that functionality, simply nest the final `<tspan>` element within an `<a>` element with an appropriate value for the `xlink:href` attribute:

```
<a xlink:href="http://www.w3.org">
<tspan x="5" dy="2em" style="font-size:10;
font-family:Arial, sans-serif;
fill:blue; stroke:blue">
http://www.w3.org/
</tspan>
</a>
```

Similarly, if you want to link the heading Scalable Vector Graphics directly to the SVG page at W3C and open that linked page in a new window, you can add this section earlier in the code:

```
<a xlink:href="http://www.w3.org/Graphics/
SVG/Overview.htm8" target="new">
<tspan x="5" y="25" style="font-size:14;
font-family:Arial, sans-serif;
stroke:#990066; fill:#990066">
<animate attributeName="y" begin="2s" dur="20s"
  from="225" to="-120"
repeatCount="indefinite"/>
Scalable Vector Graphics
</tspan>
</a>
```

Animating horizontal scrolling text

Scrolling text horizontally is also a fairly straightforward process, so you can produce ticker-tape-like effects.

The following code could form the top "frame" on a Web page, with the window on the ticker tape the size of a standard banner ad. A ticker tape like this one could be used for banner ads, news updates, and weather information, for example.

Listing 8.34 (TickerTape01.svg)

```
<?xml version="1.0" standalone="no"?>
<!DOCTYPE svg PUBLIC "-//W3C//DTD SVG 1.0//EN"
     "http://www.w3.org/TR/2001/PR-SVG-20010719/
     DTD/svg10.dtd">
<svg width="800" height="100">
<rect x="0" y="0" width="800" height="100"
style="fill:#CCFFCC;"/>
<svg x="166" y="20" width="468" height="60">
<rect x="0" y="0" width="100%" height="100%"
style="fill:white; stroke:none;"/>
<a xlink:href="mailto://Consulting@xmml.com">
<text x="700" y="40" style="stroke:green; fill:green;
font-family:Courier, monospace; font-size:20;
  font-weight:normal;">
```

```
XMML.com now provides consulting services on XML,
SVG, XSL-FO, XLink and XForms. Click here to email us.
<animate attributeName="x" from="600" to="-1000"
begin="0s" dur="20s"
repeatCount="indefinite"/>
</text>
</a>
<rect x="0" y="0" width="468" height="60"
style="stroke:#009900;
stroke-width:2; fill:none;"/>
</svg>
</svg>
```

When you are creating a ticker tape, you can easily overlook the need to scroll the text right out of its window. Notice that I have not taken the animation quite far enough to the left (see Figure 08.21). To provide a tidy end to the animation, you need to change the `to` attribute to have a value of `-1250`.

If the example is used as a banner ad, you want users to be able to link to another Web site or to send an email message for information—hence, the presence of the `<a>` element around the `<text>` element.

Figure 08.21

Scrolling text in
a ticker tape
animation.

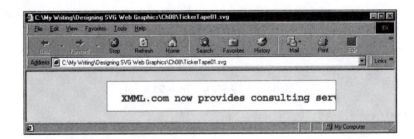

Altering text color

In Chapter 5, "Creating Navigation Bars," I showed you step-wise changes of color on mouseover and mouseout. However, SVG can also produce much more gradual color changes. For example, in Listing 8.35 you can examine a color change sequence that uses the `values` and `keyTimes` attributes on the `<animateColor>` element to animate color values of text over time:

Listing 8.35 (ColorAnimation01.svg)

```
<?xml version="1.0" standalone="no"?>
<!DOCTYPE svg PUBLIC "-//W3C//DTD SVG 1.0//EN"
    "http://www.w3.org/TR/2001/PR-SVG-20010719/
    DTD/svg10.dtd">
<svg width="300" height="100">
<rect x="0" y="0" width="100%" height="100%"
style="fill:#EEEEEE" />
<text x="20" y="40" style="fill:red; stroke:none;
font-family:Arial, sans-serif; font-size:36;">
<animateColor attributeName="fill" begin="0s"
values="red; white; blue; red" keyTimes="2s; 7s;
10s; 15s" dur="15s" repeatCount="indefinite"/>
SVGenius.com
</text>
</svg>
```

Figure 08.22 shows the animated color moving from white to blue (see the `values` attribute in the code).

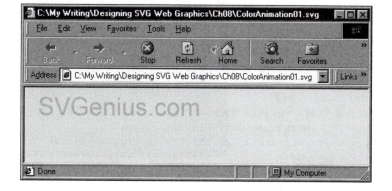

Figure 08.22

Part of a multistage color animation of text fill color.

Altering text opacity

Sometimes, you might want some text to fade gently into view or fade quietly into the sunset. By now, you probably have worked out how to create this effect, but let me give you a couple of examples.

The first example simply makes a simple piece of text visible over a period of ten seconds.

Listing 8.36 (AnimOpacityInText00.svg)

```
<?xml version="1.0" standalone="no"?>
<!DOCTYPE svg PUBLIC "-//W3C//DTD SVG 1.0//EN"
    "http://www.w3.org/TR/2001/PR-SVG-20010719/
    DTD/svg10.dtd">
<svg width="400" height="80">
<text x="20" y="50" style="font-family:Ventana,
Arial, sans-serif; font-size:20; stroke:red; fill:red">
<animate begin="0s" dur="10s" attributeName="opacity"
attributeType="CSS" from="0" to="1" fill="freeze"/>
SVG is truly dynamic and subtle!
</text>
</svg>
```

You might want a faster animation, and you might want it to repeat. You could, as shown in the following example, alter the `dur` attribute to four seconds and add a `repeatCount` attribute with value of `5`. If you want it to repeat indefinitely, you could change the value of the `repeatCount` attribute to `indefinite`.

Listing 8.37 (AnimOpacityInText01.svg)

```
<?xml version="1.0" standalone="no"?>
<!DOCTYPE svg PUBLIC "-//W3C//DTD SVG 1.0//EN"
    "http://www.w3.org/TR/2001/PR-SVG-20010719/
    DTD/svg10.dtd">
<svg width="400" height="80">
<text x="20" y="50" style="font-family:Ventana,
Arial, sans-serif; font-size:20; stroke:red; fill:red">
<animate begin="0s" dur="4s" attributeName="opacity"
attributeType="CSS" from="0" to="1"
fill="freeze" repeatCount="5"/>
SVG is truly dynamic and subtle!
</text>
</svg>
```

Another option is to create a chain of animations where an animation that makes text opaque when it finishes triggers a fade animation, which in turn triggers the first animation. In the following example, the duration of the animations gives a fairly subtle effect. By changing the duration of each animation to a shorter period, you can create a more dynamic (or intrusive) transition. The choice is yours. SVG gives you precise control so that you can change the animation to exactly the effect you want.

Listing 8.38 (AnimOpacityInText00.svg)

```
<?xml version="1.0" standalone="no"?>
<!DOCTYPE svg PUBLIC "-//W3C//DTD SVG 1.0//EN"
    "http://www.w3.org/TR/2001/PR-SVG-20010719/
     DTD/svg10.dtd">
<svg width="400" height="80">
<text x="20" y="50" style="font-family:Ventana, Arial,
sans-serif; font-size:20; stroke:red; fill:red">
<animate id="MakeVisible" begin="0s; MakeTransparent.end"
dur="4s" attributeName="opacity" attributeType="CSS"
from="0" to="1" fill="freeze" />
<animate id="MakeTransparent" begin="MakeVisible.end"
dur="8s" attributeName="opacity" attributeType="CSS"
from="1"
to="0" fill="freeze" />
SVG is truly dynamic and subtle!
</text>
</svg>
```

Animating opacity in a gradient

Now revisit one of the gradient examples and apply animations of the
`stop-opacity` properties of the gradient. After the animation is applied,
the code looks like this:

Listing 8.39 (AnimGradientOpacity01.svg)

```
<?xml version='1.0'?>
<!DOCTYPE svg PUBLIC "-//W3C//DTD SVG 1.0//EN"
    "http://www.w3.org/TR/2001/PR-SVG-20010719/
     DTD/svg10.dtd">
<svg width="800" height="600">
<defs>
<linearGradient id="MyBlueGradient"
gradientUnits="userSpaceOnUse" x1="0"
y1="0" x2="0" y2="100" >
<stop offset="10%" style="stop-color:#000066">
<animate begin="2s" attributeName="stop-opacity"
from="1" to="0" dur="3s" fill="freeze"/>
</stop>
<stop offset="75%" style="stop-color:#AAAADD">
<animate begin="5s" attributeName="stop-opacity"
from="1" to="0" dur="8s" fill="freeze"/>
```

```
</stop>
</linearGradient>
</defs>
<text x="50" y="70" style="font-family:Times, serif;
font-size:72;
fill:url(#MyBlueGradient);">
Hello SVG!
</text>
</svg>
```

As with many of the other animations in this chapter, the best way to appreciate what is going on is to run the code.

I have animated the `stop-opacity` property of both `<stop>` elements contained within the `<linearGradient>` element. Notice that I have set the duration of the first `<animate>` element to be three seconds, whereas the start time of the second animation is five seconds and its duration is eight seconds. These settings allow what is essentially a two-step fade of the text. During the first three seconds, the top part of the text fades noticeably. It doesn't fade completely because color is still being contributed to the top part of the text by the color defined in the second `<stop>` element. However, from five seconds onward, the opacity of the remaining color in the text fades slowly over an 8-second period.

You might not choose to use such slow fades. My main aim in this example is to show you that you can independently control the fade of different parts of a gradient. Of course, this same technique can be applied to other SVG elements, not just to text, and can also be applied to gradients that have multiple stop elements, not just two. The potential for subtle, controlled fades in SVG animations is enormous.

Listing 8.40 demonstrates an animation of a filter that uses the `<feTurbulence>` filter primitive.

Listing 8.40 (AnimTurbulence01.svg)

```
<?xml version="1.0" standalone="no"?>
<!DOCTYPE svg PUBLIC "-//W3C//DTD SVG 1.0//EN"
      "http://www.w3.org/TR/2001/PR-SVG-20010719/
        DTD/svg10.dtd">
<svg width="400" height="500">
<defs>
```

```
    <filter id="Turbulence1" in="SourceImage"
filterUnits="objectBoundingBox">
        <feTurbulence in="SourceAlpha" type="turbulence"
baseFrequency="0.01"
numOctaves="1" seed="0" >
<animate attributeName="baseFrequency"
values="0.01; 0.008; 0.01; 0.012; 0.01"
keyTimes="0s; 5s; 10s; 15s; 20s;"
begin ="0s" dur="20s" repeatCount="indefinite"/>
        </feTurbulence>
</filter>
</defs>
<rect x="0" y="0" width="400" height="500"
style="filter:url(#Turbulence1)"/>
</svg>
```

Figure 08.23 shows the visual appearance when `baseFrequency` has been animated to a value of approximately 0.008.

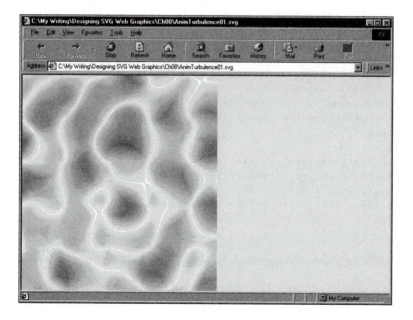

Figure 08.23

A turbulence filter primitive in the process of animation.

Listing 8.41 shows an animation of a complex of filter primitives that I adapted from an animation on the Adobe.com Web site. The visual appearance is approximately that of a floodlight scanning across some lettering over time.

Listing 8.41 (Spotlight.svg)

```
<?xml version="1.0" standalone="no"?>
<!DOCTYPE svg PUBLIC "-//W3C//DTD SVG 1.0//EN"
     "http://www.w3.org/TR/2001/PR-SVG-20010719/
        DTD/svg10.dtd">
<svg>
<defs>
<filter id="MySpot" x="-20%" y="-60%" width="150%"
height="300%" >
<feDiffuseLighting in="SourceGraphic"
lighting-color="red" result="lamp"
diffuseConstant=".8" surfaceScale="10"
resultScale=".2">
<feSpotLight
 x="200" y="150" z="15"
 pointsAtX="0" pointsAtY="100" pointsAtZ="0"
 specularExponent="10">
 <animate attributeName="pointsAtX"
values="0;100;400;100;0" begin="0s"
  dur="8s" repeatCount="indefinite"/>
      </feSpotLight>
    <animateColor attributeName="lighting-color"
values="yellow;white;red;white;yellow;"
    begin="0s" dur="8s" repeatCount="indefinite"/>
    </feDiffuseLighting>
    <feComposite in="lamp" result="lamp"
operator="arithmetic" k2="1" k3="1"/>
</filter>
</defs>
<text id="Spotlight" pointer-events="none"
style="fill:white; stroke-width:4;
stroke:white; font-size:80;
filter:url(#MySpot);" x="10" y="85">XMML.com</text>
</svg>
```

Figure 08.24 shows the "spotlight" partway through a scan of the lettering.

I hope that in this chapter I have succeeded in conveying to you a little of the exciting potential of SVG animations. I consciously have largely avoided using at this stage any animations that are interactive in nature (those are described in Chapter 11).

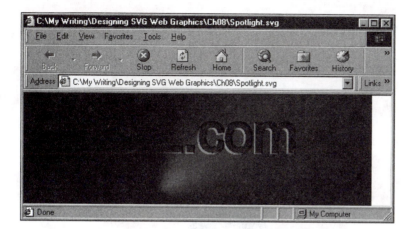

Figure 08.24

A complex animated SVG filter that looks like a spotlight playing across giant lettering.

If you have caught a glimpse of the enormous potential of SVG for producing subtle animations that go far beyond anything that is possible with bitmap graphics, please take time to experiment. The huge advantage of SVG is that you can examine how experts have produced animations that you find visually attractive or exciting. This is one of the reasons that I believe SVG will take off in a big way. I expect an explosion of interest and skills, just as there was with HTML, back in the early to mid-1990s. Of course, much more can be said about SVG animations, but that discussion needs to await another book dedicated to the topic.

9

Creating Logos
and Banner Ads

Creating Logos

In this chapter, you apply techniques you have learned in earlier chapters to produce some quasirealistic SVG Web page "furniture." My aim is primarily to show you how to use those techniques and apply them to your own graphics design needs.

If you have followed the earlier chapters sequentially, you should have a grasp of the essentials of the structure of an SVG document: SVG graphics shapes, text layout, SVG gradients, filters, and animations. Now that I have covered those key aspects of SVG, you are in a position to create semirealistic images and put combinations of those technologies to work.

Creating a logo for a customer is a common task of many graphics designers, so in this section you examine the creation of some possible logos using SVG that demonstrate the use of a variety of SVG elements.

Static logos

First, apply what you have learned so far by creating a number of static logos.

A logo reusing simple shapes

Create a simple logo using only `<text>` and `<rect>` elements for SVGenius.com. Assume that the Web page on which it will be placed has a black background, and use that in your logo too. When the logo is complete, it looks like Figure 09.01.

Figure 09.01

The completed logo.

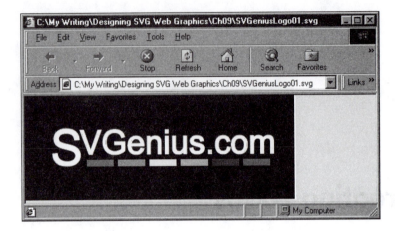

Now create the logo piece by piece. You want to place it on a Web page with a black background, so you need a black rectangle with exactly the same dimensions as the `<svg>` element to ensure that the default whitish background color of an SVG viewport is covered fully. You start with this code:

Listing 9.1 (SVGenius00.svg)

```
<?xml version="1.0" standalone="no"?>
<!DOCTYPE svg PUBLIC "-//W3C//DTD SVG 1.0//EN"
    "http://www.w3.org/TR/2001/PR-SVG-20010719/
      DTD/svg10.dtd">
<svg width="200" height="75">
<rect x="0" y="0" width="200" height="75"/>
</svg>
```

The rectangle is black because the default fill for an SVG graphic is black. If you want to express that explicitly, you could use

```
<rect x="0" y="0" width="200" height="75"
  style="fill:black; stroke:black;"/>
```

For purposes of this example, you don't have to be pixel perfect. Remember that because the stroke does take up some width, however, you might want to specify the stroke width as zero in other situations where precise placement is crucial.

Next, you want to add the text. You want a dropped initial capital, which is obviously a larger font size than the rest of the company name. Unfortunately, because SVG has no drop capitals option, you need to place the initial *S* in its own text element and adjust the `font-size` property and the `x` and `y` attributes to suit. The code for the text looks like this:

```
<text x="20" y="50" style="font-size:36; fill:white;
stroke:white;">S</text>
<text  x="42" y="42" style="font-size:24; fill:white;
stroke:white;">VGenius.com</text>
```

An alternative approach is to use one `<text>` element and two `<tspan>` elements nested within it.

Finally, you want to add the set of colored rectangles. Notice that you will use six rectangles that are identical in size. It makes sense, therefore, to define the basic rectangle in a `<rect>` element nested within the `<defs>` element, like this:

```
<defs>
<rect id="myLittleRect" width="20" height="5"/>
</defs>
```

Notice that you have added an `id` attribute of value `myLittleRect` so that you can reference this definition later, employing the SVG `<use>` element.

Having defined the size of the rectangle, you need to use it six times, not surprisingly employing the SVG `<use>` element to do so. The definition of the `<rect>` you will reuse gave its size, but specified nothing about its position or style, so you need to add `x` and `y` attributes to place the rectangles in appropriate places within the SVG graphic. You also need to style each rectangle to give the color progression you want:

```
<use x="47" y="46" xlink:href="#myLittleRect"
style="fill:red;"/>
<use x="70" y="46" xlink:href="#myLittleRect"
style="fill:#FF9900;"/>
<use x="93" y="46" xlink:href="#myLittleRect"
style="fill:#FFFF00;"/>
<use x="116" y="46" xlink:href="#myLittleRect"
```

```
style="fill:#66FF00;"/>
<use x="139" y="46" xlink:href="#myLittleRect"
style="fill:#3333FF;"/>
<use x="162" y="46" xlink:href="#myLittleRect"
style="fill:#CC00FF;"/>
```

Typically, in an SVG graphic, the ordering of elements can be quite important. In this example, the only important thing is to make sure that the large black `<rect>` comes first after the `<defs>` element, which ensures that it is the background on which everything else is placed. If you place the black rectangle later, it obscures some other part of the logo. If you place it last, every other part of the logo is covered and you see a plain black rectangle.

Putting all that together, the source code for the logo looks like this:

Listing 9.2 (SVGGeniusLogo01.svg)

```
<?xml version="1.0" standalone="no"?>
<!DOCTYPE svg PUBLIC "-//W3C//DTD SVG 1.0//EN"
     "http://www.w3.org/TR/2001/PR-SVG-20010719/
     DTD/svg10.dtd">
<svg width="200" height="75">
<defs>
<rect id="myLittleRect" width="20" height="5"/>
</defs>
<rect x="0" y="0" width="200" height="75"/>
<text x="20" y="50" style="font-size:36; fill:white;
stroke:white;">S</text>
<text   x="42" y="42" style="font-size:24; fill:white;
stroke:white;">VGenius.com</text>
<use x="47" y="46" xlink:href="#myLittleRect"
style="fill:red;"/>
<use x="70" y="46" xlink:href="#myLittleRect"
style="fill:#FF9900;"/>
<use x="93" y="46" xlink:href="#myLittleRect"
style="fill:#FFFF00;"/>
<use x="116" y="46" xlink:href="#myLittleRect"
style="fill:#66FF00;"/>
<use x="139" y="46" xlink:href="#myLittleRect"
style="fill:#3333FF;"/>
<use x="162" y="46" xlink:href="#myLittleRect"
style="fill:#CC00FF;"/>
</svg>
```

A logo using gradients

In this example, you use a couple of linear gradients to create two logos for XMML.com, one on a white background and the second on a black background. The finished version on a white background is shown in Figure 09.02.

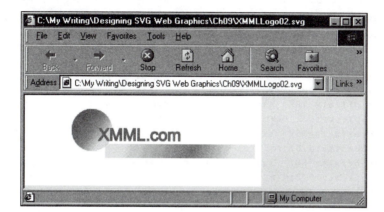

Figure 09.02

The logo for XMML.com on a white background produced using two linear gradients, one with graduated opacities.

First, create the circle with the diagonal linear gradient within it. The linear gradient needs to be defined so that the interesting part of the color transition takes place within the circle. After a little experimentation, you settle on the values for the x1, y1, x2, and y2 attributes shown in the code. To pull the deep pink up and to the left, for example, you could decrease the value of the x1 and y1 attributes.

Listing 9.3 (XMMLLogo01.svg)

```
<?xml version="1.0" standalone="no"?>
<!DOCTYPE svg PUBLIC "-//W3C//DTD SVG 1.0//EN"
      "http://www.w3.org/TR/2001/PR-SVG-20010719/
      DTD/svg10.dtd">
<svg width="350" height="130">
<defs>
<linearGradient id="MyBlueGradient"
gradientUnits="userSpaceOnUse"
x1="90" y1="0" x2="150" y2="50" >
<stop offset="10%" style="stop-color:#FF0066"/>
<stop offset="75%" style="stop-color:#EEEEFF"/>
</linearGradient>
</defs>
```

```
<ellipse cx="100" cy="50" rx="30" ry="30"
style="fill:url(#MyBlueGradient)">
</ellipse>
</svg>
```

Next, you create the horizontal bar with a similar linear gradient. However, because you want the linear gradient in the horizontal bar to have a different, more subtle appearance with varying opacities, you need to create another linear gradient and add that to the `<defs>` element:

```
<linearGradient id="MyOtherGradient"
gradientUnits="userSpaceOnUse" x1="120"
y1="40" x2="350" y2="120" >
<stop offset="10%" style="stop-color:#EEEEFF;
stop-opacity:0.2;"/>
<stop offset="55%" style="stop-color:#FF0066;
stop-opacity:0.5;"/>
<stop offset="80%" style="stop-color:#EEEEFF;
stop-opacity:0.2;"/>
</linearGradient>
```

The new linear gradient has three `<stop>` elements rather than two. You have to adjust the `x1`, `y1`, `x2`, and `y2` attributes on this gradient too, to obtain the visual effect you want. Then you create the rectangle that the linear gradient will be used to fill:

```
<rect x="120" y="70" width="220" height="20"
style="fill:url(#MyOtherGradient)"/>
```

Notice that the `stop-opacity` property for the first and third `<stop>` elements is set to 0.2. If it is set to 0.4, for example, the ends of the rectangle are still visible as squared-off ends, which isn't visually attractive. Reducing the stop-opacity below that gives, against a white background, a smooth fall-off in color.

Finally, you add the text to the logo, as you saw in Figure 09.02. The text should be placed late in the code because you want it to be displayed in front of the circle so that it overlaps it:

```
<text x="110" y="65" style="font-family:Arial,
sans-serif; font-size: 24;
fill:#FF0066; stroke:#FF0066">
XMML.com
</text>
```

Putting all that together, you can see in Listing 9.4 the code that produced Figure 09.02.

Listing 9.4 (XMMLLogo02.svg)

```
<?xml version="1.0" standalone="no"?>
<!DOCTYPE svg PUBLIC "-//W3C//DTD SVG 1.0//EN"
    "http://www.w3.org/TR/2001/PR-SVG-20010719/
    DTD/svg10.dtd">
<svg width="350" height="130">
<defs>
<linearGradient id="MyBlueGradient"
gradientUnits="userSpaceOnUse" x1="90"
y1="0" x2="150" y2="50" >
<stop offset="10%" style="stop-color:#FF0066"/>
<stop offset="75%" style="stop-color:#EEEEFF"/>
</linearGradient>
<linearGradient id="MyOtherGradient"
gradientUnits="userSpaceOnUse" x1="120"
y1="40" x2="350" y2="120" >
<stop offset="10%" style="stop-color:#EEEEFF;
stop-opacity:0.2;"/>
<stop offset="55%" style="stop-color:#FF0066;
stop-opacity:0.5;"/>
<stop offset="80%" style="stop-color:#EEEEFF;
stop-opacity:0.2;"/>
</linearGradient>
</defs>
<ellipse cx="100" cy="50" rx="30" ry="30"
style="fill:url(#MyBlueGradient)">
</ellipse>
<rect x="120" y="70" width="220" height="20"
style="fill:url(#MyOtherGradient)"/>
<text x="110" y="65" style="font-family:Arial,
sans-serif; font-size: 24;
fill:#FF0066; stroke:#FF0066">
XMML.com
</text>
</svg>
```

Suppose that you also want to explore the appearance of the logo against a black background. Simply adding a black background to Listing 9.5 leaves a fairly crude visual appearance, so you need to adjust the stop-opacity properties on both the circle and the rectangle.

The code for the logo against a black background is shown in Listing 9.5. The appearance of the logo against a black background is shown in Figure 09.03.

Listing 9.5 (XMMLLogo03.svg)

```
<?xml version="1.0" standalone="no"?>
<!DOCTYPE svg PUBLIC "-//W3C//DTD SVG 1.0//EN"
    "http://www.w3.org/TR/2001/PR-SVG-20010719/
        DTD/svg10.dtd">
<svg width="350" height="130">
<defs>
<linearGradient id="MyBlueGradient"
gradientUnits="userSpaceOnUse" x1="90"
y1="0" x2="150" y2="50" >
<stop offset="10%" style="stop-color:#FF0066;
stop-opacity:0.6"/>
<stop offset="75%" style="stop-color:#EEEEFF;
stop-opacity:0.8;"/>
</linearGradient>
<linearGradient id="MyOtherGradient"
gradientUnits="userSpaceOnUse" x1="120"
y1="40" x2="350" y2="120" >
<stop offset="10%" style="stop-color:#EEEEFF;
stop-opacity:0.2;"/>
<stop offset="55%" style="stop-color:#FF0066;
stop-opacity:0.7;"/>
<stop offset="80%" style="stop-color:#EEEEFF;
stop-opacity:0.2;"/>
</linearGradient>
</defs>
<rect width="100%" height="100%"/>
<ellipse cx="100" cy="50" rx="30" ry="30"
style="fill:url(#MyBlueGradient)">
</ellipse>
<rect x="120" y="70" width="220" height="20"
style="fill:url(#MyOtherGradient)"/>
<text x="110" y="65" style="font-family:Arial,
sans-serif; font-size: 24; fill:#FF0066;
stroke:#FF0066">
XMML.com
</text>
</svg>
```

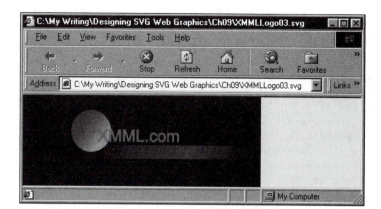

Figure 09.03

The XMML.com logo on a black background and following adjustments to the stop-opacity properties.

Animated logos

SVG offers an enormous range of possibilities for the animation of logos, whether it is the color, size, position, or opacity of individual SVG elements or some combination of them.

A simple animated logo

Figure 09.04 shows the logo you started to build in Chapter 3, "Creating Static Graphics Elements," using `<rect>` elements combined with a suitable banner for a Web page—perhaps an SVG Web page, such as those described in Chapter 12, "Creating a Simple SVG Web Site."

The starting point you reached in Chapter 4, "Using Text in SVG," having earlier laid out the rectangles and lines in Chapter 3, is shown next:

Listing 9.6 (ThreeRectLogo01.svg)

```
<?xml version='1.0'?>
<!DOCTYPE svg PUBLIC "-//W3C//DTD SVG 1.0//EN"
     "http://www.w3.org/TR/2001/PR-SVG-20010719/
     DTD/svg10.dtd">
<svg width="800" height="600">
<!-- The logo from chapter 3 is re-used here. -->
<svg x="0" y="0" width="400" height="500">
<rect x="10" y="20" width="100" height="100"
style="fill:none; stroke:#000099;
stroke-width:4;"/>
```

```
<rect x="130" y="130" width="100" height="100"
style="fill:none;
stroke:#000099; stroke-width:4;"/>
<rect x="10" y="240" width="100" height="100"
style="fill:none; stroke:#000099;
stroke-width:4;"/>
<line x1="35" y1="130" x2="110" y2="180"
style="stroke-width:5;
stroke:#000099"/>
<line x1="35" y1="230" x2="110" y2="180"
style="stroke-width:5;
stroke:#000099"/>
<rect x="18" y="130" width="100" height="100"
style="fill:none; stroke:white;
stroke-width:16;"/>
<text x="20" y="70" style="font-size:18;
stroke:#FF0066; fill:#FF0066;">
Scalable</text>
<text x="150" y="180" style="font-size:18;
stroke:#FF0066; fill:#FF0066;">
Vector</text>
<text x="20" y="290" style="font-size:18;
stroke:#FF0066; fill:#FF0066;">
Graphics</text>
</svg>
</svg>
```

Figure 09.04

The logo created using simple SVG shapes and a linear gradient.

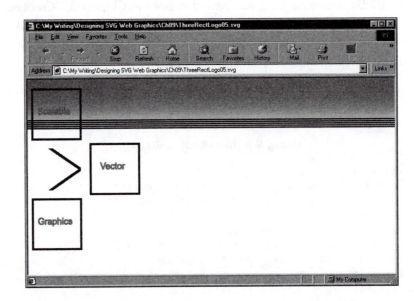

To that straightforward base, you add a banner-size background that involves a linear gradient. As you might recall, you need to define, early in your SVG document, the linear gradient within a `<LinearGradient>` element that is nested within a `<defs>` element. The code for the linear gradient looks like this:

```
<defs>
<LinearGradient id="MyPinkGradient"
gradientUnits="userSpaceOnUse" x1="0"
y1="0" x2="0" y2="120" >
<stop offset="10%" style="stop-color:#FF0066"/>
<stop offset="75%" style="stop-color:#EEEEFF"/>
</LinearGradient>
</defs>
```

The linear gradient is a vertical one, graduating from a deep pinkish color, #FF0066, at the top to a pale blue, #EEEEFF, at the bottom. You know that it is a vertical gradient because the values for the y1 and y2 attributes are different and the values for the x1 and x2 attributes are the same.

If you want to create a horizontal linear gradient, the x1 and x2 attributes would be different and the y1 and y2 attributes would be the same. If you want to create a diagonal linear gradient, both pairs of attributes would differ.

To create the gradient in the SVG image, you need to apply it as the fill in a `<rect>` element placed at the top of the page, like this:

```
<rect x="0" y="0" width="800" height="100"
style="fill:url(#MyPinkGradient);"/>
```

If you look back at Figure 09.04, you see that a series of lines is added to the bottom of the gradient to provide a deep blue contrast against the background at that part of the gradient that is a pale blue. In this instance, the lines were created using `<rect>` elements, (although you could use `<Line>` elements) and nest those in a `<g>` element, as shown in this code:

```
<g>
<rect x="0" y="82" width="800" height="1"
style="fill:#000066; stroke:#000066;
stroke-width:1"/>
<rect x="0" y="86" width="800" height="1"
```

```
style="fill:#000066; stroke:#000066;
stroke-width:1"/>
<rect x="0" y="90" width="800" height="1"
style="fill:#000066; stroke:#000066;
stroke-width:1"/>
<rect x="0" y="94" width="800" height="1"
style="fill:#000066; stroke:#000066;
stroke-width:1"/>
<rect x="0" y="98" width="800" height="1"
style="fill:#000066; stroke:#000066;
stroke-width:1"/>
</g>
```

So you now have a static logo. Add a little animation to it! You cause the middle of the three rectangles and the pair of lines that form the right-pointing arrow to be animated in from the left side of the page when the image is loaded. Remember that you have the essentially invisible rectangle with the white stroke and no fill as well as the `<text>` element containing the word *Vector* to include in this group. Because you want to animate these elements together, you enclose them in a grouping `<svg>` element, like this:

```
<svg>
<rect x="130" y="130" width="100" height="100"
style="fill:none;
stroke:#000099; stroke-width:4;"/>
<line x1="35" y1="130" x2="110" y2="180"
style="stroke-width:5;
stroke:#000099"/>
<line x1="35" y1="230" x2="110" y2="180"
style="stroke-width:5;
stroke:#000099"/>
<rect x="18" y="130" width="100" height="100"
style="fill:none; stroke:white;
stroke-width:16;"/>
<text x="150" y="180" style="font-size:18;
stroke:#FF0066; fill:#FF0066;">
Vector</text>
</svg>
```

If you compare that code carefully with the code shown in Listing 9.6, you see that some of the elements have to be reordered to bring them together so that they can be animated together within the grouping `<svg>` element.

You could use a `<g>` element as the grouping element for this task, if you prefer. I tend to use only the `<g>` element when I want to perform a transformation that can't be used on an `<svg>` element.

The group of elements extends almost 200 pixels to the right of the left edge of the image. Therefore, to start them animating from off the page, you set the `x` attribute of the `<svg>` element to `-200` and then animate them with an `<animate>` element, as shown in the following code:

```
<svg x="-200" y="0">
<animate attributeName="x" begin="0s" dur="5s"
fill="freeze" from="-200" to="0"/>
<rect x="130" y="130" width="100" height="100"
style="fill:none;
stroke:#000099; stroke-width:4;"/>
<line x1="35" y1="130" x2="110" y2="180"
style="stroke-width:5;
stroke:#000099"/>
<line x1="35" y1="230" x2="110" y2="180"
style="stroke-width:5;
stroke:#000099"/>
<text x="150" y="180" style="font-size:18;
stroke:#FF0066; fill:#FF0066;">
Vector</text>
<rect x="18" y="130" width="100" height="100"
style="fill:none; stroke:white;
stroke-width:16;"/>
</svg>
```

Notice that when the page loads, the `x` attribute of the `<svg>` element is set to `-200`. The animation described by the `<animate>` element applies to everything in the `<svg>` element because it is an immediate child element of the `<svg>` element; therefore, all the contents of the `<svg>` element are animated together, maintaining their relative positions to each other.

Hopefully, you were able to follow exactly where each addition and change to the code was to be placed. This process is shown in full in the following listing. If you are in doubt, trace the code step by step, and compare the code you read with Figure 09.04.

Listing 9.7 (ThreeRectLogo05.svg)

```
<?xml version='1.0'?>
<!DOCTYPE svg PUBLIC "-//W3C//DTD SVG 1.0//EN"
    "http://www.w3.org/TR/2001/PR-SVG-20010719/
     DTD/svg10.dtd">
<svg width="800" height="600">
<defs>
<linearGradient id="MyPinkGradient"
gradientUnits="userSpaceOnUse" x1="0"
y1="0" x2="0" y2="120" >
<stop offset="10%" style="stop-color:#FF0066"/>
<stop offset="75%" style="stop-color:#EEEEFF"/>
</linearGradient>
</defs>
<rect x="0" y="0" width="800" height="100"
style="fill:url(#MyPinkGradient);"/>
<g>
<rect x="0" y="82" width="800" height="1"
style="fill:#000066; stroke:#000066;
stroke-width:1"/>
<rect x="0" y="86" width="800" height="1"
style="fill:#000066; stroke:#000066;
stroke-width:1"/>
<rect x="0" y="90" width="800" height="1"
style="fill:#000066; stroke:#000066;
stroke-width:1"/>
<rect x="0" y="94" width="800" height="1"
style="fill:#000066; stroke:#000066;
stroke-width:1"/>
<rect x="0" y="98" width="800" height="1"
style="fill:#000066; stroke:#000066;
stroke-width:1"/>
</g>
<!-- The logo from chapter 3 is re-used here. -->
<svg x="0" y="0" width="400" height="500">
<rect x="10" y="20" width="100" height="100"
style="fill:none; stroke:#000099;
stroke-width:4;"/>
<rect x="10" y="240" width="100" height="100"
style="fill:none; stroke:#000099;
stroke-width:4;"/>
<svg x="-200" y="0">
<animate attributeName="x" begin="0s" dur="5s"
fill="freeze" from="-200" to="0"/>
<rect x="130" y="130" width="100" height="100"
style="fill:none;
stroke:#000099; stroke-width:4;"/>
```

```
<line x1="35" y1="130" x2="110" y2="180"
style="stroke-width:5;
stroke:#000099"/>
<line x1="35" y1="230" x2="110" y2="180"
style="stroke-width:5;
stroke:#000099"/>
<text x="150" y="180" style="font-size:18;
stroke:#FF0066; fill:#FF0066;">
Vector</text>
<rect x="18" y="130" width="100" height="100"
style="fill:none; stroke:white;
stroke-width:16;"/>
</svg>
<text x="20" y="70" style="font-size:18;
stroke:#FF0066; fill:#FF0066;">
Scalable</text>
<text x="20" y="290" style="font-size:18;
stroke:#FF0066; fill:#FF0066;">
Graphics</text>
</svg>
</svg>
```

A logo with rotating text messages

Now use the combined ellipses you saw in Chapter 3 to form the basis for
a simple logo for RootsPics.com. When you are creating an animated logo,
you should often create a static version first. A first attempt at a
RootsPics.com logo might look like this:

Listing 9.8 (EllipsesRootsPics01.svg)

```
<?xml version="1.0" standalone="no"?>
<!DOCTYPE svg PUBLIC "-//W3C//DTD SVG 1.0//EN"
      "http://www.w3.org/TR/2001/PR-SVG-20010719/
       DTD/svg10.dtd">
<svg width="800" height="150">
<svg x="0" y="0" width="800" height="150">
<g>
<ellipse cx="240" cy="70" rx="220" ry="30"
style="stroke:none; fill:#000099"/>
<ellipse cx="221" cy="74" rx="192" ry="22"
style="stroke:none; fill:white"/>
<text>
<tspan x="90" y="70" style="font-size:14;
```

```
font-family: Ventana, Arial, sans-serif;
fill:red; stroke:red;">
RootsPics.com
</tspan>
<tspan dx="-8em" dy="1.5em" style="font-size:12;
font-family: Ventana, Arial, sans-serif; fill:#CCCCCC;
 stroke:#CCCCCC; opacity:0.7">
For your picture needs as you explore your roots.
</tspan>
</text>
</g>
</svg>
</svg>
```

Notice that an `<svg>` element is nested within another. If you want to adjust the position of the whole logo on the page, you can simply adjust the `x` or `y` attributes of the nested `<svg>` element, and all the components move together the requisite distance because they take their position from the upper-left corner of that nested `<svg>` element.

To add some interest to the logo, add a linear gradient to the rear ellipse (the one that is dark blue) so that it graduates from a pale blue on the left to the dark blue on the right. You need to create the gradient within a `<linearGradient>` element nested within the `<defs>` element. The `<defs>` element is inserted after the outer `<svg>` element and before the inner one, like this:

```
<svg width="800" height="150">
<defs>
<linearGradient id="Gradient01">
<stop offset="20%" style="stop-color:#9999FF"/>
<stop offset="90%" style="stop-color:#000099"/>
</linearGradient>
</defs>
<svg x="0" y="0" width="800" height="150">
```

You apply the gradient to the ellipse like this:

```
<ellipse cx="240" cy="70" rx="220" ry="30"
style="stroke:none; fill:url(#Gradient01)"/>
```

and modify the text `RootsPics.com` so that the same gradient is applied to it as fill and stroke:

```
<tspan x="90" y="70" style="font-size:14;
font-family: Ventana, Arial, sans-serif;
fill:url(#Gradient01); stroke:url(#Gradient01);">
RootsPics.com
</tspan>
```

Suppose that the effect that you want to create below the RootsPics.com text is one of a mini-slide show, with three short pieces of text rotating over time to highlight some services that RootsPics.com might supply. The technique for the placement of those pieces of text is to describe them relative to each other so that for the second and third pieces of text, the `dx` attribute on the `<tspan>` element is a negative number (the second and third pieces of text are pulled back to the beginning of the line). If all three pieces of text were visible at the same time, you would have an unsightly overlap of characters.

To create the rotating text messages, you create an animation using the `targetElement` syntax mentioned briefly early in Chapter 8, "Animation: SVG and SMIL Animation." To achieve the effect you want, you need to coordinate the timings of the animations while they cycle through visible and hidden states. The first `<tspan>` should be visible when the page loads, and the other two should be hidden. You need to create animations that alter the value of the visibility property at appropriate times. The following code shows one technique to achieve this effect:

```
<tspan id="Message1" dx="-8em" dy="1.5em"
style="font-size:12;
font-family: Ventana, Arial, sans-serif; fill:#CCCCCC;
  stroke:#CCCCCC; opacity:0.7" visibility="visible">
<animate begin="0s" dur="12s" targetName="Message1"
attributeName="visibility" values="visible; hidden;
hidden; visible"
keyTimes="0s; 4s; 8s; 12s" repeatCount="indefinite" />
For your picture needs as you explore your roots.
</tspan>
```

Notice that an `id` attribute has been added to the `<tspan>` element. The `targetName` attribute of the `<animate>` element references the `<tspan>` element by means of the `id` attribute. The animation begins at 0 seconds after the page loads and has a duration of 12 seconds. At key times, the value of the visibility property is changed to either `visible` or `hidden` to

reflect the rotating messages you want at particular times. The value of the
`repeatCount` attribute indicates that this animation continues indefinitely.
Similar animations, with different timings for visibility and hiddenness, are
created for the other two `<tspan>` elements.

With all those parts put together, your final code looks like the following
code. The RootsPics.com text is static. The contents of the other three
`<tspan>` elements are in turn made visible or hidden to provide rotating
text messages within the logo.

Listing 9.9 (EllipsesRootsPics04.svg)

```
<?xml version="1.0" standalone="no"?>
<!DOCTYPE svg PUBLIC "-//W3C//DTD SVG 1.0//EN"
      "http://www.w3.org/TR/2001/PR-SVG-20010719/
        DTD/svg10.dtd">
<svg width="800" height="150"
  xmlns:xlink="http://www.w3.org/1999/xlink">
<defs>
<linearGradient id="Gradient01">
<stop offset="20%" style="stop-color:#9999FF"/>
<stop offset="90%" style="stop-color:#000099"/>
</linearGradient>
</defs>
<svg x="0" y="0" width="800" height="150">
<ellipse cx="240" cy="70" rx="220" ry="30"
style="stroke:none; fill:url(#Gradient01)"/>
<ellipse cx="221" cy="74" rx="192" ry="22"
style="stroke:none; fill:white"/>
<text>
<tspan x="90" y="70" style="font-size:14;
font-family: Ventana, Arial, sans-serif;
fill:url(#Gradient01);
stroke:url(#Gradient01);">
RootsPics.com
</tspan>
<tspan id="Message1" dx="-8em" dy="1.5em"
style="font-size:12;
font-family: Ventana, Arial, sans-serif;
fill:#CCCCCC;
stroke:#CCCCCC; opacity:0.7" visibility="visible">
<animate begin="0s" dur="12s" targetName="Message1"
attributeName="visibility" values="visible; hidden;
hidden; visible"
keyTimes="0s; 4s; 8s; 12s" repeatCount="indefinite" />
```

```
For your picture needs as you explore your roots.
</tspan>
<tspan id="Message2" dx="-21em" style="font-size:12;
font-family: Ventana, Arial, sans-serif; fill:#CCCCCC;
 stroke:#CCCCCC; opacity:0.7" visibility="hidden">
<animate begin="0s" dur="12s" targetName="Message2"
attributeName="visibility" values="hidden; visible;
hidden; hidden"
keyTimes="0s; 4s; 8s; 12s" repeatCount="indefinite" />
Photographic prints of yesteryear
</tspan>
<tspan id="Message3" dx="-15em" style="font-size:12;
font-family: Ventana, Arial, sans-serif; fill:#CCCCCC;
 stroke:#CCCCCC; opacity:0.7" visibility="hidden">
 <animate begin="0s" dur="12s" targetElement="Message3"
attributeName="visibility" values="hidden; hidden;
visible; hidden"
keyTimes="0s; 4s; 8s; 12s" repeatCount="indefinite" />
Paintings of locations of your family's roots.
</tspan>
</text>
</svg>
</svg>
```

A logo with several text animations

Now go on and use a more complex sequence of animations, and create a logo for S-V-G.com, with the slogan "SVG with more than a dash of brilliance!"

When viewed as a static image, the logo looks like the one shown in Figure 09.05. Because you will animate various letters and words within

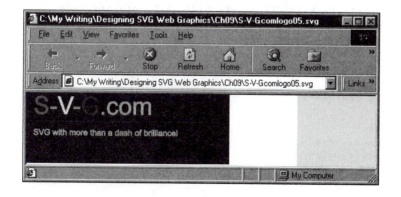

Figure 09.05

The logo for S-V-G.com.

the logo separately, you need to separate out carefully the parts you want to animate individually. The following code shows the logo before any animation is added. The code looks just like Figure 09.05 onscreen.

Listing 9.10 (S-V-Gcomlogo01.svg)

```
<?xml version="1.0" standalone="no"?>
<!DOCTYPE svg PUBLIC "-//W3C//DTD SVG 1.0//EN"
     "http://www.w3.org/TR/2001/PR-SVG-20010719/
      DTD/svg10.dtd">
<svg width="400" height="200" >
<svg x="0" y="0" width="300" height="100">
<rect x="0" y="0" width="100%" height="100%"/>
<text x="10" y="30" style="font-size:36;
font-family:Ventana, Arial, san-serif;">
<tspan dy="0m" style="fill:red; stroke:red;">
S
</tspan>
<tspan dx="0m" style="fill:#00FF33; stroke:#00FF33;">
-
</tspan>
<tspan dx="0m" style="fill:#FFFF00; stroke:#FFFF00">
V
</tspan>
<tspan dx="0m" style="fill:#00FF33; stroke:#00FF33;">
-
</tspan>
<tspan dx="0m" style="fill:#3333FF; stroke:#3333FF">
G
</tspan>
<tspan dx="0m" style="fill:#FFCC00; stroke:#FFCC00;">
.com
</tspan>
</text>
<line x1="4%" y1="40" x2="95%" y2="40"
style="stroke:#3333FF; stroke-width:1.5; opacity:1"/>
<text x="10" y="60" style="stroke:#FFCC00;
fill:#FFCC00">
<tspan dy="0em">
SVG with more than a
</tspan>
<tspan dx="0em">
dash
</tspan>
<tspan dx="0em">
of brilliance!
```

```
</tspan>
</text>
</svg>
</svg>
```

Notice that in both lines of text, you have made use of the `dx` attribute with a value of `0em`. That allows spacing to be preserved; at the same time, however, the separate `<tspan>` elements allow you to animate parts of each line of text individually.

Because you want to create the animation from a blank black background, the next step is to set the visibility property on each element to a value of `hidden`. You want to control the appearance of the content of each `<tspan>` element individually, so be sure to set the visibility to `hidden` on the `<tspan>` elements, *not* on the `<text>` elements. After that is done, the beginning state of the animated logo has a horizontal blue line on a black background with all the text hidden.

Now you animate the various parts of the logo within their individual `<tspan>` elements. The first thing you do is to make the letters `S`, `V`, and `G` (which are part of S-V-G.com) successively visible while keeping the two dashes and the `.com` hidden. At that stage, the content of the first `<text>` element looks like this:

```
<text x="10" y="30" style="font-size:36;
font-family:Ventana, Arial, san-serif;" >
<tspan dy="0m" style="fill:red; stroke:red;"
visibility="hidden">
<animate attributeName="visibility" from="hidden"
to="visible" begin="2s" dur="0.1s" fill="freeze"/>
S
</tspan>
<tspan dx="0m" style="fill:#00FF33; stroke:#00FF33;"
visibility="hidden">
-
</tspan>
<tspan dx="0m" style="fill:#FFFF00; stroke:#FFFF00"
visibility="hidden">
<animate attributeName="visibility" from="hidden"
to="visible" begin="3s" dur="0.1s" fill="freeze"/>
V
</tspan>
<tspan dx="0m" style="fill:#00FF33; stroke:#00FF33;"
visibility="hidden">
```

```
-
</tspan>
<tspan dx="0m" style="fill:#3333FF; stroke:#3333FF"
visibility="hidden">
<animate attributeName="visibility" from="hidden"
to="visible" begin="4s" dur="0.1s" fill="freeze"/>
G
</tspan>
<tspan dx="0m" style="fill:#FFCC00; stroke:#FFCC00;"
visibility="hidden">
.com
</tspan>
</text>
```

Then you add animations to the text below the line, like this:

```
<text x="10" y="60" style="stroke:#FFCC00; fill:#FFCC00">
<tspan dy="0em" visibility="hidden">
<animate attributeName="visibility" from="hidden"
to="visible" begin="5s" dur="0.1s" fill="freeze"/>
SVG with more than a
</tspan>
<tspan dx="0em" style="fill:#00FF33; stroke:#00FF33"
visibility="hidden">
<animate attributeName="visibility" from="hidden"
to="visible" begin="5.5s" dur="0.1s" fill="freeze"/>
dash
</tspan>
<tspan dx="0em" visibility="hidden">
<animate attributeName="visibility" from="hidden"
to="visible" begin="6s" dur="0.1s" fill="freeze"/>
of brilliance!
</tspan>
</text>
```

Then you add animations to make the dashes and the .com of S-V-G.com
visible, like this:

```
<text x="10" y="30" style="font-size:36;
font-family:Ventana, Arial, san-serif;" >
<tspan dy="0m" style="fill:red; stroke:red;"
visibility="hidden">
<animate attributeName="visibility" from="hidden"
to="visible" begin="2s" dur="0.1s" fill="freeze"/>
S
</tspan>
```

```
<tspan dx="0m" style="fill:#00FF33; stroke:#00FF33;"
visibility="hidden">
<animate attributeName="visibility" from="hidden"
to="visible" begin="7s" dur="0.1s" fill="freeze"/>
-
</tspan>
<tspan dx="0m" style="fill:#FFFF00; stroke:#FFFF00"
visibility="hidden">
<animate attributeName="visibility" from="hidden"
to="visible" begin="3s" dur="0.1s" fill="freeze"/>
V
</tspan>
<tspan dx="0m" style="fill:#00FF33; stroke:#00FF33;"
visibility="hidden">
<animate attributeName="visibility" from="hidden"
to="visible" begin="7s" dur="0.1s" fill="freeze"/>
-
</tspan>
<tspan dx="0m" style="fill:#3333FF; stroke:#3333FF"
visibility="hidden">
<animate attributeName="visibility" from="hidden"
to="visible" begin="4s" dur="0.1s" fill="freeze"/>
G
</tspan>
<tspan dx="0m" style="fill:#FFCC00; stroke:#FFCC00;"
visibility="hidden">
<animate attributeName="visibility" from="hidden"
to="visible" begin="7s" dur="0.1s" fill="freeze"/>
.com
</tspan>
</text>
```

The completed code listing is shown in Listing 9.11.

Listing 9.11 (S-V-Gcomlogo05.svg)

```
<?xml version="1.0" standalone="no"?>
<!DOCTYPE svg PUBLIC "-//W3C//DTD SVG 1.0//EN"
    "http://www.w3.org/TR/2001/PR-SVG-20010719/
    DTD/svg10.dtd">
<svg width="400" height="200" >
<svg x="0" y="0" width="300" height="100">
<rect x="0" y="0" width="100%" height="100%"/>
<g display="block">
<animate attributeName="display" from="block" to="none"
begin="8s" dur="0.1s" fill="freeze"/>
```

```
<animate attributeName="display" from="none" to="block"
begin="8.5s" dur="0.1s" fill="freeze"/>
<animate attributeName="display" from="block" to="none"
begin="9s" dur="0.1s" fill="freeze"/>
<animate attributeName="display" from="none" to="block"
begin="9.5s" dur="0.1s" fill="freeze"/>
<animate attributeName="display" from="block" to="none"
begin="10s" dur="0.1s" fill="freeze"/>
<animate attributeName="display" from="none" to="block"
begin="10.5s" dur="0.1s" fill="freeze"/>
<text x="10" y="30" style="font-size:36;
font-family:Ventana, Arial, san-serif;" >
<tspan dy="0m" style="fill:red; stroke:red;"
visibility="hidden">
<animate attributeName="visibility" from="hidden" to="visible"
begin="2s" dur="0.1s" fill="freeze"/>
S
</tspan>
<tspan dx="0m" style="fill:#00FF33; stroke:#00FF33;"
visibility="hidden">
<animate attributeName="visibility" from="hidden" to="visible"
begin="7s" dur="0.1s" fill="freeze"/>
-
</tspan>
<tspan dx="0m" style="fill:#FFFF00; stroke:#FFFF00"
visibility="hidden">
<animate attributeName="visibility" from="hidden" to="visible"
begin="3s" dur="0.1s" fill="freeze"/>
V
</tspan>
<tspan dx="0m" style="fill:#00FF33; stroke:#00FF33;"
visibility="hidden">
<animate attributeName="visibility" from="hidden" to="visible"
begin="7s" dur="0.1s" fill="freeze"/>
-
</tspan>
<tspan dx="0m" style="fill:#3333FF; stroke:#3333FF"
visibility="hidden">
<animate attributeName="visibility" from="hidden" to="visible"
begin="4s" dur="0.1s" fill="freeze"/>
G
</tspan>
<tspan dx="0m" style="fill:#FFCC00; stroke:#FFCC00;"
visibility="hidden">
<animate attributeName="visibility" from="hidden" to="visible"
begin="7s" dur="0.1s" fill="freeze"/>
.com
</tspan>
```

```
    </text>
  </g>
  <line x1="4%" y1="40" x2="95%" y2="40" style="stroke:#3333FF;
  stroke-width:1.5; opacity:1"/>
  <text x="10" y="60" style="stroke:#FFCC00; fill:#FFCC00">
  <tspan dy="0em" visibility="hidden">
  <animate attributeName="visibility" from="hidden" to="visible"
  begin="5s" dur="0.1s" fill="freeze"/>
  SVG with more than a
  </tspan>
  <tspan dx="0em" style="fill:#00FF33; stroke:#00FF33"
  visibility="hidden">
  <animate attributeName="visibility" from="hidden" to="visible"
  begin="5.5s" dur="0.1s" fill="freeze"/>
  dash
  </tspan>
  <tspan dx="0em" visibility="hidden">
  <animate attributeName="visibility" from="hidden" to="visible"
  begin="6s" dur="0.1s" fill="freeze"/>
  of brilliance!
  </tspan>
  </text>
  </svg>
</svg>
```

An animated logo with a gradient and filter

In this example, you create for SVGenius.com a logo that incorporates both a gradient and a filter, together with an animation. This arrangement gives you a dynamic logo through the use of animation, but some visual subtlety through the use of the filter. In production-quality SVG logos, you are likely to want to combine these aspects of SVG to create attractive and striking visual effects. The final logo is shown in Figure 09.07, but I suggest that this should be one you run onscreen.

As a first step, you create a rectangle with curved corners and fill it with a regular pattern of lines. On the lower and right edges of the rectangle, you apply a narrow drop shadow filter, by adjusting the `stdDeviation` of the `<feGaussianBlur>` element to 0.5 and the `dx` and `dy` attributes of the `<feOffset>` filter primitive. In this initial stage, the lines are simply filled with a plain color to check placement. The code at the end of this first stage is shown in Listing 9.12.

Listing 9.12 (RectLinesLogo01.svg)

```
<?xml version="1.0" standalone="no"?>
<!DOCTYPE svg PUBLIC "-//W3C//DTD SVG 1.0//EN"
     "http://www.w3.org/TR/2001/PR-SVG-20010719/
        DTD/svg10.dtd">
<svg>
<defs>
<filter id="CombinedDropShadow" width="140%" y="-20%"
height="200%">
<feGaussianBlur in="SourceAlpha" stdDeviation="0.5"
result="ShadowOut" />
<feOffset in="ShadowOut" dx="2" dy="1"
result="ShadowOnly" />
<feMerge>
   <feMergeNode in="ShadowOnly"/>
   <feMergeNode in="SourceGraphic"/>
</feMerge>
</filter>
</defs>
<svg x="150">
<rect x="5" y="55" width="300" height="80" rx="10"
ry="10" style="fill:white;
filter:url(#CombinedDropShadow)"/>
<rect x="10" y="60" width="295" height="2"
style="fill:#FF0099; stroke:none;"/>
<rect x="10" y="65" width="295" height="2"
style="fill:#FF0099; stroke:none;"/>
<rect x="10" y="70" width="295" height="2"
style="fill:#FF0099; stroke:none;"/>
<rect x="10" y="75" width="295" height="2"
style="fill:#FF0099; stroke:none;"/>
<rect x="10" y="80" width="295" height="2"
style="fill:#FF0099; stroke:none;"/>
<rect x="10" y="85" width="295" height="2"
style="fill:#FF0099; stroke:none;"/>
<rect x="10" y="90" width="295" height="2"
style="fill:#FF0099; stroke:none;"/>
<rect x="10" y="95" width="295" height="2"
style="fill:#FF0099; stroke:none;"/>
<rect x="10" y="100" width="295" height="2"
style="fill:#FF0099; stroke:none;"/>
<rect x="10" y="105" width="295" height="2"
style="fill:#FF0099; stroke:none;"/>
<rect x="10" y="110" width="295" height="2"
style="fill:#FF0099; stroke:none;"/>
<rect x="10" y="115" width="295" height="2"
```

```
style="fill:#FF0099; stroke:none;"/>
<rect x="10" y="120" width="295" height="2"
style="fill:#FF0099; stroke:none;"/>
<rect x="10" y="125" width="295" height="2"
style="fill:#FF0099; stroke:none;"/>
<rect x="10" y="130" width="295" height="2"
style="fill:#FF0099; stroke:none;"/>
</svg>
</svg>
```

Suppose that you want to add a linear gradient within the lines. An initial attempt is shown in the following code:

```
<linearGradient id="MyPinkGradient"
gradientUnits="userSpaceOnUse"
x1="150" y1="150" x2="220" y2="50" >
<stop offset="10%" style="stop-color:#EEEEFF;
stop-opacity:0.8"/>
<stop offset="50%" style="stop-color:#FF0099"/>
<stop offset="75%" style="stop-color:#EEEEFF"/>
</linearGradient>
```

I hope that you have taken or will be taking my advice about trying to visualize how a linear gradient will look onscreen by experimenting with gradients on large background rectangles. However, you need to think about an additional issue. My habit of using a nested `<svg>` element means that a new user coordinate system is created. In Figure 09.06, the linear gradient on a rectangle is inserted in the background (using the coordinate system of the outer `<svg>` element) and the gradient as it applies on my lines.

In Listing 9.13, you can see the next stage of the development where the lines on the rectangle have been filled using the linear gradient rather than a plain fill, as in the first stage. The `x1`, `y1`, `x2`, and `y2` coordinates of the `<linearGradient>` element have been adjusted to give pale blue in the lower-left and upper-right corners.

Listing 9.13 (RectLinesLogo03.svg)

```
<?xml version="1.0" standalone="no"?>
<!DOCTYPE svg PUBLIC "-//W3C//DTD SVG 1.0//EN"
    "http://www.w3.org/TR/2001/PR-SVG-20010719/
    DTD/svg10.dtd">
```

Figure 09.06

*The linear gradient is
applied according to
the coordinate sys-
tem in use in each
`<svg>` element.*

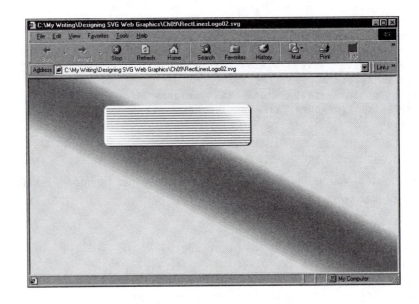

```
<svg>
<defs>
<linearGradient id="MyPinkGradient"
gradientUnits="userSpaceOnUse"
x1="200" y1="175" x2="250" y2="50" >
<stop offset="20%" style="stop-color:#EEEEFF"/>
<stop offset="50%" style="stop-color:#FF0099"/>
<stop offset="75%" style="stop-color:#EEEEFF"/>
</linearGradient>
<filter id="CombinedDropShadow" width="140%" y="-20%"
height="200%">
<feGaussianBlur in="SourceAlpha" stdDeviation="0.5"
result="ShadowOut" />
<feOffset in="ShadowOut" dx="2" dy="1"
result="ShadowOnly" />
<feMerge>
  <feMergeNode in="ShadowOnly"/>
  <feMergeNode in="SourceGraphic"/>
</feMerge>
</filter>
</defs>
<svg x="150">
<rect x="5" y="55" width="300" height="80" rx="10"
ry="10" style="fill:white;
filter:url(#CombinedDropShadow)"/>
<rect x="10" y="60" width="295" height="2"
```

```
    style="fill:url(#MyPinkGradient);
    stroke:none;"/>
  <rect x="10" y="65" width="295" height="2"
    style="fill:url(#MyPinkGradient);
    stroke:none;"/>
  <rect x="10" y="70" width="295" height="2"
    style="fill:url(#MyPinkGradient);
    stroke:none;"/>
  <rect x="10" y="75" width="295" height="2"
    style="fill:url(#MyPinkGradient);
    stroke:none;"/>
  <rect x="10" y="80" width="295" height="2"
    style="fill:url(#MyPinkGradient);
    stroke:none;"/>
  <rect x="10" y="85" width="295" height="2"
    style="fill:url(#MyPinkGradient);
    stroke:none;"/>
  <rect x="10" y="90" width="295" height="2"
    style="fill:url(#MyPinkGradient);
    stroke:none;"/>
  <rect x="10" y="95" width="295" height="2"
    style="fill:url(#MyPinkGradient);
    stroke:none;"/>
  <rect x="10" y="100" width="295" height="2"
    style="fill:url(#MyPinkGradient);
    stroke:none;"/>
  <rect x="10" y="105" width="295" height="2"
    style="fill:url(#MyPinkGradient);
    stroke:none;"/>
  <rect x="10" y="110" width="295" height="2"
    style="fill:url(#MyPinkGradient);
    stroke:none;"/>
  <rect x="10" y="115" width="295" height="2"
    style="fill:url(#MyPinkGradient);
    stroke:none;"/>
  <rect x="10" y="120" width="295" height="2"
    style="fill:url(#MyPinkGradient);
    stroke:none;"/>
  <rect x="10" y="125" width="295" height="2"
    style="fill:url(#MyPinkGradient);
    stroke:none;"/>
  <rect x="10" y="130" width="295" height="2"
    style="fill:url(#MyPinkGradient);
    stroke:none;"/>
  </svg>
  </svg>
```

Finally, you add some text for the domain name, including a simple animation that draws attention to the text of the logo, but is then static after the animation is complete:

```
<text x="-300" y="110"
style="font-family:'Times New Roman', serif;
font-size:48;
stroke:#FF0099; fill:white;
filter:url(#CombinedDropShadow)">
<animate begin="1s" dur="2s" attributeName="x"
from="-300" to="30" fill="freeze"/>
SVGenius.com
</text>
```

The final appearance of the logo, after the animation of the text is complete, is shown in Figure 09.07.

Figure 09.07

The completed logo, after the animation of the text has taken place with the drop shadow on the text and enclosing rectangle and the use of a gradient fill on the lines within the rectangle.

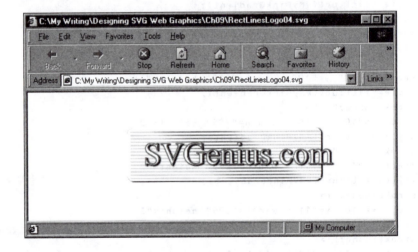

A power meter logo

I guess that you are familiar with those animated logos that resemble a power meter and announce something like "Powered by XYZ." Personally, I find some of them fairly irritating on a Web page, particularly if I am trying to digest interesting content on the page, but because constructing this type of a logo lets you put several SVG techniques into practice, it is an interesting example to develop.

First, look at how the finished product should look. Of course, because this logo is animated, I again encourage you to download and run the code. Figure 09.08 can't convey all that is going on.

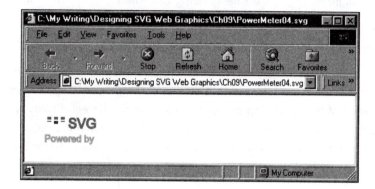

Figure 09.08

A static impression of the power meter logo.

Now you create a power meter. Various techniques produce roughly similar appearances, but the way the animation is produced is shown in the following code:

```
<svg id="MeterHolder" x="0" y="0" width="200"
height="20">
<rect id="MyMeter" x="0" y="0" width="20" height="40"
style="fill:white;
stroke:none;">
</rect>
  <rect id="Top" x="2" y="2" width="6" height="4"
style="fill:red; stroke:none"/>
  <rect id="Second" x="2" y="8" width="6" height="4"
style="fill:blue;
stroke:none"/>
  <rect id="Third" x="2" y="14" width="6" height="4"
style="fill:green;
stroke:none"/>
</svg>
```

The code is enclosed in a `<svg>` element that is later placed in the `<defs>` element and used more than once. The way the animation will be created is by changing the height of the `<svg>` element. When the height is 0, the `<svg>` element is not displayed, nor is any element nested within it. When you increase the height of the `<svg>` element to 6, the red rectangle becomes visible; when the height is increased to 10, the blue rectangle is visible; and when the height of the `<svg>` element is 14 or greater, the green rectangle is visible too. You need to animate only one attribute, therefore, the `height` attribute of the `<svg>` element, to create the appearance of all three `<rect>` elements being animated.

Notice that an `id` attribute is included on the `<svg>` element so that it can be referenced from elsewhere in the document.

You need to create three of these power meters, side by side. You make use of the SVG `<use>` element to create each one. Because you want to make each of the animating power meters have a different display, you create the animation within the `<use>` element, not within the definition of the `<svg>` element, because you can't animate referenced elements individually. It's a pity that you can't because some nice effects would be possible.

At the time this book was written, the SVG Working Group had recently been chartered to produce SVG version 2, which includes Mobile SVG. A Requirements Working Draft has recently been issued for Mobile SVG (see http://www.w3.org/TR/SVGMobile Reqs) as well as a Requirements Working Draft for SVG version 2.0 (see http://www.w3.org/TR/ SVGReqs). If you want to communicate with the SVG Working Group, the W3C has a mailing list dedicated to SVG. To subscribe, send an email message to `www-svg-request@w3.org` *with* `subscribe` *in the Subject line. SVG Working Group members have also been active on the SVG-Developers mailing list on YahooGroups.com. The SVG-Developers mailing list is probably the most active discussion forum on SVG. To subscribe, send an email to* `svg-developers-subscribe@yahoogroups.com`*.*

Note that the `height` attribute is being animated in each `<use>` element, which means that the `height` attribute of an `<svg>` element, which is what the `<use>` element stands for here, is being animated. The animation begins as soon as the page is loaded, (`begin="0s"`), lasts five seconds (`dur="5s"`), and is repeated indefinitely (`repeatCount="indefinite"`). However, the `values` attribute has a different list of values for each of the three `<use>` elements because you want the three power meters to be animated independently:

```
<use x="2" y="2" xlink:href="#MeterHolder" >
 <animate attributeName="height" begin="0s"
values="0; 20; 10; 20; 0"
dur="2.5s" fill="freeze"
 repeatCount="indefinite"/>
</use>
```

```
<use id="SecondMeter" x="12" y="2"
xlink:href="#MeterHolder"
Top.style="fill:blue">
 <animate attributeName="height"
targetElement="SecondMeter" begin="0s"
values="20; 10; 20; 0; 20"
  dur="2.5s" fill="freeze"
 repeatCount="indefinite"/>
</use>
<use id="ThirdMeter" x="22" y="2"
xlink:href="#MeterHolder"
Top.style="fill:blue">
 <animate attributeName="height"
targetElement="SecondMeter" begin="0s"
values="10; 20; 0; 20; 0"
  dur="2.5s" fill="freeze"
 repeatCount="indefinite"/>
</use>
```

The final code looks like this:

Listing 9.14 (PowerMeter04.svg)

```
<?xml version="1.0" standalone="no"?>
<!DOCTYPE svg PUBLIC "-//W3C//DTD SVG 1.0//EN"
     "http://www.w3.org/TR/2001/PR-SVG-20010719/
       DTD/svg10.dtd">
<svg width="500" height="400"
  xmlns:xlink="http://www.w3.org/1999/xlink">
<defs>
<svg id="MeterHolder" x="0" y="0" width="200"
height="20">
<rect id="MyMeter" x="0" y="0" width="20"
height="40" style="fill:white;
stroke:none;">
</rect>
 <rect id="Top" x="2" y="2" width="6" height="4"
style="fill:red; stroke:none"/>
 <rect id="Second" x="2" y="8" width="6" height="4"
style="fill:blue;
stroke:none"/>
 <rect id="Third" x="2" y="14" width="6" height="4"
style="fill:green;
stroke:none"/>
</svg>
</defs>
```

```
<svg id="PowerMeter" x="30" y="30" width="300"
height="200">
<use x="2" y="2" xlink:href="#MeterHolder" >
 <animate attributeName="height" begin="0s"
values="0; 20; 10; 20; 0"
dur="2.5s" fill="freeze"
 repeatCount="indefinite"/>
</use>
<use id="SecondMeter" x="12" y="2"
xlink:href="#MeterHolder"
Top.style="fill:blue">
 <animate attributeName="height"
targetElement="SecondMeter" begin="0s"
values="20; 10; 20; 0; 20"
   dur="2.5s" fill="freeze"
 repeatCount="indefinite"/>
</use>
<use id="ThirdMeter" x="22" y="2"
xlink:href="#MeterHolder"
Top.style="fill:blue">
 <animate attributeName="height"
targetElement="SecondMeter" begin="0s"
values="10; 20; 0; 20; 0"
   dur="2.5s" fill="freeze"
 repeatCount="indefinite"/>
</use>
<text x="0" y="40" style="font-size:14;
font-family:Arial, sans-serif;
fill:#CCCCCC; stroke:#CCCCCC">Powered by</text>
<text x="35" y="20" style="font-size:20;
font-family:Arial, sans-serif;
fill:#FF0066; stroke:#FF0066">SVG</text>
</svg>
</svg>
```

Creating Banner and Other Types of Ads in SVG

You quite likely will have heard that concern is being expressed in certain quarters about the perceived falling effectiveness of banner ads on Web pages. Yet, if you visit almost any commercial Web site, you find a huge variety of ads on many Web pages. To complete this chapter, look at some possible uses of SVG in creating these types of ads.

One key aspect of any banner or other type of ad is the facility to click through to another Web site. Information about the SVG `<a>` element, which controls this type of between-page navigation, is in Chapter 5, "Creating Navigation Bars."

The examples in this section illustrate the use of many of the SVG elements and attributes that were touched on in earlier chapters. Each of the ads is for EditITWrite.com, a (fictional) information technology editing and writing company.

A rotating text ad

The finished ad in one of its phases looks as shown in Figure 09.09.

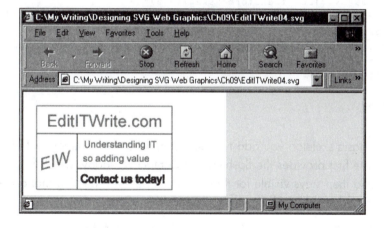

Figure 09.09

A rotating text ad for EditITWrite.com that uses the `<tref>` element and the skewY transformation.

First, you create the framework for the ad. The outline of the rectangle and the lines within it are created using a `<rect>` and three `<line>` elements. The minilogo for EditITWrite.com, the letters *EIW*, is created by applying a skew transformation on the letters. To create the logo, you use the `<tref>` element, which illustrates how it is used.

Listing 9.15 (EditITWrite01.svg)

```
<?xml version="1.0" standalone="no"?>
<!DOCTYPE svg PUBLIC "-//W3C//DTD SVG 1.0//EN"
    "http://www.w3.org/TR/2001/PR-SVG-20010719/
    DTD/svg10.dtd">
<svg width="300" height="150">
<defs>
<text id="Ref" >EIW</text>
</defs>
<rect x="20" y="20" width="200" height="120"
style="fill:white; stroke:black; stroke-width:0.5;"/>
<line x1="20" y1="60" x2="220" y2="60"
style="stroke:black; stroke-width:0.5;"/>
<line x1="80" y1="60" x2="80" y2="140"
style="stroke:black; stroke-width:0.5;"/>
<line x1="80" y1="110" x2="220" y2="110"
style="stroke:black; stroke-width:0.5;"/>
<text style="font-size:24; font-family:Arial,
sans-serif; stroke:none; stroke-width:0; fill:red;"
   x="25" y="120" transform="skewY(-15)" >
   <tref xlink:href="#Ref"/>
</text>
<text x="35" y="50" style="font-size:24;
fill:red; stroke:none; font-family:Arial, sans-serif;">
EditITWrite.com
</text>
</svg>
```

To that basic skeleton you add two animations that are independent of each
other. The first provides the flashing text Contact Us Today, which flashes
twice and then stays visible for three seconds before repeating that cycle of
flashing and visibility. The code to produce this effect is shown here:

```
<text x="85" y="130" style="fill:blue; stroke:blue;
font-size:16; font-family:Arial, sans-serif;">
<animate attributeName="visibility" begin="0s"
repeatCount="indefinite" dur="5s"
   values="visible; hidden; visible; hidden; visible;"
   keyTimes="0s; 0.5s; 1s; 1.5s; 2s;"/>
Contact us today!
</text>
```

Notice how the individual values within the `values` attribute switch from
visible to hidden more than once. This switching produces the flashing

effect. By varying the values within the `keyTimes` attribute value, you can vary the speed of the flashing.

With that second animation in place, the ad now looks as shown in Figure 09.10.

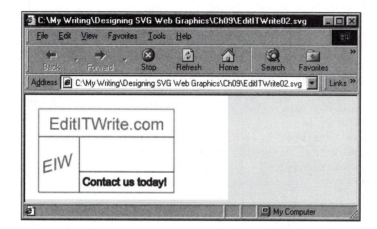

Figure 09.10

The ad after the addition of the first animation.

At that stage, the overall code resembles the code shown in Listing 9.16.

Listing 9.16 (EditITWrite02.svg)

```
<?xml version="1.0" standalone="no"?>
<!DOCTYPE svg PUBLIC "-//W3C//DTD SVG 1.0//EN"
     "http://www.w3.org/TR/2001/PR-SVG-20010719/
      DTD/svg10.dtd">
<svg width="300" height="150">
<defs>
<text id="Ref" >EIW</text>
</defs>
<rect x="20" y="20" width="200" height="120"
style="fill:white; stroke:black;
stroke-width:0.5;"/>
<line x1="20" y1="60" x2="220" y2="60"
style="stroke:black; stroke-width:0.5;"/>
<line x1="80" y1="60" x2="80" y2="140"
style="stroke:black; stroke-width:0.5;"/>
<line x1="80" y1="110" x2="220" y2="110"
style="stroke:black;
stroke-width:0.5;"/>
<text style="font-size:24; font-family:Arial,
sans-serif; stroke:none;
```

```
  stroke-width:0; fill:red;"
    x="25" y="120" transform="skewY(-15)" >
    <tref xlink:href="#Ref"/>
  </text>
  <text x="35" y="50" style="font-size:24;
  fill:red; stroke:none;
  font-family:Arial, sans-serif;">
  EditITWrite.com
  </text>
  <text x="85" y="130" style="fill:blue;
  stroke:blue; font-size:16;
  font-family:Arial, sans-serif;">
  <animate attributeName="visibility" begin="0s"
  repeatCount="indefinite"
  dur="5s"
    values="visible; hidden; visible; hidden; visible;"
    keyTimes="0s; 0.5s; 1s; 1.5s; 2s;"/>
  Contact us today!
  </text>
  </svg>
```

The second animation is a rotation of text messages that needs to communicate the three ideas of the domain name: technical editing, knowledge of information technology, and technical writing. Suppose that the three chosen messages are "Editing technical documents precisely", "Understanding IT and adding value" and "Writing clearly to communicate effectively".

Given the space constraints in the chosen design, each of the three messages needs to be split over two lines. The next step is to place the two lines of text in the available box and to make sure that the chosen text fits as static text. The code for the first message is

```
<text id="Message1">
<tspan x="90" y="80" style="font-size:14;
font-family:Arial, sans-serif; fill:red; stroke:none;">
Editing technical
</tspan>
<tspan x="90" y="100" style="font-size:14;
font-family:Arial, sans-serif; fill:red; stroke:none;">
documents precisely
</tspan>
</text>
```

Unlike with the RootsPics.com rotating message you saw earlier in this chapter, you must create an `id` attribute on the `<text>` element because all the content of the `<text>` element (the two `<tspan>` elements and their content) needs to be animated. However, you can use the animation from the RootsPics.com example as an animation visual component:

```
<animate begin="0s" dur="12s" targetName="Message1"
attributeName="visibility"
values="visible; hidden; hidden; visible"
keyTimes="0s; 4s; 8s; 12s" repeatCount="indefinite" />
```

Choose the same value for the `id` attribute as before (although this time it is on a `<text>` element), and again choose to have three messages. If you want four messages, for example, the values and `keyTimes` attributes of the animation for `Message1` could be modified as follows, assuming that you again want to have each message displayed for four seconds:

```
<animate begin="0s" dur="16s" targetName="Message1"
attributeName="visibility"
values="visible; hidden; hidden; hidden; visible"
keyTimes="0s; 4s; 8s; 12s; 16s"
repeatCount="indefinite" />
```

To complete the animation, you need to create a `<text>` element with suitable `id` attribute and `<tspan>` elements nested within. Because you know that the code for the first message is correctly positioned and animates correctly, as shown here:

```
<text id="Message1">
<animate begin="0s" dur="12s" targetName="Message1"
attributeName="visibility"
values="visible; hidden; hidden; visible"
keyTimes="0s; 4s; 8s; 12s" repeatCount="indefinite" />
<tspan x="90" y="80" style="font-size:14;
font-family:Arial, sans-serif; fill:red; stroke:none;">
Editing technical
</tspan>
<tspan x="90" y="100" style="font-size:14;
font-family:Arial, sans-serif; fill:red; stroke:none;">
documents precisely
</tspan>
</text>
```

you can use that as another visual component, making suitable changes in the `id` attribute of the `<text>` element, in the `values` attribute of the `<animate>` element and in the content of each of the two `<tspan>` elements.

To finish the ad, you need to add a link to the http://www.edititwrite.com Web site:

```
<a xlink:href="http://www.edititwrite.com/
target="new">
...
</a>
```

After those changes are made, the code looks like the code shown in Listing 9.17.

Listing 9.17 (EditITWrite03.svg)

```
<?xml version="1.0" standalone="no"?>
<!DOCTYPE svg PUBLIC "-//W3C//DTD SVG 1.0//EN"
    "http://www.w3.org/TR/2001/PR-SVG-20010719/
        DTD/svg10.dtd">
<svg width="300" height="150">
<defs>
<text id="Ref" >EIW</text>
</defs>
<a xlink:href="http://www.edititwrite.com/"
target="new">
<rect x="20" y="20" width="200" height="120"
style="fill:white; stroke:black; stroke-width:0.5;"/>
<line x1="20" y1="60" x2="220" y2="60"
style="stroke:black; stroke-width:0.5;"/>
<line x1="80" y1="60" x2="80" y2="140"
style="stroke:black; stroke-width:0.5;"/>
<line x1="80" y1="110" x2="220" y2="110"
style="stroke:black; stroke-width:0.5;"/>
<text style="font-size:24; font-family:Arial,
sans-serif; stroke:none; stroke-width:0; fill:red;"
  x="25" y="120" transform="skewY(-15)" >
  <tref xlink:href="#Ref"/>
</text>
<text x="35" y="50" style="font-size:24; fill:red;
stroke:none; font-family:Arial, sans-serif;">
EditITWrite.com
</text>
```

```
<text id="Message1">
<animate begin="0s" dur="12s" targetName="Message1"
attributeName="visibility"
values="visible; hidden; hidden; hidden;"
keyTimes="0s; 3.5s; 8s; 12s" repeatCount="indefinite" />
<tspan x="90" y="80" style="font-size:14;
font-family:Arial, sans-serif; fill:red; stroke:none;">
Editing technical
</tspan>
<tspan x="90" y="100" style="font-size:14;
font-family:Arial, sans-serif; fill:red; stroke:none;">
documents precisely
</tspan>
</text>
<text id="Message2" visibility="hidden">
<animate begin="0s" dur="12s" targetName="Message2"
attributeName="visibility"
values="hidden; visible; hidden; hidden;"
keyTimes="0s; 4s; 8s; 12s" repeatCount="indefinite"
calcMode="discrete"/>
<tspan x="90" y="80" style="font-size:14;
font-family:Arial, sans-serif; fill:red; stroke:none;">
Understanding IT
</tspan>
<tspan x="90" y="100" style="font-size:14;
font-family:Arial, sans-serif; fill:red; stroke:none;">
so adding value
</tspan>
</text>
<text id="Message3" visibility="hidden">
<animate begin="0s" dur="12s" targetName="Message3"
attributeName="visibility"
values="hidden; hidden; visible; hidden;"
keyTimes="0s; 4s; 8s; 12s" repeatCount="indefinite"
calcMode="discrete"/>
<tspan x="90" y="80" style="font-size:14;
font-family:Arial, sans-serif; fill:red; stroke:none;">
Writing clearly to
</tspan>
<tspan x="90" y="100" style="font-size:14;
font-family:Arial, sans-serif; fill:red; stroke:none;">
communicate well
</tspan>
</text>
<text x="85" y="130" style="fill:blue; stroke:blue;
font-size:16; font-family:Arial, sans-serif;">
<animate attributeName="visibility" begin="0s"
```

```
repeatCount="indefinite" dur="5s"
  values="visible; hidden; visible; hidden; visible;"
  keyTimes="0s; 0.5s; 1s; 1.5s; 2s;"/>
Contact us today!
</text>
</a>
</svg>
```

The cycling of the text works beautifully with this code, except that once in each cycle, all three pieces of text are visible together for a short time! That's not what you want! You can see the mess in Figure 09.11.

Figure 09.11

The undesirable overlap of the text messages that occurs briefly once in each 12-second cycle because of the trailing-semicolon bug.

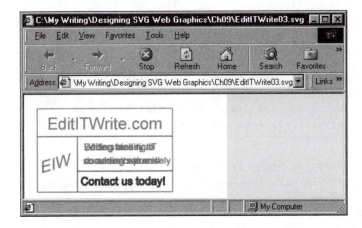

The reason for the problem? A trailing semicolon was left in each of the `values` attributes on the `<animate>` elements. After the semicolons are taken out (they have been removed from the code download), it all works beautifully. (So much trouble for three semicolons!)

The `<set>` animation element provides an alternative approach to the `<animate>` element here. When you use the `<set>` element, as shown here:

```
<text id="Message1" visibility="hidden">
<set id="Anim1" begin="0s; Anim3.end"
end="Anim1.begin+4s" attributeName="visibility"
from="hidden" to="visible" repeatCount="indefinite"/>
<tspan x="90" y="80" style="font-size:14;
font-family:Arial, sans-serif; fill:red; stroke:none;">
Editing technical
</tspan>
<tspan x="90" y="100" style="font-size:14;
font-family:Arial, sans-serif; fill:red; stroke:none;">
```

```
documents precisely
</tspan>
</text>
<text id="Message2" visibility="hidden">
<set id="Anim2" begin="Anim1.end" dur="4s"
attributeName="visibility"
from="hidden" to="visible"/>
<tspan x="90" y="80" style="font-size:14;
font-family:Arial, sans-serif; fill:red; stroke:none;">
Understanding IT
</tspan>
<tspan x="90" y="100" style="font-size:14;
font-family:Arial, sans-serif; fill:red; stroke:none;">
so adding value
</tspan>
</text>
<text id="Message3" visibility="hidden">
<set id="Anim3" begin="Anim2.end" dur="4s"
attributeName="visibility"
from="hidden" to="visible"/>
<tspan x="90" y="80" style="font-size:14;
font-family:Arial, sans-serif; fill:red; stroke:none;">
Writing clearly to
</tspan>
<tspan x="90" y="100" style="font-size:14;
font-family:Arial, sans-serif; fill:red; stroke:none;">
communicate well
</tspan>
</text>
```

the sequence of animations plays exactly as you want, with no ugly transitory overlap of text as the second and subsequent cycles of animation started. So you have two solutions to the problem: Remove the trailing semicolons, or use the `<set>` element to make the animation.

A banner ad with scrolling text

In Chapter 8, I showed you a text window with scrolling text. In that example, you create smoothly scrolling text; on this occasion, however, for another possible banner ad for EditITWrite.com, suppose that you want to have scrolling text in a traditionally sized banner ad that stops long enough for users to have a chance to read the text.

The finished ad, during part of its animation, looks like the one shown in Figure 09.12.

Figure 09.12

The EditITWrite.com banner ad during part of its animation.

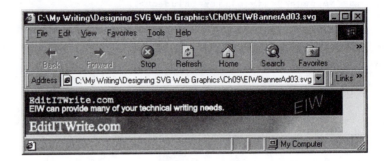

For most of the earlier examples, the precise size of the SVG image hasn't mattered too much; for a banner ad, however, the precise size matters immensely. It is 468 by 60 pixels, and that's that. So that's the dimension you must work with:

Listing 9.18 (EIWBannerAd01.svg)

```
<?xml version="1.0" standalone="no"?>
<!DOCTYPE svg PUBLIC "-//W3C//DTD SVG 1.0//EN"
     "http://www.w3.org/TR/2001/PR-SVG-20010719/
     DTD/svg10.dtd">
<svg width="468" height="60">
</svg>
```

First, you split the available space into two rectangles: the top one with 35 pixels (for two lines of scrolling text) and the lower one with 25 pixels for a static name. In the bottom rectangle, you create a filter effect that uses the background image, so the first rectangle (the background), which has a linear gradient across it, is used to provide the input to that filter process. The other two rectangles cover it completely, so you do not see anything other than its effect within the filter:

```
<rect  x="0" y="0" width="468" height="60"
style="fill:url(#MyBlueGradient);
opacity:0.5;"/>
<rect x="0" y="0" width="468" height="35"
style="fill:black; stroke:none;"/>
```

```
<rect x="0" y="35" width="468" height="25"
style="fill:#000099; filter:url(#Turbulence1);
  stroke:none;"/>
```

As shown in the preceding example, visual components from earlier chapters are available for reuse. Make use of a linear gradient that was used earlier; in this case, with the first `stop-color` property adapted to give a much bluer effect. Because the linear gradient is, by virtue of being applied to the background image, an input to the `<feTurbulence>` filter primitive, the whole of the appearance in the lower visible rectangle has an abstract bluish effect in it.

You also reuse the skewed text `EIW` in the ad, placing it far to the right. If you start using skew effects, you might find that it is invisible when you first try to use it. Intuitively, from looking at Figure 09.12, you might expect to place the `EIW` skew text at perhaps `(410,40)`. If you try that method, however, you don't see the text. It is hidden off the top of your screen, as you can confirm if you try coordinates like those and then zoom out and pan around to find the text. You should have a large outer `<svg>` element to allow for "losing" elements when you first experiment with skewing (as in Figure 09.13).

Figure 09.13

An EditITWrite.com banner ad before the addition of the scrolling text.

Listing 9.19 (EIWBannerAd02.svg)

```
<?xml version="1.0" standalone="no"?>
<!DOCTYPE svg PUBLIC "-//W3C//DTD SVG 1.0//EN"
     "http://www.w3.org/TR/2001/PR-SVG-20010719/
      DTD/svg10.dtd">
<svg width="468" height="60">
<defs>
<linearGradient id="MyBlueGradient"
```

```
gradientUnits="userSpaceOnUse" x1="90"
y1="50" x2="400" y2="500" >
<stop offset="10%" style="stop-color:#000066"/>
<stop offset="40%" style="stop-color:#FFFF00"/>
<stop offset="75%" style="stop-color:#9999FF"/>
</linearGradient>
 <filter id="Turbulence1" in="SourceImage"
filterUnits="userSpaceOnUse" >
  <feTurbulence in="BackgroundImage"
type="turbulence" baseFrequency="0.01"
    numOctaves="1" seed="0" >
  </feTurbulence>
</filter>
</defs>
<rect  x="0" y="0" width="468" height="60"
style="fill:url(#MyBlueGradient);
opacity:0.5;"/>
<rect x="0" y="0" width="468" height="35"
style="fill:black; stroke:none;"/>
<rect x="0" y="35" width="468" height="25"
style="fill:#000099; filter:url(#Turbulence1);
stroke:none;"/>
<text x="5" y="55"
style="font-family:'Times New Roman', serif;
font-size:20; stroke:white; fill:white;">
EditITWrite.com
</text>
<text style="font-size:24; font-family:Arial,
sans-serif; stroke:red;
stroke-width:0; fill:red;" x="395" y="140"
transform="skewY(-15)" >
EIW
</text>
</svg>
```

Plan to reuse parts of the scrolling text window from Chapter 8 because it is a useful visual component, after all. Make some adjustments to how it works, however, because only two lines of text can be displayed at one time.

First, you create a nested `<svg>` element that covers the black rectangle:

```
<svg x="0" y="0" width="468" height="35">
</svg>
```

Because all the scrolling text is nested within that `<svg>` element, the text cannot be visible outside it, even if you make a coding mistake.

Although you use the scrolling text window, adapting it for use here is a more significant task than most of the adaptations of visual components you have looked at so far. The first difficulty is that the text in the original is black, which does not show up well against the black background here, so you have to change the text color to yellow for the heading or white for ordinary text. The original had one smooth animation, although here you want stepped animation with two lines of text scrolling into view and then stopping long enough for them to be read. To achieve that effect, you use a `values` attribute in the `<animate>` element. To achieve the pauses in scrolling, you simply make two successive values the same so that there is no movement and therefore the pause you want:

```
<animate attributeName="y" begin="0s" dur="16s"
values="50; 15; 15; -55; -55; -130; -130 "
repeatCount="indefinite"/>
```

Suppose that you want to give a clear visual impression of text scrolling up by adding blank lines. However, a `<tspan>` element with no text in it seems to be ignored, at least by the Adobe SVG Viewer. So, you make use of the invisibility of black text against a black background and add two lines between each frame of text, which have the word *blank* in black lettering, giving an adequate visual impression of blank lines.

The text in the original scrolling box was font size 10; on this occasion, assume that 12 is more readable as white text against a black background.

The changes to the original scrolling box, therefore, were to change the fill color of all the `<tspan>` elements, change the font size except on the heading text, substitute a `values` attribute in the `<animate>` element, and reduce the `dur` attribute of the animation to correspond with the lesser amount of text than in the original. Although you have to make many adaptations to the original visual component, it still saves time compared to coding it all from scratch.

Listing 9.20 (EIWBanner03.svg)

```
<?xml version="1.0" standalone="no"?>
<!DOCTYPE svg PUBLIC "-//W3C//DTD SVG 1.0//EN"
     "http://www.w3.org/TR/2001/PR-SVG-20010719/
       DTD/svg10.dtd">
<svg width="468" height="60">
<defs>
<linearGradient id="MyBlueGradient"
gradientUnits="userSpaceOnUse" x1="90"
y1="50" x2="400" y2="500" >
<stop offset="10%" style="stop-color:#000066"/>
<stop offset="40%" style="stop-color:#FFFF00"/>
<stop offset="75%" style="stop-color:#9999FF"/>
</linearGradient>
 <filter id="Turbulence1" in="SourceImage"
filterUnits="userSpaceOnUse" >
   <feTurbulence in="BackgroundImage" type="turbulence"
baseFrequency="0.01"
      numOctaves="1" seed="0" >
   </feTurbulence>
</filter>
</defs>
<rect  x="0" y="0" width="468" height="60"
style="fill:url(#MyBlueGradient);
opacity:0.5;"/>
<rect x="0" y="0" width="468" height="35"
style="fill:black; stroke:none;"/>
<rect x="0" y="35" width="468" height="25"
style="fill:#000099; filter:url(#Turbulence1);
stroke:none;"/>
<svg x="0" y="0" width="468" height="35">
<text>
<tspan x="5" y="50" style="font-size:14;
font-family:courier, monospace;
stroke:#FFFF00; fill:#FFFF00">
<animate attributeName="y" begin="0s" dur="16s"
values="50; 15; 15; -55; -55; -130; -130 "
repeatCount="indefinite"/>
EditITWrite.com
</tspan>
<tspan x="5" dy="1em" style="font-size:12;
font-family:Arial, sans-serif; fill:white;
stroke:white;">
EIW can provide many of your technical writing needs.
</tspan>
```

```
<tspan x="5" dy="2em" style="font-size:12;
font-family:Arial, sans-serif;">
blank
</tspan>
<tspan x="5" dy="2em" style="font-size:12;
font-family:Arial, sans-serif; ">
blank
</tspan>
<tspan x="5" dy="1em" style="font-size:12;
font-family:Arial, sans-serif; fill:white;
stroke:white;">
We have expertise in XML, SVG, Java,
XHTML, JavaScript,
</tspan>
<tspan x="5" dy="1em" style="font-size:12;
font-family:Arial, sans-serif; fill:white;
stroke:white;">
Lotus Domino and other Web technologies.
</tspan>
<tspan x="5" dy="2em" style="font-size:12;
font-family:Arial, sans-serif;">
blank
</tspan>
<tspan x="5" dy="2em" style="font-size:12;
font-family:Arial, sans-serif; ">
blank
</tspan>
<tspan x="5" dy="1em" style="font-size:12;
font-family:Arial, sans-serif; fill:white;
stroke:white;">
We can translate from German, French, Spanish,
</tspan>
<tspan x="5" dy="1em" style="font-size:12;
font-family:Arial, sans-serif; fill:white;
stroke:white;">
Japanese and other languages into English.
</tspan>
</text>
</svg>
<text x="5" y="55"
style="font-family:'Times New Roman', serif;
font-size:20; stroke:white; fill:white;">
EditITWrite.com
</text>
<text style="font-size:24; font-family:Arial,
sans-serif; stroke:red;
```

```
stroke-width:0; fill:red;" x="395" y="140"
transform="skewY(-15)" >
EIW
</text>
</svg>
```

Figures 09.14, 09.15, and 09.16 show the three phases of text in the banner ad for EditITWrite.com.

Figure 09.14

The first bit of text shown in the scrolling banner ad for EditITWrite.com

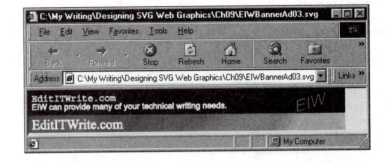

Figure 09.15

The second bit of text shown in the scrolling banner ad for EditITWrite.com

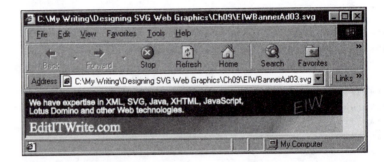

Figure 09.16

The third bit of text shown in the scrolling banner ad for EditITWrite.com

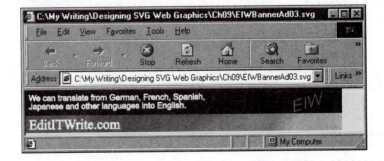

In this chapter, I have showed you how to combine several parts of the functionality provided by SVG, and I hope that you have begun to gain a feel for the power that SVG provides when these basic visual components are combined. In Chapter 10, "Embedding SVG in HTML or XHTML Pages," you go on to look at how you can embed the SVG images you want to use in an HTML or XHTML Web page.

10

Embedding SVG
in HTML or
XHTML Pages

In this chapter:

SVG and HTML

Many examples in this book have shown SVG images in isolation, with the images simply displayed on their own in a Web browser that has the Adobe SVG Viewer, in a dedicated SVG viewer such as Batik, or in a multi-namespace XML browser such as X-Smiles. In day-to-day use of SVG, one of the things you are likely to want to do routinely with an SVG image is to embed it in an HTML or XHTML Web page. In the first part of this chapter, you look at how that basic task is carried out.

Displaying an SVG image might seem to be a straightforward task, but if you are aiming to achieve cross-browser display, you need to consider several factors, as the following discussion explains.

In practice, you might well have multiple SVG images within one HTML or XHTML page, but the techniques discussed here can be applied many times in a single page, assuming that you use HTML or XHTML tables or CSS correctly for Web page positioning.

As you might know, the HTML `<embed>` tag was originally developed as a proprietary tag and is deprecated by the W3C. However, as you will see from the following discussion, the `<embed>` tag provides better cross-browser functionality for this purpose than the more "politically correct" `<object>` element. So, this chapter first looks at how to use the `<embed>` tag to embed a single SVG image.

Using the <embed> Element

Embedding an SVG image in an XHTML page using the `<embed>` element is a straightforward process. You use the `<embed>` tag with the `src`, `type`, `width`, and `height` attributes specified correctly, and it all pretty much works "out of the box"—at least with the browsers I tested: Internet Explorer 5.5, Netscape 4.7, Netscape 6, and Opera 5. The `type` attribute for an SVG image is `image/svg+xml`.

The following example embeds a simple SVG image that you used, in a slightly different version, to look at the nesting of `<svg>` elements. You see the purpose of using this particular image later in this chapter. You set it against a pale gray background so that you can easily see the boundaries of the SVG and the containing HTML or XHTML page.

Listing 10.1 (Embed01.html)

```
<html>
<head>
<meta http-equiv="content-type"
content="text/html;charset=iso-8859-1">
<title>Embedding an SVG image using
the &lt;embed&gt; element.</title>
</head>
<body bgcolor="#cccccc" leftmargin="0"
marginwidth="0" topmargin="0" marginheight="0">
<h4>The image below is an embedded SVG image.
The pale gray background is the XHTML page
background color. The white area surrounded
by a red outline is the SVG image.</h4>
<p><embed src="NestedSVG.svg" width="500"
height="400" type="image/svg+xml"></p>
</body>
</html>
```

When you try to display this HTML or XHTML page in Netscape 6, it is satisfactory and looks like the one shown in Figure 10.01.

In Internet Explorer 5.5, the appearance is similar and also satisfactory. Interestingly, a book I read recently about browser capabilities stated emphatically that no version of Internet Explorer supports the embed tag.

Figure 10.02 demonstrates that statement to be incorrect. Similarly, this syntax works in the Opera 5 browser most of the time, but occasionally, for no obvious reason, the Opera 5.02 browser doesn't display SVG correctly (see Figure 10.03). I don't know the reason.

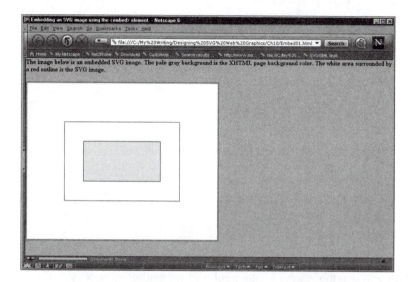

Figure 10.01

Listing 10.1 viewed in Netscape 6.0.

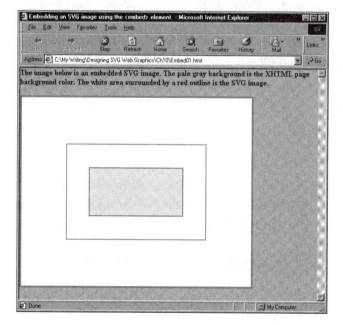

Figure 10.02

Listing 10.1 viewed in Internet Explorer 5.5.

Figure 10.03

Listing 10.1 viewed
in Opera 5.02.

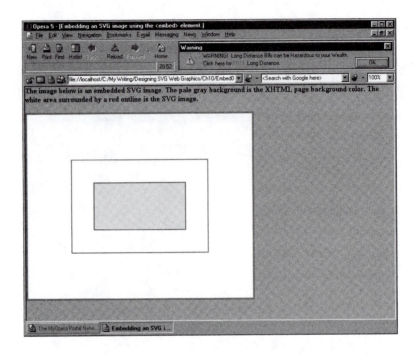

When you use the `<embed>` element and remember to specify the `src`, `type`, `width`, and `height` attributes correctly, you can reliably (with the possible exception of the occasional glitch with Opera 5) expect to see your SVG image correctly displayed in Internet Explorer 5.x, Netscape 6, Netscape 4.7, and Opera 5.

But I wonder whether you noticed the content of the `<body>` tag of the HTML page:

```
<body bgcolor="#cccccc" leftmargin="0"
marginwidth="0" topmargin="0" marginheight="0">
```

The syntax is unorthodox. You can omit all the attributes, if you want, and the appearance doesn't change much—the text moves just a little down and to the right—as you can see in Figure 10.04, from Internet Explorer 5.5.

Listing 10.2 (NestingSVG00.html)

```
<html>
<head>
<meta http-equiv="content-type"
```

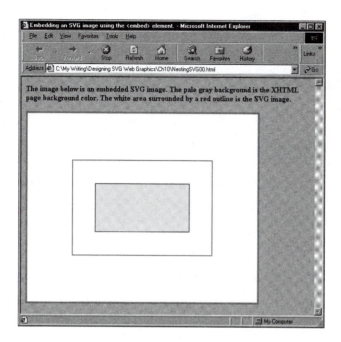

Figure 10.04

Listing 10.2
viewed in Internet
Explorer 5.5.

```
content="text/html;charset=iso-8859-1">
<title>Embedding an SVG image using
the &lt;embed&gt; element.</title>
</head>
<body bgcolor="#cccccc" >
<h4>The image below is an embedded SVG image.
The pale gray background is the
XHTML page background color. The white area
surrounded by a red outline is the SVG
image.</h4>
<p><embed src="NestedSVG.svg" width="500"
height="400" type="image/svg+xml">
</p>
</body>
</html>
```

For many, but not all, purposes, the following syntax is adequate :

```
<body bgcolor="#CCCCCC">
```

I discuss this issue of cross-browser positioning a little later in this chapter,
after you move on to look at adding scroll bars to SVG Web pages.

Adding Scroll Bars to SVG Web Pages

One of the disappointments of the Adobe SVG Viewer, at least for me, has been the omission of scroll bars (still missing as of version 2.0) when SVG images are displayed on their own as Web pages (see Chapter 12, "Creating a Simple SVG Web Site"). That omission contrasts with the many successes of the Adobe viewer. However, overcoming the omission is simple: Use the HTML `<embed>` element to provide scroll bars for a large SVG image, as Listing 10.3 shows.

Listing 10.3 (ScrollBars01.html)

```html
<html>
 <head>
  <meta http-equiv="content-type"
content="text/html;charset=iso-8859-1">
  <title>An SVG Web Page which seems to
have scroll bars!</title>
 </head>
 <body leftmargin="0" marginwidth="0"
topmargin="0"  marginheight="0">
   <embed src="NestedSVG.svg" width="1000"
height="800"
    type="image/svg+xml">
 </body>
</html>
```

If the SVG image must completely fill the screen, as with SVG Web pages, make sure that you set the margins for the body of the HTML `<body>` element to zero. Then the SVG image completely fills the page. Because the page is in HTML, however, the benefit is that the Internet Explorer browser, as shown in Figure 10.05, automatically provides scroll bars for displaying the SVG image. Of course, if you want to pan or zoom the SVG image, assuming that the page designer has not turned those facilities off, you simply hold down the Alt key (on a Windows system) and the left mouse button and then move the mouse to pan the SVG image.

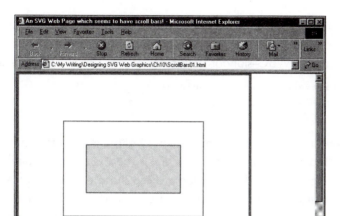

Figure 10.05

Listing 10.3 produces scroll bars for an SVG image, displayed in Internet Explorer 5.5.

You might assume that setting the `<svg>` image width and height to 100 percent, as shown in Listing 10.4, would achieve the same effect, but in fact it doesn't. The SVG image is resized to the browser window and therefore doesn't really need scroll bars, although Internet Explorer 5.5 provides a rudimentary vertical scroll bar.

Listing 10.4 (ScrollBars01b.html)

```
<html>
<head>
<meta http-equiv="content-type"
content="text/html;charset=iso-8859-1">
<title>An SVG Web Page which seems to have
scroll bars!</title>
</head>
<body leftmargin="0" marginwidth="0"
topmargin="0" marginheight="0">
<embed src="NestedSVG.svg"
 width="100%" height="100%" type="image/svg+xml">
</body>
</html>
```

As I said in the preceding section, in order to achieve zero borders in Internet Explorer 5.5, Netscape 4.7, Netscape 6, or Opera 5, you have to use several non–W3C–standard attributes on the `<body>` tag, like this:

```
<body leftmargin="0" marginwidth="0"
topmargin="0"  marginheight="0">
```

I can report to you that this combination of attributes achieves zero margins on all four browsers. The `leftmargin` and `topmargin` attributes are proprietary Internet Explorer tags. Using those ensures that the left and top page margins in Internet Explorer are zero. The `marginwidth` and `marginheight` attributes belong to a `<frame>` tag, but seem to work correctly (at least they achieve what I want them to achieve) on the `<body>` element, too.

The "correct" (W3C-approved) way to obtain zero margins is to use Cascading Style Sheets, or CSS. However, I could not find a syntax that would work on all four browsers I tested—hence, my use of an unorthodox combination of attributes that works for all four browsers.

Using the <object> Element

The `<embed>` element was deprecated by the W3C in HTML 4, although, as you've seen in earlier examples, the element still continues to perform its function, even if you have to resort to the use of slightly unorthodox syntax to achieve zero margins cross-browser. The element now preferred by W3C for displaying SVG and other objects on an HTML or XHTML Web page is the `<object>` element. However, its use is fraught with practical issues and difficulties.

First, Figure 10.06 shows what happens if you use the `<object>` element just as you used the `<embed>` element for the first example.

In Figure 10.06, you can see that part of the SVG image is obscured. Now you see the benefit of images that make use of every pixel at the edge when testing—it shows up edge problems like this one. In Internet Explorer 5.5, when an SVG image is displayed, a pseudo–3-D border is

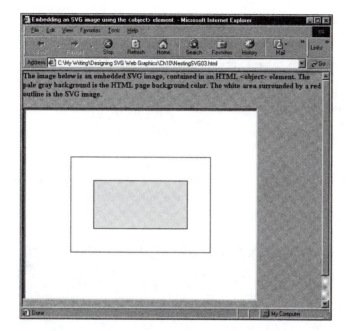

Figure 10.06

*Using the
\<object\> element
in Internet Explorer
causes the loss of a
little of the SVG
image.*

added that intrudes into the space for the SVG image. So, when your code
has dimensions (as shown in the following code) that are exactly the same
size as the SVG image, you cut off a little of the image.

Listing 10.5 (NestingSVG03.html)

```
<html>
<head>
 <meta http-equiv="content-type"
content="text/html;charset=iso-8859-1">
 <title>Embedding an SVG image using
the &lt;object&gt; element.</title>
</head>
<body bgcolor="#cccccc" leftmargin="0"
marginwidth="0" topmargin="0"
  marginheight="0">
<h4>The image below is an embedded SVG image,
contained in an HTML &lt;object&gt; element.
   The pale gray background is the HTML page
background color. The white area surrounded by a red
   outline is the SVG image.</h4>
<object data="NestedSVG.svg" width="500"
height="400" type="image/svg+xml">
```

```
<img src="Non-existent.gif" alt="Unable
to display SVG." />
</object>
<h4>Notice that the &lt;object&gt; element
imposes a border which cuts off part of the
SVG image at the
right and bottom.</h4>
</body>
</html>
```

However, if you slightly increase the `width` and `height` attributes on the `<object>` element, you can display the full image in Internet Explorer, as you can see in Figure 10.07.

Figure 10.07

Using the `<object>` element and increasing the `width` and `height` attributes allows all of the SVG image to be displayed.

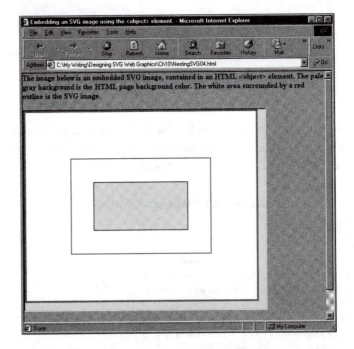

 Variations seem to exist in how different "flavors" of Internet Explorer 5.5 display this code. Not all show the 3D border, as shown in Figure 10.07. The reasons for the differences are unclear.

The code is shown in Listing 10.6.

Listing 10.6 (NestingSVG04.html)

```html
<html>
<head>
 <meta http-equiv="content-type"
content="text/html;charset=iso-8859-1">
 <title>Embedding an SVG image using
the &lt;object&gt; element.</title>
</head>
<body bgcolor="#cccccc" leftmargin="0"
marginwidth="0" topmargin="0"
  marginheight="0">
<h4>The image below is an embedded SVG image,
contained in an HTML &lt;object&gt; element.
  The pale gray background is the HTML page
background color. The white area surrounded by a red
  outline is the SVG image.</h4>
<object data="NestedSVG.svg" width="520" height="420"
type="image/svg+xml">
<img src="Non-existent.gif" alt="Unable to
display SVG." />
</object>
<h4>Notice that the &lt;object&gt; element imposes a
border which cuts off part of the SVG image at the
right and bottom.</h4>
</body>
</html>
```

In Internet Explorer (as Figure 10.07 might suggest to you), if you don't make the `width` and `height` attributes adequate, part of the SVG image is cut off. This behavior is unlike the display of GIF images, for example. If the `width` and `height` attributes are too small to display GIFs, Internet Explorer adds scroll bars, although it doesn't add them for SVG images.

Be careful not to omit the `width` and `height` attributes on the `<object>` tag if you want your SVG image to be displayed in Internet Explorer. If you do omit them, you will produce the appearance shown in Figure 10.08 (the SVG image is not displayed). This behavior is the same as when the `width` and `height` attributes are omitted in GIF images.

Figure 10.08

If you omit the width *and* height *attributes on an* <object> *tag, you produce this appearance (see Listing 10.7 for the code).*

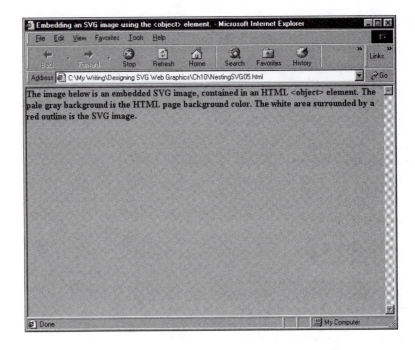

Listing 10.7 (NestingSVG05.html)

```html
<html>
<head>
 <meta http-equiv="content-type"
content="text/html;charset=iso-8859-1">
 <title>Embedding an SVG image using
the &lt;object&gt; element.</title>
</head>
<body bgcolor="#cccccc" leftmargin="0"
marginwidth="0" topmargin="0"
  marginheight="0">
<h4>The image below is an embedded SVG image,
contained in an HTML
&lt;object&gt; element.
  The pale gray background is the HTML page
background color. The white area
surrounded by a red
  outline is the SVG image.</h4>
<object data="NestedSVG.svg" type="image/svg+xml">
<img src="Non-existent.gif" alt="Unable to
display SVG." />
</object>
</body>
</html>
```

What happens if you use the `<object>` element and attempt to view your SVG image using the Netscape 6 or Opera 5 browsers? The answer is that the appearance is similar to what is shown in Figure 10.08. In other words, the SVG image is not displayed, although an appropriately sized rectangular space is reserved for its display. (However, it is displayed correctly in Netscape 4.7.)

If you want to disregard users of Netscape 6.0 and Opera 5.0 as visitors to your Web site, you can afford to use the `<object>` tag to display SVG. However, to provide the correct display in Internet Explorer 5.5, you need to be sure to add a few pixels to the `width` and `height` attributes if you want to avoid slightly cropping the right and bottom edges of your SVG image.

Netscape 6.01 seems to display the <object> element, but has other problems displaying SVG. For viewing SVG, Netscape 6.0 has been significantly more stable. Opera 5.1 seems to display the <object> element, but with a white border.

In practice, although the `<object>` element is the "correct" way to embed SVG images, using the `<embed>` element—even though it is deprecated by W3C—is the only practical way to display SVG images in a way that is compatible with the four major browsers mentioned earlier in this section.

Displaying Alternative Text or Images

So far in this chapter, I have discussed the embedding of SVG images in HTML and XHTML Web pages as though every visitor to your Web site has SVG viewing capability. But, of course, at least for a while, they might not. Adobe has an agreement with Real.com to distribute the Adobe SVG Viewer with RealPlayer (recent versions of which use SMIL) and to include the SVG Viewer with Adobe Acrobat and other products. Adobe aims, by these and other means, to have distributed 45 million copies of the SVG viewer by December 2001 and a total of 110 million by April 2002.

Within a few months of the publication of this book, many visitors to your Web site are likely, therefore, to have the Adobe viewer installed. However, for visitors to your site who do not have the viewer, or who choose not to install it, you need to provide alternative information—including information about how to download and install an SVG viewer.

Alternatives using the <embed> tag

As far as I can find out, you cannot display a message from within an `<embed>` tag that transmits a text message, such as to indicate that an SVG viewer needs to be downloaded.

A sensible strategy, then, if you choose to use the `<embed>` tag, is to place at some suitable place on the home page (or any other likely entry point to your Web site) a text message indicating the need for an SVG viewer and include a link so that site visitors can download a suitable SVG viewer, such as the Adobe viewer.

Alternatives using the <object> tag

With the `<object>` tag, you have two display options: Display a bitmap image, such as a GIF, or, if that image is not displayed, display alternative text using the `alt` attribute on the `<img>` tag, as shown in the following sample code:

Listing 10.8 (ObjectAlt01.html)

```
<html>
<head>
 <meta http-equiv="content-type"
content="text/html;charset=iso-8859-1">
 <title>Embedding an SVG image using
the &lt;object&gt; element.</title>
</head>
<body bgcolor="#cccccc" leftmargin="0"
marginwidth="0" topmargin="0"
  marginheight="0">
<h4>The image below is an embedded SVG image,
contained in an HTML
```

```
&lt;object&gt; element.
   The pale gray background is the HTML page
background color. The white area
surrounded by a red
   outline is the SVG image.</h4>
<object data="NestedSVG.svg" width="500"
height="400" type="image/svg+xml">
<img src="GetSVGViewer.gif" alt="Unable to
display SVG. Please visit http://www.Adobe.com/svg/
to download an SVG viewer." />
</object>
<h4>Notice that the &lt;object&gt; element imposes a
border which cuts off part
of the SVG image at the
right and bottom.</h4>
</body>
</html>
```

In Internet Explorer 5.5, if the alternative GIF image is not displayed, a text message advises the site visitor of the need to have an SVG viewer and gives a URL where a viewer can be downloaded.

As in so many other situations with variations in browser behavior, you have to make a choice about which of the available not totally satisfactory choices best meets your needs.

Alternatives in XML and SMIL

The X-Smiles browser, as mentioned in Chapter 1, "The Basic SVG Tool Set," is a useful test bed for exploring the use of SVG images in or with a variety of XML application languages, including SMIL, XSL-FO, and XForms.

I suggest that you check the X-Smiles Web site, http://www.x-smiles.org, for the latest information because the SMIL, XSL-FO, and XForms specifications are all under ongoing development and X-Smiles support changes almost weekly. X-Smiles provides useful sample files for download to allow you to see working syntax.

The SMIL 2.0 specification is at http://www.w3.org/TR/smil20. The XSL-FO specification, at http://www.w3.org/TR/xsl/, is referred to there as "XSL". The XForms specification is at http://www.w3.org/TR/xforms/.

As you look forward, SVG is likely to be used in many ways. It might be embedded in HTML or XHTMl, as I showed you earlier in this chapter. It undoubtedly will be used frequently with the emerging XML application languages, such as SMIL, XSL-FO, and XForms. The Mozilla browser has a project in an early stage to provide support for inline support of SVG. Similarly, the Amaya browser has limited, but growing, support for inline SVG. However, in the near term, you will need to display SVG embedded in HTML or XHTML.

11

Creating Interactive SVG Graphics

In this chapter:

Defining Interactive

SVG graphics can be *interactive*, where they respond to a variety of user-initiated events, such as clicking a mouse button, moving the mouse over a particular part of an image, or zooming and panning an SVG image.

You can create interactivity on an SVG image by using events, such as a mouse click, to initiate SVG declarative animation or to initiate scripts. This chapter demonstrates the use of declarative SVG to create interactivity based on the SVG events that are accessible to declarative syntax.

One specific type of interactivity, linking to other pages, was described in Chapter 5, "Creating Navigation Bars," in connection with the use of the SVG `<a>` element in navigation bars.

SVG Events

SVG provides an extensive range of events, which are listed in Chapter 16 of the SVG specification at http://www.w3.org/TR/SVG/. The most useful events are the click, mouseover, and mouseout events. You can also use the mousedown and mouseup events, but I find that I rarely use them.

Listing 11.1 shows the syntax for using a click event to begin an animation that uses a `<set>` element.

Listing 11.1 (BasicEvents01.svg)

```
<?xml version="1.0" standalone="no"?>
<!DOCTYPE svg PUBLIC "-//W3C//DTD SVG 1.0//EN"
    "http://www.w3.org/TR/2001/PR-SVG-20010719/
        DTD/svg10.dtd">
<svg>
<defs>
<linearGradient id="MyGreenGradient">
<stop offset="5%" style="stop-color:#006600"/>
<stop offset="95%" style="stop-color:#99FFCC"/>
</linearGradient>
</defs>
<rect x="20" y="20" width="100" height="50" rx="10" ry="10"
style="fill:url(#MyGreenGradient)">
<set begin="click" dur="3s" attributeName="fill"
from="url(#MyGreenGradient)" to="#006600"/>
</rect>
</svg>
```

A click event, formally speaking, follows a mousedown event and a mouse-up event. If you want to have separate color changes, for example, on an SVG object on mousedown and mouseup, you can use code as shown in Listing 11.2.

Listing 11.2 (BasicEvents02.svg)

```
<?xml version="1.0" standalone="no"?>
<!DOCTYPE svg PUBLIC "-//W3C//DTD SVG 1.0//EN"
    "http://www.w3.org/TR/2001/PR-SVG-20010719/
        DTD/svg10.dtd">
<svg>
<defs>
<linearGradient id="MyGreenGradient">
<stop offset="5%" style="stop-color:#006600"/>
<stop offset="95%" style="stop-color:#99FFCC"/>
</linearGradient>
<linearGradient id="MyRedGradient">
<stop offset="5%" style="stop-color:#FF9999"/>
<stop offset="95%" style="stop-color:#660000"/>
</linearGradient>
</defs>
<rect x="20" y="20" width="100" height="50" rx="10" ry="10"
style="fill:url(#MyGreenGradient)">
<set begin="mousedown" end="mouseup" attributeName="fill"
```

```
from="url(#MyGreenGradient)" to="#006600"/>
<set begin="mouseup" dur="3s" attributeName="fill"
from="#006600" to="url(#MyRedGradient)"/>
</rect>
</svg>
```

The code shown in Listing 11.2 causes the rectangle on mousedown to change its fill to plain green, which lasts until the mouseup event, when the fill changes to a reddish gradient, which lasts three seconds.

Watch out for one potential trap in the wording of the SVG specification. For the click event, for example, the specification refers to the *event attribute name* as `onclick`. If you attempt to use that term as the attribute name on an SVG element, you don't achieve the interactivity you want. You need to use `click` as the attribute name on the SVG element.

Sample SVG Images and Components Using Interactivity

In this section, I want to show you some examples of constructing SVG Web page "furniture" that demonstrates interactivity.

A mailto graphic

A mailto link on a Web page can be as simple as plain text or, in some cases, a hyperanimated irritation. In this section, you create an interactive, animated mailto graphic—one that doesn't intrude on the user experience.

The graphic looks like an envelope. When you mouse over the graphic, the "flap" opens and the text "Email me" is animated (see Figure 11.01).

First, create a static version of the graphic. I chose to create it against a black background because that seemed to give a better overall effect. Here is the code for the first static version:

Figure 11.01

The completed mailto graphic when it is not moused.

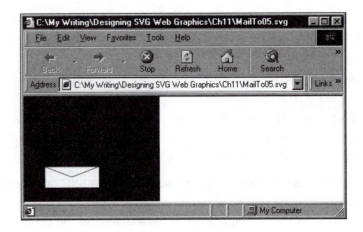

Listing 11.3 (MailTo01.svg)

```
<?xml version="1.0" standalone="no"?>
<!DOCTYPE svg PUBLIC "-//W3C//DTD SVG 1.0//EN"
     "http://www.w3.org/TR/2001/PR-SVG-20010719/
        DTD/svg10.dtd">
<svg>
<svg x="0" y="0" width="200" height="150">
<rect x="0" y="0" width="200" height="150" />
<a id="MailTo" xlink:href="mailto:consulting@andrewwatt.com">
<rect x="30" y="100" width="80" height="30"
style="fill:#FEFEFE; stroke:black;
stroke-width:0.05"/>
<line id="LeftLine" x1="30" y1="100" x2="70" y2="115"
style="stroke:black;
stroke-width:0.05"/>
<line id="RightLine" x1="70" y1="115" x2="110" y2="100"
style="stroke:black;
stroke-width:0.05"/>
</a>
</svg>
</svg>
```

Notice that I have created the graphic within its own `<svg>` element, which allows you to move it later to a suitable location on the page, if you use it as part of a larger SVG graphic. If you were planning to simply place a single SVG graphic on an HTML or XHTML Web page, you could omit the nested `<svg>` element and, most likely, center the envelope within tighter borders.

Apart from the black background rectangle, all of the graphical image is nested within an `<a>` element whose `xlink:href` attribute provides the mailto link to `consulting@AndrewWatt.com`. The remaining shapes are `<rect>` and `<line>` elements.

As the next step, you add an animation that begins when you mouse over the envelope. You create the flap of the envelope using a `<path>` element, although you could use two `<line>` elements instead:

```
<path id="OpenFlap" d="M30,100 L70,85 110,100"
style="fill:#FFFFFF;
stroke:black; stroke-width:0.1"
visibility="hidden">
<animate begin="MailTo.mouseover" attributeName="visibility"
from="hidden"
to="visible" dur="0.1s" fill="freeze"/>
<animate begin="MailTo.mouseout" attributeName="visibility"
from="visible"
to="hidden" dur="0.1s" fill="freeze"/>
</path>
```

Note that the visibility attribute for the `<path>` element is set to a value of `hidden`.

Notice that the events you make use of for animations are mouseover and mouseout. You use a pair of `<animate>` elements. The first one defines what happens when you mouse the envelope. The second defines the animation when you remove the mouse from that part of the screen.

An alternative approach is to use the `<set>` element, like this:

```
<set attributeName="visibility" begin="MailTo.mouseover"
end="MailTo.mouseout"
to="visible"/>
```

The `begin` attribute of the first `<animate>` element has a value of `MailTo.mouseover`. Recall that the `<a>` element has an `id` of value `MailTo`, so mousing any of the elements nested within the `<a>` element should cause the flap of the envelope to open. However, if you slowly move the mouse pointer over the graphic, you see that when it rests over either of the `<line>` elements, the flap closes. To avoid that problem, you need to modify the `<line>` elements by adding the `pointer-events` attribute set to a value of `none`, as shown here:

```
<line id="LeftLine" x1="30" y1="100" x2="70" y2="115"
style="stroke:black;
stroke-width:0.05" pointer-events="none"/>
<line id="RightLine" x1="70" y1="115" x2="110" y2="100"
style="stroke:black;
stroke-width:0.05" pointer-events="none"/>
```

If you want the flap of the envelope to close when you stray outside the original outline of the envelope, you can also use `pointer-events="none"` to achieve that effect:

```
<path id="OpenFlap" d="M30,100 L70,85 110,100"
style="fill:#FFFFFF;
stroke:black; stroke-width:0.1"
visibility="hidden" pointer-events="none">
```

Having made all those changes, you have an envelope that "opens" when any part of it is moused, but closes when the mouse goes outside the original outline of the envelope. The code at this stage looks like this:

Listing 11.4 (MailTo02.svg)

```
<?xml version="1.0" standalone="no"?>
<!DOCTYPE svg PUBLIC "-//W3C//DTD SVG 1.0//EN"
     "http://www.w3.org/TR/2001/PR-SVG-20010719/
        DTD/svg10.dtd">
<svg>
<svg x="0" y="0" width="200" height="150">
<rect x="0" y="0" width="200" height="150" />
<a id="MailTo" xlink:href="mailto:consulting@andrewwatt.com">
<rect x="30" y="100" width="80" height="30"
style="fill:#FEFEFE; stroke:black;
stroke-width:0.05"/>
<line id="LeftLine" x1="30" y1="100" x2="70" y2="115"
style="stroke:black;
stroke-width:0.05" pointer-events="none"/>
<line id="RightLine" x1="70" y1="115" x2="110" y2="100"
style="stroke:black;
stroke-width:0.05" pointer-events="none"/>
<path id="OpenFlap" d="M30,100 L70,85 110,100"
style="fill:#FFFFFF;
stroke:black; stroke-width:0.1"
visibility="hidden" pointer-events="none">
<animate begin="MailTo.mouseover" attributeName="visibility"
from="hidden"
```

```
to="visible" dur="0.1s" fill="freeze"/>
<animate begin="MailTo.mouseout" attributeName="visibility"
from="visible"
to="hidden" dur="0.1s" fill="freeze"/>
</path>
</a>
</svg>
</svg>
```

Now add several further animations, which I explain individually. After that, you see all of them put together with the code, as shown in the preceding example.

If you look closely at a real paper envelope, the inside of the envelope when the flap is open doesn't quite meet the corner. The next animation you add is to move down the outer edges of the two `<line>` elements:

```
<line id="LeftLine" x1="30" y1="100" x2="70" y2="115"
style="stroke:black;
stroke-width:0.05" pointer-events="none">
<animate begin="MailTo.mouseover" attributeName="y1" from="100"
to="102"
dur="0.1s" fill="freeze"/>
<animate begin="MailTo.mouseout" attributeName="y1" from="102"
to="100"
dur="0.1s" fill="freeze"/>
</line>
<line id="RightLine" x1="70" y1="115" x2="110" y2="100"
style="stroke:black;
stroke-width:0.05" pointer-events="none">
<animate begin="MailTo.mouseover" attributeName="y2" from="100"
to="102"
dur="0.1s" fill="freeze"/>
<animate begin="MailTo.mouseout" attributeName="y2" from="102"
to="100"
dur="0.1s" fill="freeze"/>
</line>
```

As before, you use `<animate>` elements in pairs—one `<animate>` for the mouseover event and the other on mouseout. That looks like lots of code for such a tiny movement, but the animation now looks, to my eye, more lifelike.

Next, you add some text to the envelope so that when the envelope is moused, the graphic looks like the one shown in Figure 11.02. (I discuss one issue relating to this text a little later in this section.)

Figure 11.02

The envelope with the first text animation implemented.

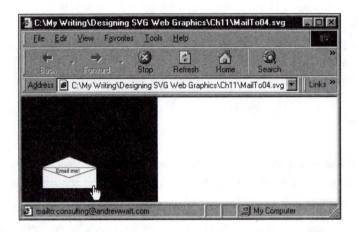

```
<text x="50" y="130" style="font-size:8; fill:green; font-fami-
ly:Arial, sans-serif;" visibility="hidden" >
<animate begin="MailTo.mouseover" attributeName="y" from="130"
to="108"
dur="0.5s" fill="freeze"/>
<animate begin="MailTo.mouseout" attributeName="y" from="108"
to="130"
dur="0.1s" fill="freeze"/>
<animate begin="MailTo.mouseover" attributeName="visibility"
from="hidden"
to="visible" dur="0.1s" fill="freeze"/>
<animate begin="MailTo.mouseout" attributeName="visibility"
from="visible"
to="hidden" dur="0.1s" fill="freeze"/>
Email me!</text>
```

The text in this code is hidden except when the envelope is moused, as reflected by the visibility attribute of the `<text>` element having a value of `hidden`. The code contains two pairs of animations. The first one moves the text up from the bottom of the envelope to a position nicely nested within the flap over a period of a half-second by animating the `y` attribute of the `<text>` element. When the mouse is removed, it snaps back to its position more quickly. However, the visibility of the text is being animated at the same time. The second pair of animate elements makes the text visible when the envelope is moused, and makes it hidden when the mouse is removed.

You might be quite happy with that effect as a simple mailto graphic, but now you add further animations to it. In Chapter 8, "Animation: SVG and

SMIL Animation," I demonstrated chained animations, a technique you can make use of here.

First, you need to add an `id` attribute to the `<animate>` element from which you want to chain the new animations:

```
<animate id="TextUp" begin="MailTo.mouseover" attributeName="y"
from="130" to="108"
dur="0.5s" fill="freeze"/>
```

After the text is animated upward, you can animate it down and increase its size so that it fills the envelope. When that task is done, the final appearance of the envelope looks like the one shown in Figure 11.03.

```
<animate id="TextDownAgain" begin="TextUp.end+0.1s"
attributeName="y" from="108" to="130"
dur="0.5s" fill="freeze"/>
<animate id="TextAcross" begin="TextUp.end+0.1s"
attributeName="x" from="50" to="35"
dur="0.5s" fill="freeze"/>
<animate id="TextGrow" begin="TextUp.end+0.1s"
attributeName="font-size" from="8" to="16"
dur="0.5s" fill="freeze"/>
<animate id="TextBackAcross" begin="MailTo.mouseout"
attributeName="x" from="35" to="50"
dur="0.01s" fill="freeze"/>
<animate id="TextShrink" begin="MailTo.mouseout"
attributeName="font-size" from="16" to="8"
dur="0.01s" fill="freeze"/>
```

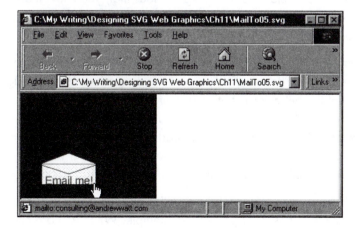

Figure 11.03

The envelope after the second text animation has been added.

Each of the first three `<animate>` elements has a `begin` attribute with a value of `TextUp.end+0.1s`. In other words, after the text animates the envelope, a pause of 0.1 second occurs, and these three animations begin. Each has a duration of 0.5 second, and simultaneously the text is animated down to the bottom of the envelope. It is moved across to the left a little, to allow for the effect of the third animation, which increases the font size from 8 to 16.

The final two of the five `<animate>` elements help you restore the original state of the text so that it is ready for another mouseover to happen. With those two pieces of code, you move the text back across to the right a little and shrink it back to a font size of 8. Remember that you separately have a mouseout event that sets the visibility back to `hidden`:

```
<animate begin="MailTo.mouseout" attributeName="visibility"
from="visible"
to="hidden" dur="0.01s" fill="freeze"/>
```

and one that returns the `y` attribute of the `<text>` element to `130`:

```
<animate id="TextDown" begin="MailTo.mouseout" attributeName="y"
from="108" to="130"
dur="0.01s" fill="freeze"/>
```

That final mouseout animation isn't necessary if all the animations are allowed to complete, but a visitor to the site might mouse out before the animation is complete. Even if the visitor does that, you know that—with all these mouseout animations—you return the `<text>` element to the state it was in before the mouseover event.

If you have been following this example step-by-step, you might have encountered weird behavior as you use this animation, and you might have noticed that the behavior is not consistent. What is probably happening is that the animated text is crossing the mouse pointer and causing the same problem as the `<line>` elements did earlier in this chapter. If you add to the `<text>` element a `pointer-events` attribute with a value of `none`, that problem is solved and the animation works nicely.

You might have been struggling to visualize how all the animations interact and interrelate in this latter part of the example. When you are chaining animations, the situation can become complex. Therefore, I encourage you to work through the example step-by-step and observe exactly what happens as you make each change. You can learn a great deal about how to put together visual components, which is what SVG animations are.

Many changes are made in this last part of the example, so you should see the code in full so that you are clear about how it all fits. Feel free to experiment with it, changing attributes and timings, for example, to produce different visual effects. Keep a copy of the original, though, just in case you get in a tangle from which you can't free yourself.

Listing 11.5 (MailTo05.svg)

```
<?xml version="1.0" standalone="no"?>
<!DOCTYPE svg PUBLIC "-//W3C//DTD SVG 1.0//EN"
    "http://www.w3.org/TR/2001/PR-SVG-20010719/
     DTD/svg10.dtd">
<svg>
<svg x="0" y="0" width="200" height="150">
<rect x="0" y="0" width="200" height="150" />
<a id="MailTo" xlink:href="mailto:consulting@andrewwatt.com">
<animate begin="mouseover" />
<rect x="30" y="100" width="80" height="30"
style="fill:#FEFEFE; stroke:black;
stroke-width:0.05"/>
<text x="50" y="130" style="font-size:8; fill:green;
font-family:Arial, sans-serif;" pointer-events="none"
visibility="hidden">
<animate id="TextUp" begin="MailTo.mouseover" attributeName="y"
from="130" to="108"
dur="0.5s" fill="freeze"/>
<animate id="TextDown" begin="MailTo.mouseout" attributeName="y"
from="108" to="130"
dur="0.01s" fill="freeze"/>
<animate begin="MailTo.mouseover" attributeName="visibility"
from="hidden"
to="visible" dur="0.1s" fill="freeze"/>
<animate begin="MailTo.mouseout" attributeName="visibility"
from="visible"
to="hidden" dur="0.01s" fill="freeze"/>
<animate id="TextDownAgain" begin="TextUp.end+0.1s"
attributeName="y" from="108" to="130"
dur="0.5s" fill="freeze"/>
<animate id="TextAcross" begin="TextUp.end+0.1s"
attributeName="x" from="50" to="35"
dur="0.5s" fill="freeze"/>
```

```
<animate id="TextGrow" begin="TextUp.end+0.1s"
attributeName="font-size" from="8" to="16"
dur="0.5s" fill="freeze"/>
<animate id="TextBackAcross" begin="MailTo.mouseout"
attributeName="x" from="35" to="50"
dur="0.01s" fill="freeze"/>
<animate id="TextShrink" begin="MailTo.mouseout"
attributeName="font-size" from="16" to="8"
dur="0.01s" fill="freeze"/>
Email me!
</text>
<line id="LeftLine" x1="30" y1="100" x2="70" y2="115"
style="stroke:black;
stroke-width:0.05" pointer-events="none">
<animate begin="MailTo.mouseover" attributeName="y1" from="100"
to="102"
dur="0.1s" fill="freeze"/>
<animate begin="MailTo.mouseout" attributeName="y1" from="102"
to="100"
dur="0.1s" fill="freeze"/>
</line>
<line id="RightLine" x1="70" y1="115" x2="110" y2="100"
style="stroke:black;
stroke-width:0.05" pointer-events="none">
<animate begin="MailTo.mouseover" attributeName="y2" from="100"
to="102"
dur="0.1s" fill="freeze"/>
<animate begin="MailTo.mouseout" attributeName="y2" from="102"
to="100"
dur="0.1s" fill="freeze"/>
</line>
<path id="OpenFlap" d="M30,100 L70,85 110,100"
style="fill:#FFFFFF;
stroke:black; stroke-width:0.1"
visibility="hidden" pointer-events="none">
<animate begin="MailTo.mouseover" attributeName="visibility"
from="hidden"
to="visible" dur="0.1s" fill="freeze"/>
<animate begin="MailTo.mouseout" attributeName="visibility"
from="visible"
to="hidden" dur="0.1s" fill="freeze"/>
</path>
</a>
</svg>
</svg>
```

Simple text rollovers

On Web sites where simplicity of design is employed creatively, a navigation "bar" might consist simply of a series of appropriately placed words that have attached rollover capability and are linked to the appropriate pages.

Suppose that you are creating a nostalgia photos-and-paintings site named RootsPics.com and you want to create simple text links, including rollovers, from the home page to pages such as Photographs, Paintings, Order Tracking, and Contact Details. You might attempt to lay the foundation for creating a simple text-navigation bar like this:

Listing 11.6 (RootsPics01.svg)

```
<?xml version="1.0" standalone="no"?>
<!DOCTYPE svg PUBLIC "-//W3C//DTD SVG 1.0//EN"
     "http://www.w3.org/TR/2001/PR-SVG-20010719/
     DTD/svg10.dtd">
<svg width="800" height="150">
<svg x="0" y="0" width="800" height="150">
<text x="10" y="25" style="font-family: Arial, sans-serif;
font-size:24; fill:#990066; stroke:#990066;">
RootsPics.com
</text>
<text x="10" y="50" style="font-family: Arial, sans-serif;
font-size:14; fill:#990066; stroke:none;">
Photographs Paintings Order Tracking Contact Details
</text>
</svg>
</svg>
```

A problem exists, however, if you want to create separate rollovers for each page. If you do, you need separate animations for each link, so you need to split up the second `<text>` element into four `<tspan>` elements. Later, you add to each `<tspan>` element rollovers and links to the appropriate pages.

Listing 11.7 (RootsPics02.svg)

```
<?xml version="1.0" standalone="no"?>
<!DOCTYPE svg PUBLIC "-//W3C//DTD SVG 1.0//EN"
     "http://www.w3.org/TR/2001/PR-SVG-20010719/
     DTD/svg10.dtd">
```

```
<svg width="800" height="150">
<svg x="0" y="0" width="800" height="150">
<text x="10" y="25" style="font-family: Arial, sans-serif;
font-size:24; fill:#990066; stroke:#990066;">
RootsPics.com
</text>
<text>
<tspan x="10" y="50" style="font-family: Arial, sans-serif;
font-size:14; fill:#990066; stroke:none;">
Photographs
</tspan>
<tspan dx="1em" style="font-family: Arial, sans-serif;
font-size:14; fill:#990066; stroke:none;">
Paintings
</tspan>
<tspan dx="1em" style="font-family: Arial, sans-serif;
font-size:14; fill:#990066; stroke:none;">
Order Tracking
</tspan>
<tspan dx="1em" style="font-family: Arial, sans-serif;
font-size:14; fill:#990066; stroke:none;">
Contact Details
</tspan>
</text>
</svg>
</svg>
```

Notice that you need to state an absolute position for the first `<tspan>` element and then link the position of all the others to that position by using the `dx` attribute, which basically indicates that other `<tspan>` elements are positioned a little further along the same horizontal line. Note that you repeat the style information for each `<tspan>` element; otherwise, they are displayed as the default color, which is black.

You next need to add the rollover effect for each piece of text. That task involves recognizing the mouseover and the mouseout events and changing the color appropriately. For this example, choose bright green as the rollover color. After changing the color, you animate the stroke from a value of `none` to the same green color as the fill. This action gives a heavier weight to the text that is moused. An alternative approach is to change the `font-weight` attribute.

The rollover effect is the same for each of the four pieces of text, so after you have correctly created the rollover for one piece of text, you have a visual component you can reuse on the other three.

Listing 11.8 (RootsPics04.svg)

```
<?xml version="1.0" standalone="no"?>
<!DOCTYPE svg PUBLIC "-//W3C//DTD SVG 1.0//EN"
     "http://www.w3.org/TR/2001/PR-SVG-20010719/
      DTD/svg10.dtd">
<svg width="800" height="150">
<svg x="0" y="0" width="800" height="150">
<text x="10" y="25" style="font-family: Arial, sans-serif;
font-size:24; fill:#990066; stroke:#990066;">
RootsPics.com
</text>
<text>
<tspan x="10" y="50" style="font-family: Arial, sans-serif;
font-size:14; fill:#990066; stroke:none;">
<animate begin="mouseover" dur="0.1s" attributeName="fill"
from="#990066" to="#00CC00" fill="freeze"/>
<animate begin="mouseover" dur="0.1s" attributeName="stroke"
from="none" to="#00CC00" fill="freeze"/>
<animate begin="mouseout" dur="0.1s" attributeName="fill"
from="#00CC00" to="#990066" fill="freeze"/>
<animate begin="mouseout" dur="0.1s" attributeName="stroke"
from="#00CC00" to="none" fill="freeze"/>
Photographs
</tspan>
<tspan dx="1em" style="font-family: Arial, sans-serif;
font-size:14; fill:#990066; stroke:none;">
<animate begin="mouseover" dur="0.1s" attributeName="fill"
from="#990066" to="#00CC00" fill="freeze"/>
<animate begin="mouseover" dur="0.1s" attributeName="stroke"
from="none" to="#00CC00" fill="freeze"/>
<animate begin="mouseout" dur="0.1s" attributeName="fill"
from="#00CC00" to="#990066" fill="freeze"/>
<animate begin="mouseout" dur="0.1s" attributeName="stroke"
from="#00CC00" to="none" fill="freeze"/>
Paintings
</tspan>
<tspan dx="1em" style="font-family: Arial, sans-serif;
font-size:14; fill:#990066; stroke:none;">
<animate begin="mouseover" dur="0.1s" attributeName="fill"
from="#990066" to="#00CC00" fill="freeze"/>
<animate begin="mouseover" dur="0.1s" attributeName="stroke"
from="none" to="#00CC00" fill="freeze"/>
```

```
<animate begin="mouseout" dur="0.1s" attributeName="fill"
from="#00CC00" to="#990066" fill="freeze"/>
<animate begin="mouseout" dur="0.1s" attributeName="stroke"
from="#00CC00" to="none" fill="freeze"/>
Order Tracking
</tspan>
<tspan dx="1em" style="font-family: Arial, sans-serif;
font-size:14; fill:#990066; stroke:none;">
<animate begin="mouseover" dur="0.1s" attributeName="fill"
from="#990066" to="#00CC00" fill="freeze"/>
<animate begin="mouseover" dur="0.1s" attributeName="stroke"
from="none" to="#00CC00" fill="freeze"/>
<animate begin="mouseout" dur="0.1s" attributeName="fill"
from="#00CC00" to="#990066" fill="freeze"/>
<animate begin="mouseout" dur="0.1s" attributeName="stroke"
from="#00CC00" to="none" fill="freeze"/>
Contact Details
</tspan>
</text>
</svg>
</svg>
```

An alternative approach to the mouseover and mouseout animations using the `<animate>` element is to use `<set>` elements.

You now should have the rollovers working correctly on each of the four linking pieces of text, so you can complete the functionality by adding links to each of the pieces of text. This time, because the pieces of text need to be nested within the linking `<a>` elements, you have to be careful to create the correct nesting (see Figure 11.04). An alternative approach is to create the containing `<a>` element first, and then nest the static elements, and then nest the animation elements within those `<a>` elements. Be careful to nest the first `<a>` element immediately after the opening `<text>` element and before the first `<tspan>` element. The first closing `</a>` element follows the closing `</tspan>` element. Also, if you are cutting and pasting the `<a>` tags with their `xlink:href` attributes in place, be sure to customize the value of the `xlink:href` attribute to suit each link.

Listing 11.9 (RootsPics05.svg)

```
<?xml version="1.0" standalone="no"?>
<!DOCTYPE svg PUBLIC "-//W3C//DTD SVG 1.0//EN"
    "http://www.w3.org/TR/2001/PR-SVG-20010719/
    DTD/svg10.dtd">
```

```
<svg width="800" height="150">
<svg x="0" y="0" width="800" height="150">
<text x="10" y="25" style="font-family: Arial, sans-serif;
font-size:24; fill:#990066; stroke:#990066;">
RootsPics.com
</text>
<text>
<a xlink:href="Photographs.html">
<tspan x="10" y="50" style="font-family: Arial, sans-serif;
font-size:14; fill:#990066; stroke:none;">
<animate begin="mouseover" dur="0.1s" attributeName="fill"
from="#990066" to="#00CC00" fill="freeze"/>
<animate begin="mouseover" dur="0.1s" attributeName="stroke"
from="none" to="#00CC00" fill="freeze"/>
<animate begin="mouseout" dur="0.1s" attributeName="fill"
from="#00CC00" to="#990066" fill="freeze"/>
<animate begin="mouseout" dur="0.1s" attributeName="stroke"
from="#00CC00" to="none" fill="freeze"/>
Photographs
</tspan>
</a>
<a xlink:href="Paintings.html">
<tspan dx="1em" style="font-family: Arial, sans-serif;
font-size:14; fill:#990066; stroke:none;">
<animate begin="mouseover" dur="0.1s" attributeName="fill"
from="#990066" to="#00CC00" fill="freeze"/>
<animate begin="mouseover" dur="0.1s" attributeName="stroke"
from="none" to="#00CC00" fill="freeze"/>
<animate begin="mouseout" dur="0.1s" attributeName="fill"
from="#00CC00" to="#990066" fill="freeze"/>
<animate begin="mouseout" dur="0.1s" attributeName="stroke"
from="#00CC00" to="none" fill="freeze"/>
Paintings
</tspan>
</a>
<a xlink:href="OrderTracking.html">
<tspan dx="1em" style="font-family: Arial, sans-serif;
font-size:14; fill:#990066; stroke:none;">
<animate begin="mouseover" dur="0.1s" attributeName="fill"
from="#990066" to="#00CC00" fill="freeze"/>
<animate begin="mouseover" dur="0.1s" attributeName="stroke"
from="none" to="#00CC00" fill="freeze"/>
<animate begin="mouseout" dur="0.1s" attributeName="fill"
from="#00CC00" to="#990066" fill="freeze"/>
<animate begin="mouseout" dur="0.1s" attributeName="stroke"
from="#00CC00" to="none" fill="freeze"/>
Order Tracking
</tspan>
```

```
</a>
<a xlink:href="ContactDetails.html">
<tspan dx="1em" style="font-family: Arial, sans-serif;
font-size:14; fill:#990066; stroke:none;">
<animate begin="mouseover" dur="0.1s" attributeName="fill"
from="#990066" to="#00CC00" fill="freeze"/>
<animate begin="mouseover" dur="0.1s" attributeName="stroke"
from="none" to="#00CC00" fill="freeze"/>
<animate begin="mouseout" dur="0.1s" attributeName="fill"
from="#00CC00" to="#990066" fill="freeze"/>
<animate begin="mouseout" dur="0.1s" attributeName="stroke"
from="#00CC00" to="none" fill="freeze"/>
Contact Details
</tspan>
</a>
</text>
</svg>
</svg>
```

Figure 11.04

The completed text-navigation bar with rollover.

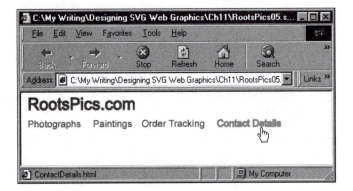

A more complex text rollover

Now that you're building up step-by-step, you can follow the techniques in this section to create a significantly more complex text rollover.

Imagine (or, in my case, fantasize) that XMML.com is a design company with offices in New York, Amsterdam, San Francisco, and Tokyo and that you want to create a suitably sophisticated, understated banner or logo on the corporate Web page.

When viewed statically, the banner might look pretty much like the one shown in Figure 11.05.

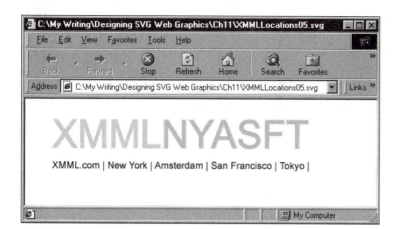

Figure 11.05

The unmoused state of the XMML.com text rollover.

However, you still want the banner to have interesting and intriguing built-in interactivity. You want to achieve a design where the letters indicating each major office have their own rollover capability. Incorporated into that rollover is not only a color change in the letter but also the display of contact details for that office.

If you want to animate each office separately, you need to nest the initials for each office separately in their own `<tspan>` elements because you need to have SVG elements to which you can apply selected animations.

If you choose to animate both the `stroke` and `fill` properties for each office, you need two `<animate>` or `<animateColor>` elements for mouseover and an additional two elements for mouseout. So your first step toward the final interactive banner looks like this, with the mouseover and mouseout animations inserted for the company initials, XMML:

Listing 11.10 (XMMLLocations01.svg)

```
<?xml version="1.0" standalone="no"?>
<!DOCTYPE svg PUBLIC "-//W3C//DTD SVG 1.0//EN"
    "http://www.w3.org/TR/2001/PR-SVG-20010719/
    DTD/svg10.dtd">
<svg width="800" height="300">
<text x="40" y="70" style="font-size:48; font-family:Arial,
sans-serif; stroke:#CCCCCC; fill:#CCCCCC;">
<tspan id="XMML" style="stroke:#FFCCCC; fill:#FFCCCC;">
<animateColor begin="mouseover" dur="0.1s" attributeName="fill"
from="#FFCCCC" to="#FF3333" fill="freeze"/>
```

```
<animateColor begin="mouseover" dur="0.1s"
attributeName="stroke" from="#FFCCCC" to="#FF3333"
fill="freeze"/>
<animateColor begin="mouseout" dur="0.1s" attributeName="fill"
from="#FF3333" to="#FFCCCC" fill="freeze"/>
<animateColor begin="mouseout" dur="0.1s" attributeName="stroke"
from="#FF3333" to="#FFCCCC" fill="freeze"/>
XMML
</tspan>
<tspan id="NY">
NY
</tspan>
<tspan id="A">
A
</tspan>
<tspan id="SF">
SF
</tspan>
<tspan id="T">T
</tspan>
</text>
<text x="40" y="100" style="font-family:Arial, sans-serif;
font-size:14;" >
XMML.com | New York | Amsterdam | San Francisco | Tokyo |
</text>
</svg>
```

When you place the mouse over the text XMML, both the fill and stroke are animated to a red color from a grayish pink. When you mouse out the red, color returns to its original grayish pink color.

Because you want to have the same mouseover and mouseout functionality on each of the letters representing the branch offices, you have a visual component for the animation you want:

```
<animateColor begin="mouseover" dur="0.1s" attributeName="fill"
from="#FFCCCC" to="#FF3333" fill="freeze"/>
<animateColor begin="mouseover" dur="0.1s"
attributeName="stroke" from="#FFCCCC" to="#FF3333"
fill="freeze"/>
<animateColor begin="mouseout" dur="0.1s" attributeName="fill"
from="#FF3333" to="#FFCCCC" fill="freeze"/>
<animateColor begin="mouseout" dur="0.1s" attributeName="stroke"
from="#FF3333" to="#FFCCCC" fill="freeze"/>
```

You can create an individualized color change on mouseover by simply adapting the `to` attribute on the "mouseover" `<animateColor>` element to a specific color and then change the "mouseout" `<animateColor>` element to start at the correct color.

Remember that you need to change all the `from` and `to` attributes because the XMML has a different start and mouseover color in both stroke and fill.

After you have added the mouseover and mouseout visual components to each location, the code looks like this:

Listing 11.11 (XMMLLocations02.svg)

```
<?xml version="1.0" standalone="no"?>
<!DOCTYPE svg PUBLIC "-//W3C//DTD SVG 1.0//EN"
    "http://www.w3.org/TR/2001/PR-SVG-20010719/
        DTD/svg10.dtd">
<svg width="800" height="300">
<text x="40" y="70" style="font-size:56; font-family:Arial,
sans-serif; stroke:#CCCCCC; fill:#CCCCCC;">
<tspan id="XMML" style="stroke:#FFCCCC; fill:#FFCCCC;">
<animateColor begin="mouseover" dur="0.1s" attributeName="fill"
from="#FFCCCC" to="#FF3333" fill="freeze"/>
<animateColor begin="mouseover" dur="0.1s"
attributeName="stroke" from="#FFCCCC" to="#FF3333"
fill="freeze"/>
<animateColor begin="mouseout" dur="0.1s" attributeName="fill"
from="#FF3333" to="#FFCCCC" fill="freeze"/>
<animateColor begin="mouseout" dur="0.1s" attributeName="stroke"
from="#FF3333" to="#FFCCCC" fill="freeze"/>
XMML
</tspan>
<tspan id="NY">
<animateColor begin="mouseover" dur="0.1s" attributeName="fill"
from="#CCCCCC" to="#33FF33" fill="freeze"/>
<animateColor begin="mouseover" dur="0.1s"
attributeName="stroke" from="#CCCCCC" to="#33FF33"
fill="freeze"/>
<animateColor begin="mouseout" dur="0.1s" attributeName="fill"
from="#33FF33" to="#CCCCCC" fill="freeze"/>
<animateColor begin="mouseout" dur="0.1s" attributeName="stroke"
from="#33FF33" to="#CCCCCC" fill="freeze"/>
NY
</tspan>
<tspan id="A">
```

```
<animateColor begin="mouseover" dur="0.1s" attributeName="fill"
from="#CCCCCC" to="#FF9900" fill="freeze"/>
<animateColor begin="mouseover" dur="0.1s"
attributeName="stroke" from="#CCCCCC" to="#FF9900"
fill="freeze"/>
<animateColor begin="mouseout" dur="0.1s" attributeName="fill"
from="#FF9900" to="#CCCCCC" fill="freeze"/>
<animateColor begin="mouseout" dur="0.1s" attributeName="stroke"
from="#FF9900" to="#CCCCCC" fill="freeze"/>
A
</tspan>
<tspan id="SF">
<animateColor begin="mouseover" dur="0.1s" attributeName="fill"
from="#CCCCCC" to="#9900FF" fill="freeze"/>
<animateColor begin="mouseover" dur="0.1s"
attributeName="stroke" from="#CCCCCC" to="#9900FF"
fill="freeze"/>
<animateColor begin="mouseout" dur="0.1s" attributeName="fill"
from="#9900FF" to="#CCCCCC" fill="freeze"/>
<animateColor begin="mouseout" dur="0.1s" attributeName="stroke"
from="#9900FF" to="#CCCCCC" fill="freeze"/>
SF
</tspan>
<tspan id="T">
<animateColor begin="mouseover" dur="0.1s" attributeName="fill"
from="#CCCCCC" to="#FFFF00" fill="freeze"/>
<animateColor begin="mouseover" dur="0.1s"
attributeName="stroke" from="#CCCCCC" to="#FFFF00"
fill="freeze"/>
<animateColor begin="mouseout" dur="0.1s" attributeName="fill"
from="#FFFF00" to="#CCCCCC" fill="freeze"/>
<animateColor begin="mouseout" dur="0.1s" attributeName="stroke"
from="#FFFF00" to="#CCCCCC" fill="freeze"/>
T
</tspan>
</text>
<text x="40" y="100" style="font-family:Arial, sans-serif;
font-size:14;" >
XMML.com | New York | Amsterdam | San Francisco | Tokyo |
</text>
</svg>
```

At rest, the appearance is no different from the original code; when any of the locations is moused, however, it changes color on both mouseover and mouseout, such as the green color for the New York location, as shown in Figure 11.06.

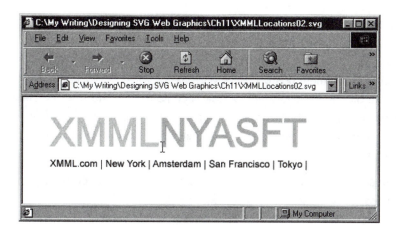

Figure 11.06

Mouseover of the letters NY causes a color change.

When the large-font initials are moused, you want them to not only change color but also to replace the general location list underneath with contact information that is specific to that location. To achieve that effect, you need to add interactive functionality to hide the general text information as well as to show location-specific contact information.

First, you add an animation to the general locations list contained in this code:

```
<text x="40" y="100" style="font-family:Arial, sans-serif;
font-size:14;" >
XMML.com | New York | Amsterdam | San Francisco | Tokyo |
</text>
```

Suppose that you want to hide the locations list when individual locations are moused and show it again when the mouse is removed. You need eight `<animate>` elements, therefore: four to hide the information when a location is moused and four to reveal it again when the mouse is moved away. First, you create two animations that hide the location information when NY is moused and show it again when the mouse moves away:

```
<text x="40" y="100" style="font-family:Arial, sans-serif;
font-size:14;" >
<animate attributeName="visibility" begin="NY.mouseover"
dur="0.1s" from="visible" to="hidden" fill="freeze"/>
<animate attributeName="visibility" begin="NY.mouseout"
dur="0.1s" from="hidden" to="visible" fill="freeze"/>
XMML.com | New York | Amsterdam | San Francisco | Tokyo |
</text>
```

Note that the `begin` attribute for the `<animate>` element is
`NY.mouseover`, meaning that when the element with an `id` of value
`NY` is moused, the animation should begin. Correspondingly, the other
`<animate>` element has a `begin` attribute of value `NY.mouseout`.
Because all the text you want to hide is contained in one `<text>` element,
you animate the visibility property from `visible` to `hidden` and back
again. In a moment, you see how to achieve a similar effect for groups of
elements.

You need to apply similar animations to correspond to each of the other
locations, so that section of code expands to this:

```
<text x="40" y="100" style="font-family:Arial, sans-serif;
font-size:14;" >
<animate attributeName="visibility" begin="NY.mouseover"
dur="0.1s" from="visible" to="hidden" fill="freeze"/>
<animate attributeName="visibility" begin="NY.mouseout"
dur="0.1s" from="hidden" to="visible" fill="freeze"/>
<animate attributeName="visibility" begin="A.mouseover"
dur="0.1s" from="visible" to="hidden" fill="freeze"/>
<animate attributeName="visibility" begin="A.mouseout"
dur="0.1s" from="hidden" to="visible" fill="freeze"/>
<animate attributeName="visibility" begin="SF.mouseover"
dur="0.1s" from="visible" to="hidden" fill="freeze"/>
<animate attributeName="visibility" begin="SF.mouseout"
dur="0.1s" from="hidden" to="visible" fill="freeze"/>
<animate attributeName="visibility" begin="T.mouseover"
dur="0.1s" from="visible" to="hidden" fill="freeze"/>
<animate attributeName="visibility" begin="T.mouseout"
dur="0.1s" from="hidden" to="visible" fill="freeze"/>
XMML.com | New York | Amsterdam | San Francisco | Tokyo |
</text>
```

As you can see in Figure 11.07, when the `NY` abbreviation is moused, the
color of the initials changes and the general location information is hidden.

Finally, you need to add more animations so that when the initials for the
location are moused, the specific location information is displayed. You
create the specific location information in a grouping `<g>` element so that
you can look at how to use animation of the display property here (rather
than the visibility property you used earlier in this example).

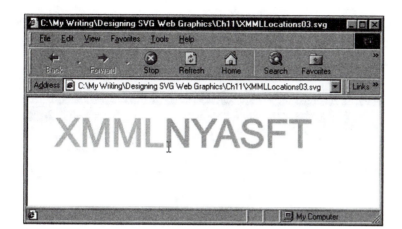

Figure 11.07

Mousing the letters NY causes the general location information to be hidden.

So, for the New York office, you need the following code:

```
<g id="NYSpecificLocationInformation" display="none">
<animate attributeName="display" begin="NY.mouseout" dur="0.1s"
from="visible" to="none" fill="freeze"/>
<animate attributeName="display" begin="NY.mouseover" dur="0.1s"
from="none" to="visible" fill="freeze"/>
<text>
<tspan x="40" y="100" style="font-family:Arial, sans-serif;
font-size:14;" >
New York Office Address Information
</tspan>
<tspan x="40" dy="1em" style="font-family:Arial, sans-serif;
font-size:14;" >
New York Office Email: NewYork@XMML.com
</tspan>
</text>
</g>
```

Remember that you want the general information to be hidden unless the NY initials are moused, so the default value of the `display` attribute on the grouping `<g>` element is `none`. When the NY initials are moused, the specific location information is displayed; when the mouse moves away, the value of the `display` attribute returns to its default value of `none`; and so the specific location information is again hidden.

The same interactivity is created for each of the other locations.

As you can see in Figure 11.08, when the A initial is moused, the general location information is hidden and the specific location contact information is made visible.

Figure 11.08

Mousing the letter A causes a color change in the letters, the general location information to be hidden, and the specific location information for Amsterdam to become visible.

Take a look at the final code for the animation. Now is the best time to do it—when it is (I hope) fresh in your mind.

Listing 11.12 (XMMLLocations05.svg)

```
<?xml version="1.0" standalone="no"?>
<!DOCTYPE svg PUBLIC "-//W3C//DTD SVG 1.0//EN"
     "http://www.w3.org/TR/2001/PR-SVG-20010719/
      DTD/svg10.dtd">
<svg width="800" height="300">
<text x="40" y="70" style="font-size:56; font-family:Arial,
sans-serif; stroke:#CCCCCC; fill:#CCCCCC;">
<tspan id="XMML" style="stroke:#FFCCCC; fill:#FFCCCC;">
<animateColor begin="mouseover" dur="0.1s" attributeName="fill"
from="#FFCCCC" to="#FF3333" fill="freeze"/>
<animateColor begin="mouseover" dur="0.1s"
attributeName="stroke" from="#FFCCCC" to="#FF3333"
fill="freeze"/>
<animateColor begin="mouseout" dur="0.1s" attributeName="fill"
from="#FF3333" to="#FFCCCC" fill="freeze"/>
<animateColor begin="mouseout" dur="0.1s" attributeName="stroke"
from="#FF3333" to="#FFCCCC" fill="freeze"/>
XMML
</tspan>
<tspan id="NY">
<animateColor begin="mouseover" dur="0.1s" attributeName="fill"
```

```
from="#CCCCCC" to="#33FF33" fill="freeze"/>
<animateColor begin="mouseover" dur="0.1s"
attributeName="stroke" from="#CCCCCC" to="#33FF33"
fill="freeze"/>
<animateColor begin="mouseout" dur="0.1s" attributeName="fill"
from="#33FF33" to="#CCCCCC" fill="freeze"/>
<animateColor begin="mouseout" dur="0.1s" attributeName="stroke"
from="#33FF33" to="#CCCCCC" fill="freeze"/>
NY
</tspan>
<tspan id="A">
<animateColor begin="mouseover" dur="0.1s" attributeName="fill"
from="#CCCCCC" to="#FF9900" fill="freeze"/>
<animateColor begin="mouseover" dur="0.1s"
attributeName="stroke" from="#CCCCCC" to="#FF9900"
fill="freeze"/>
<animateColor begin="mouseout" dur="0.1s" attributeName="fill"
from="#FF9900" to="#CCCCCC" fill="freeze"/>
<animateColor begin="mouseout" dur="0.1s" attributeName="stroke"
from="#FF9900" to="#CCCCCC" fill="freeze"/>
A
</tspan>
<tspan id="SF">
<animateColor begin="mouseover" dur="0.1s" attributeName="fill"
from="#CCCCCC" to="#9900FF" fill="freeze"/>
<animateColor begin="mouseover" dur="0.1s"
attributeName="stroke" from="#CCCCCC" to="#9900FF"
fill="freeze"/>
<animateColor begin="mouseout" dur="0.1s" attributeName="fill"
from="#9900FF" to="#CCCCCC" fill="freeze"/>
<animateColor begin="mouseout" dur="0.1s" attributeName="stroke"
from="#9900FF" to="#CCCCCC" fill="freeze"/>
SF
</tspan>
<tspan id="T">
<animateColor begin="mouseover" dur="0.1s" attributeName="fill"
from="#CCCCCC" to="#FFFF00" fill="freeze"/>
<animateColor begin="mouseover" dur="0.1s"
attributeName="stroke" from="#CCCCCC" to="#FFFF00"
fill="freeze"/>
<animateColor begin="mouseout" dur="0.1s" attributeName="fill"
from="#FFFF00" to="#CCCCCC" fill="freeze"/>
<animateColor begin="mouseout" dur="0.1s" attributeName="stroke"
from="#FFFF00" to="#CCCCCC" fill="freeze"/>
T
</tspan>
</text>
```

```
<text x="40" y="100" style="font-family:Arial, sans-serif;
font-size:14;" >
<animate attributeName="visibility" begin="NY.mouseover"
dur="0.1s" from="visible" to="hidden" fill="freeze"/>
<animate attributeName="visibility" begin="NY.mouseout"
dur="0.1s" from="hidden" to="visible" fill="freeze"/>
<animate attributeName="visibility" begin="A.mouseover"
dur="0.1s" from="visible" to="hidden" fill="freeze"/>
<animate attributeName="visibility" begin="A.mouseout"
dur="0.1s" from="hidden" to="visible" fill="freeze"/>
<animate attributeName="visibility" begin="SF.mouseover"
dur="0.1s" from="visible" to="hidden" fill="freeze"/>
<animate attributeName="visibility" begin="SF.mouseout"
dur="0.1s" from="hidden" to="visible" fill="freeze"/>
<animate attributeName="visibility" begin="T.mouseover"
dur="0.1s" from="visible" to="hidden" fill="freeze"/>
<animate attributeName="visibility" begin="T.mouseout"
dur="0.1s" from="hidden" to="visible" fill="freeze"/>
XMML.com | New York | Amsterdam | San Francisco | Tokyo |
</text>
<g id="NYSpecificLocationInformation" display="none">
<animate attributeName="display" begin="NY.mouseout" dur="0.1s"
from="visible" to="none" fill="freeze"/>
<animate attributeName="display" begin="NY.mouseover" dur="0.1s"
from="none" to="visible" fill="freeze"/>
<text>
<tspan x="40" y="100" style="font-family:Arial, sans-serif;
font-size:14;" >
New York Office Address Information
</tspan>
<tspan x="40" dy="1em" style="font-family:Arial, sans-serif;
font-size:14;" >
New York Office Email: NewYork@XMML.com
</tspan>
</text>
</g>
<g id="AmsterdamSpecificLocationInformation" display="none">
<animate attributeName="display" begin="A.mouseout" dur="0.1s"
from="visible" to="none" fill="freeze"/>
<animate attributeName="display" begin="A.mouseover" dur="0.1s"
from="none" to="visible" fill="freeze"/>
<text>
<tspan x="40" y="100" style="font-family:Arial, sans-serif;
font-size:14;" >
Amsterdam Office Address Information
</tspan>
```

```
<tspan x="40" dy="1em" style="font-family:Arial, sans-serif;
font-size:14;" >
Amsterdam Office Email: Amsterdam@XMML.com
</tspan>
</text>
</g>
<g id="SanFranciscoSpecificLocationInformation" display="none">
<animate attributeName="display" begin="SF.mouseout" dur="0.1s"
from="visible" to="none" fill="freeze"/>
<animate attributeName="display" begin="SF.mouseover" dur="0.1s"
from="none" to="visible" fill="freeze"/>
<text>
<tspan x="40" y="100" style="font-family:Arial, sans-serif;
font-size:14;" >
San Francisco Office Address Information
</tspan>
<tspan x="40" dy="1em" style="font-family:Arial, sans-serif;
font-size:14;" >
San Francisco Office Email: SanFrancisco@XMML.com
</tspan>
</text>
</g>
<g id="TokyoSpecificLocationInformation" display="none">
<animate attributeName="display" begin="T.mouseout" dur="0.1s"
from="visible" to="none" fill="freeze"/>
<animate attributeName="display" begin="T.mouseover" dur="0.1s"
from="none" to="visible" fill="freeze"/>
<text>
<tspan x="40" y="100" style="font-family:Arial, sans-serif;
font-size:14;" >
Tokyo Office Address Information
</tspan>
<tspan x="40" dy="1em" style="font-family:Arial, sans-serif;
font-size:14;" >
Tokyo Office Email: Tokyo@XMML.com
</tspan>
</text>
</g>
</svg>
```

You have used `<animate>` or `<animateColor>` elements in the example as you have built it up. An alternative approach is to use the `<set>` element. The file XMMLLocations05set.svg shows the `<set>` element being used to produce the same functionality as shown in Listing 11.12.

NOTE

Hopefully, you no longer are intimidated by long SVG code listings. If you can break it down into its component parts, it all becomes clear fairly quickly.

A menu with an animated filter rollover

A filter property of an SVG element is just another property that can be animated, as far as an SVG rendering engine is concerned. Therefore, you can create rollover effects using SVG filters in response to mouseover and mouseout events.

The example in this section reuses the drop shadow filter you created in Chapter 7, "Using SVG Filters." The drop shadow effect is already created, and you use it here as a visual component in a menu to add a rollover drop shadow effect.

As a first step, you nest the embryonic menu in a nested `<svg>` element to make the menu easy to relocate on the page. In a menu, the font size needs to be reduced, so you also reduce the value of the `stdDeviation` attribute on the `<feGaussianBlur>` element in the filter. The rollover effect can be added to the `<text>` element by simply using the following code:

```
<set begin="mouseover" end="mouseout" attributeName="filter"
     to="url(#CombinedDropShadow)" />
```

When the text is not moused, the value of the `filter` attribute is `none`. When the text is moused, the `<set>` element changes the value of the filter property of the `<text>` element to refer to the combined drop shadow filter. In addition, the text must have hyperlinking functionality; therefore, I have nested the `<text>` element within an `<a>` element. With one menu choice created, the code is shown in Listing 11.13.

Listing 11.13 (ShadowRollover01.svg)

```
<?xml version="1.0" standalone="no"?>
<!DOCTYPE svg PUBLIC "-//W3C//DTD SVG 1.0//EN"
     "http://www.w3.org/TR/2001/PR-SVG-20010719/
      DTD/svg10.dtd">
<svg>
<defs>
```

```
<filter id="CombinedDropShadow" width="140%" y="-20%"
height="200%">
<feGaussianBlur in="SourceAlpha" stdDeviation="1"
result="ShadowOut"/>
<feOffset in="ShadowOut" dx="2" dy="2" result="ShadowOnly"/>
<feMerge>
  <feMergeNode in="ShadowOnly"/>
  <feMergeNode in="SourceGraphic"/>
</feMerge>
</filter>
</defs>
<svg x="0" y="0">
<a xlink:href="AboutUs.html" >
<text x="10" y="30" style="font-family:Arial, sans-serif;
font-size:16;
stroke:#CC0099; fill:#CC0099; filter:none;">
<set begin="mouseover" end="mouseout" attributeName="filter"
to="url(#CombinedDropShadow)" />
About Us</text>
</a>
</svg>
</svg>
```

The contents of the `<a>` element in this code are now a simple visual component with the needed rollover functionality; therefore, you cut and paste those to add links to additional pages, giving you the final code shown in Listing 11.14.

Listing 11.14 (ShaddowRollover02.svg)

```
<?xml version="1.0" standalone="no"?>
<!DOCTYPE svg PUBLIC "-//W3C//DTD SVG 1.0//EN"
    "http://www.w3.org/TR/2001/PR-SVG-20010719/
     DTD/svg10.dtd">
<svg>
<defs>
<filter id="CombinedDropShadow" width="140%" y="-20%"
height="200%">
<feGaussianBlur in="SourceAlpha" stdDeviation="1"
result="ShadowOut" />
<feOffset in="ShadowOut" dx="2" dy="2" result="ShadowOnly" />
<feMerge>
  <feMergeNode in="ShadowOnly"/>
  <feMergeNode in="SourceGraphic"/>
```

```
</feMerge>
</filter>
</defs>
<svg x="0" y="0">
<a xlink:href="AboutUs.html" >
<text x="10" y="30" style="font-family:Arial, sans-serif; font-
size:16;
stroke:#CC0099; fill:#CC0099; filter:none;">
<set begin="mouseover" end="mouseout" attributeName="filter"
to="url(#CombinedDropShadow)" />
About Us</text>
</a>
<a xlink:href="Products.html" >
<text x="10" y="60" style="font-family:Arial, sans-serif;
font-size:16;
stroke:#CC0099; fill:#CC0099; filter:none;">
<set begin="mouseover" end="mouseout" attributeName="filter"
to="url(#CombinedDropShadow)" />
Products</text>
</a>
<a xlink:href="Consultancy.html" >
<text x="10" y="90" style="font-family:Arial, sans-serif;
font-size:16;
stroke:#CC0099; fill:#CC0099; filter:none;">
<set begin="mouseover" end="mouseout" attributeName="filter"
to="url(#CombinedDropShadow)" />
Consultancy</text>
</a>
<a xlink:href="ContactUs.html" >
<text x="10" y="120" style="font-family:Arial, sans-serif;
font-size:16;
stroke:#CC0099; fill:#CC0099; filter:none;">
<set begin="mouseover" end="mouseout" attributeName="filter"
to="url(#CombinedDropShadow)" />
Contact Us</text>
</a>
</svg>
</svg>
```

When you are adding additional links, you must adjust the `xlink:href`
attribute of the `<a>` element, the `y` attribute of the `<text>` element, and the
text contained within the `<text>` element. The appearance of the final
menu is shown in Figure 11.09.

Figure 11.09

The text menu with the drop shadow rollover effect showing the drop shadow on a moused link.

A dynamic menu

Now look at creating a dynamic menu, using SVG declarative animation. First, take a look at how the finished menu will look. When the menu is closed, it looks similar to the one shown in Figure 11.10. When the menu is open, it looks like the one shown in Figure 11.11.

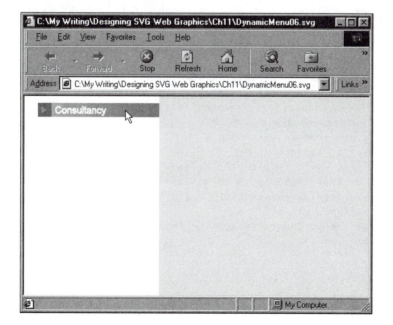

Figure 11.10

The menu in the closed position.

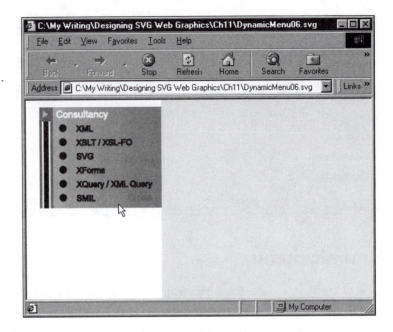

Figure 11.11

The dynamic menu
when it is opened.

You create the closed appearance and the sliding menu tree separately and later put them together. First, create the square with the flashing triangle:

Listing 11.15 (DynamicMenu01.svg)

```
<?xml version="1.0" standalone="no"?>
<!DOCTYPE svg PUBLIC "-//W3C//DTD SVG 1.0//EN"
    "http://www.w3.org/TR/2001/PR-SVG-20010719/
        DTD/svg10.dtd">
<svg width="200" height="300">
<svg x="20" y="10">
<rect x="0" y="0" width="20" height="20" style="fill:#669999"/>
<path d="M5,5 L5,15 13,10 z" style="fill:#669966; stroke:none">
<animate attributeName="fill" begin="0s" dur="1s" val-
ues="#669966; #FFFF00;
#669966" repeatCount="indefinite"/>
</path>
</svg>
</svg>
```

Nothing should be unfamiliar there. Add the grayish rectangle that includes a linear gradient, and use white text against that darkish gray background.

Because a click on this graphic will be the stimulus to opening the menu, you add an `id` attribute to the nested `<svg>` element. The code now looks like this:

Listing 11.16 (DynamicMenu02.svg)

```
<?xml version="1.0" standalone="no"?>
<!DOCTYPE svg PUBLIC "-//W3C//DTD SVG 1.0//EN"
      "http://www.w3.org/TR/2001/PR-SVG-20010719/
       DTD/svg10.dtd">
<svg width="200" height="300">
<svg id="Menu" x="20" y="10">
<defs>
<linearGradient id="MyGrayGradient">
<stop offset="5%" style="stop-color:#555555"/>
<stop offset="95%" style="stop-color:#AAAAAA"/>
</linearGradient>
</defs>
<rect x="0" y="0" width="20" height="20" style="fill:#669999"/>
<path d="M5,5 L5,15 13,10 z" style="fill:#669966; stroke:none">
<animate attributeName="fill" begin="0s" dur="1s" val-
ues="#669966; #FFFF00; #669966" repeatCount="indefinite"/>
</path>
<rect x="20" y="0" width="160" height="20"
style="fill:url(#MyGrayGradient); stroke:none;"/>
<text x="25" y="15" style="fill:white; stroke:white; font-
size:14; font-family:Arial, sans-serif;">
Consultancy
</text>
</svg>
</svg>
```

Move on to create the part of the menu that appears when the main part is clicked. For now, you should be concerned only with getting the layout to fit together correctly. The `<animate>` element simply gives some impression of what the opening of the menu looks like.

Listing 11.17 (DynamicMenu03.svg)

```
<?xml version="1.0" standalone="no"?>
<!DOCTYPE svg PUBLIC "-//W3C//DTD SVG 1.0//EN"
      "http://www.w3.org/TR/2001/PR-SVG-20010719/
       DTD/svg10.dtd">
<svg>
```

```
<svg x="0" y="0" width="180" height="150">
<defs>
<linearGradient id="MyOtherGrayGradient">
<stop offset="5%" style="stop-color:#CCCCCC"/>
<stop offset="95%" style="stop-color:#999999"/>
</linearGradient>
</defs>
<animate attributeName="y" begin="0s" dur="4s" from="-150"
to="0"
fill="freeze"/>
<rect x="20" y="0" width="160" height="150" style="fill:red;
stroke:red;"/>
<rect x="0" y="0" width="3" height="100%"
style="fill:#669999;stroke:#669999"/>
<rect x="4" y="0" width="2" height="100%" style="fill:white;
stroke:white"/>
<rect x="7" y="0" width="6" height="100%"
style="fill:#000099;stroke:#000099"/>
<rect x="14" y="0" width="2" height="100%" style="fill:white;
stroke:white"/>
<rect x="17" y="0" width="3" height="100%"
style="fill:#669999;stroke:#669999"/>
<rect x="20" y="0" width="160" height="100%"
style="fill:url(#MyOtherGrayGradient);
stroke:none;"/>
</svg>
</svg>
```

If you are wondering why a `<rect>` element is there with red stroke and red fill, I use that technique in fitting other elements together. If I don't have the positioning absolutely correct, some red shows through, so I know where I need to do some fine-tuning of the position.

Also notice that the `from` attribute of the `<animate>` element has a value of `-150`. The starting point is then 150 pixels above the top of the screen.

Next, you need to get the text etc. that offers links to the various available consultancy services.

```
<circle cx="35" cy="15" r="5" style="fill:#000099;
stroke:#000099"/>
<text id="FirstOption" x="55" y="20" style="fill:#000099;
stroke:#000099">
XML
</text>
<circle cx="35" cy="35" r="5" style="fill:#000099;
```

```
stroke:#000099"/>
<text id="SecondOption" x="55" y="40" style="fill:#000099;
stroke:#000099">
XSLT / XSL-FO
</text>
<circle cx="35" cy="55" r="5" style="fill:#000099;
stroke:#000099"/>
<text id="SecondOption" x="55" y="60" style="fill:#000099;
stroke:#000099">
SVG
</text>
<circle cx="35" cy="75" r="5" style="fill:#000099;
stroke:#000099"/>
<text id="SecondOption" x="55" y="80" style="fill:#000099;
stroke:#000099">
XForms
</text>
<circle cx="35" cy="95" r="5" style="fill:#000099;
stroke:#000099"/>
<text id="SecondOption" x="55" y="100" style="fill:#000099;
stroke:#000099">
XQuery / XML Query
</text>
<circle cx="35" cy="115" r="5" style="fill:#000099;
stroke:#000099"/>
<text id="SecondOption" x="55" y="120" style="fill:#000099;
stroke:#000099">
SMIL
</text>
```

Now comes the moment of truth. How will they look when they are put
together? Will the animation work? One thing you must remember is that
because the slide-down menu you created second will appear from behind
the top-level menu, it must appear earlier in the document than the top-level
menu.

Listing 11.18 (DynamicMenu04.svg)

```
<?xml version="1.0" standalone="no"?>
<!DOCTYPE svg PUBLIC "-//W3C//DTD SVG 1.0//EN"
    "http://www.w3.org/TR/2001/PR-SVG-20010719/
    DTD/svg10.dtd">
<svg width="200" height="300">
<svg x="20" y="-150" width="200" height="130">
<defs>
```

```
<linearGradient id="MyGrayGradient">
<stop offset="5%" style="stop-color:#CCCCCC"/>
<stop offset="95%" style="stop-color:#999999"/>
</linearGradient>
</defs>
<animate attributeName="y" begin="Menu.click" dur="1s" from="
-150" to="25" fill="freeze"/>
<rect x="0" y="0" width="160" height="150" style="fill:red;
stroke:red;"/>
<rect x="0" y="0" width="3" height="100%"
style="fill:#669999;stroke:#669999"/>
<rect x="4" y="0" width="2" height="100%" style="fill:white;
stroke:white"/>
<rect x="7" y="0" width="6" height="100%"
style="fill:#000099;stroke:#000099"/>
<rect x="14" y="0" width="2" height="100%" style="fill:white;
stroke:white"/>
<rect x="17" y="0" width="3" height="100%"
style="fill:#669999;stroke:#669999"/>
<rect x="20" y="0" width="160" height="100%"
style="fill:url(#MyGrayGradient); stroke:none;"/>
<circle cx="35" cy="15" r="5" style="fill:#000099;
stroke:#000099"/>
<text id="FirstOption" x="55" y="20" style="fill:#000099;
stroke:#000099">
XML
</text>
<circle cx="35" cy="35" r="5" style="fill:#000099;
stroke:#000099"/>
<text id="SecondOption" x="55" y="40" style="fill:#000099;
stroke:#000099">
XSLT / XSL-FO
</text>
<circle cx="35" cy="55" r="5" style="fill:#000099;
stroke:#000099"/>
<text id="SecondOption" x="55" y="60" style="fill:#000099;
stroke:#000099">
SVG
</text>
<circle cx="35" cy="75" r="5" style="fill:#000099;
stroke:#000099"/>
<text id="SecondOption" x="55" y="80" style="fill:#000099;
stroke:#000099">
XForms
</text>
<circle cx="35" cy="95" r="5" style="fill:#000099;
stroke:#000099"/>
```

```
<text id="SecondOption" x="55" y="100" style="fill:#000099;
stroke:#000099">
XQuery / XML Query
</text>
<circle cx="35" cy="115" r="5" style="fill:#000099;
stroke:#000099"/>
<text id="SecondOption" x="55" y="120" style="fill:#000099;
stroke:#000099">
SMIL
</text>
</svg>
<rect x="0" y="0" width="200" height="10" style="fill:white;
stroke:white"/>
<svg id="Menu" x="20" y="10">
<defs>
<linearGradient id="MyGrayGradient">
<stop offset="5%" style="stop-color:#555555"/>
<stop offset="95%" style="stop-color:#AAAAAA"/>
</linearGradient>
</defs>
<rect x="0" y="0" width="20" height="20" style="fill:#669999"/>
<path d="M5,5 L5,15 13,10 z" style="fill:#669966; stroke:none">
<animate attributeName="fill" begin="0s" dur="1s" val-
ues="#669966; #FFFF00; #669966" repeatCount="indefinite"/>
</path>
<rect x="20" y="0" width="160" height="20"
style="fill:url(#MyGrayGradient); stroke:none;"/>
<text x="25" y="15" style="fill:white; stroke:white; font-
size:14; font-family:Arial, sans-serif;">
Consultancy
</text>
</svg>
</svg>
```

Already, the code looks fairly hefty, but you still have a few things to do to create a fully functional menu. You need to add `<a>` elements to provide the linking functionality, and you need to provide rollover effects, both on the text in the menu and on the `<circle>` elements that are acting as bullets for the available choices. And, of course, you need animation to allow the slide-down menu to close when the top-level menu is clicked again—at least, you would if the user wasn't going to take one of the available choices from the menu.

When you have added the link and rollovers, the code for the SVG consultancy option looks like this:

```
<a id="SVGChoice" xlink:href="SVGConsultancy.html">
<circle cx="35" cy="55" r="5" style="fill:#000099;
stroke:#000099">
<animate begin="SVGChoice.mouseover" dur="0.01s"
attributeName="fill" from="#000099" to="#FF0066" fill="freeze"/>
<animate begin="SVGChoice.mouseout" dur="0.01s"
attributeName="fill" from="#FF0066" to="#000099" fill="freeze"/>
</circle>
<text id="SecondOption" x="55" y="60" style="fill:#000099;
stroke:#000099">
<animate begin="SVGChoice.mouseover" dur="0.01s"
attributeName="fill" from="#000099" to="#FF0066" fill="freeze"/>
<animate begin="SVGChoice.mouseout" dur="0.01s"
attributeName="fill" from="#FF0066" to="#000099" fill="freeze"/>
<animate begin="SVGChoice.mouseover" dur="0.01s"
attributeName="stroke" from="#000099" to="#FF0066"
fill="freeze"/>
<animate begin="SVGChoice.mouseout" dur="0.01s"
attributeName="stroke" from="#FF0066" to="#000099"
fill="freeze"/>
SVG
</text>
</a>
```

Now put all that together. Take time to walk through the code, and make sure that you understand it. If part of it puzzles you, rewind a little and check the explanations earlier in this section so that, gradually, the purpose of each part of the code becomes clearer.

Listing 11.19 (DynamicMenu06.svg)

```
<?xml version="1.0" standalone="no"?>
<!DOCTYPE svg PUBLIC "-//W3C//DTD SVG 1.0//EN"
      "http://www.w3.org/TR/2001/PR-SVG-20010719/
       DTD/svg10.dtd">
<svg width="200" height="300">
<svg x="20" y="-150" width="200" height="130">
<defs>
<linearGradient id="MyGrayGradient">
<stop offset="5%" style="stop-color:#CCCCCC"/>
<stop offset="95%" style="stop-color:#999999"/>
</linearGradient>
</defs>
<animate attributeName="y" begin="Menu.click" dur="1s" from="-
150" to="25" fill="freeze"/>
```

```
<animate attributeName="y" begin="MenuClose.click" dur="1s"
from="25" to="-150" fill="freeze"/>
<rect x="0" y="0" width="160" height="150" style="fill:red;
stroke:red;"/>
<rect x="0" y="0" width="3" height="100%"
style="fill:#669999;stroke:#669999"/>
<rect x="4" y="0" width="2" height="100%" style="fill:white;
stroke:white"/>
<rect x="7" y="0" width="6" height="100%"
style="fill:#000099;stroke:#000099"/>
<rect x="14" y="0" width="2" height="100%" style="fill:white;
stroke:white"/>
<rect x="17" y="0" width="3" height="100%"
style="fill:#669999;stroke:#669999"/>
<rect x="20" y="0" width="160" height="100%"
style="fill:url(#MyGrayGradient); stroke:none;"/>
<a id="XMLChoice" xlink:href="XMLConsulting.html">
<circle cx="35" cy="15" r="5" style="fill:#000099;
stroke:#000099">
<animate begin="XMLChoice.mouseover" dur="0.01s"
attributeName="fill" from="#000099" to="#FF0066" fill="freeze"/>
<animate begin="XMLChoice.mouseout" dur="0.01s"
attributeName="fill" from="#FF0066" to="#000099" fill="freeze"/>
</circle>
<text id="FirstOption" x="55" y="20" style="fill:#000099;
stroke:#000099">
<animate begin="XMLChoice.mouseover" dur="0.01s"
attributeName="fill" from="#000099" to="#FF0066" fill="freeze"/>
<animate begin="XMLChoice.mouseout" dur="0.01s"
attributeName="fill" from="#FF0066" to="#000099" fill="freeze"/>
<animate begin="XMLChoice.mouseover" dur="0.01s"
attributeName="stroke" from="#000099" to="#FF0066"
fill="freeze"/>
<animate begin="XMLChoice.mouseout" dur="0.01s"
attributeName="stroke" from="#FF0066" to="#000099"
fill="freeze"/>
XML
</text>
</a>
<a id="XSLTChoice" xlink:href="XSLTXSLFOConsultancy.html">
<circle cx="35" cy="35" r="5" style="fill:#000099;
stroke:#000099">
<animate begin="XSLTChoice.mouseover" dur="0.01s"
attributeName="fill" from="#000099" to="#FF0066" fill="freeze"/>
<animate begin="XSLTChoice.mouseout" dur="0.01s"
attributeName="fill" from="#FF0066" to="#000099" fill="freeze"/>
</circle>
```

```
<text id="SecondOption" x="55" y="40" style="fill:#000099;
stroke:#000099">
<animate begin="XSLTChoice.mouseover" dur="0.01s"
attributeName="fill" from="#000099" to="#FF0066" fill="freeze"/>
<animate begin="XSLTChoice.mouseout" dur="0.01s"
attributeName="fill" from="#FF0066" to="#000099" fill="freeze"/>
<animate begin="XSLTChoice.mouseover" dur="0.01s"
attributeName="stroke" from="#000099" to="#FF0066"
fill="freeze"/>
<animate begin="XSLTChoice.mouseout" dur="0.01s"
attributeName="stroke" from="#FF0066" to="#000099"
fill="freeze"/>
XSLT / XSL-FO
</text>
</a>
<a id="SVGChoice" xlink:href="SVGConsultancy.html">
<circle cx="35" cy="55" r="5" style="fill:#000099;
stroke:#000099">
<animate begin="SVGChoice.mouseover" dur="0.01s"
attributeName="fill" from="#000099" to="#FF0066" fill="freeze"/>
<animate begin="SVGChoice.mouseout" dur="0.01s"
attributeName="fill" from="#FF0066" to="#000099" fill="freeze"/>
</circle>
<text id="SecondOption" x="55" y="60" style="fill:#000099;
stroke:#000099">
<animate begin="SVGChoice.mouseover" dur="0.01s"
attributeName="fill" from="#000099" to="#FF0066" fill="freeze"/>
<animate begin="SVGChoice.mouseout" dur="0.01s"
attributeName="fill" from="#FF0066" to="#000099" fill="freeze"/>
<animate begin="SVGChoice.mouseover" dur="0.01s"
attributeName="stroke" from="#000099" to="#FF0066"
fill="freeze"/>
<animate begin="SVGChoice.mouseout" dur="0.01s"
attributeName="stroke" from="#FF0066" to="#000099"
fill="freeze"/>
SVG
</text>
</a>
<a id="XFormsChoice" xlink:href="XFormsConsultancy.html">
<circle cx="35" cy="75" r="5" style="fill:#000099;
stroke:#000099">
<animate begin="XFormsChoice.mouseover" dur="0.01s"
attributeName="fill" from="#000099" to="#FF0066" fill="freeze"/>
<animate begin="XFormsChoice.mouseout" dur="0.01s"
attributeName="fill" from="#FF0066" to="#000099" fill="freeze"/>
</circle>
<text id="SecondOption" x="55" y="80" style="fill:#000099;
stroke:#000099">
```

```
<animate begin="XFormsChoice.mouseover" dur="0.01s"
attributeName="fill" from="#000099" to="#FF0066" fill="freeze"/>
<animate begin="XFormsChoice.mouseout" dur="0.01s"
attributeName="fill" from="#FF0066" to="#000099" fill="freeze"/>
<animate begin="XFormsChoice.mouseover" dur="0.01s"
attributeName="stroke" from="#000099" to="#FF0066"
fill="freeze"/>
<animate begin="XFormsChoice.mouseout" dur="0.01s"
attributeName="stroke" from="#FF0066" to="#000099"
fill="freeze"/>
XForms
</text>
</a>
<a id="XQueryChoice" xlink:href="XQueryConsultancy.html">
<circle cx="35" cy="95" r="5" style="fill:#000099;
stroke:#000099">
<animate begin="XQueryChoice.mouseover" dur="0.01s"
attributeName="fill" from="#000099" to="#FF0066" fill="freeze"/>
<animate begin="XQueryChoice.mouseout" dur="0.01s"
attributeName="fill" from="#FF0066" to="#000099" fill="freeze"/>
</circle>
<text id="SecondOption" x="55" y="100" style="fill:#000099;
stroke:#000099">
<animate begin="XQueryChoice.mouseover" dur="0.01s"
attributeName="fill" from="#000099" to="#FF0066" fill="freeze"/>
<animate begin="XQueryChoice.mouseout" dur="0.01s"
attributeName="fill" from="#FF0066" to="#000099" fill="freeze"/>
<animate begin="XQueryChoice.mouseover" dur="0.01s"
attributeName="stroke" from="#000099" to="#FF0066"
fill="freeze"/>
<animate begin="XQueryChoice.mouseout" dur="0.01s"
attributeName="stroke" from="#FF0066" to="#000099"
fill="freeze"/>
XQuery / XML Query
</text>
</a>
<a id="SMILChoice" xlink:href="SMILConsultancy.html">
<circle cx="35" cy="115" r="5" style="fill:#000099;
stroke:#000099">
<animate begin="SMILChoice.mouseover" dur="0.01s"
attributeName="fill" from="#000099" to="#FF0066" fill="freeze"/>
<animate begin="SMILChoice.mouseout" dur="0.01s"
attributeName="fill" from="#FF0066" to="#000099" fill="freeze"/>
</circle>
<text id="SecondOption" x="55" y="120" style="fill:#000099;
stroke:#000099">
```

```
<animate begin="SMILChoice.mouseover" dur="0.01s"
attributeName="fill" from="#000099" to="#FF0066" fill="freeze"/>
<animate begin="SMILChoice.mouseout" dur="0.01s"
attributeName="fill" from="#FF0066" to="#000099" fill="freeze"/>
<animate begin="SMILChoice.mouseover" dur="0.01s"
attributeName="stroke" from="#000099" to="#FF0066"
fill="freeze"/>
<animate begin="SMILChoice.mouseout" dur="0.01s"
attributeName="stroke" from="#FF0066" to="#000099"
fill="freeze"/>
SMIL
</text>
</a>
<a>
<text id="MenuClose" x="130" y="120" style="fill:red;
stroke:none; font-size:14">
Close
</text>
</a>
</svg>
<rect x="0" y="0" width="200" height="10" style="fill:white;
stroke:white"/>
<svg id="Menu" x="20" y="10">
<defs>
<linearGradient id="MyGrayGradient">
<stop offset="5%" style="stop-color:#555555"/>
<stop offset="95%" style="stop-color:#AAAAAA"/>
</linearGradient>
</defs>
<rect x="0" y="0" width="20" height="20" style="fill:#669999"/>
<path d="M5,5 L5,15 13,10 z" style="fill:#669966; stroke:none">
<animate attributeName="fill" begin="0s" dur="1s" val-
ues="#669966; #FFFF00; #669966" repeatCount="indefinite"/>
</path>
<rect x="20" y="0" width="160" height="20"
style="fill:url(#MyGrayGradient); stroke:none;"/>
<text x="25" y="15" style="fill:white; stroke:white; font-
size:14; font-family:Arial, sans-serif;">
Consultancy
</text>
</svg>
</svg>
```

If you have, as you might in a production, two or three of these, you have a reasonably sized download on your hands.

Links using SVG

Because SVG documents or document fragments are commonly used as navigation graphics in Web pages, you should understand fully how to make use of SVG linking functionality. That aspect of SVG interactivity was covered in Chapter 5.

Zooming, Panning and Scrolling SVG Images

Conforming SVG viewers are required to provide the zooming and panning of SVG images. The details of how that is done are left to the implementation in individual SVG viewers.

However, in some situations, you may not want a user to be able to use zooming and panning. In this type of situation, you can disable zooming by setting the `zoomAndPan` attribute on the outer `<svg>` element to a value of `disable`:

```
<svg zoomAndPan="disable">
```

The only other value that the `zoomAndPan` attribute might take is `magnify`, which is the default. If the `zoomAndPan` attribute is not mentioned in an `<svg>` element, therefore, zooming and panning are enabled.

Adding a `zoomAndPan` attribute to a nested `<svg>` element has no effect on whether zooming and panning are enabled. The `zoomAndPan` attribute on the outer `<svg>` element defines the setting image-wide.

Zooming

In the Adobe SVG Viewer version 2.0, you access zooming functionality by right-clicking on the SVG image. A menu is then displayed with several options, of which the first three relate to zooming.

Alternatively, you can hold down the Ctrl key and drag out an area with the mouse.

Panning

Just as with zooming, the detailed way in which panning is implemented varies from one SVG viewer to another.

To pan an image in the Adobe Viewer on a Windows platform, hold down the Alt key and then hold down the left mouse button. The cursor then changes to an open hand, as you can see in Figure 11.12.

Figure 11.12

Panning an SVG image (note the open-hand cursor).

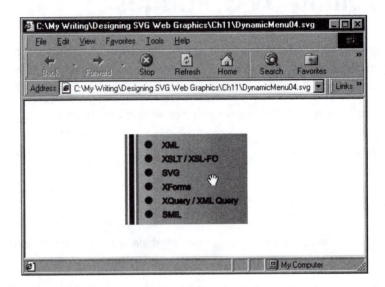

Scrolling

At the time this book was written, none of the SVG viewers provided scrolling functionality—at least not using the familiar browser scroll bars. The technique for providing scroll bars for an SVG image is described in Chapter 10, "Embedding SVG in HTML or XHTML Pages."

In this chapter, you have seen some examples of using SVG to produce the interactivity of types that are commonly used on Web pages. The techniques you have seen can be adapted for use with other SVG shapes. If you have grasped these techniques, you have a good base for applying your own creativity to create dynamic, interactive SVG Web page furniture.

12

Creating a Simple
SVG Web Site

In this chapter:

Creating an Entire Web Page with SVG

In this chapter, I introduce you to the concept of using SVG images as part of the graphics "furniture" of HTML or XHTML Web pages. I also want you to consider that SVG can be potentially a "single language" Web authoring package. In other words, you can create Web sites only with SVG, or primarily using SVG.

At first sight, it might seem odd superficially to use a graphics technology to create Web pages when such a significant part of the content of Web pages is text based. This chapter looks realistically at the practicalities of using SVG as a one-stop Web authoring technology.

In case you are skeptical that this can be done, take a look at Figure 12.01, where you can see that a Web page produced only in SVG can look pretty much like an HTML or XHTML Web page.

Creating Web Pages with a "Graphics" Language

I have tried hard in the preceding 11 chapters not to let too much of my excitement about SVG show through—but in a way, I hope that I have failed. In this

Figure 12.01

An early SVG-only home page at http://www.svgspider.com/default.svg.

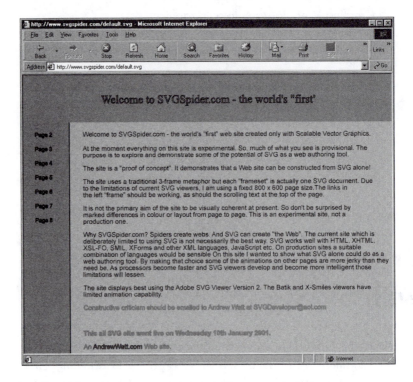

chapter, I feel I should tell you more up front how excited I am about SVG as a possible one-stop, XML-based Web authoring solution.

You might be asking yourself whether I am crazy. Are you wondering whether I have forgotten that SVG is a *graphics* format?

The answer, of course, is that I haven't forgotten that SVG is *called* Scalable Vector *Graphics*. But, I also am fully aware (and if you have read earlier chapters, I hope that you too are aware) that SVG is a graphics format unlike anything you have ever seen. A couple of steps back in the history of SVG development, it was based on PostScript—which is very much a page layout language. Furthermore, an SVG file remains editable at all times, unlike bitmap images and Flash .swf files.

I spend a significant part of this chapter discussing the pros and cons of SVG as a Web authoring technology. If you like to see and do, feel free to skip ahead to the section "Creating SVG Web Pages." In time, you need to think about the more general issues too, but first you might want to *see* how you can use SVG to produce Web pages.

Characteristics of an ideal Web authoring technology

Take a step backward, and list some characteristics you might like an "ideal" Web page authoring language to have. Then have a look at how SVG measures up to these desirable traits.

This list shows the characteristics for my version of an ideal modern Web authoring language:

- It is XML-based.
- It can be created statically or dynamically.
- It can lay out Web pages.
- It includes graphics capabilities.
- It can be styled using Cascading Style Sheets.
- It includes text layout facilities.
- It can be animated.
- It can be scripted.
- It can be combined with other XML-technologies, including XHTML and Xforms.
- It can (potentially) be used with streaming technologies, including multimedia.
- It can be used for high-quality printouts.

A few years ago, such a list of ideal qualities wouldn't have been on many people's list—or on mine, that far back. But starting today, and looking forward rather than back, I see all those qualities as important. I don't claim that SVG scores 100 percent on each of those qualities, but I would claim that it does score high enough on many of these qualities to be seriously considered as a Web authoring technology, despite the fact that it has *graphics* in its name.

Now examine the relevance of each of these points, and consider whether and how well SVG scores.

It should be XML based

SVG *is* XML, by which I mean that SVG is an application language of XML. Why is that concept important? The practical reality is that the future of (much of) the Web will be based on XML. Particularly important from the point of view of the professional graphics designer is that the part of the Web that pays those salaries will be the part based on XML. If you are not already XML savvy, now is the time to begin that process. If you don't pay attention to XML, the Web will increasingly pass you by. Whether you like XML or hate it, you have little chance of escaping the need to use it, if you have clients using the Web commercially.

It can be created statically or dynamically

Web pages were, way back in the early 1990s, almost exclusively created statically: An HTML coder wrote each page *by hand*, and when the page needed to be updated, that person updated it by hand, too. As the demand for immediate information that is updated as events happen (for example, share prices) increased, it became important that Web pages could be created "on the fly" (dynamically using server-side technologies). That can be done to produce HTML or XHTML using a variety of technologies (Java servlets, JavaServer Pages [JSP], and others, for example).

Similarly, SVG can be created both statically and dynamically. As I indicated in earlier chapters, SVG can be created statically using a tool as simple as a text editor; for many graphic designers, however, the tool of choice for at least some tasks that produce SVG images are vector graphics drawing packages, such as Jasc WebDraw, Adobe Illustrator, or Corel Draw. After using a drawing package to produce an SVG image, those with sufficient understanding of SVG will tweak the generated code as necessary.

Additionally, SVG images—and Web pages—can be created dynamically using, for example, the Extensible Stylesheet Language Transformations (XSLT). Data is stored as plain XML, or in an XML-enabled database, but can be transformed by XSLT into SVG images or Web pages that are dynamically updated as the raw data (held as XML or in a relational database management system) is updated.

It can lay out Web pages

Clearly, any Web authoring technology must be able to lay out Web pages. Ideally, it should be able to lay them out with pixel precision.

SVG scores well in this area. Because it includes CSS2 absolute positioning, SVG elements—whether they are text or graphics—can be laid out "pixel perfect" onscreen. This concept is important when you are creating SVG for traditional graphics uses, but is also useful when you are laying out larger areas of SVG text, such as on a Web page.

In addition, the availability of nested `<svg>` elements allows you to create visual components or complete Web page layouts and to position them on the page with pixel precision.

If you are used to creating, as a designer, the look of a Web site or page in a bitmap graphics package, such as Photoshop, which is then coded into HTML or XHTML by an HTML coder, I hope that you can see the huge workflow advantage if the layout created by a graphic designer in Jasc WebDraw, Corel Draw, or Adobe Illustrator can be exported directly as SVG Web pages. The need for the HTML coder middleman disappears in some settings, and, assuming that the designer has a grasp on SVG, increased efficiency is possible.

SVG also allows more flexibility and ease of use in layout than does HTML or XHTML used without CSS. You don't need complicated nested tables to achieve a particular layout. You want a block placed? Just create an SVG visual component, nested perhaps within an `<svg>` element, and, making due allowance for the SVG painter's model, place it where you want it to appear.

It includes graphics capabilities

Any Web authoring technology needs to have graphics capabilities. If you have ever used text-only access to the Web, you realize the truth of that statement. Clearly, SVG, as a graphics technology, scores high in this area. The Web would have been a much more visually exciting place if HTML had had years ago a fraction of the graphics power that SVG has.

That both the text and graphics parts of SVG Web pages are in the same SVG document offers advantages. At the practical level, you need to master only one skill set to allow the authoring of both text and graphics. For the individual Web developer or graphic designer, the need to master essentially one skill set opens up new business opportunities. For the corporate employee, who is more likely to be a specialist, these issues might be less important.

The unity of text and graphics in SVG applies at a technical level, too. SVG text and graphics can be styled using the same CSS stylesheet, and both text and graphics in an SVG Web page can be scripted.

It can be styled using Cascading Style Sheets

As Web sites increase in size, the demands on a developer's time to maintain the site increase greatly. The use of Cascading Style Sheets (CSS) makes it possible to update the look and feel of a Web site by changing only one file—an external CSS style sheet.

With SVG, you can also style text on an SVG Web page. However, the exciting additional benefit is that if the SVG graphics have been appropriately created, you can also update the look and feel of both the graphics and the text throughout a Web site by changing only one CSS style sheet. The potential efficiency benefits of maintaining and updating Web sites are enormous. The use of CSS with SVG is discussed in more detail in Chapter 13, "Designing Your SVG for Use with CSS."

It includes text-layout facilities

Any Web page authoring technology must be able to lay out text on the page. Although SVG can do this task, that is not one of its strongest points, at least with respect to one aspect where it scores less well than HTML or XHTML. When a browser window is resized in HTML, the flow of text alters to adjust to, for example, the new screen width. SVG-based text cannot, at least for now, do that. An SVG rendering engine cannot automatically insert line breaks or perform word wrapping. The width of the display of SVG using `<text>` and `<tspan>` elements is fixed and does not change if the browser window is resized.

The absence of automatic line breaks is undoubtedly a disadvantage. However, because more and more Web pages are increasingly likely to be generated dynamically, this lack is less of a practical handicap than it might first appear because line length can readily be calculated programmatically. In addition, after you become used to the connection between `<text>` and `<tspan>` elements, as demonstrated in Chapter 4, "Using Text in SVG," laying out text sensibly for chosen page sizes is a straightforward process. The more the `<tspan>` element is used within a single `<text>` element on a Web page, the easier and quicker the process becomes.

In addition, SVG has a `<foreignObject>` element that can, in principle, allow the import of HTML or XHTML into a designated area on an SVG Web page. Potentially, that element could allow a form of automatic word wrapping in HTML or XHTML modules nested within an SVG Web page. However, at the time this book was written, the Adobe SVG viewer had not yet implemented the `<foreignObject>` element, although the X-Smiles browser and the Amaya browser have implemented the `<foreignObject>` element to some degree. Hopefully, the developers of SVG viewers can make this useful facility fully available to the SVG community soon.

It can be animated

As you have seen in Chapter 8, "Animation: SVG and SMIL Animation," SVG has powerful animation facilities. The animation of SVG elements, whether text or more traditional graphics, might be produced without the need for learning scripting languages. I don't want to understate the power of scripting for certain uses, but SVG provides powerful animation facilities by means of its native declarative syntax.

It can be scripted

The Document Object Model (DOM) of an SVG Web page can be manipulated using, for example, ECMAScript (JavaScript). This situation opens up substantial possibilities in addition to those provided by the SVG declarative syntax, for interactivity under user control.

The Document Object Model provides an application programming interface (API) to give access to create, modify, or delete parts of an HTML or XML document. SVG has its own Document Object Model that allows programmatic control of parts of an SVG document. A discussion of the DOM is beyond the scope of this book, but if you want to explore that part of SVG, books covering that topic are sure to be available soon.

It can be combined with other XML technologies, including XHTML and XForms

The combining of SVG with XML-based technologies can be considered under two headings.

First, in a conventional Web browser with an SVG viewer plug-in, you can make use of the SVG `<foreignObject>` element so that HTML or XHTML can be embedded within an SVG document. After SVG viewers implement the `<foreignObject>` element, this provides one technique of mixing SVG with other XML technologies in such a way that all can be viewed within a conventional Web browser.

The second approach to combining SVG with other XML technologies is the availability of genuine XML-enabled browsers, such as the X-Smiles browser, which allows combinations of SVG with XSL-FO, XForms, or SMIL (Synchronized Multimedia Integration Language). The combination of SVG and XForms looks likely to provide a powerful combination for the creation of dynamic interactive Web pages.

These types of combinations allow SVG to perform a significant role in multilanguage, multimedia Web applications.

It can (potentially) be used in multimedia presentations

SVG, as an XML-based technology, is ideally suited to being used together with SMIL to therefore provide integrated access to a growing range of XML-based multimedia opportunities. A full consideration of the potential of SVG in multimedia is beyond the scope of this book, although some early examples are available at http://www.xsmiles.org/.

SVG can, in principle, also be mixed with XML-based speech technologies, such as VoiceXML. Exciting possibilities lie ahead with such combinations of technology.

It can be used for high-quality printouts

For an individual Web user, this characteristic might not be important; for corporations that have to provide documentation to many thousands of users, however, the ability to store data as XML and to present it graphically as SVG for all uses (on the Web, on mobile browsers, or on paper, for example) has significant potential advantages. Think of the time and money saved compared to having to create different graphics on paper and for Web display. Within that change are threats to some individuals' livelihood and new opportunities opened up to others.

Some individuals have little need to print graphics because their business is solely Web based. However, companies of significant size are likely to want to present information on paper as well as on the Web.

SVG has the advantage of being able to be accurately positioned on paper. Although you can use pixel sizes or absolute measures for layout onscreen, you can equally use centimeters or inches to define placement when you print. The page for presentation on paper might be different from the one shown onscreen, but you can easily adapt the XSLT, or other server-side technology, to produce alternative presentations for screen or paper media.

Who Might Use SVG As a Web Authoring Tool?

This section describes some advantages of using SVG Web pages for professional graphics designers and for amateurs interested in a simple technology for creating Web pages.

Graphics design professionals already do the design work for Web pages in many companies. But their work is limited to designing—with implementation, by coding into HTML or XHTML, being carried out by others with specialized HTML knowledge. SVG can empower the graphics designer who understands the essentials of SVG.

Graphics packages such as the current versions of Corel Draw, Adobe Illustrator, and Jasc WebDraw can produce SVG-coded Web pages directly from the drawings made with the package. Those pages can be used as is for static Web pages, tweaked to add, for example, interactive or animated extras or used as templates for the creation of servlets or JavaServer Pages or other server-side technologies that produce SVG Web pages. New workflows are likely to open up, therefore, involving the interaction of SVG-savvy graphics designers with server-side programmers.

Of course, another possibility—at least in the short term—is to create SVG Web pages using vector graphics drawing tools to allow clients to see working SVG Web sites, including working links and rollovers, for example, as prototypes of a more traditional HTML or XHTML Web site. This situation could allow graphics designers to take a much more active stake in the development of the final working version of a site and free them from the occasional frustrations that occur when HTML coders don't reflect the designers' design ideas. When a prototype Web site can be created directly using Jasc WebDraw or Adobe Illustrator, interaction with the client can be direct and efficient to the potential benefit of both parties.

The fact that vector graphics packages already exist might discourage some graphics designers from getting their hands dirty with coding SVG by hand. But the availability of those same tools gives talented graphics designers potentially greater control and greater involvement in the creation of the Web pages they have designed. When you work in that way and also understand SVG well enough to be able to tweak the code whenever necessary or when you are adding visual components, you have a powerful, creative tool. Put it to good use!

Creating SVG Web Pages

To create an SVG Web page, you can work just as you have up to this point in the book—an SVG Web page is simply another type of SVG image. If you have been working with a vector graphics package, such as

CorelDRAW 10, simply open a new image with suitable dimensions and start laying out the page. Alternatively, you can choose one of the Web templates, intended presumably to be saved as HTML, although nothing stops you from saving it as SVG and tweaking any aspect of it to suit the visual display you intend. With CorelDRAW 10, you can also open HTML files and potentially save them again as SVG files to form templates for your SVG Web pages.

If you have been creating SVG by hand coding, simply create a simple template to use for all your pages, something like this:

```
<?xml version="1.0" standalone="no"?>
<!DOCTYPE svg PUBLIC "-//W3C//DTD SVG 1.0//EN"
    "http://www.w3.org/TR/2001/PR-SVG-20010719/
    DTD/svg10.dtd">
<svg width="800" height="580">
</svg>
```

Then simply lay out the SVG Web page. It's just another SVG document or image.

Of course, you can also create more complex templates, if you have a need for or like particular Web page layouts.

Laying out SVG Web pages

In Chapter 2, "SVG Document Overview," I introduced you to the idea of nesting `<svg>` elements within the `<svg>` element that constitutes the SVG image or document or, in this case, Web page. When you are laying out pages, having at least some of the parts of the page nested within `<svg>` elements is helpful. If the nested `<svg>` element has a group of shapes or text, for example, contained within it, they all are positioned within that `<svg>` element. Moving the `<svg>` element preserves all the relative positioning of parts of a graphic, including the animations. Working this way can save lots of tedious tweaking of positioning attribute values. You create the relative positioning you want within the `<svg>` element. Then you leave it alone and move the group of elements by altering the x and y attributes of the `<svg>` element.

Laying out an SVG Web page has a couple of limiting factors that will hopefully soon be removed, partly by the further development of SVG viewers to more fully implement the SVG Recommendation.

The first limitation is that the Adobe and other SVG viewers, in their initial implementations, viewed scroll bars as unnecessary. The user community brought the omission to the attention of Adobe and was told that Adobe had "heard" the user community's views. Hopefully, by the time you read this book, the Adobe viewer will have translated that "hearing" into the implementation of scroll bars in the Adobe SVG Viewer. Without scroll bars being provided by SVG viewers, a visitor who sees a sizeable SVG image—whether it is an SVG Web page or a map or technical diagram, for example—is forced to make use of the SVG panning mechanism. Panning is useful for some purposes, but does not provide the control that scrolling in either a horizontal or vertical dimension does.

The second, hopefully temporary, limitation is the absence of functionality for the SVG `<image>` element to import or include other SVG documents. After that functionality is implemented, you can split your Web pages into components, with some similarities to frames, and just import the necessary page components into a full Web page. This process can make the creation and maintenance of SVG Web pages an easier proposition.

Now I show you how to lay out an SVG Web page using the technologies that are already available. I am assuming that you have already done the planning for the visual appearance and navigation of an SVG site and that you want to implement that plan.

First, you need to decide on the dimensions of the Web page you want to create. Because of the absence of scroll bars now, this decision is more important than for an HTML or XHTML Web page. For prototype sites, such as SVGSpider.com, I recommend using a page size of 800 x 600 pixels. That size means essentially that you are assuming that the vast majority of likely visitors have a monitor that can display 800 x 600 pixels or higher. Sales statistics for monitors indicate that the most common size now being sold is capable of displaying at least 1024 x 768 pixels; for now, at least, I feel that the page size should be based on the needs of someone using an 800 x 600 pixel display. Set the `width` attribute on the document element, `<svg>`, to 800 and the `height` attribute to 600. If you want to be sure that your entire Web page is displayed onscreen, you might want to reduce the page size to take into account the pixels lost by the interface of various Web browsers. I also include within the `<svg>` element namespace declarations, as shown in the following code skeleton:

```
<?xml version="1.0" standalone="no"?>
<!DOCTYPE svg PUBLIC "-//W3C//DTD SVG 1.0//EN"
     "http://www.w3.org/TR/2001/PR-SVG-20010719/
       DTD/svg10.dtd">
<svg width="800" height="600"
     xmlns:xlink="http://www.w3.org/1999/xlink"
     xmlns = 'http://www.w3.org/2000/svg'>
</svg>
```

Now look at laying out a straightforward "three-frame" SVG Web page, using a version of http://www.svgspider.com/default.svg as the material for discussion. Because the page is a three-frame design (although it's contained in a single document), you work through the creation of each part of the page separately.

The code for the "top frame" looks like this:

```
<!-- Top "frame" -->
<rect x="0" y="0" width="800" height="100"
style="fill:#999999;"/>
<svg x="166" y="20" width="468" height="60">
<text x="700" y="40" style="stroke:black; fill:red;
font-family:'Times New
Roman', serif; font-size:24; font-weight:normal;">
Welcome to SVGSpider.com - the world's "first" all Scalable
Vector Graphics web
site.
<animate attributeName="x" from="650" to="-900" begin="0s"
dur="20s"
repeatCount="indefinite"/>
</text>
<rect x="0" y="0" width="468" height="60" style="stroke:red;
stroke-width:2; fill:none;"/>
</svg>
```

The first `<rect>` element creates a background gray color for the top frame. Its width is the same as the `<svg>` element for the Web page.

Next, you nest an `<svg>` element that represents a rectangle the same size as a typical banner ad on the Web. In this sample Web page, the rectangle simply contains horizontally scrolling text, although it can contain any

`<svg>` or bitmap image of the defined size. It was centered on the page by virtue of a little mental arithmetic when defining the value of the `x` attribute.

Use of the `<text>` element is straightforward. Remember that when a font name with more than one word is used, like Times New Roman, it must be enclosed in quotes. Also, if you used double quotes for the `style` attribute, you must use single quotes for the font name. Or, if you used single quotes for the `style` attribute, you must use double quotes for the font name:

```
<animate attributeName="x" from="650" to="-900" begin="0s"
dur="20s"
repeatCount="indefinite"/>
```

This animation produces the ticker tape effect in the top frame. Because the animated text is nested within the `<svg>` element, it becomes visible only when its `x` attribute is contained within the width of the `<svg>` element. However, if you mouse the scrolling text and select some of it, you can produce bizarre effects, with the selected text becoming visible outside the `<svg>` element. The initial value of the `x` attribute was chosen to place the scrolling text out of sight and sufficiently to the right to cause a delay before it appears onscreen. Some people prefer to have a ticker tape already visible when the page loads, in which case you might want to set to 400 or so the initial value of the `x` attribute of the `<text>` element, reflected also in the `from` attribute of the `<animate>` element.

The speed of the text across the screen is determined by the difference in the x coordinates defined by the `from` and `to` attributes of the `<animate>` element as well as the duration of the animation. If you make the animation too fast, the text flickers and is difficult to read. Make it too slow, and the reader might become bored and move on. You find that the speed that can be comfortably read depends on, among other things, the color of the text and the color of the background, which is static:

```
<rect x="0" y="0" width="468" height="60" style="stroke:red;
stroke-width:2; fill:none;"/>
```

The final part of the top frame is a red frame placed around the ticker tape. Notice that the `<rect>` element is last in the code and therefore would normally be painted in front of the scrolling text. However, it is defined in the example with the `fill` property set to `none`, so no problem exists. If you want to create a contrasting background for the scrolling text, as I have done at `http://www.svgspider.com/Page08.svg`, you need to position this `<rect>` element earlier in the document than the `<text>` element that contains the scrolling text; otherwise, a solid color for the rectangle's fill would prevent you and your users from seeing the scrolling text.

Here is the code for the left frame, which—although it's fairly long—is simple, consisting mostly of a simple visual component for each link. The code is formatted so that the repeating nature of the structure is obvious:

```
<!-- Left "frame" -->
<rect x="0" y="100" width="100" height="600"
style="fill:red;"/>
<a xlink:href="Page02.svg">
<text style="fill:black; stroke:black; font-size:12;" x="25"
y="130" >
Page 2
</text>
</a>
<a xlink:href="Page03.svg">
<text style="fill:black; stroke:black; font-size:12;" x="25"
y="160" >
Page 3
</text>
</a>
<a xlink:href="Page04.svg">
<text style="fill:black; stroke:black; font-size:12;" x="25"
y="190" >
Page 4
</text>
</a>
<a xlink:href="Page05.svg">
<text style="fill:black; stroke:black; font-size:12;" x="25"
y="220" >
Page 5
</text>
</a>
<a xlink:href="Page06.svg">
<text style="fill:black; stroke:black; font-size:12;" x="25"
y="250" >
Page 6
</text>
</a>
<a xlink:href="Page07.svg">
<text style="fill:black; stroke:black; font-size:12;" x="25"
y="280" >
```

```
Page 7
</text>
</a>
```

The first `<rect>` element creates the red background color, 100 pixels wide, for the left frame.

Each hyperlink to another page on the SVGSpider.com Web site is nested within an SVG `<a>` element. Each `<a>` element has an `xlink:href` attribute with a value appropriate to the page being linked to. The `<text>` element for the link to Page 2 defines the style of the text and the text to be displayed on the page.

After you have the first link visual component created and working correctly, you can simply copy and paste it, adjust the value of the `y` attribute, and amend the text to reflect the page being linked to. After you have created the first visual component, creating the others is simple.

Look at the code for the "main frame," which, again, should be fairly easy for you to follow. I have removed most of the page content, to conserve space:

```
<!-- Main Frame -->
<rect style="fill:#CCCCCC;" x="100" y="100" width="700"
height="500"/>
<rect style="fill:black;" x="100" y="100" width="2"
height="700"/>
<text x="130" y="130" style="font-family:Arial, sans-serif;
font-size:14;
font-weight:normal;">
Welcome to SVGSpider.com - the world's "first" web site created
only with
Scalable Vector Graphics.</text>
<text>
<tspan x="130" y="160" style="font-family:Arial, sans-serif;
font-size:14;
font-weight:normal;">
At the moment everything on this site is experimental. So, much
of what you see
is provisional. The
</tspan>
<tspan x="130" dy="1em" style="font-family:Arial,sans-serif;
font-size:14;
font-weight:normal;">
purpose is to explore and demonstrate some of the potential of
```

```
SVG as a web
authoring tool.
</tspan>
<tspan x="130" dy="2em" style="font-family:Arial,sans-serif;
font-size:14;
font-weight:normal;">
The site is a "proof of concept". It demonstrates that a Web
site can be
constructed from SVG alone!
</tspan>
<!-- Lots more page code went here. -->
</text>
```

Note that two `<rect>` elements are at the beginning of this frame. The first `<rect>` element creates a rectangle 700 pixels wide and 500 pixels high. Together with your top and left "frames," the rectangle fully occupies the 800 x 600 pixel space defined by the outer `<svg>` element. The second `<rect>` element is only two pixels wide and provides a piece of black decoration alongside the right edge of the left frame. For that, you could have used, alternatively, a `<line>` element.

All the text content on the page is contained in one `<text>` element, within which are contained a number of `<tspan>` elements, only three of which are shown in the preceding code. Notice that the position of the first `<tspan>` element is defined with absolute values for the `x` and `y` attributes. Thereafter, I use on the `<tspan>` elements a `dy` attribute indicating that the difference in the y coordinate is equivalent to one em, a measure of letter size. Lines of text within a paragraph typically might be separated with `dy` equal to 1em or 1.5em. Paragraph separation might be indicated by a `dy` value of 2em.

And, of course, don't omit the closing `</svg>` tag at the end of the page.

Creating an SVG Web page isn't hard, is it?

Handling semi-resizable SVG Web pages

One of the disappointing aspects of SVG Web pages is that if you use fixed widths and height for the outer `<svg>` element, you likely end up with an off-white band on the right side of your Web page. Getting rid of that band isn't too difficult. Take a look at the following code:

Listing 12.1 (Resizable01.svg)

```
<?xml version="1.0" standalone="no"?>
<!DOCTYPE svg PUBLIC "-//W3C//DTD SVG 1.0//EN"
    "http://www.w3.org/TR/2001/PR-SVG-20010719/
    DTD/svg10.dtd">
<svg width="100%" height="100%">
<rect x="0%" y="0%" width="100%" height="100%"/>
<rect x="25%" y="10%" width="50%" height="50%"
style="fill:white; stroke:white;"/>
<text x="26%" y="15%">
<tspan>
Hello, here is some test text.
</tspan>
<tspan x="26%" dy="1.5em">
A second line of test text.
</tspan>
</text>
</svg>
```

What you have is a solid black rectangle as your page background, which is 100 percent the size of the width and height of the browser window. However, you size the browser window, for example, as shown in Figure 12.02 and Figure 12.03. In front of that is a white rectangle that, similarly, is 50 percent of the width and 50 percent of the height of the browser window.

Of course, the two resizable rectangles do not need to be different colors—that simply makes it easier for you to see onscreen what is happening when the browser window is resized. If they were both white, the text would appear to be repositioned as the browser window is resized.

Figure 12.02

A full-width view of the resizable areas on the skeleton SVG Web page.

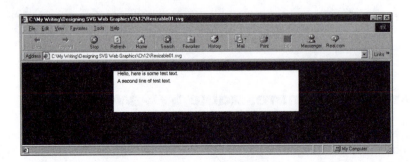

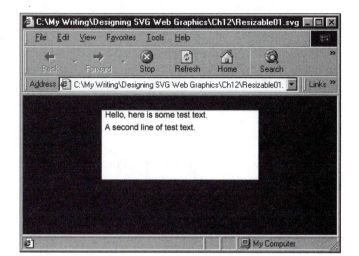

Figure 12.03

The same SVG Web page as shown in Figure 12.02, but with the browser window narrower.

This technique doesn't give you the flowing text of HTML or XHTML in the browser, but it does give you a way of presenting textual data fairly symmetrically positioned in the browser window rather than the lopsided appearance that would occur otherwise. It has limits, though. If you make the browser window tiny, you can hide a significant part of the text when line lengths are normal. In that scenario, HTML would also have difficulty coping with the scroll bars taking up a significant proportion of the width of the browser window.

Applying a similar technique gives you two color sidebars, as shown in the following code:

Listing 12.2 (Resizable03.svg)

```
<?xml version="1.0" standalone="no"?>
<!DOCTYPE svg PUBLIC "-//W3C//DTD SVG 1.0//EN"
    "http://www.w3.org/TR/2001/PR-SVG-20010719/
    DTD/svg10.dtd">
<svg width="100%" height="100%">
<rect x="0%" y="0%" width="25%" height="100%"
style="fill:#000099;stroke:white"/>
<rect x="75%" y="0%" width="25%" height="100%"
style="fill:#000099;stroke:white"/>
<rect x="25%" y="10%" width="50%" height="50%"
style="fill:white; stroke:white;"/>
<text x="26%" y="15%" style="fill:#000099; stroke:#000099">
```

```
<tspan>
Hello, here is some test text.
</tspan>
<tspan x="26%" dy="1.5em">
A second line of test text.
</tspan>
</text>
</svg>
```

This code provides you with a design for SVG Web pages that would look similar on either 800 x 600 or 1024 x 768 screen resolutions.

In the preceding code, you could have used, as an alternative approach, the `font-weight` property on the text and set the `stroke` property to `none`.

Listing 12.3 provides a slightly different possible solution. The sliding panels are on each side of the main, central text area, but when the browser window is less than fully open, the window clearly needs to be resized because the text in both the left and right blue areas is truncated, as you can see in Figure 12.04.

Figure 12.04

When the browser window does not display the full text in the left and right sidebars, they slide "behind" the central text portion, giving a clear visual cue that the browser window needs to be larger.

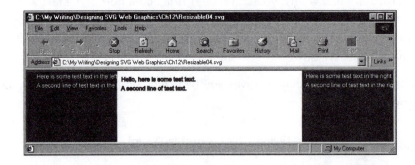

Listing 12.3 (Resizable04.svg)

```
<?xml version="1.0" standalone="no"?>
<!DOCTYPE svg PUBLIC "-//W3C//DTD SVG 20001102//EN"
        "http://www.w3.org/TR/2000/CR-SVG-20001102/DTD/svg-
20001102.dtd">
<svg width="100%" height="100%">
<rect x="0%" y="0%" width="25%" height="100%"
style="fill:#000099;stroke:white"/>
<text x="20" y="15" style="fill:#FFFFFF; stroke:none">
<tspan>
```

```
Here is some test text in the left frame.
</tspan>
<tspan x="20" dy="1.5em">
A second line of test text in the left frame.
</tspan>
</text>
<rect x="75%" y="0%" width="25%" height="100%"
style="fill:#000099;stroke:white"/>
<text x="76%" y="15" style="fill:#FFFFFF; stroke:none">
<tspan>
Here is some test text in the right frame.
</tspan>
<tspan x="76%" dy="1.5em">
A second line of test text in the right frame.
</tspan>
</text>
<rect x="25%" y="10%" width="50%" height="50%"
style="fill:white;
stroke:white;"/>
<text x="26%" y="15%" style="fill:#000099; stroke:#000099">
<tspan>
Hello, here is some test text.
</tspan>
<tspan x="26%" dy="1.5em">
A second line of test text.
</tspan>
</text>
</svg>
```

Navigating SVG Web Pages

In this section, I discuss how to navigate around SVG Web pages, not navigate between Web pages (which was discussed in Chapter 5, "Creating Navigation Bars").

It might seem strange that I have to raise the topic at all, but the SVG specification offers new navigation facilities not available in HTML: zooming and panning. However, at least in early implementations of SVG viewers, at least one important normal tool missing is missing also: scroll bars.

First, look at the good news—zooming and panning—and then look at the situation regarding scroll bars.

Zooming SVG Web pages

SVG images are vector images, of course, and are stored as text descriptions. They can therefore readily be viewed at different sizes. Such zooming facilities are readily available in several SVG viewers.

In the Adobe SVG Viewer, simply right-click on an SVG image, and you see the menu shown in Figure 12.05.

Figure 12.05

The menu made visible when you are right-clicking in the Adobe SVG Viewer. Note the options to zoom in and zoom out.

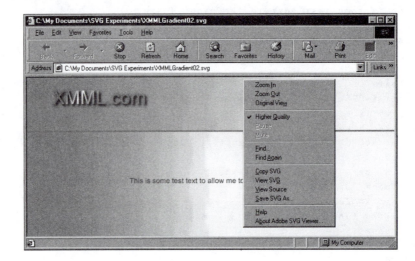

To zoom in on an image, simply click on the Zoom In option, and the image is magnified within the constraints of the size of the containing `<svg>` element. The area that is magnified is centered on the spot on which you right-clicked, so make sure that you right-click on the part of the image you are interested in seeing more closely.

From the size at which an image is initially displayed, you can zoom in four times. After that, the Zoom In option is grayed out, and you can choose only to zoom out or to start again with the Original View option.

If you start from the original view, you can zoom out four times, at which point the Zoom Out option is grayed out. In practice, zooming out from the original view isn't really helpful. It's more useful when you have zoomed in a little too far and want to go back one step.

Panning SVG Web pages

This technique was described in Chapter 11, "Creating Interactive SVG Graphics." In the Adobe viewer on the Windows platform, for example, you hold down the Alt key and hold down the left mouse button. The cursor changes to a clenched hand, like the pointer in Adobe Acrobat Reader, and you can then move the image in any direction you choose. It allows diagonal movement, which isn't practical with conventional scroll bars, but accurately scrolling vertically or horizontally is less easily done.

Scrolling SVG

At the time this book was written, none of the SVG viewers had implemented scroll bars for viewing large SVG images. Hopefully, that shortcoming will be remedied. In Chapter 10, "Embedding SVG in HTML or XHTML Pages," I showed you how to work around that situation by embedding a large SVG image or Web page within an HTML or XHTML shell.

Some Sample Page Layouts

In other chapters in this book, I have shown you a variety of techniques to create SVG for use as Web graphics. In this section, I describe more of the capabilities of SVG as a Web page layout language.

A "three frame" layout

Love them or hate them, frame-based HTML page layouts are still in wide use. SVG lets you create "frames" within SVG Web pages without difficulty.

For an example of an all-SVG Web site using a three-frame layout, check out http://www.svgspider.com/default.svg. To view the source code, simply right-click on the SVG Web page and choose the View Source option.

Collapsing menus

You might have seen menus that collapse to the left side of the screen crafted within HTML or XHTML pages using JavaScript. Similar effects are also possible using SVG declarative animation. A simple implementation is available for viewing online at http://www.svgspider.com/Page06.svg.

Take a look at how this effect is created. To create any interactive SVG, you need to be monitoring certain events or creating some controls. In this case, you create a pair of simple controls, one to open the collapsing menu and the other to close it. Here is the code for the controls:

```
<g id="controls">
<g id="Open">
 <ellipse cx="54" cy="45" rx="34" ry="12" style="fill:red;" />
 <text x="40" y="50" pointer-events="none" style="fill:white;
   font-weight:bold;">Open</text>
</g>
<g id="Close">
 <ellipse cx="54" cy="80" rx="34" ry="12" style="fill:red "/>
 <text x="38" y="85" pointer-events="none" style="fill:white;
   font-weight:bold;">Close</text>
</g>
</g>
```

Note that the Open and Close controls each have their own `id` attribute. You need to make use of that when you create the animation:

```
<svg width="150">
<animate attributeName="width" values="150; 0"
begin="Close.click" dur="3s"
fill="freeze"/>
<animate attributeName="width" values="0; 150"
begin="Open.click" dur="3s"
fill="freeze"/>
```

The appearance of a collapsing and opening side menu is created, as shown in some earlier examples, by animating an attribute of an `<svg>` element. To close the menu, you use an `<animate>` element that has this code:

```
begin="Close.click"
```

which indicates that the animation begins when the element whose `id` attribute is `Close` is clicked.

Similarly, this code:

```
begin="Open.click"
```

means that when the element whose `id` attribute has the value `Open` is clicked, the width of the menu increases from 0 pixels to 150.

The animation is slow so that you can follow what is happening when you are viewing it on the Web page. In a production environment, you might set the duration as `0.1s` so that the menu snaps open and closed.

Animated menus

You have seen in earlier chapters of this book many animations that are focused on relatively small SVG graphics. Creating animations that are continually active within parts of an SVG Web page is clearly possible. Creating animations that are visually attractive or interesting while avoiding intrusive and irritating animations for the user who wants to read text close by can be difficult. Figure 12.06 shows a slow and gentle continuous animation that takes place behind the labels in a navigation bar on an

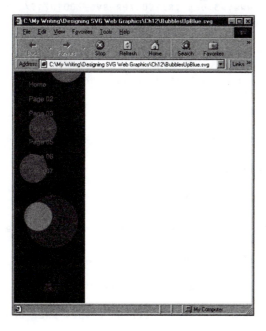

Figure 12.06

An SVG animation used in a left frame behind a text menu navigation bar.

SVG Web page. Of course, the figure can show only a snapshot of a continually moving animation. If you want to see this animation live online, visit http://www.svgspider.com/BubblesUpBlue.svg.

The code that follows might at first glance look intimidating, but the idea behind it is simple. You have a left frame with a solid color background. In front of that background is a succession of "bubbles"—SVG `<circle>` elements—of various sizes, colors, and opacities being animated upward at different speeds. The multiple different characteristics lead to many different overlap effects, some attractive and some intriguing. In front of the animated bubbles are the `<text>` elements nested within `<a>` elements that provide navigation. Because of the SVG painter's model, the bubbles seem to slip smoothly behind the text for the links.

Health warning: Code like the code shown in Listing 12.4 has a built-in temptation for you to make "just one more adjustment." You have been warned!

Listing 12.4 (BubblesUpBlue.svg)

```
<?xml version='1.0'?>
<!DOCTYPE svg PUBLIC "-//W3C//DTD SVG 1.0//EN"
     "http://www.w3.org/TR/2001/PR-SVG-20010719/
       DTD/svg10.dtd">
<!-- Simulation of multi-coloured bubbles percolating up
through "water" -->
<svg width="800" height="600">
<rect x="0" y="0" width="150" height="600"
style="fill:#000066"/>
<circle cx="40" cy="700" r="30" style="fill:white;
opacity:0.5">
<animate attributeName="cy" attributeType="XML" begin="0s"
from="700" to="-50"
dur="10s" repeatCount="indefinite"/>
</circle>
<circle cx="50" cy="700" r="30" style="fill:white;
opacity:0.6">
<animate attributeName="cy" attributeType="XML" begin="9s"
from="700" to="-50"
dur="5s" repeatCount="indefinite"/>
</circle>
<circle cx="20" cy="700" r="10" style="fill:white;
opacity:0.5">
<animate attributeName="cy" attributeType="XML" begin="4s"
from="700" to="-50"
```

```
dur="10s" repeatCount="indefinite"/>
</circle>
<circle cx="60" cy="700" r="30" style="fill:yellow;
opacity:0.5">
<animate attributeName="cy" attributeType="XML" begin="0s"
from="700" to="-50"
dur="6s" repeatCount="indefinite"/>
</circle>
<circle cx="100" cy="700" r="25" style="fill:white;
opacity:0.6">
<animate attributeName="cy" attributeType="XML" begin="1s"
from="700" to="-50"
dur="7s" repeatCount="indefinite"/>
</circle>
<circle cx="80" cy="700" r="55" style="fill:white;
opacity:0.3">
<animate attributeName="cy" attributeType="XML" begin="6s"
from="700" to="-50"
dur="9s" repeatCount="indefinite"/>
</circle>
<circle cx="110" cy="700" r="35" style="fill:yellow;
opacity:0.6">
<animate attributeName="cy" attributeType="XML" begin="10s"
from="700" to="-50"
dur="7s" repeatCount="indefinite"/>
</circle>
<circle cx="120" cy="700" r="10" style="fill:red; opacity:0.5">
<animate attributeName="cy" attributeType="XML" begin="7s"
from="700" to="-50"
dur="10s" repeatCount="indefinite"/>
</circle>
<circle cx="60" cy="700" r="10" style="fill:red; opacity:0.5">
<animate attributeName="cy" attributeType="XML" begin="1s"
from="700" to="-50"
dur="8s" repeatCount="indefinite"/>
</circle>
<circle cx="70" cy="700" r="10" style="fill:red; opacity:0.5">
<animate attributeName="cy" attributeType="XML" begin="3s"
from="700" to="-50"
dur="11s" repeatCount="indefinite"/>
</circle>
<circle cx="90" cy="700" r="20" style="fill:red; opacity:0.4">
<animate attributeName="cy" attributeType="XML" begin="1s"
from="700" to="-550"
dur="8s" repeatCount="indefinite"/>
</circle>
<g id="navbar">
```

```
<a xlink:href="default.svg">
<text x="30" y="30" style="font-family:Arial, sans-serif;
font-size:14;
font-weight:normal;
   stroke:red; fill:red;">Home</text>
</a>
<a xlink:href="Page02.svg">
<text x="30" y="60" style="font-family:Arial, sans-serif;
font-size:14;
font-weight:normal;
   stroke:red; fill:red;">Page 02</text>
</a>
<a xlink:href="Page03.svg">
<text x="30" y="90" style="font-family:Arial, sans-serif;
font-size:14;
font-weight:normal;
   stroke:red; fill:red;">Page 03</text>
</a>
<a xlink:href="Page04.svg">
<text x="30" y="120" style="font-family:Arial, sans-serif;
font-size:14;
font-weight:normal;
   stroke:red; fill:red;">Page 04</text>
</a>
<a xlink:href="Page05.svg">
<text x="30" y="150" style="font-family:Arial, sans-serif;
font-size:14;
font-weight:normal;
   stroke:red; fill:red;">Page 05</text>
</a>
<a xlink:href="Page06.svg">
<text x="30" y="180" style="font-family:Arial, sans-serif;
font-size:14;
font-weight:normal;
   stroke:red; fill:red;">Page 06</text>
</a>
<a xlink:href="Page07.svg">
<text x="30" y="210" style="font-family:Arial, sans-serif;
font-size:14;
font-weight:normal;
   stroke:red; fill:red;">Page 07</text>
</a>
</g>
s</svg>
```

You can see a more psychedelic version in Figure 12.07 and online at http://www.svgspider.com/BubblesLava01.svg.

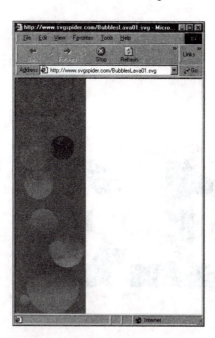

Figure 12.07

*A version of the bub-
bling SVG menu giv-
ing a psychedelic
effect by means
of multiple linear
gradients.*

SVG Web pages are in their early days. The first SVG Web page, on SVGSpider.com, went live in January 2001. Authors of SVG Web pages are only beginning to discover how best to lay out pages. However, for the reasons mentioned earlier in this chapter, I expect to see explosive growth in the authoring of SVG Web pages, to match the growth in Flash Web pages, although, hopefully, with a little more emphasis on user experience than is evident on some Flash sites.

13

Designing SVG for
Use with CSS

In this chapter:

Cascading Style Sheets

As you have created examples in earlier chapters, you simply created SVG elements as you went along. If you wanted to define the style of a particular element, you simply inserted a style attribute that contained a list of CSS properties that described how that element was to be rendered onscreen. Sometimes, not just when you used animations as visual components, you copied and pasted lengthy chunks of SVG syntax, and the copied text often had lengthy style elements.

> *A Cascading Style Sheet (CSS) contains one or more rules that associate the name of an element, or specific subclasses of an element, with a particular visual styling. Cascading Style Sheet information might be applied inline with styling properties or exist as a separate external style sheet.*

That approach is a quick, easy, and accurate technique when you are creating simple SVG graphics; when it comes to the maintenance of large SVG graphics or Web pages, however, you face a potential cost in terms of time spent to carry out site maintenance.

Maintenance of a site is one of the biggest costs, in terms of both time and money, relating to any but the smallest Web sites. So, it makes good business sense for the owners of significantly sized sites and who might be users of SVG text and graphics to seek to achieve efficiency savings by planning ahead to achieve easier maintenance of their sites.

Maintenance of a traditional Web site can often involve changes to the color scheme of a Web site (often carried out by HTML coders) or to its traditional bitmap graphics (typically carried out by graphics designers). A frequent scenario is that a client wants some sort of color-based makeover. With sites that use bitmap graphics, the availability of Cascading Style Sheets (CSS), technology benefits, the efficiency of the HTML coders who can change the appearance of text by adjusting a single Style sheet (assuming that the necessary planning was done). However, traditional Web graphics designers cannot easily edit their images in the same way, so any maintenance that involves images can be a time-consuming and expensive process.

SVG opens up new possibilities for efficient, timely, and less expensive redesigns of Web sites, even if the redesign involves some or all of the graphics on the site. These advantages are potentially available whether the Web site makes use of traditional HTML or XHTML Web pages or the more innovative or experimental SVG Web pages (see Chapter 12, "Creating a Simple SVG Web Site").

Of course, if you design a Web site to take advantage of the SVG redesign speed, at least as far as styling is concerned, you can gain significant benefits during earlier phases of a Web design project when you are interacting with some clients. If you are in a client meeting and you are told that the shade of green you are using in the text and graphics is just a little too dark or light or whatever, you can simply adjust the Cascading Style Sheet immediately and get a decision from your clients after they have seen the options side by side.

In this chapter, I can only describe for you the fundamentals of a substantial topic. CSS properties are defined in either the CSS2 specification or the SVG specification itself. To have a full appreciation of the range of CSS properties and where you can find their definitive description, consult Chapter 6.1 of the SVG specification at http://www.w3.org/TR/SVG/ and the CSS2 Recommendation at http://www.w3.org/TR/REC-CSS2.

So how do you gain the benefits that using CSS and SVG together can bring to site maintenance? To make use of the advantages of CSS, you—as is often the case with anything to do with the creation of Web sites—need to plan ahead.

Planning Your Text and Graphics

One key issue you need to decide at some stage in a project is which aspects of your images and text on a Web page share colors or other CSS2 properties. Depending on how you plan a site, you can do this at an early stage, while the site is being created, or you can do it after the design is final and you know which colors are shared between text and graphics. It all depends on how you work.

Using styling basics

SVG uses styling properties in three basic ways. The first is to define color or other obviously visual properties. The second is to define parameters, like font-family and font-size. The third is to define aspects of SVG filters and clipping paths, for example, that affect how an SVG element is rendered.

Style can be applied to SVG elements in ways similar to those by which style can be applied to HTML or XHTML elements. SVG has two ways to apply style inline, which you have seen in earlier chapters, plus a `<style>` element and the option to use external Style sheets. I describe those separately.

Inline style

In the examples in earlier chapters, I have typically shown you inline style where the style attribute of an SVG graphics object or text contains a list of CSS properties that describe the onscreen presentation of the graphics shape.

For example, this code

```
<text x="50" y="50"   style="fill:red; stroke:red;
font-style:italic; font-size:48;">
```

tells you that the `fill` and `stroke` properties of the text are red and that the `font-style` property is italic. The amalgam of these individual CSS properties is applied to create the final appearance of the text. You could have produced the same visual appearance by splitting the CSS properties from the style attribute and defining them using individual SVG attributes, like this:

```
<text x="50" y="50"  fill="red" stroke="red"
font-style="italic"  font-size="48">
```

In practice, if you are using external style sheets, as I describe shortly, you can overrule the effect of an external style sheet or SVG `<style>` element by using either of the two inline syntaxes shown here. However, unless you have compelling reasons for doing so in a particular situation, such as preserving the look and feel of a corporate logo, I suggest that you avoid mixing the two techniques because you lose at least part of the benefit of external style sheets for maintenance.

Neither of the inline syntaxes helps you in your quest for easier page or site maintenance, so they aren't considered further here.

The SVG <style> element

The `<style>` element allows a style sheet to be embedded directly within an SVG image or document, in a way that is similar to their use with HTML or XHTML (with which you might already be familiar).

Now create a simple style sheet within a `<style>` element to apply a specified fill and stroke to two rectangles in an SVG image. Here is the code:

Listing 13.1 (StyleElement02.svg)

```
<?xml version="1.0" standalone="no"?>
<!DOCTYPE svg PUBLIC "-//W3C//DTD SVG 1.0//EN"
     "http://www.w3.org/TR/2001/PR-SVG-20010719/
       DTD/svg10.dtd">
<svg>
<style type="text/css">
rect {
   stroke: red;
   fill: #CCCCFF;
```

```
        stroke-width:2;
        }
</style>
<rect x="20" y="20" width="300" height="150"/>
<rect x="120" y="95" width="100" height="50"/>
</svg>
```

The output, as shown in Figure 13.01, shows that the same style has been applied to each of the two rectangles, although no style attribute, or list of presentation attributes, is on either rectangle. So, your style sheet, contained in the `<style>` element, is working.

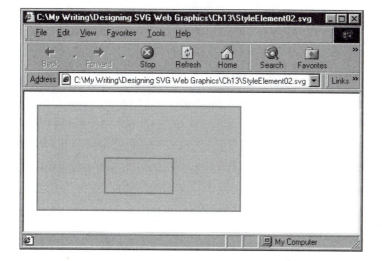

Figure 13.01

The same style applied to two rectangles using the SVG `<style>` element.

The `type` attribute of the `<style>` element is essential. If you delete it from the preceding code, you see simply a single black rectangle because the SVG rendering engine requires the `type` attribute to be present. (In fact, two black rectangles are there, one in front of the other, but you can't see that.) In its absence, the SVG rendering engine cannot interpret the styling information within the `<style>` element, so the default fill and stroke, both black, are applied to each `<rect>` element.

Just in case you are not already familiar with CSS syntax, take a closer look at the working part of the CSS syntax contained inside the `<style>` element:

```
rect {
    stroke: red;
    fill: #CCCCFF;
    stroke-width:2;
    }
```

A typical Style sheet is made up of a succession of rules, although in this simple example you used only one CSS rule. The preceding quoted code, taken in its entirety, is a CSS rule. The word *rect* is a CSS *selector* and defines to which elements the style rule will be applied. In this example, the word *rect* indicates that it is applied to `<rect>` elements. Because nothing indicates otherwise, the style is applied to all `<rect>` elements in the document (or at least to all `<rect>` elements for which no more specific CSS rule exists).

Then follows the opening curly bracket, followed by a succession of CSS *declarations*. Each CSS declaration consists of the name of a CSS property followed by a colon and then the value of the CSS property. When more than one CSS declaration is within the CSS rule, as in the example, each declaration is separated by a semicolon from the declaration that follows it.

The SVG specification indicates that you require a more complex syntax for a style sheet embedded in a `<style>` element—the use of an XML CDATA section, as shown in the following code:

Listing 13.2 (StyleElement03.svg)

```
<?xml version="1.0" standalone="no"?>
<!DOCTYPE svg PUBLIC "-//W3C//DTD SVG 1.0//EN"
     "http://www.w3.org/TR/2001/PR-SVG-20010719/
     DTD/svg10.dtd">
<svg>
<style type="text/css">
<![CDATA[
rect {
    stroke: red;
    fill: #CCCCFF;
    stroke-width:2;
    }
]]>
</style>
<rect x="20" y="20" width="300" height="150"/>
<rect x="120" y="95" width="100" height="50"/>
</svg>
```

The only difference is that the first thing nested within the start tag of the `<style>` element is

```
<![CDATA[
```

and the last thing before the end tag, `</style>`, is

```
]]>
```

In some settings where you want to use an internal Style sheet, you might find that you need to make use of a CDATA section. Certain CSS rules make use of the `>` character, which would confuse the SVG rendering engine (which would treat it as the closing character of a start or end tag, which didn't exist). So, if you are using the SVG `<style>` element with CSS rules that use these types of characters, you would be wise to use the CDATA section syntax.

However, when you consider external Style sheets, such CDATA sections are not required.

External Style sheets

To achieve the full potential maintenance benefits, you need to make use of external Style sheets. To create the same visual appearance as in the `<style>` element example, you need to remove the CSS rule from the `<style>` element and place it into an external Style sheet. In addition, you need to inform the SVG viewer that an external Style sheet will be applied to the SVG image and indicate where the Style sheet is located and what type of content it has.

First, you move the Style sheet to an external Style sheet, ExternalCSS01.css, which contains this code:

Listing 13.3 (ExternalCSS01.css)

```
rect {
    stroke: red;
    fill: #CCCCFF;
    stroke-width:2;
    }
```

Then, you modify the SVG document, now named ExternalCSS01.svg, so that it looks like this:

Listing 13.4 (ExternalCSS01.svg)

```
<?xml version="1.0" standalone="no"?>
<!DOCTYPE svg PUBLIC "-//W3C//DTD SVG 1.0//EN"
    "http://www.w3.org/TR/2001/PR-SVG-20010719/
       DTD/svg10.dtd">
<?xml-stylesheet type="text/css" href="ExternalCSS01.css" ?>
<svg>
<rect x="20" y="20" width="300" height="150"/>
<rect x="120" y="95" width="100" height="50"/>
</svg>
```

You can see that the `<style>` element has been removed so that no styling information whatsoever is contained within the SVG file. However, you see this XML processing instruction:

```
<?xml-stylesheet type="text/css" href="ExternalCSS01.css" ?>
```

which indicates that an external style sheet should be applied. The `type` attribute tells you that the type is `text/css`, meaning a Style sheet. The `href` attribute tells you that it is in the same directory, in a file named ExternalCSS01.css. If you try to view ExternalCSS01.svg, you see the same visual appearance as you saw in Figure 13.02, demonstrating that you have correctly linked to the external style sheet.

Figure 13.02

The SVG document linked to the external Cascading Style Sheet produces the same visual appearance as shown in Figure 13.01. Note the different filenames in the two figures.

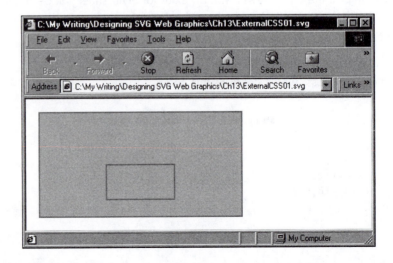

Using class attributes

So far, you have seen only how to use CSS selectors to define the application of a particular style on all elements of the same name. However, you might well want to style some `<rect>` elements in one way and other `<rect>` elements in another way.

One technique to do that is to use class selectors. You do that in two parts. First, a class attribute is added to one or more elements in the SVG, like this:

```
<rect class="Back" x="20" y="20" width="300" height="150"/>
```

and then you use a new syntax for the selector:

```
rect.Back
```

to apply any CSS declarations selectively to the appropriate elements. The syntax of the class selector is that the element name comes first, followed by a full stop, followed by the value of the class attribute on the SVG elements to which the selector applies.

If you create another Style sheet, therefore, ExternalCSS02.css:

Listing 13.5 (ExternalCSS02.css)

```
rect.Back
    {
    stroke: red;
    fill: #CCCCFF;
    stroke-width:4;
    }
rect.Front
    {
    stroke: #000099;
    fill:white;
    stroke-width:2;
    }
```

you can also modify the SVG to add a class attribute to each `<rect>` element:

Listing 13.6 (ExternalCSS02.svg)

```
<?xml version="1.0" standalone="no"?>
<!DOCTYPE svg PUBLIC "-//W3C//DTD SVG 1.0//EN"
     "http://www.w3.org/TR/2001/PR-SVG-20010719/
        DTD/svg10.dtd">
<?xml-stylesheet type="text/css" href="ExternalCSS02.css" ?>
<svg>
<rect class="Back" x="20" y="20" width="300" height="150"/>
<rect class="Front" x="120" y="75" width="100" height="50"/>
</svg>
```

When you display the resulting SVG with the styling information supplied from the external Style sheet, you see the result shown in Figure 13.03.

Figure 13.03

The "Front" and "Back" CSS2 class selectors cause the front and back rectangles to be styled differently.

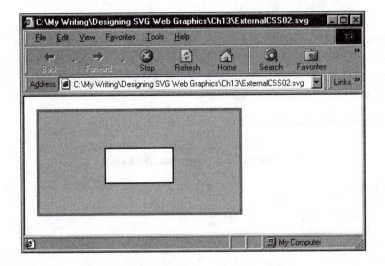

Class selectors can also be used to apply style to SVG elements that share a common value of a class attribute but are on different element types. For example, if you want a rectangle and text to share a common style, you can add the same class attribute to each one, like this:

```
<rect class="Back" x="20" y="20" width="300" height="150"/>
<text class="Back" x="30" y="40">
This is "Back" text
</text>
```

Then, if one or more selectors were defined that matched the `"Back"` class, the corresponding CSS style declarations would be applied. You can produce a modified style sheet, ExternalCSS03.css:

Listing 13.7 (ExternalCSS03.css)

```
.Back
    {
    stroke: red;
    fill: #CCCCFF;
    stroke-width:1;
    }
.Front
    {
    stroke: #000099;
    fill:white;
    stroke-width:1;
    }
text.Back
    {
    font-size: 18;
    }
text.Front
    {
    font-size: 14;
    }
```

and a modified SVG document:

Listing 13.8 (ExternalCSS03.svg)

```
<?xml version="1.0" standalone="no"?>
<!DOCTYPE svg PUBLIC "-//W3C//DTD SVG 1.0//EN"
    "http://www.w3.org/TR/2001/PR-SVG-20010719/
    DTD/svg10.dtd">
<?xml-stylesheet type="text/css" href="ExternalCSS03.css" ?>
<svg>
<rect class="Back" x="20" y="20" width="300" height="150"/>
<text class="Back" x="30" y="40">
This is "Back" text
</text>
<rect class="Front" x="120" y="75" width="100" height="50"/>
<text class="Front" x="130" y="100">
"Front" text
</text>
</svg>
```

Remember, of course, to modify the `<?xml-stylesheet ?>` processing instruction so that the correct style sheet is linked.

The first `<rect>` element is matched by the `.Back` selector (which matches any element of the `Back` class) and so has a red stroke and pale blue fill. The first `<text>` element also matches the `.Back` selector and has the same stroke and fill, but also matches the `text.Back` selector and therefore is of font size 18. The `<rect>` element does not, of course, match the `text.Back` selector. Similarly the `.Front` and `text.Front` selectors apply to the second `<rect>` and second `<text>` elements, respectively.

The result of applying the Style sheet shown in Listing 13.7 to the SVG image shown in Listing 13.8 is illustrated in Figure 13.04.

Figure 13.04

Applying the CSS selectors to both text and rectangle elements.

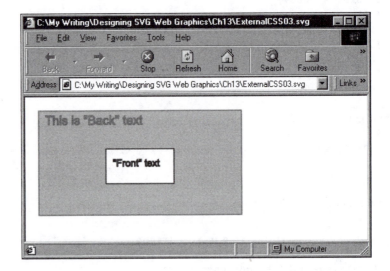

Using id attributes

You might want to apply a unique style to only one element in an SVG document. CSS provides a way of doing that, by using an `id` attribute on the chosen SVG element. In any valid XML document—and, therefore, in all SVG documents—the `id` attribute on any element must be unique. You can therefore apply a style selectively to any SVG element identified by an `id` attribute.

You can apply an `id` attribute to a `<rect>` element like this:

```
<rect id="1234" class="Front" x="120" y="75" width="100"
height="50"/>
```

and refer to it in the accompanying Style sheet like this:

```
#1234
   {
   opacity: 0.2;
   }
```

If you refer to the CSS2 specification, you notice that it refers to the ID selectors (uppercase), although SVG elements have an `id` attribute (lower-case). If you attempt to create an `ID` (uppercase) attribute on an SVG element and use it to access an external style sheet, expect to find that any rules you define that supposedly refer to the `ID` (uppercase) attribute are ignored (in the Adobe viewer) or might generate an error message.

When you put all this together and apply the ID selector to the element with the `id` attribute, the onscreen appearance looks like the one shown in Figure 13.05. Note that the stroke of the smaller rectangle is less obvious because it is semitransparent and that more of the fill of the background rectangle shows through the semitransparent fill of the smaller rectangle.

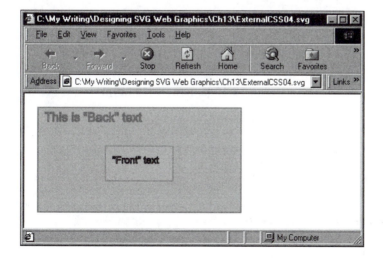

Figure 13.05

The ID selector causes the fill and stroke of the rectangle to be semitransparent.

The final style sheet looks like this:

Listing 13.9 (ExternalCSS04.css)

```
.Back
    {
    stroke: red;
    fill: #CCCCFF;
    stroke-width:1;
    }
.Front
    {
    stroke: #000099;
    fill:white;
    stroke-width:1;
    }
text.Back
    {
    font-size: 18;
    }
text.Front
    {
    font-size: 14;
    }
#1234
    {
    opacity: 0.2;
    }
```

The SVG document, including the `id` attribute, looks like this:

Listing 13.10 (ExternalCSS04.svg)

```
<?xml version="1.0" standalone="no"?>
<!DOCTYPE svg PUBLIC "-//W3C//DTD SVG 1.0//EN"
    "http://www.w3.org/TR/2001/PR-SVG-20010719/
    DTD/svg10.dtd">
<?xml-stylesheet type="text/css" href="ExternalCSS04.css" ?>
<svg>
<rect class="Back" x="20" y="20" width="300" height="150"/>
<text class="Back" x="30" y="40">
This is "Back" text
</text>
<rect id="1234" class="Front" x="120" y="75" width="100"
height="50"/>
```

```
<text class="Front" x="130" y="100">
"Front" text
</text>
</svg>
```

In this section, I have described some of the CSS syntax as it applies to SVG; if you want to fully understand CSS, however, the definitive references are the W3C CSS specifications. The CSS Level 1 specification is at http://www.w3.org/TR/1999/REC-CSS1-19990111, and the CSS Level 2 Recommendation, on which the SVG implementation of CSS is based, is at http://www.w3.org/TR/1998/REC-CSS2-19980512. Chapter 6 of the SVG specification is the major source of further SVG-specific styling information.

Understanding the scope of Cascading Style Sheets

In Chapter 10, "Embedding SVG in HTML or XHTML Pages," I explained how to embed SVG images in HTML or XHTML. In Chapter 12, I mentioned how to use stand-alone SVG Web pages. I have also briefly mentioned the use of SVG with other XML namespaces. You should consider each of these situations separately when you are using Style sheets.

SVG in HTML and XHTML

In this situation are two totally separate parse trees—one for the containing HTML or XHTML document and the second for the SVG. Visually, the HTML or XHTML and the SVG are presented in a unified way; behind the scenes, however, they remain separate. The CSS styling for the HTML or XHTML document is derived from inline style properties and any internal or external style sheets. The fact that those style properties are applied in the containing HTML or XHTML document has no implication that the SVG document is affected by them. Similarly, any styling information in the SVG image or document is confined to it and has no direct effect on styling within the containing document.

However, if both the HTML or XHTML document and the SVG document reference the same external Style sheet and the HTML and SVG documents are appropriately structured, the same styles are applied on the HTML or XHTML part of the Web page and in the SVG images.

You can achieve this synchronization in various ways. One possibility is to use a selector within the style sheet that applies to all text, in both the HTML page and the SVG document. For example, the following CSS rule ensures that all paragraph text in the HTML or XHTML document and in the SVG document would be similarly styled:

```
p, text
    {
    font-size:12;
    font-family:Arial, sans-serif;
    stroke: red;
    fill: red;
    }
```

Another approach is to use class attributes on selected HTML and SVG elements, use the CommonToBoth class, and use a rule something like this:

```
.CommonToBoth
    {
    font-size:12;
    font-family:Arial, sans-serif;
    stroke: red;
    fill: red;
    }
```

Stand-alone SVG documents

In this scenario, the situation is simple: Any style information defined within the SVG document applies across the whole document.

Mixed SVG and XML

When SVG and content from other XML namespaces are mixed in one document, such as in some of the examples on http://www.xsmiles.org/, one parse tree has elements from different namespaces contained within it. The SVG specification does not define how the presence of more than one source of style sheet information will interact.

To maintain control of the styling of SVG within this type of multi-name-space document, you can use the style attribute on SVG elements (as in most of the examples in this book) or use `class` or `id` attributes to apply styling information from a style sheet in a focused way.

Nested SVG

Specific issues arise in the case of nested SVG.

In some earlier chapters, I encouraged you to use nested `<svg>` elements to create reusable SVG visual components. What happens if you reuse SVG visual components that already possess `<style>` elements and nest them in SVG documents that also have `<style>` elements? Here is an example, which demonstrates that situation:

Listing 13.11 (NestedSVGCSS.svg)

```
<?xml version="1.0" standalone="no"?>
<!DOCTYPE svg PUBLIC "-//W3C//DTD SVG 1.0//EN"
      "http://www.w3.org/TR/2001/PR-SVG-20010719/
       DTD/svg10.dtd">
<svg width="500" height="400">
<style type="text/css">
<![CDATA[
text {
      font-size:18;
      font-family:Arial, sans-serif;
      stroke:red;
      fill:red
      }
]]>
</style>
<text x="20" y="20">
This is text in the outer &lt;svg&gt; element
</text>
<svg x="100" y="100" width="300" height="200">
<style type="text/css">
text {
      font-size:10;
      font-family: Arial, sans-serif;
      stroke:blue;
      fill:blue;
      }
</style>
```

```
<rect x="1" y="1" width="298" height="198" style="stroke:red;
stroke-width:2;
fill:none;"/>
<rect x="50" y="50" width="200" height="100"
style="fill:#EEEEEE;
stroke:blue;"/>
<text x="20" y="20">
This is text in the nested &lt;svg&gt; element
</text>
<text x="40" y="170" style="font-size:14; stroke:green;
fill:green">
<tspan>
This is individually styled text in
</tspan>
<tspan dx="-14em" dy="1em" >the nested &lt;svg&gt; element
</tspan>
</text>
</svg>
</svg>
```

In Figure 13.06, you can see that all text, with the exception of the individually styled `<text>` element late in the code, have the same visual appearance. The `<style>` element in the outer `<svg>` element that worked correctly before the nested `<style>` element was added has been overridden by the `<style>` element that occurs later in the document. It appears, therefore, that if you are using nested `<svg>` elements and have multiple `<style>` elements, you can make use of the style information in only the final `<style>` element in the document.

One work-around solution is to add a class rule in each style sheet and place corresponding class attributes on each `<text>` element.

But what happens if the imported or nested SVG image accesses style information in an external Style sheet? Processing instructions, other than those before the outer `<svg>` element, are ignored. This situation raises issues about how to apply differential styling to a containing and imported SVG document. You must use `class` or `id` attributes to achieve any selective styling.

In addition, you should be aware of the difference in the treatment of an imported `<svg>` element. An imported SVG image is treated as a wholly separate parse tree. If it has a processing instruction referring to an external Style sheet, that instruction is processed normally.

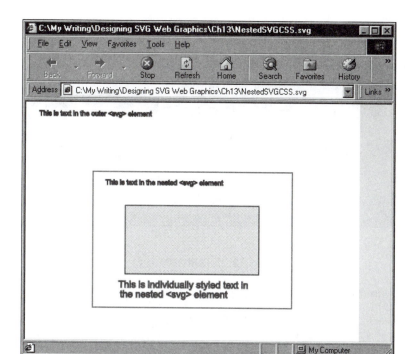

Figure 13.06

The result of running Listing 13.11.

Sample Design: SVG and CSS

This section looks at a simplified but quasirealistic scenario using CSS. Take a look at Figure 13.07. It is also available on the Web at http://www.xmml.com/XMML01.svg as well as in the download for this book. The code for the simplified page is shown in Listing 13.7. Suppose that your task is to alter the orange (#FF6600) in the original and that your client isn't quite sure what color he wants as a replacement. Perhaps a quiet green?

Using external Style sheets seems an ideal solution, particularly if the client changes his mind again about the dominant color.

Your first task is to identify which parts of the page contain the color the client wants to change. Take a look at the figure and the code and see whether you can spot the necessary changes.

Figure 13.07

The simplified XMML.com Web page before the required makeover.

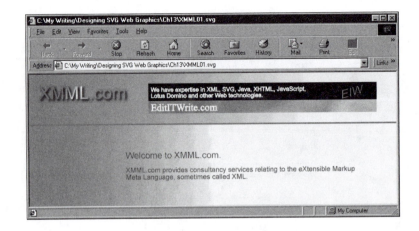

Listing 13.12 (XMML01.svg)

```
<?xml version="1.0" standalone="no"?>
<!DOCTYPE svg PUBLIC "-//W3C//DTD SVG 1.0//EN"
    "http://www.w3.org/TR/2001/PR-SVG-20010719/
      DTD/svg10.dtd">
<svg>
<defs>
<linearGradient id="PenGradient"
  x1="50" y1="50" x2="110" y2="90"
gradientUnits="userSpaceOnUse">
<stop offset="10%" style="stop-color:#999999"/>
<stop offset="50%" style="stop-color:white"/>
<stop offset="100%" style="stop-color:#FF6600"/>
</linearGradient>
<linearGradient id="MyFirstGradient">
<stop offset="5%" style="stop-color:#FF6600"/>
<stop offset="75%" style="stop-color:#FFFFCC"/>
</linearGradient>
<linearGradient id="MySecondGradient">
<stop offset="10%" style="stop-color:#FF6600"/>
<stop offset="50%" style="stop-color:#FFFFCC"/>
</linearGradient>
<filter id="CombinedDropShadow" width="140%" y="-20%"
height="200%">
<feGaussianBlur in="SourceAlpha" stdDeviation="2"
result="ShadowOut"/>
<feOffset in="ShadowOut" dx="3" dy="3" result="ShadowOnly"/>
<feMerge>
 <feMergeNode in="ShadowOnly"/>
 <feMergeNode in="SourceGraphic"/>
</feMerge>
</filter>
```

```
</defs>
<rect width="100%" height="100" fill="url(#MyFirstGradient)"/>
<rect y="100" width="100%" height="3" fill="#999999"/>
<rect y="103" width="100%" height="500"
fill="url(#MySecondGradient)"/>
<text x="20" y="50" style="font-family:Ventana, Arial,
sans-serif;
font-size:36;
fill:url(#PenGradient); stroke:none;
filter:url(#CombinedDropShadow)">
XMML.com
</text>
<svg x="200" y="150" width="500" height="400">
<text x="0" y="20">
<tspan x="0" dy="0"
 style="font-family:Arial, sans-serif; font-size:18;
 stroke:none; fill:#666666;">
Welcome to XMML.com.
</tspan>
<tspan x="0" dy="2em"
 style="font-family:Arial, sans-serif; font-size:14;
 stroke:none; fill:#666666;">
XMML.com provides consultancy services relating to the
eXtensible Markup
</tspan>
<tspan x="0" dy="1em"
 style="font-family:Arial, sans-serif; font-size:14;
 stroke:none; fill:#666666;">
Meta Language, sometimes called XML.
</tspan>
</text>
</svg>
<a xlink:href="http://www.edititwrite.com/default.svg"
target="new">
<svg x="247" y="20" width="468" height="60">
<defs>
<linearGradient id="MyBlueGradient"
gradientUnits="userSpaceOnUse" x1="90"
y1="50" x2="400" y2="500" >
<stop offset="10%" style="stop-color:#FF6600"/>
<stop offset="40%" style="stop-color:#FFFF00"/>
<stop offset="75%" style="stop-color:#9999FF"/>
</linearGradient>
 <filter id="Turbulence1" in="SourceImage"
filterUnits="userSpaceOnUse" >
   <feTurbulence in="BackgroundImage" type="turbulence"
baseFrequency="0.01"
     numOctaves="1" seed="0" >
```

```
      </feTurbulence>
   </filter>
   </defs>
   <rect   x="0"  y="0"  width="468"  height="60"
   style="fill:url(#MyBlueGradient);
   opacity:0.5;"/>
   <rect  x="0"  y="0"  width="468"  height="35"  style="fill:black;
   stroke:none;"/>
   <rect  x="0"  y="35"  width="468"  height="25"  style="fill:#000099;
   filter:url(#Turbulence1);  stroke:none;"/>
   <svg  x="0"  y="0"  width="468"  height="35">
   <text>
   <tspan  x="5"  y="50"  style="font-size:14;  font-family:courier,
   monospace;
   stroke:#FF6600;  fill:#FF6600">
   <animate  attributeName="y"  begin="0s"  dur="16s"  values="50; 15;
   15; -55; -55;
   -130; -130 "
   repeatCount="indefinite"/>
   EditITWrite.com
   </tspan>
   <tspan  x="5"  dy="1em"  style="font-size:12;  font-family:Arial,
   sans-serif;
   fill:white;  stroke:white;">
   EIW  can  provide  many  of  your  technical  writing  needs.
   </tspan>
   <tspan  x="5"  dy="2em"  style="font-size:12;  font-family:Arial,
   sans-serif;">
   blank
   </tspan>
   <tspan  x="5"  dy="2em"  style="font-size:12;  font-family:Arial,
   sans-serif; ">
   blank
   </tspan>
   <tspan  x="5"  dy="1em"  style="font-size:12;  font-family:Arial,
   sans-serif;
   fill:white;  stroke:white;">
   We  have  expertise  in  XML,  SVG,  Java,  XHTML,  JavaScript,
   </tspan>
   <tspan  x="5"  dy="1em"  style="font-size:12;  font-family:Arial,
   sans-serif;
   fill:white;  stroke:white;">
   Lotus  Domino  and  other  Web  technologies.
   </tspan>
   <tspan  x="5"  dy="2em"  style="font-size:12;  font-family:Arial,
   sans-serif;">
   blank
   </tspan>
```

```
<tspan x="5" dy="2em" style="font-size:12; font-family:Arial,
sans-serif; ">
blank
</tspan>
<tspan x="5" dy="1em" style="font-size:12; font-family:Arial,
sans-serif;
fill:white; stroke:white;">
We can translate from German, French, Spanish,
</tspan>
<tspan x="5" dy="1em" style="font-size:12; font-family:Arial,
sans-serif;
fill:white; stroke:white;">
Japanese and other languages into English.
</tspan>
</text>
</svg>
<text x="5" y="55" style="font-family:'Times New Roman', serif;
font-size:20;
stroke:white; fill:white;">
EditITWrite.com
</text>
<text style="font-size:24; font-family:Arial, sans-serif;
stroke:red;
stroke-width:0; fill:#FF6600;" x="395" y="140"
transform="skewY(-15)" >
EIW
</text>
</svg>
</a>
</svg>
```

A careful look at the image and code shows six places where the orange color occurs. In case you didn't spot them, orange is used separately in the gradients in the top and main parts of the SVG page, in the gradient for the XMML.com logo, and in three places in the banner ad (the gradient to which the filter is applied, the first line of the scrolling text, and the EIW logo to the right of the ad).

Assume that all occurrences of the orange need to be changed to the quiet green that your client wants.

When doing this type of task, I usually split it into two steps. The first is to go through the files and remove the style attributes that I want to put into the external Style sheet. Then I add to each of those elements a class attribute to correspond to the style properties I have removed.

For example, the style attribute on the final `<stop>` element of the first linear gradient:

```
<linearGradient id="PenGradient"
  x1="50" y1="50" x2="110" y2="90"
gradientUnits="userSpaceOnUse">
<stop offset="10%" style="stop-color:#999999"/>
<stop offset="50%" style="stop-color:white"/>
<stop offset="100%" style="stop-color:#FF6600"/>
</linearGradient>
```

is replaced by a class attribute of value `Class1`:

```
<linearGradient id="PenGradient"
  x1="50" y1="50" x2="110" y2="90"
gradientUnits="userSpaceOnUse">
<stop offset="10%" style="stop-color:#999999"/>
<stop offset="50%" style="stop-color:white"/>
<stop class="Class1" offset="100%" />
</linearGradient>
```

The same process is carried out for the other five occurrences of the color.

Then I create an external style sheet that, hopefully, maintains the original appearance:

Listing 13.13 (XMML02.css)

```
.Class1
    {
    stop-color:#FF6600;
    fill:#FF6600;
    stroke:#FF6600;
    }
```

Remember that a color might have been applied to different CSS properties. In the example, the orange color was used in the `stop-color` property of four separate `<stop>` elements in separate linear gradients and the `fill` or `stroke` properties of text. To ensure that all are appropriately accounted for, make sure that the rule has a class selector—the initial full stop indicates that it applies to all elements, whatever the element name, that have a class attribute of value `Class1`.

The files available for download, XMML02.svg and XMML02.css, show the process at that stage.

The final step is to modify the color (as in this case) or another CSS property you want to change in the site makeover.

Figure 13.08 shows the result of using a quiet green to replace the orange.

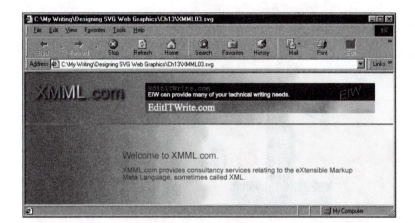

Figure 13.08

The test page after restructuring to allow the use of an external style sheet and having made a color change to a quiet green.

The final external Style sheet looks as shown in Listing 13.14.

Listing 13.14 (XMML03.css)

```
.Class1
    {
    stop-color:#669966;
    fill:#669966;
    stroke:#669966;
    }
```

The revised SVG code that accesses the Style sheet is available for download as XMML03.svg.

Styling SVG using external Style sheets can save you lots of time and make your use of SVG more enjoyable and efficient. To gain the benefits takes just a little planning. Now you need to move on to the situation where you make a mistake and time seems to disappear. Efficient debugging of SVG is something anyone who does any serious SVG development needs to master.

14

When Things Go Wrong

In this chapter:

Minimizing Errors

Inevitably, at some time during your use of SVG, things go wrong. Particularly during your first efforts to hand-code or to tweak by hand some code that was generated by a vector drawing package, you might find things going visibly awry. In this chapter, I describe an approach to keep serious errors to a minimum, discuss symptoms of commonly occurring errors, and show you an approach to diagnosing and solving problems that you might inadvertently create.

I hope that you don't get the wrong idea from this chapter and come away with the impression that SVG is impossibly complex. It isn't. However, things can go wrong in a number of ways, particularly in the learning phase. Being aware of them and of the solutions might save you time and increase the fun you have creating SVG images.

Avoiding Problems by Using Good Coding Practice

I suggest that you change, particularly during your early attempts at hand coding, only one thing at a time, whether that is adding an element, altering an attribute, or adding or refining some animation.

Let me repeat that: *Change only one thing at a time when you are learning SVG coding.* It helps your sanity!

If you change more than one thing at a time and you move from having an SVG image that is displayed correctly to one that isn't displayed as you want or, worse, isn't displayed at all, diagnosing and fixing can be quite a tussle. In the interest of sparing yourself avoidable frustration, change one thing at a time and view the result in an SVG viewer after each step.

This is good advice when you are working with the code for complex images too. You can make lots of potential tweaks that can cause problems. You might, in a flight of creative fancy, change five or ten things, one after the other, without checking the effect, and then find that the nice image is now broken and that you can remember only nine of the ten things you tweaked.

You get the idea. Work logically and systematically—it saves time and frustration in the long run.

Use an XML-aware editor

One aid to avoiding problems when coding SVG is to use an XML-aware editor. You can craft, on Windows systems, SVG images in the simplest text editor, like Notepad. However, I suggest that you think seriously about obtaining an XML-aware text editor.

An XML-aware text editor provides two simple but important aids. You can typically check to see whether the SVG document is well formed. In other words, the XML-aware text editor identifies whether your code conforms to the XML rules, and, if it doesn't, the editor identifies the line on which your first syntax error exists.

Often in parallel with the ability to check for well-formedness, an XML-aware text editor also has a color-coding facility for your code. If you omit quotation marks on an attribute or forget the closing angled bracket on an element, you have some assistance by means of an unusual color pattern in identifying exactly where the problem is.

One XML-aware text editor I like is XML Writer. It is by no means the most sophisticated XML editor around, although it does the simple, basic things well and without fuss. My strongest recommendation is that, for a basic everyday tool, it doesn't get in the way. Further information on XML Writer is available from http://www.xmlwriter.com/. A 30-day free evaluation version is usually available.

Many other XML editors are available that also have evaluation downloads. For further options, take a look at http://www.xmlsoftware.com or a similar site, for a list of XML tools. Some HTML editors, such as Allaire Homesite, can provide color coding, but without the ability to check XML well-formedness, they are of limited help.

Of course, an XML-aware editor doesn't solve all your problems. For example, covering over your nice image with a plain rectangle is perfectly legal, although not sensible. The editor doesn't point out that if you intended for the rectangle to be the background, but forgot about the SVG painter's model and placed the rectangle late in the document, it covers up something else. Nor does the editor prevent you from trying to place white text on a white background.

Construct visual components

Just as making one change and testing the effect is sensible, constructing complex SVG images and documents as visual components is helpful. If you have created and tested an SVG visual component, you know that the component was working and, assuming that you pasted it into the correct part of the document, is unlikely to have caused the problem. Because you might have imported a text component with black text to display on your nice, new black background, however, it is always possible that the component is indeed the problem.

Handling Common Error Symptoms

First, deal with a couple of the most common symptoms you are likely to encounter when you first try to code SVG by hand. The first symptom is when nothing is displayed. The second is that only some of the parts of the image are displayed.

Nothing is displayed

Getting into this position is easy. Even minor syntax errors can cause an SVG document or element to fail to be displayed.

For example, if you make a simple mistake, like omitting a closing quotation mark in the following simple SVG, which ought to display a simple rectangle with a blue outline, the browser window is blank as in Figure 14.01.

Listing 14.1 (FailToDisplay01.svg)

```
<?xml version="1.0" standalone="no"?>
<!DOCTYPE svg PUBLIC "-//W3C//DTD SVG 1.0//EN"
    "http://www.w3.org/TR/2001/PR-SVG-20010719/
    DTD/svg10.dtd">
<svg>
<rect x="100" y="100" width="100"
style="fill:none;stroke:#0000CC; stroke-width:2;/>
</svg>
```

The error in this simple code that prevents anything from being displayed is that the closing quotation mark on the style attribute of the `<rect>` element has been omitted. If you add the closing quote, the rectangle is displayed, but not properly—at least not until you specify a height attribute for the `<rect>` element.

Figure 14.01

The code in Listing 14.1 fails to display anything, but an error message appears in the browser status bar.

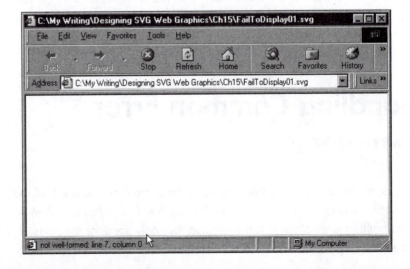

Pause to consider why this failure to display anything happens. An SVG viewer is designed to render SVG elements from the beginning of the SVG document to the end. If the viewer processes an SVG element or group of elements without an error occurring, it renders that element or group and moves on to the next one. On the first occasion that the viewer encounters an error, it does not render that element or group.

Returning to the rectangle example, the viewer was unable to render the rectangle because its syntax was incorrect. No element appeared earlier in the document that can be rendered, so nothing could be rendered, and the SVG image was blank.

Another cause of a blank screen is when an error occurs in the syntax of the `<svg>` element that encloses the SVG document. For example, a missing quote on the `x` attribute of the document's `<svg>` element causes a blank screen:

Listing 14.2 (FailToDisplay02.svg)

```
<?xml version="1.0" standalone="no"?>
<!DOCTYPE svg PUBLIC "-//W3C//DTD SVG 1.0//EN"
     "http://www.w3.org/TR/2001/PR-SVG-20010719/
      DTD/svg10.dtd">
<svg x="400 y="300">
<rect x="100" y="100" width="100"
   style="fill:none;stroke:#0000CC;
          stroke-width:2;/>
</svg>
```

The rationale is similar to that for the preceding example. The SVG viewer stops rendering when it encounters the first error—in this case, on the `<svg>` element—and it doesn't even attempt to render any other elements.

Here is a challenge for you. Can you spot in the following code why the image (a transparent rectangle with a blue outline) fails to be displayed?

Listing 14.3 (FailToDisplay03.svg)

```
<?xml version="1.0" standalone="no"?>
<!DOCTYPE svg PUBLIC "-//W3C//DTD SVG 1.0//EN"
     "http://www.w3.org/TR/2001/PR-SVG-20010719/
      DTD/svg10.dtd">
```

```
<svg x="400" y="300">
<rect x="100" y="100" width="100" height="100"
  style="fill:none;stroke:0000CC;
         stroke-width:2;"/>
</svg>
```

The problem is in the `stroke` property of the style attribute. I have omitted the # that precedes the six-character definition of the color! The syntax of the rectangle is incorrect. Therefore, it is not rendered.

Another possible reason that an image, or part of it, might fail to be displayed is the introduction of a duplicate attribute. For example, if you mistakenly create two `y2` attributes, as shown here:

```
<line x1="50" y2="50" x2="750" y2="50" style="stroke:white;
fill:white;"/>
```

you can expect to get an error message that says something like `duplicate attribute: line XX, column XX`, which basically means that you have created two identically named attributes on an element, which is illegal in XML and therefore in SVG. Because the syntax is illegal, an SVG viewer ought not to display the `<line>` element.

Here is another, simplified example that tripped me up when I was trying to create a multiply-nested bunch of `<svg>` elements. Again, try to spot the problem before reading the explanation:

Listing 14.4 (FailToDisplay04.svg)

```
<?xml version="1.0" standalone="no"?>
<!DOCTYPE svg PUBLIC "-//W3C//DTD SVG 1.0//EN"
    "http://www.w3.org/TR/2001/PR-SVG-20010719/
    DTD/svg10.dtd">
<svg>
<svg id="MeterHolder" x="0" y="0" width="200" height="200">
<rect id="MyMeter" x="0" y="0" width="20" height="40"
style="fill:white; stroke:none;">
 <rect x="2" y="2" width="6" height="4" style="fill:red;
stroke:none"/>
 <rect x="2" y="10" width="6" height="4" style="fill:red;
stroke:none"/>
</rect>
</svg>
</svg>
```

The problem arises because the first `<rect>` element was split into its start and end tags (in preparation for adding an animation at a later stage), and the two other `<rect>` elements were inserted in the wrong place. The outer `<rect>` element has its end tag last and is therefore rendered last. As far as the user is concerned, nothing is rendered to the screen. What is happening is that the outer rectangle with the white fill is rendered last and therefore covers over the two other rectangles because of the way in which the SVG painter's model works. To fix the problem, simply move the end tag `</rect>`, as shown in the following code snippet:

```
<rect id="MyMeter" x="0" y="0" width="20" height="40"
style="fill:white; stroke:none;">
</rect>
 <rect x="2" y="2" width="6" height="4" style="fill:red;
stroke:none"/>
 <rect x="2" y="10" width="6" height="4" style="fill:red;
stroke:none"/>
```

One practical tip is to avoid using white or whatever matches the background of your image, in the early stages of exploring a new idea. If you have something being visibly rendered, the use of another color helps you track down the problem more quickly.

You can cause a blank image in lots of other ways. If you get that problem, take a particularly careful look at the early part of the document. Check the spelling of the element name, and ensure that an opening quotation mark has a corresponding closing quotation mark. If the opening quotation mark is a double quote character, make sure that the closing one is too. If the opening quote is an apostrophe, make sure that the closing one is the same. Check the spelling of attribute names, and remember that SVG is case sensitive.

Only some parts of the image are displayed

This problem has lots of possible causes. A partial display arises in part from the way in which an SVG viewer is supposed to handle errors. It processes elements starting from the beginning and displays each element it views as having correct syntax. The first element the viewer encounters with a serious syntax error isn't displayed. Any elements after that one aren't displayed either.

The key to tracking down this kind of problem is to work out which elements *are* displayed. Work through the source code, in document order, and see what is displayed, it is likely (though not absolutely certain) that the first element you encounter that is not displayed is the one that contains the error.

The following code has syntax errors in all but the first `<rect>` element. Can you spot them—and fix the code so that each rectangle is displayed? The answers are at the end of this chapter, but I encourage you to try to spot the problems yourself.

Listing 14.5 (PartDisplays01.svg)

```
<?xml version="1.0" standalone="no"?>
<!DOCTYPE svg PUBLIC "-//W3C//DTD SVG 1.0//EN"
     "http://www.w3.org/TR/2001/PR-SVG-20010719/
        DTD/svg10.dtd">
<svg>
<rect x="20" y="20" width="100" height="50" />
<rect x="20" y="90" width="100" height="50" />
<rect x"20" y="160" width="100" height="50" />
<rect x="20" y="230" width="100" hieght="50" />
<rect x="20" y="300" width="100" height="50" style="fill;red;
stroke:red;"/>
</svg>
```

It was working earlier and doesn't work now

This type of problem is fairly common. Typically, the scenario is that you have a nice static SVG, you decide that you want to animate some part of the image, you introduce the necessary animation elements, you fail to get the animation you want, and part of the image that was previously displayed correctly disappears.

The cause is similar to what you saw earlier. When you introduce an animation element that contains an error, the element being animated isn't displayed because that element has an error and can't be rendered. At that point, the SVG viewer stops trying to render elements later in the document but displays any SVG elements that were processed without producing an error.

Look at the image and decide which elements have been rendered correctly. If you can remember the code clearly, decide which is the first element that ought to have been rendered but wasn't. The error is likely to be somewhere in the code of that element.

You might have made simple syntax errors in the animation element, like those shown in Listing 14.5. Or, you might have forgotten to indicate that the animation element is an empty element. For example, the `<animate>` element should look like this, with the `/>` at the end:

```
<animate ..... />
```

not like this:

```
<animate ....  >
```

because the SVG processor expects an

```
</animate>
```

end tag somewhere later in the document and you almost certainly won't have provided one.

It doesn't animate

This problem has two likely causes.

The first is that a syntax error is somewhere in the animation element, whether that is an `<animate>` element, an `<animateMotion>` element, an `<animateColor>` element, an `<animateTransform>` element, or a `<set>` element. Did you include all the necessary attributes? If you omitted the `attributeName` attribute, for example, the SVG rendering engine doesn't know which attribute you want it to animate, so the animation fails. Similarly, if you omit the `dur` attribute, it doesn't know how long that color change, or whatever, is supposed to take, so it can't start it. Or, you might have forgotten to tell the SVG rendering engine when the animation was supposed to begin because you omitted the `begin` attribute.

Check carefully for missing quotation marks in attribute values. Check too for any misspelling of attribute names, and remember that SVG (because it is XML) is case sensitive.

You can happily animate a rectangle using this code:

```
<animate begin="5s" dur="5s" attributeName="x" from="100"
to="200" fill="freeze"/>
```

but this code doesn't work:

```
<animate begin="5s" dur="5s" attributename="x" from="100"
to="200" fill="freeze"/>
```

because the `N` of `attributeName` needs to be uppercase to be correctly recognized. Similar problems can occur if you misspell the element name. Remember that it is `<animateColor>` and `<animateTransform>`, and that case is important.

Now look at an example of inserting the animation element in the wrong place. You want to animate a rectangle, and you produce the code shown in Listing 14.6. You find that the rectangle is displayed okay, but it doesn't animate:

Listing 14.6 (WrongAnimation.svg)

```
<?xml version="1.0" standalone="no"?>
<!DOCTYPE svg PUBLIC "-//W3C//DTD SVG 1.0//EN"
      "http://www.w3.org/TR/2001/PR-SVG-20010719/
        DTD/svg10.dtd">
<svg x="400" y="300">
<animate begin="5s" dur="5s" attributeName="x" from="100"
to="200" fill="freeze"/>
<rect x="100" y="100" width="100" height="100"
  style="fill:none;stroke:#0000CC;
        stroke-width:2;"/>
</svg>
```

The `<animate>` element is attempting to animate the `x` attribute of the outer `<svg>` element, which you can't do. The code shown in Listing 14.7 works because it is now animating the `x` attribute of the `<rect>` element.

Listing 14.7 (RightAnimation.svg)

```
<?xml version="1.0" standalone="no"?>
<!DOCTYPE svg PUBLIC "-//W3C//DTD SVG 1.0//EN"
      "http://www.w3.org/TR/2001/PR-SVG-20010719/
        DTD/svg10.dtd">
```

```
<svg x="400" y="300">
<rect x="100" y="100" width="100" height="100"
  style="fill:none;stroke:#0000CC;
         stroke-width:2;">
<animate begin="2s" dur="5s" attributeName="x" from="100"
to="200"
fill="freeze"/>
</rect>
</svg>
```

Killer white space appears

This potential pitfall belongs in one sense in the preceding section, but is so
subtle and potentially frustrating if you are not aware of it that I have given
it a section to itself. Worse, if you fall into this trap, the Adobe viewer gives
you no hint that anything is wrong, simply saying `Done`, which usually indicates that everything is fine, although in this case it isn't. To illustrate the
problem, go back and adapt one of the chained animation pieces of code
so that it looks like this:

Listing 14.8 (WrongWhitespace.svg)

```
<?xml version="1.0" standalone="no"?>
<!DOCTYPE svg PUBLIC "-//W3C//DTD SVG 1.0//EN"
     "http://www.w3.org/TR/2001/PR-SVG-20010719/
      DTD/svg10.dtd">
<svg width="300" height="100">
<rect id="MaroonRect" x="10" y="15" width="10" height="10"
style="fill:#990066;">
<animate begin="PinkAnim.begin+ 2s" dur="10s"
attributeName="width" from="10"
to="250"/>
</rect>
<rect id="PinkRect" x="10" y="45" width="10" height="10"
style="fill:pink;">
<animate id="PinkAnim" begin="2s" dur="10s"
attributeName="width" from="10"
to="250"/>
</rect>
<rect id="YellowRect" x="10" y="75" width="10" height="10"
style="fill:#FFFF00;">
<animate begin="PinkAnim.begin+4s " dur="10s"
attributeName="width" from="10"
```

```
to="250"/>
</rect>
</svg>
```

If you try this code, you find that the pink and maroon animations work exactly as you would expect but that the yellow animation doesn't work. The problem is buried in the syntax for the value of the `begin` attribute:

```
begin="PinkAnim.begin+4s "
```

No white space is allowed at the beginning or end of the `syncbase` value. If you remove the space character after `4s`, the animation works correctly. Yet white space is allowed on either side of the `+` sign, as shown here:

```
begin="PinkAnim.begin+ 2s"
```

That is one example you might stumble across if you use syncbase values in your animations.

Also, be aware that the same problem can prevent event-based animations from working.

The weird trailing semicolon appears

Another subtle syntax sensitivity you should be aware of when you are creating animations is what I call the weird trailing-semicolon issue. Here is a piece of code, extracted from http://www.svgspider.com/Page02.svg, that illustrates the problem. If you want to test your diagnostic skills, read and test the following code, to see whether you can spot what is causing the animation problem. Figure 14.02 shows the position at the end of a fairly weird animation.

Listing 14.9 (CurtainsSemicolon01.svg)

```
<?xml version="1.0" standalone="no"?>
<!DOCTYPE svg PUBLIC "-//W3C//DTD SVG 1.0//EN"
     "http://www.w3.org/TR/2001/PR-SVG-20010719/
      DTD/svg10.dtd">
<svg width="600" height="600">
<svg x="50" y="-200">
<rect style="fill:black" x="250" y="260" height="100"
width="150"/>
<rect style="fill:white" x="255" y="265" height="90"
```

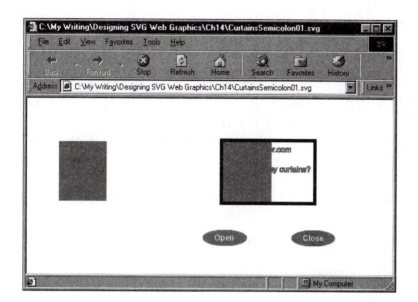

Figure 14.02

The odd position obtained at the end of a weird animation, caused by the trailing-semicolon issue.

```
width="140"/>
<text style="font-family:Arial; font-size:12; fill:red;
stroke:red" x="275"
y="280">SVGSpider.com</text>
<text style="font-family:Arial; font-size:12; fill:red;
stroke:red" x="260"
y="310">
Do you like my curtains?
</text>
<rect style="fill:red" x="255" y="265" height="90" width="1" >
<animate attributeName="width" values="1; 75; 1" dur="5s"
begin="0s" />
<animate id="close3" attributeName="width" attributeType="XML"
values="1; 75"
dur="2.5s"
begin="button2.click" fill="freeze"/>
<animate id="open" attributeName="width" attributeType="XML"
values="75; 1"
dur="2.5s"
begin="button1.click" fill="freeze"/>
</rect>
<rect style="fill:red" x="394" y="265" height="90" width="1">
<animate attributeName="width" values="1; 75; 1" dur="5s"
begin="0s"/>
<animate attributeName="x" values="394; 322; 394"
attributeType="XML" dur="5s"
begin="0s"/>
```

```
<animate id="close1" attributeName="width" attributeType="XML"
values="1; 75;"
dur="2.5s"
begin="button2.click" fill="freeze"/>
<animate id="close2" attributeName="x" attributeType="XML" val-
ues="394; 322;"
dur="2.5s"
begin="button2.click" fill="freeze" />
<animate id="open" attributeName="width" attributeType="XML"
values="75; 1"
dur="2.5s"
begin="button1.click" fill="freeze"/>
<animate id="open" attributeName="x" attributeType="XML" val-
ues="322; 394"
dur="2.5s"
begin="button1.click" fill="freeze" />
</rect>
<g id="controls">

<g id="button1">
<ellipse cx="258" cy="410" rx="34" ry="12" style="fill:red;" />
<text pointer-events="none" x="242" y="414" style="fill:white;
font-weight:bold;">Open</text>
</g>
<g id="button2">
        <ellipse cx="395" cy="410" rx="34" ry="12"
style="fill:red "/>
        <text pointer-events="none" x="379" y="414"
style="fill:white;
font-weight:bold;">Close</text>
</g>
</g>
</svg>
</svg>
```

Did you find the problems? Ah, you were looking for only one? Debugging doesn't come as neatly packaged as that in real life. The problems arise in the following lines of code:

```
<animate id="close1" attributeName="width" attributeType="XML"
values="1; 75;"
dur="2.5s"
begin="button2.click" fill="freeze"/>
```

```
<animate id="close2" attributeName="x" attributeType="XML"
values="394; 322;"
dur="2.5s"
begin="button2.click" fill="freeze" />
```

If you remove the final semicolons at the end of each values attribute (replace `75;` with `75` and replace `322;` with `322`), the code is executed correctly. You can obtain three different erroneous animations by leaving one semicolon in either values attribute list or by including both. At least that's what happens with those syntax changes in Adobe SVG Viewer version 2.0.

The same problem lay behind the weird overlay of rotating text messages I mentioned in relation to the next-to-last example in Chapter 9, "Creating Logos and Banner Ads."

Because I normally (in CSS, for example) include a final semicolon, this problem caused me frequent additional problems.

If I now find a genuinely weird piece of animation behavior in an SVG animation, the trailing semicolon is high on my list of likely culprits. My guess is that it's likely a bug in the Adobe SVG Viewer.

Diagnosing and Solving Problems

In this section, I discuss a number of miscellaneous problems you might encounter and suggest some solutions. Some of the following sections are based simply on the problem or symptom as it might affect you; others depend on the error messages displayed by an SVG viewer.

The Adobe SVG Viewer displays a number of error messages in Internet Explorer in the browser status bar. Some of these error messages are helpful, some less so. Some, like the first example, are true, even if they're just a little insulting.

The "Junk after document element" message

I have only once received this not encouraging message from the Adobe SVG Viewer. I was experimenting with a new SVG filter and copying the filter within a `<defs>` element; I then inadvertently pasted the `<defs>` element in front of the `<svg>` element (rather than nested within it). The Adobe viewer interpreted the `<defs>` element as the document element and interpreted everything after the end `</defs>` tag as "junk." I guess that put me in my place!

If you are cutting and pasting SVG code, be sure that you don't inadvertently paste it in the wrong place.

The "No Element Found" message

Sometimes, when you are editing, you might see an error message from the Adobe viewer that says `no element found, line XX, column XX`. You see this error if you have nested an `<svg>` element within another one and have closed only one of the `</svg>` elements—typically, if you add an end `</svg>` tag at the line given in the error message that fixes the problem.

A similar error message might arise if you have nested one grouping `<g>` element within another and then provided only one end `</g>` tag. However, in that case, the error message might not always indicate the exact point where you need to insert a `</g>` tag, particularly if you have a complex set of nested grouping `<g>` elements. The error message might indicate one place you can insert an end tag, but that might not create exactly the nested structure you want.

Links that don't work

In my experience, the most common cause by far of links that don't work is when you forget to include the `xlink:href` attribute, expressed properly.

This line works in HTML but not in SVG:

```
<a href="http://www.SVGSpider.com/default.svg">SVG Spider</a>
```

For SVG, you need this:

```
<a xlink:href="http://www.SVGSpider.com/default.svg">SVG
Spider</a>
```

Similarly, for mailto links, this line would work in HTML or XHTML but not in SVG:

```
<a href="mailto://Consulting@AndrewWatt.com">Consulting
Services</a>
```

For a working mailto link in SVG, you need this line:

```
<a xlink:href="mailto://Consulting@AndrewWatt.com">Consulting
Services</a>
```

Don't forget to use the correct attribute name, `xlink:href`.

Comments

If you are having real problems with a particular piece of SVG (hopefully, it's a complex piece, but at the beginning anything can seem complex), you might want to start commenting out parts of your SVG document. This technique can be useful for trying to work out exactly what is going on—or going wrong—with, for example, a complex SVG filter or animation.

Commenting out parts of an SVG image can also be useful, however, with simpler problems. Suppose that you are having problems in getting some text to display (or so you think) and your code looks something like this:

Listing 14.10 (Diagnose01.svg)

```
<?xml version="1.0" standalone="no"?>
<!DOCTYPE svg PUBLIC "-//W3C//DTD SVG 1.0//EN"
    "http://www.w3.org/TR/2001/PR-SVG-20010719/
    DTD/svg10.dtd">
<svg width="300" height="200">
<rect x="50" y="50" width="200" height="100" style="fill:black;
stroke:black"/>
<text x="60" y="70" >
Hello SVG World!
</text>
</svg>
```

Suppose also that you are wrestling with this problem. You just can't see what you have done wrong and are frustrated that your text isn't displayed.

You can comment out the rectangle so that the SVG rendering engine doesn't process it and therefore doesn't display it, like this:

Listing 14.11 (Diagnose01WithComments.svg)

```
<?xml version="1.0" standalone="no"?>
<!DOCTYPE svg PUBLIC "-//W3C//DTD SVG 1.0//EN"
    "http://www.w3.org/TR/2001/PR-SVG-20010719/
    DTD/svg10.dtd">
<svg width="300" height="200">
<!--
<rect x="50" y="50" width="200" height="100" style="fill:black;
stroke:black"/>
-->
<text x="60" y="70" >
Hello SVG World!
</text>
</svg>
```

Now that the black rectangle is removed from the display, you can see that the black text is displayed correctly against the whitish default background. You realize that forgetting to define the style attribute for the text means that it is also black, and black text on a black rectangle isn't easy to see or read.

So far, so good. In practice, you might try blocking out parts of an SVG document that already contains comments, in code a little like this:

Listing 14.12 (Comments01.svg)

```
<?xml version="1.0" standalone="no"?>
<!DOCTYPE svg PUBLIC "-//W3C//DTD SVG 1.0//EN"
    "http://www.w3.org/TR/2001/PR-SVG-20010719/
    DTD/svg10.dtd">
<svg width="300" height="200">
<rect x="50" y="50" width="200" height="100" style="fill:black;
stroke:black"/>
<text>
<!-- My first clever <tspan> line. -->
<tspan x="60" y="70" style="fill:red; stroke:red; font-size:14;
font-weight:bold;">
Hello SVG World!
```

```
</tspan>
<!-- My second clever <tspan> line. -->
<tspan x="60" y="90" style="fill:red; stroke:red; font-size:14;
font-weight:bold;">
A second line.
</tspan>
<!-- My third clever <tspan> line. -->
<tspan x="60" y="110" style="fill:red; stroke:red; font-
size:14; font-weight:bold;">
A third line.
</tspan>
</text>
</svg>
```

The code is nicely commented, but that nice commenting lays a potential trap for you if you plan to use `<!--` and `-->` comments for diagnosing problems.

Suppose that in your efforts at diagnosing some problem, you want to comment out all the text within the `<text>` element, with the code looking like this:

Listing 14.13 (Comments02.svg)

```
<?xml version="1.0" standalone="no"?>
<!DOCTYPE svg PUBLIC "-//W3C//DTD SVG 1.0//EN"
     "http://www.w3.org/TR/2001/PR-SVG-20010719/
       DTD/svg10.dtd">
<svg width="300" height="200">
<rect x="50" y="50" width="200" height="100" style="fill:black;
stroke:black"/>
<!--
<text>
<!-- My first clever <tspan> line. -->
<tspan x="60" y="70" style="fill:red; stroke:red; font-size:14;
font-weight:bold;">
Hello SVG World!
</tspan>
<!-- My second clever <tspan> line. -->
<tspan x="60" y="90" style="fill:red; stroke:red; font-size:14;
font-weight:bold;">
A second line.
</tspan>
<!-- My third clever <tspan> line. -->
<tspan x="60" y="110" style="fill:red; stroke:red; font-size:14;
font-weight:bold;">
```

```
A  third  line.
</tspan>
</text>
-->
</svg>
```

Can you see the problem? You have placed the opening `<!--` and closing `->` correctly to comment out all of the `<text>` element, *if only* it didn't already have comments within it. In XML, you cannot nest comments within other comments.

In this simple example, which was working before you inserted the illegal comments, the Adobe viewer helpfully shows the problem as seen in Figure 14.03.

You have a well-formedness error at line 10, column 4: You have opened a second comment nested within the one you just added. If you are using an XML editor with color coding, that might help you as you add the `-->` to close the comment (which is also illegal) in your document.

Spotting what is going on is easy when you have short, simple, already-working code. When you have complex SVG images, possibly heavily commented, which are already not working (otherwise, why would you be doing this?) and you add another error by illegally nesting comments, untangling the code can be a nightmare if you are unaware of this potential pitfall.

Figure 14.03

Error, with indicative error message in the status bar, caused by incorrectly inserting comments in code.

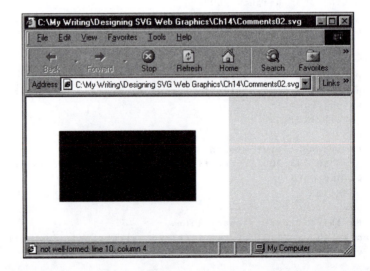

By all means, comment your code. To avoid the pitfall I just described, bring your comments up to just before a major SVG element, like this:

```
<!-- My very complex text element does marvellous things, and I
am really proud of it. It has lovely <tspan> elements. -->
<text>
...
</text>
```

rather than split many comments within code blocks. To comment out the whole text block, simply add a comment, like this:

```
<!-- My very complex text element does marvellous things, and I
am really proud of it.
It has lovely <tspan> elements. -->
<!-- This comment comments out the whole text block for diagno-
sis
<text>
...
</text>
and closes legally here. -->
```

All this is legal and likely to help you to diagnose that frustrating problem rather than add to your woes.

I hope that these various techniques help you diagnose and correct any errors in your SVG code. If you are struggling and desperate, the best source of general online help on SVG is the SVG-Developers mailing list on YahooGroups.com.

Here are the answers to the display problem shown in Listing 14.5. The second `<rect>` element had a missing opening quote on the `y` attribute. The third had a missing equals sign on the `x` attribute. The fourth had the name of the height attribute misspelled as `hieght`. The final `<rect>` had a semicolon rather than a colon between `fill` and `red`.

In this chapter, I have introduced you to many types of problems you might face while creating or tweaking SVG code. If you have created working code, you should follow my advice to then change one thing at a time. This strategy can help you avoid getting into a morass of errors that takes lots of time and frustration to escape. In listing a number of possible pitfalls, I hope that I haven't frightened you off from coding SVG. It takes care and patience, but—after you master the basics—it is often fun.

Part III

Looking Ahead

15

Planning and Building SVG Components

In this chapter:

Visual Components Defined

One key concept I hope that I have communicated to you in the earlier chapters of this book is that SVG opens up exciting new possibilities for creating visual components.

The SVG specification makes clear that the idea of visual components was in the mind of the SVG designers, although it doesn't explicitly use the term *visual components*.

Visual components in SVG can be created at various levels. The important point is to appreciate that careful planning of SVG visual components can help you reuse parts of graphics you have already created, therefore making you, as a practitioner of SVG Web graphic design, more efficient and better able to compete in what is already a highly competitive graphics marketplace. My prediction is that competition will become significantly more fierce.

Envisioning XML and Visual Components

In this book, I have largely avoided discussing the technical details of XML, as opposed to specific issues relating to SVG. However, you might find that envisioning the idea of SVG visual components in their XML context is helpful.

XML entities

Every XML document begins with a top-level, invisible entity—the document entity—that can contain one or many other entities. Those other entities can be contained within the document entity or be stored externally, typically on a computer file system.

You can look on these XML entities as predefined nonvisual components. The important thing to realize is that you can define your own entities and then use them as often as you want in XML documents.

An XML processor recognizes a few built-in entities. For example, to be able to use the `<` and `>` left and right angle brackets, in XML you must "escape" them as `&lt;` and `&gt;`, respectively. You don't need to declare those. An XML processor is already aware of what they mean.

If you want to have a paragraph in an XML document that refers to the "`<svg>` element," you need to write something like this:

```
&lt;svg&gt; element
```

Then the XML processor doesn't try to process the text `<svg>` as though it were a live SVG element.

XML allows for several specific entity types that I don't consider in detail here. For purposes of this chapter, just be aware that entities can be considered as units of information, or *storage objects*.

Clearly, the document entity contains or accesses all other entities that make up an XML document. Similarly, one of the entities that a document entity contains or accesses can contain or access another entity.

Although you do not think in those terms all the time, an XML document is therefore made up of a hierarchy of entities that can contain other entities. In this discussion, thinking of XML entities as components (not visual components, but rather the component physical parts of an XML document) can be helpful.

If you move on from the general situation of an XML document and think of how an SVG document is put together, it also is composed of entities. That isn't too surprising because SVG is an application language of XML. In SVG, each of those entities, with the exception of the document entities, are likely to have a visible effect, given the nature of what SVG is.

Just as with XML entities, SVG visual components can exist in various sizes that can individually be self-contained or contain or access other visual components.

The very flexibility of how SVG visual components can be structured or interrelated means in part that some planning is necessary.

Types of SVG visual components

As I have just mentioned, SVG visual components can be constructed in many, many ways. In this section, I want you to look briefly at some of the ways in which it can be done.

Perhaps the most coarsely grained type of SVG visual component is the separate SVG document or document fragment. If you have created any HTML or XHTML Web pages using frames, you are already familiar with the concept.

The visual space of the browser window is filled using at least two, and typically three, frames. Each frame that is part of a frameset is filled with the content of a separate HTML or XHTML file.

The same principle can be applied to SVG. If you have an SVG Web page, for example, each "frame" of it can be constructed by importing an external SVG file, in much the same way as an HTML frameset was made up. For example, the containing SVG document might look pretty much like this:

Listing 15.1 (Frameset.svg)

```
<?xml version="1.0" standalone="no"?>
<!DOCTYPE svg PUBLIC "-//W3C//DTD SVG 1.0//EN"
     "http://www.w3.org/TR/2001/PR-SVG-20010719/
     DTD/svg10.dtd">
<svg width="100%" height="600">
<!-- Import the top frame -->
<svg x="20%" y="0" width="100%" height="100">
<image x="0" y="0" width="100%" height="100%"
  xlink:href="TopFrame.svg"/>
</svg> <!-- Top frame ends here -->
<!-- Import the left frame -->
<svg x="0" y="0" width="20%" height="600">
```

```
<image x="0" y="0" width="100%" height="100%"
 xlink:href="LeftFrame.svg"/>
</svg> <!-- Left frame ends here -->
<!-- Import the main frame -->
<svg x="20%" y="100" width="80%" height="500">
<image x="0" y="0" width="100%" height="100%"
 xlink:href="MainFrame.svg"/>
</svg> <!-- Main frame ends here -->
</svg>
```

Each of the three SVG files accessed by the `<image>` elements would be functioning as a visual component. For example, the left frame might conventionally be a navigation bar that can be reused exactly as it is in all the (main) pages of a Web site.

At the time this book was written, I was still waiting for the Adobe SVG Viewer to support the code you have just looked at. Until Adobe provides complete support for the `<image>` element, this type of SVG visual component—although potentially one of the most useful—essentially isn't usable. I hope that Adobe fills that gap soon, perhaps even by the time you read this book.

Understanding the <svg> Element and Visual Components

As I have indicated in earlier chapters, you can nest `<svg>` elements within an outer `<svg>` element. In some senses, that nesting functionally does the same thing as using an `<image>` element to import separate SVG files, each nested within its own outer `<svg>` element.

One use of such nested `<svg>` elements is as a grouping element. Another is for use as independent visual components. Because the `<svg>` element that ultimately is nested can be used as the outer `<svg>` element of a separate component during testing, you can develop all the content of the `<svg>` element as a separate document fragment.

In a team setting, assuming that the size and other relevant parameters of the (to be) nested `<svg>` element are sufficiently clear, individual members of the design team can implement separate parts of a complex SVG image or Web page.

After each team member has created the `<svg>` element assigned to her and the elements have been tested, they can be pasted into one SVG document that makes use of the visual components created by individual designers.

The <use> element

In Chapter 2, "SVG Document Overview," I discussed the SVG `<use>` element. It provides the straightforward reuse of visual components within a single SVG document.

If you want to create an SVG image of the United States flag, for example, you need to have a substantial number of identical stars. Rather than redefine those one at a time, creating one correctly sized and shaped star and then accessing it multiple times by using the `<use>` element makes much more sense. This process cuts down the length of the SVG code a little and means that the code for a star has to be tested only once. Testing the code for each `<use>` element should be straightforward because, apart from adjusting the `x` and `y` attributes to ensure correct placement of each star, there are no differences between each example.

The stars wouldn't be the only reusable component in the Stars and Stripes because the stripes can also be reused.

The <defs> element

The `<defs>` element, as described in Chapter 2, also helps you to reuse code. If you want to use a gradient in more than one element in an image, for example, you simply define the gradient once and refer to it twice or more. That technique saves code and also saves time for testing the gradient.

Multiple uses in a component

When I showed you how to create navigation bars in Chapter 5, "Creating Navigation Bars," you saw how you can create one `<a>` element and all its content and, after that is working correctly, copy it to create further parts of a navigation bar—adjusting positioning attributes and the target of the `xlink:href` attribute, of course. Reuse on that small scale prevents typing mistakes from being introduced.

Use in multiple documents

At a deeper level, a navigation bar can be saved in its own file for copying and pasting into another application later. A limit must exist on how many ways a horizontal text navigation bar, for example, can be created. Of course, its colors and other characteristics are adapted in its new use, but the basic structure and function remain the same. So why not reuse the good code you already have at hand?

Using Components that Save Time and Work

As you gather experience with SVG and increase your stock of working SVG code, the reuse of that careful effort you invested earlier is sensible.

An important question is how you structure and store the visual components you have created. I return to that question later.

Saving debugging time

When you cut and paste code from previous SVG projects, you are, or ought to be, using code that has been well tested. You likely invested time in carefully constructing that code and testing its animations, interactivity, and links, for example, to ensure that they were working as you want them to.

Of course, when you reuse that code, you likely do not want to use it exactly in its original form. As you tweak some attribute values or refine some animation timing, you have to be careful not to introduce new errors into code that was previously working.

From time to time, you inevitably will make a syntax error as you adjust the code to its new purpose. If you have taken my advice to change one thing at a time and to test the static display and animations frequently, you likely know what changes you have made since the code last worked correctly. Those changes are where you should be focusing your debugging task. When you have made only one or two changes since last viewing the result, you have only one or two places to look, and spotting the error shouldn't take long.

If you have made ten or a dozen changes since you last checked whether the SVG was being displayed correctly, you have only yourself to blame if you can't even remember what two or three of the changes were. If you code in that way, expect to have some long, frustrating debugging sessions. I don't enjoy those one bit and try to code in such a way as to make them rare occurrences. I suggest that because you won't enjoy debugging, you should carefully follow a step-by-step approach on each part of an SVG project.

Breaking down the barriers to using components fully

At the time this book was written, some of the most helpful aspects of SVG for fully exploiting SVG components are missing. The biggest single omission is the absence of any implementation of the SVG `<image>` element that can include or import existing SVG images.

Hopefully, by the time you read this chapter, Adobe might have implemented the SVG image-import part of the `<image>` element. That facilitates the reuse of SVG components, pretty much along the lines of the XML entities I discussed in the early part of this chapter.

Creating a Plug-In Component and Making It Mobile

I pointed out to you earlier that the Adobe SVG Viewer does not now support the import of external SVG images using the `<image>` element. However, after the viewer has that functionality, you can add a whole new dimension to the reuse of code. Reusing code as separate files in some settings makes lots of sense.

Most of this chapter has been pretty abstract, so take a look at a practical issue that arises when you are trying to make an SVG visual component fully reusable.

One advantage of using nested `<svg>` elements—whether in a single document or using the `<image>` element to import an external SVG file or visual component—is the ability a separate `<svg>` element gives you to reposition a complex graphic on a Web page.

Consider the following adaptation from one of the logos I showed you in Chapter 9, "Creating Logos and Banner Ads." In Listing 15.2, you can see that I have used a nested `<svg>` element to contain the main rectangle, the group of lines, and the text. That graphic can be moved around the page—but in only one dimension. You can move the graphic horizontally within another `<svg>` element, but if you want to move it vertically, you need to amend each `y` attribute. Although that's not a complex task, with just a little more planning, it is an avoidable one.

Listing 15.2 (RectLinesLogo05.svg)

```
<?xml version="1.0" standalone="no"?>
<!DOCTYPE svg PUBLIC "-//W3C//DTD SVG 1.0//EN"
     "http://www.w3.org/TR/2001/PR-SVG-20010719/
      DTD/svg10.dtd">
<svg>
<defs>
<linearGradient id="MyGreenGradient"
gradientUnits="userSpaceOnUse"
x1="150" y1="150" x2="220" y2="50" >
<stop offset="10%" style="stop-color:#DDFFDD;
stop-opacity:0.8"/>
```

```
<stop offset="50%" style="stop-color:#99FF99; "/>
<stop offset="75%" style="stop-color:#DDFFDD"/>
</linearGradient>
<filter id="CombinedDropShadow" width="140%" y="-20%"
height="200%">
<feGaussianBlur in="SourceAlpha" stdDeviation="0.5"
result="ShadowOut" />
<feOffset in="ShadowOut" dx="2" dy="1" result="ShadowOnly" />
<feMerge>
  <feMergeNode in="ShadowOnly"/>
  <feMergeNode in="SourceGraphic"/>
</feMerge>
</filter>
</defs>
<svg x="30">
<rect x="5" y="55" width="300" height="80" rx="10" ry="10"
style="fill:white;
filter:url(#CombinedDropShadow)"/>
<rect x="10" y="60" width="295" height="2"
style="fill:url(#MyGreenGradient);
stroke:none;"/>
<rect x="10" y="65" width="295" height="2"
style="fill:url(#MyGreenGradient);
stroke:none;"/>
<rect x="10" y="70" width="295" height="2"
style="fill:url(#MyGreenGradient);
stroke:none;"/>
<rect x="10" y="75" width="295" height="2"
style="fill:url(#MyGreenGradient);
stroke:none;"/>
<rect x="10" y="80" width="295" height="2"
style="fill:url(#MyGreenGradient);
stroke:none;"/>
<rect x="10" y="85" width="295" height="2"
style="fill:url(#MyGreenGradient);
stroke:none;"/>
<rect x="10" y="90" width="295" height="2"
style="fill:url(#MyGreenGradient);
stroke:none;"/>
<rect x="10" y="95" width="295" height="2"
style="fill:url(#MyGreenGradient);
stroke:none;"/>
<rect x="10" y="100" width="295" height="2"
style="fill:url(#MyGreenGradient);
stroke:none;"/>
<rect x="10" y="105" width="295" height="2"
style="fill:url(#MyGreenGradient);
stroke:none;"/>
```

```
<rect x="10" y="110" width="295" height="2"
style="fill:url(#MyGreenGradient);
stroke:none;"/>
<rect x="10" y="115" width="295" height="2"
style="fill:url(#MyGreenGradient);
stroke:none;"/>
<rect x="10" y="120" width="295" height="2"
style="fill:url(#MyGreenGradient);
stroke:none;"/>
<rect x="10" y="125" width="295" height="2"
style="fill:url(#MyGreenGradient);
stroke:none;"/>
<rect x="10" y="130" width="295" height="2"
style="fill:url(#MyGreenGradient);
stroke:none;"/>
<text x="-300" y="110" style="font-family:'Times New Roman',
serif; font-size:48;
stroke:#339933; fill:white; filter:url(#CombinedDropShadow)">
<animate begin="1s" dur="2s" attributeName="x" from="-300"
to="30" fill="freeze"/>
SVGenius.com
</text>
</svg>
</svg>
```

If you look at the y attribute of the nested `<svg>` element and the other elements in this code, you see that you can subtract 50 from each y attribute within the nested `<svg>` element and add 50 to the y attribute of the nested `<svg>` element, as shown here:

```
<svg x="30" y="50">
<rect x="5" y="5" width="300" height="80" rx="10" ry="10"
style="fill:white;
filter:url(#CombinedDropShadow)"/>
<rect x="10" y="10" width="295" height="2"
style="fill:url(#MyGreenGradient);
stroke:none;"/>
<rect x="10" y="15" width="295" height="2"
style="fill:url(#MyGreenGradient);
stroke:none;"/>
<rect x="10" y="20" width="295" height="2"
style="fill:url(#MyGreenGradient);
stroke:none;"/>
<rect x="10" y="25" width="295" height="2"
style="fill:url(#MyGreenGradient);
stroke:none;"/>
```

```
<rect x="10" y="30" width="295" height="2"
style="fill:url(#MyGreenGradient);
stroke:none;"/>
<rect x="10" y="35" width="295" height="2"
style="fill:url(#MyGreenGradient);
stroke:none;"/>
<rect x="10" y="40" width="295" height="2"
style="fill:url(#MyGreenGradient);
stroke:none;"/>
<rect x="10" y="45" width="295" height="2"
style="fill:url(#MyGreenGradient);
stroke:none;"/>
<rect x="10" y="50" width="295" height="2"
style="fill:url(#MyGreenGradient);
stroke:none;"/>
<rect x="10" y="55" width="295" height="2"
style="fill:url(#MyGreenGradient);
stroke:none;"/>
<rect x="10" y="60" width="295" height="2"
style="fill:url(#MyGreenGradient);
stroke:none;"/>
<rect x="10" y="65" width="295" height="2"
style="fill:url(#MyGreenGradient);
stroke:none;"/>
<rect x="10" y="70" width="295" height="2"
style="fill:url(#MyGreenGradient);
stroke:none;"/>
<rect x="10" y="75" width="295" height="2"
style="fill:url(#MyGreenGradient);
stroke:none;"/>
<rect x="10" y="80" width="295" height="2"
style="fill:url(#MyGreenGradient);
stroke:none;"/>
<text x="-300" y="60" style="font-family:'Times New Roman',
serif; font-size:48;
stroke:#339933; fill:white; filter:url(#CombinedDropShadow)">
<animate begin="1s" dur="2s" attributeName="x" from="-300"
to="30" fill="freeze"/>
SVGenius.com
</text>
</svg>
```

After that is done, moving the graphic either vertically or horizontally is a straightforward process. You simply modify the value of the y or x attribute of the nested <svg> element, and the whole graphic can be relocated and the relative positions, including the animation, maintained.

As a generalized way of stating this concept, making the x and y attributes of elements within a potential visual component as close to zero as possible is helpful. Sometimes you might want to consciously leave a margin for some purpose, but the closer to zero the positioning attributes of the contained elements, the fuller control of positioning you have by using the x and y attributes of the outer `<svg>` element of the visual component. When that outer `<svg>` element becomes a nested `<svg>` element, positioning of the entire visual component is straightforward, depending simply on adjusting its x and y attributes.

Building a Portfolio of Visual Components

One of the issues that hits you as time passes and you build up a portfolio of SVG images is just where you can find that filter or animation you liked so much and that would be just right to make use of again.

Structuring a portfolio

I am working through this issue with my own collection of visual components. The fact that I, as you have seen, tend to make heavy use of nested `<svg>` elements has the advantage that I can break out those nested `<svg>` elements and simply copy them to separate files. Because they have an outer `<svg>` element, they are legal SVG document fragments and can stand alone in a file and be displayed by an SVG viewer.

I usually give visual components very long filenames, such as DiagonalGradientThreeStops01.svg or DiagonalGradientThreeStopsAnimated01.svg, which tells me at least a little about the nature of the visual component.

One of the more problematic areas, even when using very long filenames, is how best to store and use filters. Creating a nice filter can take quite a bit of effort, and yet it might contain multiple filters. I give those names such as FilterWhichDoesSomethingNice.svg. The visual effect is what I am most likely to remember them by, not any specific combination of SVG filter primitives.

Within each file, you can make use of the `<desc>` element to document important details of what the SVG does. Using the `<desc>` element, described in Chapter 2, is more convenient than using ordinary XML comments.

Backing up

I don't know how thorough you are about making backups of images or Web pages you create, but I suggest that you give serious thought to a backup strategy for your growing library of SVG visual components.

Those SVG visual components, properly used, are a significant asset for your graphics design activities, so it pays to take care of them. Think about how regularly you should back them up.

Of course, one side to this issue might make you less inclined to back up locally: You already have an off-site backup on the Web! All your SVG images on the Web are continuously accessible to you (barring server failure at your or your client's Web hosting company). I suggest that you don't rely solely on that and take active steps to store your visual components safely.

If you go on to build up your SVG skills, you can add to your library of SVG components all the more quickly. Chapter 16, "Building Your SVG Skills," looks at how you can build on your SVG skills.

16

Building Your SVG Skills

In this chapter:

Combining Your Skills

I hope that in this book I have communicated to you something of the power and flexibility of SVG and also whetted your appetite to learn more about SVG. I have been able to give you, in the space available, only an introduction to some of the more commonly used facets of SVG.

As I have introduced you to the concept of SVG visual components, I hope that you have appreciated that SVG has enormous flexibility to allow you to express your own creative instincts. That creative potential can be fully realized, however, only when you fully understand SVG.

In earlier chapters, I have introduced you to what I anticipate to be typical uses of SVG images on the Web—as navigation bars, buttons, animations, banners, and banner ads, for example. I have introduced you to many SVG elements and attributes, but, inevitably, haven't been able to cover everything.

I have tried to split topics up in ways I hope will help you grasp how SVG handles that particular aspect. Yet the likely way for you to produce attractive SVG graphics is, in practice, to combine many of the techniques that have been presented to you individually.

Interactive SVG

SVG gives enormous scope to incorporate interactivity and animation. I have shown you interactions and animations using simple, often individual, graphical elements and shapes. In production settings, you might use more complex, perhaps grouped, graphics shapes and animate those on complex paths. The techniques you have been shown are time-based and event-based visual components that you can, and should, experiment with. Combining those visual components is what allows you to release your creative instincts through SVG.

SVG and ECMAScript

In this book, I have focused primarily on what SVG is capable of: using the declarative XML-compliant syntax alone. However, a huge area for potential development is the combination of ECMAScript (JavaScript) with SVG to produce animations or programmatic interactivity that SVG is incapable of producing alone.

JavaScript can dynamically alter characteristics of an SVG document by altering the Document Object Model, or DOM, for the document. In addition to allowing you to produce animations that closely resemble those produced using the SVG animation elements, you can create powerful interactions that declarative SVG cannot produce.

One useful tutorial site on using JavaScript with SVG is at http://www.kevlindev.com.

An SVG Mindset

SVG is different from any Web graphics format that has ever been available. If you are to make the best use of SVG, therefore, you have to reexamine many thought patterns you take for granted. Out goes the notion, for example, that you can display only 256 colors in many of your Web images. With the arrival of SVG, you have no reason not to have 24-bit color.

When you are creating SVG, you need a mindset that is half designer and half programmer. Or, perhaps more accurately, you need a mindset that is fully designer and fully programmer. I must admit that when I first started using SVG, I found it difficult to think of the design aspects of a Web image or Web page while also trying to struggle through the exploration of how SVG syntax worked. You might find the same thing to be true.

The cure for that semifrozen mindset is practice. Just experiment with the various techniques I have shown you. Take a look at some of the existing graphics you have created, and try to imagine how you might create them, or something similar, in SVG. As you work your way toward those visual targets, you will gradually find—perhaps with moments of sudden insight— that you are gaining progressively greater control over the SVG images you are producing.

Creating and using visual components

Twenty years or so ago, computer programmers normally developed mono- lithic programs, a little like the way many graphics designers now produce a Web image. I am not trying to insult or provoke anyone—I am simply saying that graphics designers often work in a way that computer program- mers have now discarded, partly because the work is, for the programmer, inefficient or cannot be updated frequently or easily.

You produce a final image that works, but changing it or updating it, for example, is—or can be—a major task. Just as programmers took some time to adapt to the arrival of object-oriented programming techniques, with the exception of a few far-sighted pioneers not immediately grasping the poten- tial, the same situation might be true with SVG graphics. To conceive of visual components that are reusable demands a change in mindset, which takes time to work through the graphic design profession.

Visualize the image you want to create, and then break that image down into its possible component parts. For each of those components, work out how you would create that visual component. After you have created the individual components, you should be able to follow the earlier examples of putting together these types of components.

Although this approach might seem strange at first, it isn't too different from the way you perhaps work in a conventional graphics package. Rather than make a particular choice from a Photoshop or Paint Shop Pro menu and adjust its settings, you choose an SVG element, or combination of elements, that produce a similar effect.

This technique might feel different because the visual components you are creating in SVG feel so much like that—like visual components you create—whereas the familiar menus of your favorite graphics program feel comfortable to you. But you are using or creating visual components. Think a little about the effects in your favorite graphics program.

Embedding SVG in XML

In Chapter 10, "Embedding SVG in HTML or XHTML Pages," I discussed how to embed an SVG image within an HTML or XHTML document. However, the characteristics of XML-based languages mean that they can be mixed if a particular syntax form, XML namespaces, is used correctly. The W3C Recommendation that defines this concept is the Namespaces in XML Recommendation; the full text is at http://www.w3.org/TR/1999/REC-xml-names-19990114.

To use SVG in this way, you need to make clear that all the SVG elements you have become familiar with are associated with a Uniform Resource Identifier (URI), specifically http://www.w3.org/2000/svg. You do that by using a namespace declaration that is a special attribute with the following syntax:

```
xmlns:svg="http://www.w3.org/2000/svg">
```

In the following example, I declared the SVG namespace in the outer `<xmml:document>` element. Thereafter, all SVG elements have an `svg` prefix separated from the element name by a colon.

Listing 16.1 (Namespaces.xml)

```
<?xml version="1.0" standalone="no"?>
<xmml:document
  xmlns:xmml="http://www.xmml.com/"
  xmlns:svg="http://www.w3.org/2000/svg">
<svg:svg width="500" height="400" >
<svg:g>
<svg:animateTransform attributeName="transform" type="rotate"
values="0 150 100; 360 150 100" begin="0s" dur="10s" />
```

```
<svg:rect x="1" y="1" width="298" height="198"
style="stroke:red; stroke-width:2;
fill:none;"/>
<svg:rect x="50" y="50" width="200" height="100"
style="fill:#EEEEEE;
stroke:blue;"/>
</svg:g>
</svg:svg>
</xmml:document>
```

Thus, `<svg:svg>` is the familiar `<svg>` element but in a more specific identity that, together with the namespace declaration, allows SVG elements to be mixed with elements from other XML namespaces that would each have their own namespace URI and namespace prefix. When you are using namespace prefixes correctly, the XML processor knows which element belongs to which namespace, or, if you prefer, to which XML-based language the element belongs.

The X-Smiles multi-namespace browser, as mentioned in Chapter 1, "The Basic SVG Tool Set," allows SVG to be mixed with other XML namespaces, such as for the Extensible Stylesheet Language Formatting Objects (XSL-FO), Extended Forms, XForms, and Synchronized Multimedia Integration Language (SMIL).

The use of SVG with one or more other XML namespaces can be expected to increase significantly during the next couple of years. For example, RealPlayer seems to be adopting SMIL; therefore, SVG images can be integrated seamlessly with this type of multimedia presentations.

Similarly, SVG images can be displayed on the Web using XSL-FO. Some simple examples are online at http://www.xsl-fo.com/. To view these types of SVG images within XSL-FO, you need to use the X-Smiles browser or the Antenna House XSL Formatter (http://www.antennahouse.com/).

Both the X-Smiles browser and the Antenna House XSL Formatter are under continuing development, so I have not included any code at this stage because details might change during the period preceding publication. However, if this area interests you, I encourage you to visit both Web sites and download the processors to experiment. If you have a particular interest in XSL-FO, take a look at the XSL-FO mailing list, at http://www.yahoogroups.com/group/XSL-FO/.

Understanding SVG and internationalization

In the introduction to this book, I mentioned that SVG had advantages in the area of the internationalization of Web sites. Take a look at the basics of the technique that makes SVG useful in this context.

Suppose that you want to create a site for SVGenius.com for speakers of English, German, and French. The code in Listing 16.2 produces a simple multilingual logo with one of four appearances onscreen, depending on the language settings in the SVG viewer or Web browser.

Listing 16.2 (International02.svg)

```
<?xml version="1.0" standalone="no"?>
<!DOCTYPE svg PUBLIC "-//W3C//DTD SVG 1.0//EN"
    "http://www.w3.org/TR/2001/PR-SVG-20010719/
     DTD/svg10.dtd">
<svg>
<rect x="50" y="50" rx="5" ry="5" width="200" height="80"
style="fill:#CCCCFF;
stroke:#000099"/>
<text x="90" y="80" style="fill:#000099; stroke:#000099;
font-size:18; font-family:Arial, sans-serif;">
SVGenius.com
</text>
<switch>
<text x="120" y="110" style="stroke:#000099; fill:#000099;
font-size:20;"
systemLanguage="en">
Hello!
</text>
<text x="110" y="110" style="stroke:#000099; fill:#000099;
font-size:20;"
systemLanguage="fr">
Bonjour!
</text>
<text x="100" y="110" style="stroke:#000099; fill:#000099;
font-size:20;"
systemLanguage="de">
Guten Tag!
</text>
<text x="52" y="110" style="stroke:#000099; fill:#000099;
font-size:12;">
```

```
Sorry, we don't speak your language.
</text>
</switch>
</svg>
```

The SVG `<switch>` element indicates that no more than one of the elements nested within it is displayed. If you step through the options one at a time, you see that the first option is `systemLanguage="en"`, meaning English. If the system language is English, the greeting contained within that `<text>` element is displayed and the other options within the `<switch>` element are ignored.

However, if `systemLanguage` is not English, the next `<text>` element is evaluated. If it has a value of `fr` (French), the greeting `Bonjour!` is displayed. If that fails, `systemLanguage` is evaluated on the third `<text>` element, and if `systemLanguage` is set for German, the greeting `Guten Tag!` is displayed.

A `<switch>` element should have a default setting. In this case, the message `Sorry, we don't speak your language` is displayed if none of the three earlier `<text>` elements nested within the `<switch>` element matches the current system language.

At the time this book was written, the Adobe SVG Viewer had not implemented the `systemLanguage` attribute, so the figures produced from Listing 16.2 show the Batik SVG Viewer. If you want to test the code, choose Language from the Options menu. A window is displayed that allows you to add or remove system languages, for the purposes of the Batik viewer. You might have chosen more than one language. For example, if you set French and German, the French greeting is displayed because it is the first element within the `<switch>` element that satisfies the condition. All later elements, including the one with `systemLanguage="de"`, are ignored.

The Batik setting for English seems idiosyncratic to me. It uses `"en"` to indicate English-US, which should be `"en-us"`. Making an allowance for that, if you set the language to English-US, the greeting shown in Figure 16.01 is displayed.

Figure 16.01

The greeting displayed when the system language is English.

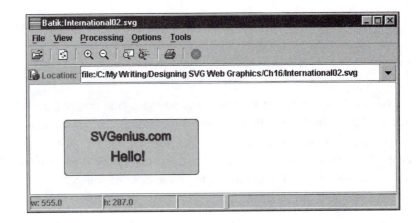

If you alter the system language to include German but neither `"en"` nor `"fr"` (French), the greeting that is displayed is the one shown in Figure 16.02.

Finally, if you change the system language to German, you see the output shown in Figure 16.03.

In practice, of course, the system language is set depending on the user's location and personal language preferences, and they see the greeting in only their own language.

Similarly, if you want to create internationalized animated graphics, you can apply the same techniques. For example, you can create a trilingual ticker tape message using code something like this:

Figure 16.02

The greeting displayed when the system language is French.

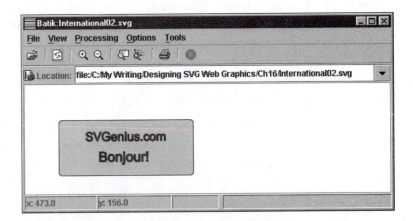

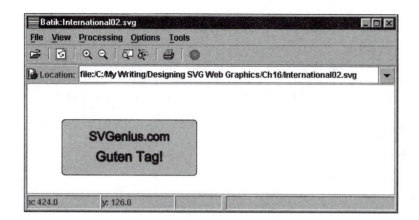

Figure 16.03

The greeting displayed when the system language is German.

Listing 16.3 (International03.svg)

```
<?xml version="1.0" standalone="no"?>
<!DOCTYPE svg PUBLIC "-//W3C//DTD SVG 1.0//EN"
     "http://www.w3.org/TR/2001/PR-SVG-20010719/
       DTD/svg10.dtd">
<rect x="0" y="0" width="800" height="100"
style="fill:#CCFFCC;"/>
<svg x="166" y="20" width="468" height="60">
<rect x="0" y="0" width="100%" height="100%" style="fill:white;
stroke:none;"/>
<a xlink:href="mailto://Consulting@SVGenius.com">
<switch>
<text x="700" y="40" style="stroke:green; fill:green;
font-family:Courier,
monospace; font-size:20;
 font-weight:normal;" systemLanguage="en">
SVGenius.com offers consulting services on SVG. Click here to
contact us.
<animate attributeName="x" from="600" to="-1000" begin="0s"
dur="20s"
repeatCount="indefinite"/>
</text>
<text x="700" y="40" style="stroke:green; fill:green;
font-family:Courier,
monospace; font-size:20;
 font-weight:normal;" systemLanguage="fr">
SVGenius.com provides consulting services on SVG. Click here to
contact us.
<animate attributeName="x" from="600" to="-1000" begin="0s"
dur="20s"
repeatCount="indefinite"/>
```

```
</text>
<text x="700" y="40" style="stroke:green; fill:green;
font-family:Courier,
monospace; font-size:20;
  font-weight:normal;" systemLanguage="de">
SVGenius.com provides consulting services on SVG. Click here to
contact us.
<animate attributeName="x" from="600" to="-1000" begin="0s"
dur="20s"
repeatCount="indefinite"/>
</text>
</switch>
</a>
<rect x="0" y="0" width="468" height="60"
style="stroke:#009900;
stroke-width:2; fill:none;"/>
</svg>
</svg>.03
```

Unfortunately, I can't show you the various output from the system language settings. The Adobe SVG Viewer doesn't yet display SVG on the basis of the value of the `systemLanguage` attribute, and Batik is limited in its animation capabilities. Hopefully, by the time you read this book, you can run the code in one or both of those SVG viewers.

Clipping Paths

Finally, I want to show you a technique using SVG clipping paths, which you can use to great creative effect. What a clipping path does is similar to taking a pair of scissors and cutting out a shape. SVG allows you to "cut out" noncontinuous shapes, such as text.

The final clipping path looks like the one shown in Figure 16.04.

If you look closely at the fill of the lettering, you might recognize that the left part of the text is filled with an image of a sunset, of which you see the full version in Figure 16.05.

The right part of the text is filled with the painting shown in Figure 16.06.

Figure 16.04

An SVG clipping path used with two bitmap images to create interesting text.

Figure 16.05

The sunset bitmap used for the left part of the clipping path shown in Figure 16.04.

Figure 16.06

A painting of a seal, used as the fill for the right part of the clipping path image shown in Figure 16.04.

Take a look at how this is done:

Listing 16.4 (Clipping01.svg)

```
<?xml version='1.0'?>
<!DOCTYPE svg PUBLIC "-//W3C//DTD SVG 1.0//EN"
      "http://www.w3.org/TR/2001/PR-SVG-20010719/
        DTD/svg10.dtd">
<svg width="800" height="600">
<defs>
  <g id="ClipElement">
     <clipPath id="Clip1">
     <text x="20" y="80" class="Clipstyle">Clipping Path</text>
     </clipPath>
  </g>
<style type="text/css">
  <![CDATA[
    .Clipstyle
     {stroke:#FF0000;
      stroke-width:3;
      font-family: Verdana,Arial, sans-serif;
      font-size:72;
      font-weight:bold;}
        ]]>
</style>
</defs>
<rect x="0" y="0" width="800" height="100"
style="fill:black;"/>
<svg x="80" width="600" height="100">
  <g id="bitmapfill">
    <image x="10" y="20" width="250" height="100"
xlink:href="Sunset.jpg"
     style="clip-path:url(#Clip1)" />
    <image x="260" y="0" width="380" height="100"
xlink:href="SealCropped.jpg"
     style="clip-path:url(#Clip1)" />
  </g>
</svg>
</svg>
```

Let me walk you through that code, step by step. Much of it happens within the `<defs>` element:

```
<defs>
  <g id="ClipElement">
     <clipPath id="Clip1">
     <text x="20" y="80" class="Clipstyle">Clipping Path</text>
```

```
        </clipPath>
    </g>
  <style type="text/css">
   <![CDATA[
    .Clipstyle
      {stroke:#FF0000;
       stroke-width:3;
       font-family: Verdana, Arial, sans-serif;
       font-size:72;
       font-weight:bold;}
          ]]>
  </style>
  </defs>
```

The business end is the `<clipPath>` element, which you see in the early part of the `<defs>` element. The `<clipPath>` element contains the SVG elements to which the image that is being clipped will be applied. In this instance, the images will be applied to a `<text>` element that contains the text `Clipping Path`. Notice that the `<text>` element has a `Clipstyle` class attribute.

The second part of the content of the `<defs>` element is a `<style>` element that, in a CDATA section, describes the font family, font size, or font weight, for example, for the text element contained within the `<clipPath>` element. The `".Clipstyle"` CSS selector ensures that the declarations that follow are applied to the text.

How does the visual appearance of the sunset and seal images get into the text? That happens within the main body of the SVG document:

```
<g id="bitmapfill">
   <image x="10" y="20" width="250" height="100"
xlink:href="Sunset.jpg"
     style="clip-path:url(#Clip1)" />
   <image x="260" y="0" width="380" height="100"
xlink:href="SealCropped.jpg"
     style="clip-path:url(#Clip1)" />
  </g>
```

The first `<image>` element indicates that, starting at a position of (10,20) and with a width of 250, the referenced image, Sunset.jpg, should be displayed with a clip-path property of `url(#Clip1)`, which references the `<clipPath>` element you saw a little earlier in the `<defs>` element.

The sunset image is displayed as far as 260 pixels across (a starting position of 10, specified by the `x` attribute plus a 250-pixel width).

Then the second `<image>` element comes into play. That image starts at `x="260"`. In other words, it abuts nicely the first image. If you look carefully at Figure 16.04, you can see the join in the first vertical line of the *n* of *Clipping*.

The left part of the text has the sunset image clipped to the shape of the text defined in the `<clipPath>` element. In the right part of the text. the seal image is clipped to the shape of the latter part of the text.

Suppose that you want to reposition the image so that the yellowish color of the sunset appears a little lower:

Listing 16.5 (Clipping02.svg)

```
<?xml version='1.0'?>
<!DOCTYPE svg PUBLIC "-//W3C//DTD SVG 1.0//EN"
    "http://www.w3.org/TR/2001/PR-SVG-20010719/
      DTD/svg10.dtd">
<svg width="800" height="600">
<defs>
 <g id="ClipElement">
    <clipPath id="Clip1" opacity="0.1">
    <text x="20" y="80" class="Clipstyle">Clipping Path</text>
    </clipPath>
 </g>
<style type="text/css">
 <![CDATA[
   .Clipstyle
    {stroke:#FF0000;
     stroke-width:3;
     font-family: Verdana,Arial, sans-serif;
     font-size:72;
     font-weight:bold;}
       ]]>
</style>
</defs>
<rect x="0" y="0" width="800" height="100"
style="fill:black;"/>
<svg x="80" width="600" height="100">
 <g id="bitmapfill">
  <image x="10" y="40" width="250" height="100"
xlink:href="Sunset.jpg"
```

```
      style="clip-path:url(#Clip1)" />
   <image x="260" y="0" width="380" height="100"
xlink:href="SealCropped.jpg"
      style="clip-path:url(#Clip1)" />
  </g>
 </svg>
 </svg>
```

You simply alter the y attribute of the first `<image>` element from 20 to 40, and the image moves down within the clipping path by 20 pixels.

If you want to reverse the images, simply swap over the filenames in the two `<image>` elements.

Clearly, the use of bitmaps in text gives you great creative potential.

To see a similar image online, take a look at http://www.svgspider.com/Page04.svg. The clipping path is displayed on a background whose color you can animate.

Speaking of animations, if the `<image>` element has an x attribute, there's nothing to stop you from animating it, right?

Listing 16.6 (Clipping03.svg)

```
<?xml version='1.0'?>
<!DOCTYPE svg PUBLIC "-//W3C//DTD SVG 1.0//EN"
       "http://www.w3.org/TR/2001/PR-SVG-20010719/
       DTD/svg10.dtd">
<svg width="800" height="600">
<defs>
  <g id="ClipElement">
     <clipPath id="Clip1" opacity="0.1">
     <text x="20" y="80" class="Clipstyle">Clipping Path</text>
     </clipPath>
  </g>
<style type="text/css">
  <![CDATA[
   .Clipstyle
    {stroke:#FF0000;
     stroke-width:3;
     font-family: Verdana,Arial, sans-serif;
     font-size:72;
     font-weight:bold;}
       ]]>
```

```
</style>
</defs>
<rect x="0" y="0" width="800" height="100"
style="fill:black;"/>
<svg x="80" width="600" height="100">
 <g id="bitmapfill">
   <image x="10" y="20" width="250" height="100"
xlink:href="SealCropped.jpg"
     style="clip-path:url(#Clip1)" />
   <image x="260" y="20" width="380" height="100"
xlink:href="Sunset.jpg"
     style="clip-path:url(#Clip1)" >
     <animate attributeName="x" from="10" to="260" begin="2s"
dur="4s" fill="freeze" repeatCount="1"/>
   </image>
 </g>
</svg>
</svg>
```

Take a look at those scudding clouds blowing on a breeze within your text! Beautiful! Be sure to run the code to get an idea of what is possible.

SVG is enormously powerful. I hope that this glimpse of what is possible, such as this animated clipping path example, makes you want to dive in and experiment. The water is lovely!

17

The Future of SVG

In this chapter:

Where Does SVG Fit in a Web Graphics Strategy?

The history of computing is littered with good technologies that lose out to better-marketed technologies. Will that be the future of SVG—to be consigned to the dustbin of computer history, like the IBM operating system OS/2, which lost out to Microsoft Windows a decade ago?

Or, will SVG meet a practical need of both corporate and individual Web developers and designers?

What is the future of SVG?

I suspect that the answer to this question is something that will be of great importance to many readers of this book as well as to many who don't read it, perhaps because they are unaware that the question is so important to their professional futures as Web graphic designers.

Do the intentions of the designers of SVG look like they will come to fruition? Will SVG replace *many* uses of bitmap graphics? Remember that that is what the SVG requirements document anticipated SVG would do. If it replaces some of those uses, which ones are likely to be affected?

What about the head-to-head competition of the W3C open-source vector graphics standard for the Web and the heavily used proprietary vector graphics format, Macromedia Flash? Will SVG even dent the market share of Flash? Will

SVG grow solely at the expense of bitmap graphics? Or, do Flash designers have good cause to worry that the open-source SVG will erode their current dominant market position?

As with many important questions, the issues involved aren't simple ones. Significant commercial interests are at stake.

Early in the writing phase of this book, Adobe announced that it intended to distribute *100 million* copies of the Adobe SVG Viewer by around April 2002. Part of that huge distribution will take place in association with the distribution of RealPlayer and part in association with sales of Adobe Web and graphics products. If Adobe achieves its goal, and I have no reason to doubt that it will, SVG will clearly have a critical mass of viewers in the marketplace.

After the Adobe SVG Viewer achieves that critical mass, as surely it will, the two vector graphics formats can go head-to-head in direct competition.

The Adobe SVG Viewer is now technically superior to any other options. If the other SVG viewers, such as Batik, don't catch up, or if major browser vendors don't implement SVG natively, the possibility (some would say danger) exists that a dominant Adobe SVG Viewer could make SVG a quasi-proprietary technology. For the health of SVG, the Adobe Viewer needs competition.

Most of this chapter looks at the potential use of SVG in isolated market segments because they are easiest to analyze (or speculate about).

For static graphics

As you have seen throughout this book, SVG can readily produce the simple static graphics that form the bread and butter of Web page graphics furniture. This area is, or has been until recently, the almost exclusive home territory of bitmap graphics, such as GIFs and JPGs. However, JPEGs are likely to retain their dominance for displaying photographic images on the Web.

Recently, I was carrying out a Web-based research project (unrelated to this book) in a part of the Web that I had never seriously looked at. The thing that struck me was the increased use of Flash graphics for straightforward Web page furniture.

If Flash is already able to displace bitmap graphics from at least some basic use on Web sites, there's no reason that SVG graphics might not also make a significant impact in the same sphere.

Indeed, SVG will have a huge advantage over Flash in making inroads into that area. That the source code for SVG images is always visible makes it likely that many Web users will examine the SVG graphics used in that way to see what is there, behind the covers. Those Web users will either learn from what they see or (with human nature what it is) "borrow" code that produces visual effects they like.

That universal access to source code is how the use of HTML exploded a few years back. I fully expect to see the use of SVG explode in a similar manner. But you must keep one important difference in mind: When the use of HTML exploded, the number of Web users was perhaps measured in a relatively small number of millions. Now, users are measured in hundreds of millions. The number of authors won't equal the number of users, but the number of Web authors has also grown substantially in recent years.

Just how huge and how fast will the explosion of SVG use be?

For animated graphics

Animated graphics is an area where I see SVG (and, to some extent, Flash) likely to make progressive inroads into the use of animated bitmap graphics. The subtle and controllable effects that can be produced in SVG far exceed anything possible with a GIF of acceptable size. PNGs are perhaps less inferior to SVG, but PNG hasn't really ever reached critical mass, unlike the use of animated GIFs.

Already, I am seeing the increasing use of simple Flash animations in basic animated Web page furniture. SVG is fully a match for Flash in this area, I believe, and, again, as far as grabbing market share, has the enormous advantage of being open source. Non-expert users of SVG will quickly get up to speed to a degree, either by learning from the code of others or by straightforward code theft. Whatever the morals of that practice, the practical impact will be, in my view, a huge growth in the use of SVG by non-experts for producing relatively simple Web page furniture.

Java applets

Many readers won't be making much use of Java applets but, for completeness, I'll briefly mention how SVG might affect that use.

For some uses, SVG-animated graphics will be go head-to-head with existing uses for Java applets. For example, in Chapter 8, "Animation: SVG and SMIL Animation," you created a scrolling window of text that uses SVG to provide functionality for which a Java applet typically might have been used. Similarly, the SVG banner ad with scrolling text might have been implemented previously as a Java applet.

If many millions of Web users have the Adobe SVG Viewer, not to mention the alternatives, the number of site visitors capable of viewing SVG might soon exceed the number who are capable of, or who have chosen to be capable of, viewing Java applets.

SVG animations alone might significantly displace the use of Java applets. More sophisticated Java applets might be more resistant to the impact of SVG, but even those are likely to find competition from SVG combined with JavaScript for at least some uses.

For interactive graphics

As I demonstrated in Chapter 5, "Creating Navigation Bars," SVG Web furniture can provide all the navigation functionality needed on a Web page. Creating some visually attractive rollover and similar effects is a straightforward process.

In this area, I see SVG having an impact on the use of HTML or XHTML with scripting languages. For many new users, the ability to create rollovers and other effects by using a simple text editor that uses SVG or by examining or acquiring other people's code will lead to a growth in interactive SVG graphics. This process is, in my opinion, more intuitive and more efficient than using a scripting language and multiple bitmap images.

For Web authoring

When I first announced the existence of SVGSpider.com, I was amazed and somewhat shocked by the vitriolic reaction of a few individuals who strongly, passionately, believed that SVG ought not to be used for authoring Web pages.

I was unable then, and am unable now, to understand the depth of animosity that the experiment generated because the proprietary vector format, Flash, was being widely and routinely used for exactly that purpose already. With that background, it was obvious, at least to me, that SVG would make a great XML-based Web page authoring tool.

Flash demonstrated, as did SVGSpider.com, that creating Web pages solely from vector content is entirely possible.

As I have shown you in Chapter 12, "Creating a Simple SVG Web Site" (and with the demonstrations on SVGSpider.com), SVG is a capable Web page authoring technology.

Will SVG displace HTML? I expect that it will, probably more slowly than its impact in the graphics market. But after non-expert people start experimenting with SVG to produce Web page graphics and realize that SVG can be used equally to author whole Web pages, I expect to see the substantial growth of SVG in this arena.

SVG and Macromedia Flash

For many people reading this book, this is the $64,000 dollar question: What impact does SVG have on Flash? For a few, the impact of the impending competition between SVG and Flash will be measured in many millions of dollars rather than in tens of thousands. For smaller players, making the right choice might make the difference to how well, if at all, their graphics design career progresses.

In several earlier sections in this chapter, I have touched on comparisons of SVG and Flash—but how do I view the overall picture? Will the well-established Flash crowd out the young pretender, SVG? Will the open-source, W3C standard SVG dethrone Flash? Or will both succeed, with a huge decline in bitmap graphics on the Web? Or will Flash and SVG carve out separate niches on the Web?

At the time I wrote this chapter, the SVG specification, although essentially complete, was not a full W3C Recommendation, although it is likely to be by the time this book appears in print. Flash, on the other hand, at version 5 is a fairly mature technology. However, SVG has the potential benefit of having familiar vector graphics drawing tools, such as Corel Draw 10 and Adobe Illustrator 9, being able to export SVG. In addition, Jasc, which made the successful bitmap editor Paint Shop Pro, has produced WebDraw, a capable drawing package focused directly on SVG that promises to be a comprehensive SVG authoring package, including SVG animations.

Significant changes were made from Flash 4 to Flash 5 that demanded of users some additional new learning. Those who have already invested that time and effort might have an understandable reluctance to spend time exploring an alternative, competing technology. However, as additional SVG-enabled animation tools come to market, a significant number of Flash designers are likely to at least explore the alternative tools.

Because those tools were not yet marketed at the time I wrote this chapter, the relative futures of Flash and SVG in that arena are uncertain. I expect that the numbers of users who hand-code SVG animations will be small, so much of the competition will center on the usability and power of the animation tools for Flash and SVG. Can Macromedia improve an already powerful tool? Are a significant number of Flash designers finding Flash too complex? Will Adobe, or someone else, produce an SVG animation tool with a Photoshop-like interface that provides a seductive, but perhaps not easy, path for Photoshop users to transition to SVG? Or, will a code-concealing approach be seen as inadequate? Perhaps that is where Jasc sees an opportunity, by providing in WebDraw an SVG drawing and animation tool with simultaneous access to the SVG code.

Of course, I don't know the answers to some of those questions. Nor, I suspect, does anyone else now. It is simply too early to know what the future focus of the competition between SVG and Flash will be. But, if I were a Flash developer, I might be wearing a worried frown on my forehead.

The Future of SVG

Someone once said something like, "Predictions are a risky business, particularly with respect to the future!" So I am possibly being foolhardy in trying to predict what the future holds for SVG.

Let me put my head right on the chopping block. I believe that SVG has an exciting future. I can see SVG replacing bitmap graphics for many uses and also providing potent competition for the existing proprietary Web vector graphics format: Macromedia Flash.

I can also visualize SVG, in addition to its effect on bitmap and proprietary vector graphics, making an impact in the traditional HTML and XHTML Web graphics space. I expect to see SVG make a major impact as part of the content to be displayed by a new generation of multi-namespace XML browsers. Take a look at some of those points in a little more detail.

SVG, because it is XML, has a fundamental advantage over bitmap graphics and over Flash in a Web whose future will be, like it or not, increasingly XML based. I am not suggesting that XML capabilities cannot be grafted on to Flash (they already have been, to a degree, in Flash 5), but Flash is not XML based, nor is it likely that it ever will be. If Flash becomes an XML-based vector format, that will be, in my view, Macromedia's acknowledgment of defeat. Given the contribution of Flash to the Macromedia bottom line, that concession is not something the company would make lightly.

I hope to see quality implementations of SVG in Internet Explorer and the Netscape browser. With the wide availability of the Adobe SVG Viewer, the impetus for native support might be stifled or delayed.

Factors influencing the future of SVG

When you are thinking about the future of SVG, keep in mind several factors.

You need to be realistic. You need to be aware of the fact that SVG is barely a completed first version of a new technology. A nonproprietary graphics technology, based on XML and always editable, has never been available. Your mindset for even thinking about creating Web graphics needs to undergo a paradigm shift.

Perhaps most radical is that the source code for Web SVG images will be accessible to many, many thousands of interested viewers of SVG. The techniques of creating simple or sophisticated SVG graphics will all be available for study, as was the case with HTML Web pages a few years back. Just as there was an explosion of interest in creating Web pages with HTML, I expect a similar explosion of interest in creating SVG Web graphics. After all, studying the techniques, and copying or adapting the techniques, of the skilled users of SVG Web graphics has never been easier.

Using SVG with HTML or XHTML

In the short term, this is likely to be a core use of SVG on the Web. Most current Web pages are HTML with limited uptake of XHTML 1.0. Using SVG images to replace static and animated bitmap images and to potentially replace Flash graphics has advantages. SVG images can be downloaded significantly more quickly than bitmap graphics. In addition, SVG images can produce subtleties of transitions and interactivity that are difficult or impossible to achieve with bitmap Web graphics. The superiority of a vector graphics approach for some Web graphics has been demonstrated by the explosion in the use of Flash on the Web.

One practical issue is how quickly ordinary users will have the capability to view SVG. Until the major browsers incorporate the ability to display SVG natively, users will need to download SVG viewers (probably the Adobe SVG Viewer for now). But the Adobe ambition to have distributed 100 million SVG viewers by spring 2002 means that the time when SVG reaches critical mass for those viewing HTML or XHTML Web pages cannot be far away.

Using SVG with bitmap graphics

In Chapter 16, "Building Your SVG Skills," I briefly touched on the possible use of SVG with existing bitmap graphics in clipping paths. I encourage you to think of those existing bitmap graphics that are worth saving as visual components. They have limitations as visual components because they are no longer editable in GIF, JPEG, or PNG format. But they do have at least some potential for reuse.

Creative designers will explore many other potential uses of bitmap graphics with SVG. Whether a better understanding of how to create SVG images will supplant that use remains to be seen. But using bitmap images as the input to animated SVG clipping paths, for example, has the potential for many interesting visual effects.

SVG As a Web Authoring Tool

In Chapter 12, I showed you a little of what SVG is capable of as a "single-language" Web authoring technology. For some Web authors, I would imagine that having to learn only one language to produce viable XML-based Web pages will be an attraction. That approach will inevitably be looked down on by those in the happy position of working in a team environment where each team member has one or more XML specializations.

Creating SVG Dynamically

In the introduction to this book, I mentioned the commercial pressures operating on Web-enabled businesses wherever they might be situated.

Many e-businesses will have SVG created dynamically on the server side, perhaps in a real-time graphing of stock market prices for selected stocks or weather information, such as overnight temperature for growers of frost-sensitive crops.

Those continually updated images could be created server-side using SVG. For some of the graphing, as opposed to graphical, uses of SVG, little interaction might occur between graphics designers and server-side programmers. For other uses, however, that interaction might be considerable. If you, as a graphic designer, have some worthwhile understanding of how to code SVG, your relationship with server-side coders might be a much more enjoyable and productive one.

SVG, SMIL Animation, and SMIL 2.0

SVG can be one component being included in XML-based multimedia presentations. SVG natively includes SMIL Animation capabilities, yet SVG images are not limited to being stand-alone images: They have enormous potential as part of an XML-based, multi-namespace multimedia future.

Imagine creating graphically rich animated company reports or brochures—using SVG in combination with SMIL or XSL-FO. The creative opportunities are likely to be substantial for those with the requisite understanding, foresight, and combination of skills.

Using SVG with XForms

SVG Web pages lack the ability to convey to the Web server the information entered on forms. By combining SVG with the forthcoming XForms standard, a powerful, XML-based, forms-capable Web authoring environment becomes possible. You can see a hint of what might be possible already by experimenting with the SVG and XForms capabilities in the X-Smiles browser.

For the latest version of the XForms specification, visit http://www.w3.org/TR/xforms/.

Using SVG with XSL-FO

SVG can be embedded in XSL-FO. XSL-FO, surprisingly, can be used to display text-based information on the Web, which opens up new metaphors of use on Web sites. It becomes possible to "turn pages," as it were, on an XSL-FO Web site. Whether that will be seen as preferable by users compared to the scrolling facility you have become used to remains to be seen.

The future for SVG is bright. In addition, Web graphics designers who build skills in SVG early will be in a good position to explore and exploit the huge potential that SVG brings to Web graphics. In this book, I could only scratch the surface of SVG's enormous capabilities, but I hope that I have been able to impart to you at least some of the essential SVG skills and also help you glimpse the great future that lies ahead of SVG.

Don't be left behind!

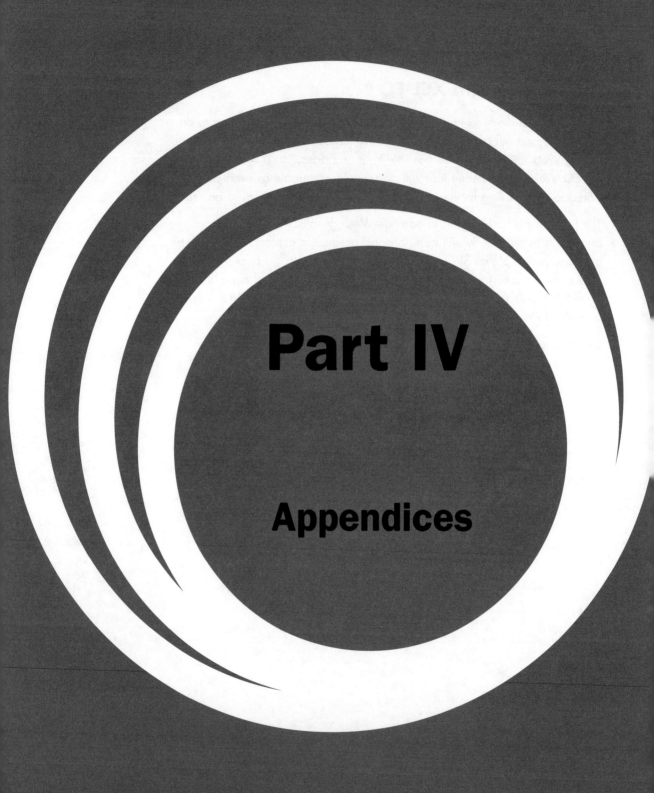

Part IV

Appendices

A

Online SVG and XML Resources

In this appendix:

- SVG at the W3C
- SVG Viewers
- SVG Tools
- SVG Tutorials and Demos
- SVG References
- Server-Side SVG
- XML Resources

SVG at the W3C

For all W3C URLs listed here, a URL is automatically updated, wherever possible, to allow you to see the latest version of a specification. If you are interested in closely following developments at the W3C, you can frequently visit http://www.w3.org/tr/ to see recently announced drafts or final specifications.

Style activity

SVG draws heavily on Cascading Style Sheets Level 2, CSS2. The CSS2 specification is at http://www.w3.org/TR/REC-CSS2.

SVG specifications: http://www.w3.org/TR/SVG/

The SVG specification is, at the time this book was written, a Proposed Recommenda on at the W3C. The URL in this section points to the most up-to-date version a any time.

SMIL Animation: http://www.w3.org/TR/smil-animation

At the time this book was written, SMIL Animation is a W3C Proposed Recommendation.

SMIL 2.0: http://www.w3.org/TR/smil20

SMIL 2.0, the Synchronized Multimedia Integration Language, has substantially extended the capabilities of SMIL 1.0 (see http://www.w3.org/TR/REC-smil). In common with some other parts of the XML family, SMIL is being modularized to permit its use with other XML-based applications, such as SVG and XHTML.

XML Linking Language (XLink): http://www.w3.org/TR/xlink

XLink is a full W3C Recommendation.

SVG Viewers

X-Smiles Viewer

Further information is available at http://www.x-smiles.org/. You can download the X-Smiles viewer from http://www.x-smiles.org/download.html.

Adobe SVG Viewer

You can download this product from http://www.adobe.com/svg/viewer/install/main.html.

SVG Tools

Jasc WebDraw: http://www.jasc.com/webdraw.asp?

WebDraw was described in Chapter 1. It provides close to round-trip management of SVG, allowing the creation of graphics visually but also allowing the tweaking of the SVG source code by hand.

Adobe Illustrator: http://www.adobe.com/products/illustrator/main.html

Illustrator 9 has useful SVG functionality.

Mayura Draw: http://www.mayura.com/

Mayura Draw is a limited SVG drawing tool.

Corel Draw 10: http://www.corel.com

Corel Draw 10 is a surprisingly useful SVG drawing, and potential Web page authoring, tool.

SVG Tutorials and Demos

As with all rapidly developing technologies, a choice of tutorial and demonstration sites must be a personal one. The sites listed in this section provide a range of perspectives. If you take time to browse the sites, and take a look at the source code on each one, you simply have to be learning more about SVG as you go.

Adobe.com: http://www.adobe.com/svg/

Adobe has an excellent SVG-oriented section on its Web site. From there, you can download the Adobe SVG Viewer, view some useful SVG tutorials, and examine some attractive samples of SVG.

Specifically, Adobe provides some basic online tutorials at http://www.adobe.com/svg/tutorial/intro.html, and some demo SVG images are at http://www.adobe.com/svg/demos/main.html.

SVGSpider.com: http://www.svgspider.com/default.svg

This is one of my own Web sites and was, I believe, the world's first "all SVG" Web site. Its purpose was and is to act as "proof of concept" about what is possible with SVG as a Web authoring tool.

Burning Pixel: http://www.burningpixel.com/svg/

Ron Lussier's Web site has a number of useful SVG demos, including a demo SVG Web site, which happens to be, in the prototype version, embedded within HTML pages.

KevlinDev.com: http://www.kevlindev.com

Kevin Lindsey's site has some nice SVG demos using declarative SVG. He also provides a number of demo images that achieve animation or interactivity through using JavaScript with SVG.

PinkJuice.com: http://www.pinkjuice.com/SVG/

At Tobias Reif's site, you can get some good SVG demos. Some of them look unimpressive in the small GIF version on the front page, but have hidden depths when you open the full SVG version.

Amino's SVG Laboratory: http://www.greenthing.net/svg/index.html

Laura Brown's site has a number of SVG demos and links to other SVG sites.

Battle Bots: http://www.battlebots.com/ svg_info.asp

This interesting demonstration site uses SVG graphics with robotic battle bots. It also has some sophisticated use of SVG. However, be aware that some download times are significant.

Skeeter-s.com: http://skeeter-s.com/svg

The SVG section at Steve Bowen's Web site is devoted to the early exploration of SVG in the Mozilla browser. Use Netscape 6 rather than Internet Explorer at this site, and visit the Mozilla SVG project at http://www.mozilla.org/projects/svg/.

SVG References

Zvon.org: http://www.zvon.org/ index.php?nav_id=zvonindex

Zvon has a number of useful references online for SVG and other XML technologies. It has an SVG element reference, with two versions: one in HTML and one in SVG. To view the latter, you obviously need an SVG viewer, such as those listed in Chapter 1, "The Basic SVG Tool Set."

Server-Side SVG

A number of tools are available to create SVG on the server dynamically. They focus mostly on charting or diagrams.

SVGObjects.com: http://www.svgobjects.com

This site produces SVG using the Apple WebObjects server-side technology.

Corda's PopChart Image Server: http://www.corda.com

The PopChart Image Server, in its Professional version, is capable of generating SVG charts. This professional tool is for sizeable Web sites.

XML Resources

A vast number of XML resources are on the Web. In this appendix, I can give only a few that are either generally useful or that link to other useful sites.

World Wide Web Consortium: http://www.w3.org

The place for definitive information on XML can be intimidating and overwhelming. If you are a newcomer to XML, visit this place from time to time, but not to find introductory tutorials.

From the top of the URL, you can link to Technical Reports, which is where you can access up-to-date drafts of a whole raft of XML technologies. Also linkable from the home page is a page describing W3C "Activities," which gives a perspective on the thinking behind much of the current and likely future W3C activity.

XML Tools: http://www.xmlsoftware.com

XMLSoftware.com is a useful general XML tool site.

XML.com: http://www.xml.com

This site a good source of general information on XML. It has a small, if infrequently updated, section devoted to SVG news.

XMLHack.com: http://www.xmlhack.com

This good source of news about general XML topics has a searchable archive, and you can browse its material by topic of interest. Browse the SVG section for recent significant events.

Zvon.org: http://www.zvon.org/index.php?nav_id=zvonindex

Zvon provides several online XML references and tutorials. The URL points to the Site Index, where the available tutorials and reference material are listed.

B

SVG Glossary

The purpose of this glossary is twofold. First, it helps you understand terms used in this book. Second, as you move beyond the scope of this book, this glossary provides a foundation to aid you in understanding other documents describing technical issues relating to SVG.

Words appearing in italics within the definitions indicate that those words are defined elsewhere in this glossary.

Animation Target   The *attribute* that is the target of an SVG animation. The animation target is designated by assigning an appropriate value to the `attributeName` attribute.

Attribute   A way of describing a characteristic of an SVG element. Attributes must conform to XML syntax requirements, with the form `attribute="value"` or `attribute='value'`. You have a choice whether to use double or single quotes, but you must use only one of these on any individual attribute. If you fail to use quotes, the SVG document is not *well formed*.

Basic Shapes   Predefined common graphical *shapes* that include the `<rect>`, `<circle>`, `<ellipse>`, `<line>`, `<polyline>`, and `<polygon>` elements.

Canvas   The space (potentially infinite) where an SVG image can be rendered. In practice, the rendering of SVG occurs in a finite rectangular area of the canvas—the *viewport*.

CDATA Section   An XML section designed to contain character data, not intended to be parsed as XML. One use in SVG is within a `<style>` element to contain an internal style sheet.

Container Element An element that can have graphics elements and other container elements as child elements. The SVG container elements are `<svg>`, `<g>`, `<defs>`, `<symbol>`, `<clipPath>`, `<mask>`, `<pattern>`, `<marker>`, `<a>`, and `<switch>`.

Document A well-formed XML document that describes an SVG image. The document may contain or link to other images, in either SVG or other formats.

Document fragment In SVG, consists of any number of SVG elements contained within an `<svg>` element.

Document Object Model A representation of the structure of an SVG image that provides an application programming interface (API) accessible by scripting languages, such as JavaScript.

Element A basic unit of the structure of an XML and SVG documents that can possess attributes. An element has start and end tags, in pairs, or can be expressed as an empty element tag.

Fill An attribute of many SVG elements that defines how an SVG *shape* other than the *stroke* will be painted inside the path defining the shape.

Filter In SVG, a series of graphical operations that produce a new visual appearance built up by applying to graphics elements a range of mathematically based *filter primitives* within an SVG `<filter>` element. Examples of SVG filter effects are drop shadow and bevel.

Filter Primitive A graphical operation that forms part of an SVG filter, represented as an SVG element, such as `<feGaussianBlur>` or `<feMerge>`. Filter primitives can be combined in a variety of ways to produce sophisticated filter effects.

Global Attributes A series of XLink attributes available for use on any SVG element. The attributes are `xlink:type`, `xlink:href`, `xlink:actuate`, `xlink:show`, `xlink:role`, `xlink:title`, and `xlink:arcrole`.

Graphics Element One of the element types that can cause graphics to be drawn on the target SVG canvas. They include but are not confined to SVG *shapes*. Available graphics elements are `<circle>`, `<ellipse>`, `<image>`, `<line>`, `<path>`, `<polygon>`, `<polyline>`, `<rect>`, `<text>`, and `<use>`.

Graphics Referencing Element   A graphics element that uses a reference to a different document or file (SVG or other format) or to an SVG element as the source of its graphical content. SVG 1.0 provides two graphics-referencing elements: `<image>` and `<use>`.

Original Value   The value maintained in the Document Object Model, or DOM, during an SVG animation. A separate *presentation value* is used to produce the changing visual appearance onscreen.

Paint   Paint represents how color is presented on the SVG canvas. SVG supports three types of paint: color, gradients, and patterns. Paint includes both color and alpha values.

Painter's Model   A conceptual picture of the way in which an SVG rendering engine (viewer) "paints" or re-creates an SVG image. It has some similarities to the effect of applying oil paint on a canvas.

Path   A mathematical description of the outline of an SVG *shape*. In addition to the predefined *basic shapes*, it can be represented by the `<path>` element (see Chapter 3).

Presentation Attributes   Styling in SVG can be added inline using the style attribute or individual presentation attributes, such as `fill` and `font-family`.

Presentation Value   The value of an attribute that is used to define the visual appearance at any moment during an SVG animation. The presentation value that changes as a function of time. A separate *original value* of the attribute is maintained in the Document Object Model.

Shape   A graphics element that is defined by some combination of straight lines and curves. In SVG, the shapes provided are `<circle>`, `<ellipse>`, `<line>`, `<path>`, `<polygon>`, `<polyline>`, and `<rect>`.

String   A sequence of characters that may be rendered within an SVG `<text>` element.

Stroke   The paint applied to the outline of an SVG shape or characters in a text string. The stroke attribute can specify paint type, width, opacity, and other characteristics that affect the appearance of an object.

SVG   Scalable Vector Graphics.

Viewport   The rectangular area where SVG is rendered; part of the potentially infinite SVG *canvas*.

Viewport Coordinate System   The coordinate system within the current viewport.

Viewport Space   A synonym for viewport coordinate system.

W3C   World Wide Web Consortium, an international cross-industry organization that helps develop and promote vendor-neutral technology standards for the Web.

Well-formed   A term to describe an SVG (or other XML) document that complies with the syntax required by the *XML* 1.0 Recommendation. For example, elements must be properly nested within each other, and *attribute* values must be enclosed in quotes.

XML   Extensible Markup Language. SVG is an application of XML and therefore uses the syntax required by the XML 1.0 Recommendation.

C

What's on the Web Site

In this appendix:

- SVGSpider
- Source Files
- Feedback

SVGSpider

Much of the beauty of SVG is its ability to manipulate and animate images, so visit SVGSpider at www.svgspider.com/default.svg. SVGSpider provides the full-motion implementations of many of the examples in this book. Be sure you have the most recent version of an SVG Viewer (try Adobe's, downloadable from www.adobe.com) and away you go.

Source Files

See a listing in this book you want to work with and manipulate? Simply go to the New Riders web site (www.newriders.com), insert this book's ISBN (0735711666) in the search box and you'll have access to download all the listings found in this book.

Feedback

I hope you have enjoyed reading *Designing SVG Web Graphics* and I would value your constructive suggestions for how the book might be improved or which SVG topics you think need to be covered in more depth. To reach me either use the feedback form on the New Riders Web site or email me at Andrew@SVGSpider.com. I can't promise to reply individually to emails because of the sheer volume but will certainly read and carefully consider all comments received.

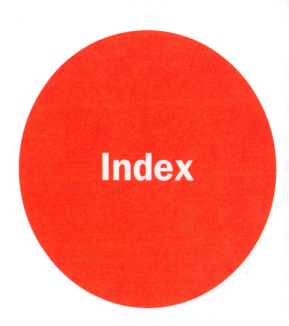

Index

Y

Z

Solutions from experts you know and trust.

www.informit.com

OPERATING SYSTEMS

WEB DEVELOPMENT

PROGRAMMING

NETWORKING

CERTIFICATION

AND MORE...

**Expert Access.
Free Content.**

New Riders has partnered with **InformIT.com** to bring technical information to your desktop. Drawing on New Riders authors and reviewers to provide additional information on topics you're interested in, **InformIT.com** has free, in-depth information you won't find anywhere else.

- **Master the skills you need, when you need them**

- **Call on resources from some of the best minds in the industry**

- **Get answers when you need them, using InformIT's comprehensive library or live experts online**

- **Go above and beyond what you find in New Riders books, extending your knowledge**

As an **InformIT** partner, **New Riders** has shared the wisdom and knowledge of our authors with you online. Visit **InformIT.com** to see what you're missing.

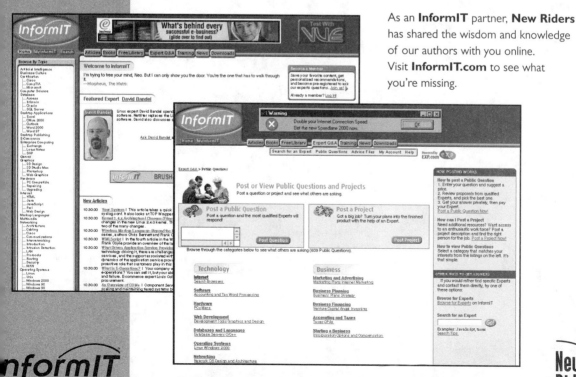

www.informit.com ▪ www.newriders.com

VOICES THAT MATTER

Inside Dreamweaver 4
Anne-Marie Yerks, John Pickett
0735710848
$44.99 (with CD-ROM)
Learn how long-time Dreamweaver users make it really perform! These users share their secrets and give you learning activities that present the new features of Dreamweaver.

Dreamweaver 4 Magic
Al Sparber
0735710465
$45.00 (with CD-ROM)
"If you are serious about Web work, this book will take you to a new level and you won't look back either."
   —an online reviewer

**Flash Web Design:
The v5 Remix**
Hillman Curtis
0735710988
$45.00
"The Hillman Curtis deconstruction method of teaching Flash is invaluable. Not only does he teach you the concepts, but by looking at Flash animations in a deconstructive mode you will be able to determine how they were created."
   —an online reviewer

**Flash ActionScript
for Designers: Drag,
Slide, Fade**
Brendan Dawes
0735710473
$45.00
In response to the high demand for ActionScripting books! *Drag, Slide, Fade* explains and explores the power of ActionScript for those who design it. The text is supported by four-colored visuals and annotated codes.

**Generator/Flash Web
Development**
Richard Alvarez, Jason Taylor, Matthew Groch
0735710805
$34.99 (with CD-ROM)
"With the publication of Generator/Flash Web Development, the technology world has found a new bible. From conception to completion, this book will take projects to new heights. The knowledge demonstrated by Alvarez, Taylor, and Groch is vast, as are the possibilities that this book will open."
   —an online reviewer

Flash to the Core
Joshua Davis
0735711046
$45.00 Coming Soon
Unlike any other Flash book on the market! Joshua Davis shares his cutting-edge techniques and coding secrets. These methods are guaranteed to challenge and inspire all professional readers.

New Riders

W W W . N E W R I D E R S . C O M

NEW RIDERS HAS WHAT YOU NEED TO MASTER PHOTOSHOP 6.

Photoshop 6 Shop Manual
Donnie O'Quinn
ISBN: 0735711305
$39.99

**Photoshop 6 Photo-
Retouching Secrets**
Scott Kelby
ISBN: 0735711461
$39.99

**Photoshop 6 Down
& Dirty Tricks**
Scott Kelby
ISBN: 073571147X
$39.99

Photoshop 6 Artistry
Barry Haynes,
Wendy Crumpler
ISBN: 0735710376
$59.99

Photoshop 6 Web Magic
Jeff Foster
ISBN: 0735710368
$45.00

**Bert Monroy: Photorealistic
Techniques with Photoshop
and Illustrator**
Bert Monroy
ISBN: 0735709696
$49.99

Photoshop 6 Effects Magic
Rhoda Grossman, Sherry London
ISBN: 073571035X
$45.00

New
Riders

WWW.NEWRIDERS.COM

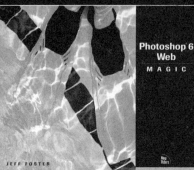

Jakob Nielsen

Designing
Web Usability

Designing Web Usability
Jakob Nielsen
ISBN: 156205810X
$45.00

Flash Web Design: the v5 remix
Hillman Curtis
ISBN: 0735710988
$45.00

Photoshop 6 Web Magic
Jeff Foster
ISBN: 0735710368
$45.00

<designing web graphics.3>
Lynda Weinman
ISBN: 1562059491
$55.00

The Art & Science of Web Design
Jeffrey Veen
ISBN: 0789723700
$45.00

<creative html design.2>
Lynda Weinman and
William Weinman
ISBN: 0735709726
$39.99

Don't Make Me Think!
Steve Krug
ISBN: 0789723107
$35.00

The Authors. The Content. The Timeliness.

What it takes to be a classic.

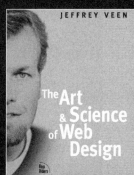

New
Riders

WWW.NEWRIDERS.COM